Athens

The Truth

D1287844

Athens

The Truth

Searching for Mános
Just Before the Bubble Burst

David Cade

Tales of Orpheus

British Library Cataloguing in Publication Data. A catalogue record for this book is available from the British Library.

First published 2013
Tales of Orpheus
TreeTops, Mardu,
Shropshire SY7 8QG,
United Kingdom.

The author's website is at:
www.davidcade.net

Cover Art:
Laurent de Commines,
Peintre & Décorateur,
Paris, 2013.

ISBN: 0-9552090-3-X
ISBN-13: 978-0-9552090-3-1

Πάντα στον νου σου νάχεις την Ιθάκη.

Hold Itháki ever in your mind.

Το φθάσιμον εκεί είν' ο προορισμός σου.

Your arrival there is your destiny.

Αλλά μη βιάζεις το ταξείδι διόλου.

But do not hurry the journey at all.

Καλλίτερα χρόνια πολλά να διαρκέσει

Better that it take many years,

και γέρος πια ν' αράξεις στο νησί,

that you be old by the time you reach the island,

πλούσιος με όσα κέρδισες στον δρόμο,

and rich with all you've gained along the way,

μη προσδοκώντας πλούτη να σε δώσει η Ιθάκη.

not expecting Itháki to give you riches.

- from the poem 'Ιθάκη' (Itháki),
by Constantínos Caváfy, 1863 - 1933.

Contents

Notes

To assist with the proper pronunciation of Greek terms, a stress mark indicates the syllable to be emphasized. This emphasis is important. Firstly, of course, it helps with correct pronunciation. But secondly, where Greek words have two or more syllables the stressing of a particular one helps to specify meaning. As an example, if you step into a Greek handicrafts shop, or you're invited into a Greek home, you may well observe a fine woven Greek rug upon the floor or displayed proudly upon a wall. If you exclaim 'What a *háli*!' (HAR-lee), rather than 'What a *halí*!' (har-LEE), you could cause great dismay, if not offence. For a carpet is a '*halí*', but a '*háli*' is a mess!

Where the Anglicization of a word doesn't vary much from the Greek, I've used a transliteration of the original as an acknowledgement of how greatly Greece has influenced our language, thought, and culture. For example: the Greek words *cháos* and *écstasis*, or the mellifluous *Aristotéles* (Ah-ris-to-TEL-ees) instead of the abrupt and comparatively brutal English transliteration 'Aristotle'. However, there are some Anglicizations which I have not avoided as they differ markedly from the original terms and have become commonplace. For example, the rather grand Anglicized adjectives 'Tyrrhenian' and 'Panathenean' are quite removed from the Greek *Tyrrinikó* and *Panathinaïkó*.

Eagle-eyed readers may also occasionally note what may appear to be discrepancies or inconsistencies in spelling. It should be borne in mind however that in Modern Greek subtle distinctions are sometimes indicated by way of slightly different forms of the same word. For example, the name George may appear as either *Yiórgos* or as *Yeórghios*. The first is the familiar and warmer form, as in the name of the popular singer Yiórgos Daláras. *Yeórghios*, however, is formal, as in the names of many Greek statesmen - although, interestingly, not usually in the case of the American-born ex-prime minister Yiórgos Papandréou.

So that people who have been quoted in this book should not experience any public embarrassment for having been open with me in conversation, I've replaced most people's names with pseudonyms.

॰

With respect for readers of all beliefs, the dating indications CE and BCE (Common Era, and Before the Common Era) are used throughout this book, instead of the traditional abbreviations AD and BC (Anno Domini, and Before Christ) although CE and BCE indicate exactly the same periods as AD and BC, respectively.

Αθήνα

Η Αλήθεια

Αναζητώντας τον Μάνο
Λίγο Πριν Σκάσει η Φούσκα

1

Introduction

Searching for Mános

My journey to Athens began 50 years ago, on the South Pacific island of Viti Levu, Fiji. Enveloped one morning in the heady fragrance of one of Planet Earth's most gorgeously-scented flowers, the little frangipani, delicate creamy-white with an eye of intense yellow, I sat under the great arching leaves of a banana tree and held, almost to the point of caressing, a brand-new transistor-radio. Despite the strong sun and the trenchant tropical heat, I remember too how all the brilliant-red petals of the hibiscus bushes which surrounded me on every side that mid-morning, still sparkled as brightly and vividly as they had when I'd been up first thing at dawn, full of excitement. But now, three or four hours later, ever so slowly turning the dial backwards and forwards, I was all agog in that South Pacific paradise with rich new layers of aural sensation, sounds that were totally foreign, exotic, bewitching, and magical.

That morning, in 1962, I had become an eight-year-old, and the big heavy radio on my lap, about the same size as an A4 page, was my one, but very great, birthday present. My parents, having fled grey damp Britain after the trauma of the Second World War and just two years before I'd been born in the cool south of New Zealand, were ecstatic to be living in Fiji, and so for my birthday they'd hit Suva's duty-free shops determined to splash out. And now here it was: a luxurious radio, 'Made in Japan', gleaming with complicated wavebands, with silver switches and sensitive dials, an extendable aerial like a long chrome fishing-rod, and the whole thing protected within a durable case of highly-polished richly-smelling deep-brown leather! That morning that transistor seemed to me the most marvellous object in the universe. But this was mostly because the music it produced was something I'd never before encountered: the strange music of the East. Fiji had, and still has, a large Indian population, and so whether the music that was being broadcast in those days was Carnatic, Hindi, or comprised of the greatly popular 'filmi' songs of Indian cinema, I found all of it absolutely mesmerising. But why did it so hit the eight-year-old me, like an asteroid from outer space, why was I so captivated by it, while my parents, and their friends, and the few other white boys amongst my classmates, either sniggered at it or were indifferent to it? I have no idea.

Some years later we were settled in Christchurch, New Zealand, and during my first year at an all-boys secondary school there an architecturally splendid new science-block was opened. Its corridors, labs, and seminar rooms had all been lined and floored with fresh pungently-scented New Zealand timbers. These woods, however, smelt sweetest and most strongly in the building's little theatre, which unlike all of the other spaces had no windows and was dark. With its tall science-lab taps and deep basins built into the great raised bench that stood directly in front of the blackboard, this room had been designed specifically for serious demonstrations in physics, chemistry, and biology. But one afternoon, after lunch, when we'd all expected to return to the classroom for more miserable maths or suchlike, our teacher announced a surprise, a treat: a film in the fine new theatre! We were then all single-filed in a state of considerable excitement over to the science-block and up into the steep rake of its little 'cinema'. A projector started up behind us, its reels clicking as they turned, the lights were killed, and then in the blackness there suddenly leapt upon the screen - in that little space in a small school in the Antipodes - an intensely bright light, the daylight of some unknown, undreamt-of, unimagined, and very far distant land. In the vivid luminosity of that remote place we boys gazed upon stone and marble monuments; dense concrete apartment buildings, such as simply didn't exist anywhere in our country; we saw crowded streets with people passing up and down in fashionable summer clothing, wearing dark glasses and looking sophisticated; and I can also remember trains, and trams, and trolleys. This place, apparently, was the city of Athens, a large and thriving *metrópolis* that none of us young Kiwi boys knew anything about, other than, of course, it once having been a very important part of Ancient Greece.

The film was a well-produced documentary, a forerunner of the TV travel programme, and with that intense effulgence which had burst upon the screen in the film's opening moments, there had come a rippling surge of tinkling music, a magical entrancing vibration of sound that we boys, of mainly English and Irish stock, had never before heard: the music of Athens and of Greece. But unlike my classmates, I instantly and somehow 'recognised' it. There was something about it that flashed me back to the Eastern music of my transistor, to those exotic sounds that had suddenly gone from my life when our family departed sunny Fiji. Now, here in cool and temperate New Zealand, alongside the rapture of the warm and glowing images of that faraway country upon the screen, a related music fluttered in like a flight of delicate glasslike wings, a flock of gentle *bouzoúkia*, beating and soaring in and around phrases of beautiful plaintive melody.

Eleven years old, I sat there devastated. I had known of course that Greece was a place of antiquities, of old columns and carved stones and very many statues, often connected with the tales of Homer, the Iliad and the Odyssey, and each year on ANZAC day there were references to the six hundred or so New Zealand soldiers who'd died in Greece's defence during the Second World War. But this rippling, magical, glasslike music was an aspect of Greece that was completely new - unexpected, a revelation. But such was the gulf at that time between we lads down there in the South Seas and the lands of far-distant Europe, in the Northern Hemisphere and truly the other side of the globe from us, that it did not, or could not, even occur to me that one could at least go to a library and find out what instruments those were that gave off such remarkable sounds. I was just too much in awe, too removed. It was simply music 'from far beyond', from 'heaven', from a foreign world an incomprehensible thousands of miles away, music from a continent which people said it took months to reach, by ship. And as the film had purely been meant as a treat, a diversion apparently granted us on a whim, back in the classroom there was no follow-up to it, not even a 'So what did you think of that then, boys? Any questions?'

The profound sensations of that afternoon didn't enter my world again for four more years. I was at another school now, in Wellington, the capital of New Zealand, and two hours' of dishing out ice-creams in a dairy every afternoon, once classes were over, meant that for the first time in my life I had a reasonable and regular amount of pocket-money, as well as the freedom to spend it as I liked. I chose to buy my first LPs - big glossy beautifully-produced twelve-inch sleeves encasing works like Brahms's Third Symphony, The Haydn Variations, Tchaikovsky's First Piano Concerto, and excerpts from the Messiah. And then one day I noticed amongst the racks a small new section of records. Altogether it held no more than about fifteen discs, and all of their titles, in some strange alphabet, were completely incomprehensible. Ah, that must be music for the Greeks, I thought.

Wellington about that time had become home to quite a lot of Greeks, most of them having arrived in New Zealand during the 1950s and 60s, although a small Hellenic community had already been established by Greek immigrants earlier in the century. Because New Zealand's first settlers came mostly from England, Scotland, Ireland, and Wales, I'd always been aware of groupings like the Caledonians and the Hibernians, and even, in Christchurch, the Cambrians, each such society keeping up an identification with 'home', with 'the old country'. But we all understood the Greeks to be distinctly different. Their *diasporá*, and their nostalgia for their homeland, rather like that of the Jews and Armenians, was considered born of some particular suffering or hardship and difficulties associated with identity. Furthermore, 'the Greeks', in as much as we were aware of them, were known to be strongly connected to their local church, just as members of the Jewish *diasporá* tend to cluster about synagogues. To this day, all over the globe, to be Greek is generally to belong to the Greek Orthodox Church, and so Greek events as far from Greece as Wellington, Auckland, Melbourne or Adelaide were, and are still, generally linked to a local Orthodox Church, at the heart of each Greek community. So for most of the seven million members of the Greek *diasporá* scattered around the world, they're more than simply people of Greek descent. Although naturalised and often long-settled in other countries, Greeks generally remain essentially and proudly 'Greeks'.

While I was at school in the New Zealand capital, the only sizeable groups of identifiable 'foreigners' in the city were these 'Greeks', and some Chinese, and both were to be seen in similar sorts of occupations. Although many of the incoming Greeks had been farmers in their own country, they hadn't been able to afford New Zealand land, and so instead they turned mostly to running fish and chip shops, simple restaurants, various kinds of small stores, and 'milk bars'. In the early 1960s there were roughly seventy such Greek-owned businesses in downtown Wellington, but in the 1970s this particular schoolboy only ever encountered Greeks when he wandered into one of the downtown milk bars. These 'milk bars' were generally old-fashioned narrow cafés with fixed high-backed seating all along one wall, fifties style, as in old railway-carriages. They were the kind of place you popped into for a coffee, a tea, or a milk-shake, alongside maybe a small traditional steak-and-kidney pie, a sausage roll, or a custard slice. In those days in New Zealand few businesses played background music and those which did usually just tuned into a local radio station, so I failed to connect the people running these places with the extraordinary music of that soundtrack I'd been exposed to at school in Christchurch. But with the appearance of the strange new LPs the link with the local Greek community was obvious and it wasn't long before I'd parted with some of my pocket-money to make an exploratory purchase. I chose María Farandoúri singing Míkis Theodorákis's song-cycle 'Ένας Όμηρος' (*Énas Ómiros*, The Hostage). When I got it home and played it I was once again mesmerised. So back I went and bought another. And then many more. My parents thought I was mad, that something rather questionable had begun, possibly even something for us all to be ashamed about, so I didn't dare breathe a word of my passion to a soul at school.

The lyrics of the songs on these discs were of course meaningless to me and so it was all, to my mind, simply 'Greek Music'. But I did prefer some melodies or collections more than I did others, and I figured that this was simply because some were just 'better' than the rest. Though I loved nearly all of this music, I never once realised or even suspected that the songs that totally arrested me had all been written by one composer. Yes, I was so intimidated by the Greek titling on the discs and sleeves that I never persevered to find clues as to who was responsible for which track! And as more and more Greek records arrived in that one Wellington shop that stocked them, I saw that there was a great deal of Greek music in existence and assumed that there must therefore be many Greek song-writers, as indeed there were. Little did I know that the total number of Greek composers and singers in existence was nothing short of astounding.

And then, in the midst of all this discovery, a BBC series featuring the Greek singer Nána Moúskouri and other international performers suddenly started appearing on New Zealand television. Although the content of this series mainly featured all sorts of Western pop- and folk-songs of the time, a couple of tunes in every programme were Greek. So for the first time I was treated to seeing some of the magical words and melodies of Greece flowing directly from a performer. However, although Moúskouri would often introduce her Greek songs with a brief explanation, she didn't usually announce who had written either the music or the words. Thus, amazingly, it was to take me another thirty years to realise that of all the many talented composers of Greek music the one who touched me most strongly, right back at the time of those first discoveries in Wellington, was Mános Hadjidákis.

Some deep inner urge for greater exoticism eventually propelled me away from the land I'd been born in. In 1967 an Australian comedy had been a huge success in cinemas throughout New Zealand. 'They're a Weird Mob' had alerted all of us to the many Italian and Greek immigrants who were flooding into Australia at about that time. So when I took up residence at the age of twenty-one in sunny sub-tropical Sydney, with all its sparkling light, the blue of its magnificent harbour, its people in light clothing nearly all the year round, and with exciting Greek shops and cafés to be found dotted throughout the city and suburbs, I felt as if I'd actually implanted myself in that extraordinary Mediterranean place I'd seen on the screen all those years before while in cool and rather English Christchurch.

Within months of settling in Sydney, I found in a downtown classical record-shop a brand-new just-released LP from Germany featuring a splendid Greek tenor, a Michael Theodore. Not only was this very fine tenor completely unknown to me, but at the New South Wales Conservatorium of Music he was also unknown to all of my fellow singing students, as well as to my teacher who had only recently been performing with the Vienna Volksoper. There was a photograph of Theodore on the album's front cover, leaning over a grand piano at which sat that other great Greek composer Míkis Theodorákis. Theodore's real name was Mihális Theodórou but when a glittering career in Germany had beckoned it was simplified for his German audience to Michael Theodore. And then after singing leading roles in opera his outstanding voice was thankfully preserved forever on a flood of fine German LPs, including in 1974 his only recording in Greek.

The music of 'Michael Theodore singt griechische Lieder von Mikis Theodorakis und Manos Hadzidakis' was, for me, perfection. Theodore had a voice that was high, pure, strong, and sharp - comparable to Mario Lanza's. And on this particular disc he was accompanied by a large orchestra that flew luxuriantly and excitedly all about him, filling in wherever he paused with the most delicate, intricate, and filigreed of Eastern ornamentations. The sound was luscious, sunny, euphoric, and full of positive energy. And of course each song dripped with the glorious and unbeatably melliflu-ous sounds of the Greek tongue. The titling and sleeve-notes were unfortunately all in German - a language I could've studied at school but was disinclined to on account of what the Nazis had inflicted on my grandparents and uncle during the course of the war - but it was pretty clear that most of the songs were by Theodorákis. I could easily have worked out exactly which song had been written by which composer but I was just too intoxicated by the overall sound of the entire collection to ever bother.

Through this recording though, and by way of my many others, I perceived that the music of Theodorákis was mainly for the morning: it was rousing, strong, optimistic, full of fight and determination. It shone with leadership. And I sensed an understanding of the words would add considerably to one's appreciation of the great power of the work, for with Theodorákis you often feel an important message is being propounded, that weighty and momentous things are underway, that profound change must occur - and is about to occur! In those wonderful three years I spent in Sydney, Theodorákis accompanied me daily from little flats in Elizabeth Bay, Gladesville, and Glebe, to all my places of work, study, and pleasure, in and around the city. But several songs which Theodore sang seemed more appropriate for the evening. They were songs for dreaming, songs of longing, songs for reflection, for savouring the truths, the beauties, and the sadnesses of life. Their melodies were accompanied by rich and emotionally-satisfying harmonies, never driving one at all after the meaning of the words, but strongly suggesting starlit evenings, warm breezes, the lapping of waves upon a shore, or light cotton curtains blowing in open windows on hot sultry nights.

I played that record so often I was quite fearful I would wear away the sound. All my other Greek discs took second place. The twelve tracks of that one glorious recording became imprinted on my mind, and as I walked Sydney's lovely sub-tropical streets, basking in the warmth and the whole Mediterranean feel of those harbour-side suburbs where I lived, the melodies of that recording played themselves involuntarily and almost ceaselessly inside my head. I couldn't escape them, nor did I ever want to. I was amazed each day at how the orchestra simply started up in my brain without my even willing it. And I felt, or believed, or really I suppose I pretended, that I was actually in the great 'mythological' city of Athens. And I was blissfully happy there, though I knew full well I wasn't really there at all! And so I came to believe that the Greek capital itself must surely be a city a million times more exciting than that which I was so enjoying there and then in Australia.

Arriving in London in the grey grim winter of 1979, I was delighted to find, quite by chance, opposite Foyles Bookshop in Charing Cross Road, in the shadow of the giant white Centrepoint building and amongst a bunch of ugly dilapidated Victorian terraces, a tiny Greek bookshop. Inside, it was all dishevelled, crammed with Greek books in mostly plain cream or white covers, modest, studious, and academic-looking. I surveyed the shop's contents with a thirst, and eventually, right at the back, hidden on a low shelf just an inch or so above the floor, I found a shallow pile of Greek sheet-music. This was my first sighting of the actual notation from which the magical music arose! In amongst that heap I even detected a song by Mános Hadjidákis, a tune made famous in Greece by the actress and singer Alíki Vougiouklάki, a voluptuous blonde of the 50s and 60s, very much like Brigitte Bardot, and whose image adorned the front cover. Of course I purchased the song without a moment's hesitation, but it wasn't until I moved to Oxford several years later that I acquired a small piano and was then able, for the first time, to produce the deliciously charming music of Hadjidákis with my own hands - though still I didn't recognise that I found his music so much more fulfilling than that of any other Greek composer.

Thirteen years later, teaching in inner-city schools in deeply unprivileged areas of Manchester proved quite a grind, for maintaining order and discipline in those classrooms challenged we staff far more than the actual teaching. I was devoted to the work and at times it was rewarding, but I knew my heart lay elsewhere. I just wasn't sure of the location. While studying Drama and Theatre Arts at the University of Birmingham I'd so revelled in our studies and performances of plays by Evripídis, Aristophánes, Aeschýlos, and Sophoclés that I'd made my way one afternoon to the Department of Modern Languages for a chat with a couple of lecturers who were Greek. They assured me there was an abundance of theatrical life in Athens but due to my total lack of proficiency in Greek they were understandably doubtful of my chances of working there. Nevertheless the hankering remained, and while I was teaching in Manchester the urge towards things Greek was sufficiently strong to hurl me down by train one weekend to London, purely in order to make my way to a music shop that I'd heard was in the Greek and Turkish quarter of Haringey. My mission was to try to find recordings of that mysterious 'right kind of Greek music' - the music of Hadjidákis, though I still didn't know it. Over the course of several hours in that little store its kind and accommodating owner allowed me to sample sufficient recordings to head back north with half a dozen LPs that offered satisfactory music although none of them, I observed many years later, actually featured any Hadjidákis. They were enough, however, to salve my remaining days in the difficult classrooms of inner-city Manchester. The Haringey oasis also sold a few Greek music-books, and so, in addition to the LPs, I returned home with five books of songs by Theodorákis and a song-cycle by Hadjidákis.

Back in Manchester these music-books were 'all Greek to me', not only in terms of the impenetrable lyrics, in an alphabet I'd still to fathom, but in terms of their musical notation. The Hadjidákis was the most difficult. Its notes were often so foreign and seemed so 'wrong'. The melody lines needed to be sung as I played, for their notes were not included in the accompaniments, but the accompaniments, played by themselves, were strange and seemed to fight the melodies! Thus, to produce the intended overall effect by oneself, to play those accompaniments and to sing the difficult melodies at the same time, was a struggle. Furthermore, occasionally coming to a bar and finding that on the first beat one was required to play one chord with one hand and a completely different and highly discordant couple of notes with the other, simply repelled me. Many of the time-signatures also vexed. Five beats in a bar - a group of three followed by a group of two? Or nine beats in bar - one group of three, followed by three groups of two! And on top of this, some of these pieces were clearly meant to go like the clappers! What absolutely lunatic music was this? It went against all my training in classical music. Surely this particular collection couldn't be translated into any of those glorious Greek recordings I'd found so mesmerising? All six volumes of music were very soon shelved and abandoned.

From the late 1980s I lived and worked in Sa'udi Arabia and Kuwait and spent some of my holidays in Egypt. Being Muslim countries, public concerts were held only in very rare circumstances and seldom was music ever heard in cafés or restaurants. Nevertheless, in all three countries a great deal of recorded music was available for purchase, mainly on tape but eventually on CD. I thus bought literally hundreds of recordings and soon isolated those Arabic singers who sang the Arabic music I liked most. I was also captivated by the considerable similarities I perceived between Arabic music and Greek music, for, except for the language or dialects in which the melodies were sung, much Arabic music seemed remarkably and inexplicably akin to a particular strand of the popular music of Greece! However, I didn't pursue a connection. I didn't even reflect upon the close geographical proximity of these two Eastern regions. Instead, I simply swirled in delight amidst all the exotic Arabic sounds of Egypt, Lebanon, Turkey, Syria, Sa'udi, Kuwait, and the Emirates.

Unfortunately, my enjoyment of Arabic music was frequently defiled by a dark and distressing shadow. Angry bearded *mutawwa'în*, Sa'udi Arabia's religious policemen from 'The Ministry for the Prevention of Vice and Protection of Virtue', would quite frequently appear red-faced, bulgey-eyed, furious, and ranting at the doors of music-shops while customers browsed. They'd stand on the threshold and loudly demand of shop-assistants that the volume of the music be turned right down, so that it could barely be heard, or, just as often, that it be switched off altogether, so that all these little shops selling music, selling joy, selling the expression of the human heart, would then be plunged into a kind of emotional darkness, into pits of guilt and shame. Several times I witnessed some demented *muttawa*, eyes flashing, stamp his way across a shop floor to loudly harangue and poke at some young Arab male who'd dared to venture outdoors in Western clothing, instead of the standard flowing white *thobe* and *ghoutra* head-dress. So except for the warmth of the sun, for visits to beauty-spots far out in the desert, for the astounding generosity of Arab hospitality at dinners and feasts, and for all the fascinating music of Arabia, my overall experience of the Islamic Middle East was killing.

One of the greatest joys of returning to London in the late 1990s, beside escaping the stifling sterility and suppression of Islamic lands, was being able to tune into 'LGR', London Greek Radio, a station that broadcasts from the heart of the Greek community in the suburb of Haringey. LGR gives the British capital a spread of Greek music that is rapturous, particularly at night when they play the recordings of all the great Greek singers of *laïká* and *éntechno*, forms of Greek song which are heavily romantic in nature, extremely melodic, usually flooded with rippling *bouzoúkia*, and of course always dripping with the honeyed vowels of the Greek language. Many scholars, academics, performers, and lovers of classical music automatically chant with total conviction the age-old received opinion that Italian is the most beautiful tongue in which to sing, but I have to very strongly and firmly object that this is simply not true. When one just gets over the strange and seemingly-forbidding written form of the Greek alphabet, and words that usually give Westerners no clue as to their meanings, and one just listens to sung Greek, then it is found that it's not just as beautiful as sung Italian: it is more so. Simply purchase the two finest collections of songs by Hadjidákis that currently exist, 'Romaïkí Agorá' (EMI, 1986) and 'Laïkí Agorá' (EMI, 1987), and there is no argument. The four discs in these two collections present superb performances and arrangements of the finest of all the many songs that Hadjidákis wrote between the years 1947 and 1985.

Long after moving away from hectic and busy London, and despite having lived since then in a stunningly beautiful picture-book location in Canterbury and later on the edge of Snowdonia National Park, before settling in the hills of South Shropshire, I realised, for the first time in my life, that I was seriously discontent. I was living in glorious countryside, with all the time in the world for my creative projects and pursuits, with everything else in my life seeming as good as could possibly be, but something was clearly lacking. Eventually I set myself to working out what it was.

Since the time I first plunged into the Internet, in 1992, while working at the very well-equipped Faculty of Medicine at Kuwait University, the Web has of course progressed at a rapid pace. At the end of 1992, a good few months after the 'Information Super Highway' had exploded into being, I noted with disappointment that there were literally no web-pages whatsoever on Greek music or Greek composers. But ten years later there were dozens! And so with the turn of the new millennium I began to learn a great deal, to find snippets of data on Greek artists, writers, poets, and composers, and in amongst those initial sprinklings, of course, many details about the great Mános Hadjidákis and Míkis Theodorákis. And some of the things I discovered were electrifying. The most enlightening finds were those newspaper articles, interviews, and sundry pieces of prose in which Hadjidákis had set out what could be described as having been his philosophy of song. I saw that he had said that for him the urge to sing was a mystical personal experience, but, at the same time, he believed singing was also an activity of socially binding importance. The song he therefore sought to create existed at a point between the whispered intensity of the personal and private prayer and the unleashed exhilaration of a full-blown public love affair. He'd wanted to create melodies so intoxicating and commanding that they'd threaten one's peace of mind! Thus the ideal song was to be neither a prop for vain and strutting youths nor a passing distraction for the tired, the bored, or the monied. In fact, Hadjidákis had indicated that he wished his songs to stand against all of the invading tides of fashion, superficiality, and falsity.

Though these discoveries were a revelation, explaining so much of the power of the music that had charmed me for years, I didn't immediately respond to them in any truly massive way. I took no action other than deciding to rigorously devote at least one hour first thing every morning to mastering those Hadjidákis accompaniments and melodies that I'd given up on in Manchester, fifteen years earlier. But that was hard work enough! Because as I tried to get those odd melodies, rhythms, and dissonances into my head and under my skin, for many months the first hour of each day began with real frustration at the keyboard, frequently marked by the flinging out aloud of furious curses. It took me almost two years to get on top of them, but eventually all those elements of the music which once vexed and offended me in the playing were transformed. With perseverance they suddenly began to pass, quickly and easily, to resolve with great satisfaction, and to add the most delicious moments of appetizing pungency and spiciness to the performance of the music. I had, at last, broken through, right into the heart of the composer's world.

Mános Hadjidákis was born in 1925, in the city of Xánthi, in Thrace (or Thráki, as it is called by Greeks), in the extreme north-east of Greece, about ninety miles from today's border with Turkey. While his father was a lawyer from Crete, his mother, with whom Hadjidákis maintained a strong relationship all his life, came from Hadrianópolis, or Edirne as it has generally been called by Turks following its fall to them in the 14th century. Hadrianópolis, as the city is still referred to by Greeks, is now in the most western part of Turkish territory, in that part of Thrace that is close to both Bulgaria and Greece. Today there are roughly 130,000 ethnic Turks (or 'Greek Muslims' as the Greek government prefers to term them) living in western Thrace (under Greek control), while in the town of Xánthi, where Hadjidákis was born, these 'Greek Muslims' compose roughly half of the current population. Most Muslims in north-eastern Greece generally look to Turkey in terms of culture and identity, despite Greek courts having outlawed reference to these people as being 'Turkish', and despite their being, in fact, citizens of Greece. Thus, while they and Christians in the region live and function side by side, there are some who do so only warily and uncomfortably. Between older and more conservative members of the two communities there's little interaction. However, younger members today tend to be more placable and less given to observing their differences.

Back in 1923, two years before Hadjidákis's birth, Muslims constituted 67% of the population of western Thrace. They were generally ethnic Turks, long-established in the area, who were exempted from the tragic and massive 1923 population exchange of Christians and Muslims between Greece and Turkey that was agreed under the Convention of Lausanne. So it was in a region that had only recently been freed from centuries of Turkish domination, in an area of significantly mixed Greco-Turkish culture, and in a landscape dotted with Turkish minarets but where people also danced to the fox-trot and tango, that Hadjidákis the child responded to the various colourful and exotic stimuli which were all about him and exhibited his very early signs of musical aptitude. At the unusually young age of four he began piano lessons and soon after also began playing the violin and the accordion.

In 1932 his parents parted and Mános and his sister, Miránda, moved south with their mother and continued their schooling in Athens. As a teenager during and following the period when Greece was occupied by the Nazis, Hadjidákis laboured on the Piraeus docks, made beer in the old brewery in the locality of Fix, sold ice, assisted a photographer, and worked as a nurse in a military hospital. At the same time, however, he studied musical theory at the Greek National Music School and read philosophy at the University of Athens. In 1943 he met the budding Greek poet Níkos Gátsos, who became his life-long mentor and friend. Then in 1944 while he was attending drama classes at the Athens 'Art Theatre', founded and run by the internationally famous director Károlos Koun, Hadjidákis made his first appearance as a composer. Fortunately Koun persuaded the student that his musical abilities exceeded his acting talents, and thus Hadjidákis created music for Art Theatre productions of plays by the likes of Tennessee Williams, Federico García Lorca, and Arthur Miller, for a full fifteen years thereafter. Additionally, during the last years of the Nazi occupation he toured Greece as pianist to the theatre group of the Greek Resistance Movement. At one point during this affiliation a member of a right-wing organization savagely attacked the young accompanist and shattered his front teeth. Never too bothered about his appearance, Mános wasn't much concerned about the damage and it was thirty years before he got the teeth attended to, but he was so seriously disturbed by the outrage and violence of the attack that he determined to remove himself from the front lines of political activism from that moment onwards.

Beside the productions at the Art Theatre, Hadjidákis also began achieving elsewhere. In 1946 he began writing for Greek and foreign films, becoming in 1960 the first Greek composer to receive an Oscar, although for the acclaim that he received throughout his life for such cinematic work he felt little regard. In 1948 his collection of ten piano pieces 'For a Little White Seashell, Opus 1' achieved the honour of public performance by the great American pianist Julius Katchen. The pieces were of a style clearly Greek but also redolent of some of the works of the Polish and Russian classical composers Szymanowski and Prokofiev. So the very next year conservative Greek society was shocked to hear Hadjidákis delivering a lecture in praise of *rebétika*, the 'low-life' songs of Greece's early 20th century refugee camps, or slums, formed largely as a result of Greece's traumatic Asia Minor Disaster of 1914 to 1923 and the tragic displacement, or 'population exchange', which followed it. Athenian conservative displeasure did not, however, deter the young composer and soon he was producing all sorts of music based upon the reviled *rebétika*: ballet music; further songs and piano works; and music incidental to dramas ranging from ancient tragedy to Shakespeare to modern classics. In 1950 Hadjidákis presented his first music for ancient drama: music for the first two plays, Agamémnon and Choephóroe, from Aeschýlos's Orésteia. And at about this time he also began collaborating with one of Greece's finest 20th century poets, Ághelos Sikelianós.

In 1959 Hadjidákis agreed to introduce to the wider Greek public an old chum from his years in the Greek Resistance Movement. Míkis Theodorákis, a determinedly left-wing activist, had composed melodies for Yiánnis Rítsos's tragic cycle of eight lyrical but highly politically-charged poems entitled 'Epitáphios', and Míkis had then asked his famous and accomplished friend Mános to orchestrate and record them for him. Hadjidákis produced a cycle that was dramatic, musically profound, and of a quality such that it demanded to be listened to, intently, in awe and in silence. Theodorákis, however, was dissatisfied. Rather strangely, he wanted an arrangement of Epitáphios's tragic lyrics which everyone, of 'low culture' and high, street-sweeper or dentist, would want to sing along to! So Theodorákis went away and created his own version. Sung by Grigóris Bithikótsis, it was close in sound and style to the *rebétika* of the slums. It was raw. Thus began a most unusual competition, between two remarkably different recordings of one work. Many Greeks today relish the myth that the two versions produced such enmity between Mános and Míkis that the two composers fell out, went their separate ways, and didn't speak to each other again for years. But this is dramatic invention and quite untrue. Although the general public embraced Theodorákis's version more enthusiastically than they did Hadjidákis's, the two composers remained firm friends.

While Mános continued creating his own new form of Greek music, based upon the modes and motifs prevalent in his birthplace and in Asia Minor, that adjacent land-mass now known as Turkey but historically referred to as either Asia Minor or Anatolía (Anatolía meaning 'The East'), he instituted and financed a competition for serious avant-garde Greek composers, and thus in 1962 helped bring the budding Iánnis Xenákis, the French composer of Greek descent, to wider international attention. The following year he founded 'The Athens Experimental Orchestra', introducing and conducting many new works by further serious contemporary Greek composers. Then shortly after Hadjidákis arrived in New York in 1966, to prepare a theatrical adaptation of one of his musicals, Greece fell under the repressive military régime of the colonels, the régime still spoken of in Greece today as the Júnta (pronounced Húda, as in the 'hood' of a car). Partly because of the *coup d'état* and partly because of the news that he apparently now owed an extremely high amount of tax in Greece, Mános chose to remain in New York, and while there to produce a great many more compositions in different forms.

In 1972 the colonels suddenly suggested a deal. Wanting the internationally famous Greek Oscar-winner to appear to be on their side, as one of their supporters, they proposed that in exchange for a cancellation of all his outstanding taxes he should simply return to Greece and consent to being photographed as happy in their company. The exile agreed, and ever since he has unfortunately and wrongfully been considered in many Greek minds as a political right-winger, if not a traitor. That Hadjidákis remained essentially a cultural subversive, and no typical conservative, was demonstrated only a year after his return to Athens when he set up his café-theatre *Polýtropon* as an outlet by which he might experiment in new musical forms. He was now also absolutely open about his sexuality, such honest public disclosure constituting an act of integrity thought very brave of similarly eminent figures in progressive countries of the time, never mind in strongly Orthodox and very traditional Greece.

When the military dictatorship ended in 1974 Hadjidákis once again became active in the nation's cultural affairs. From 1975 to 1977 he headed the Greek Opera, from 1975 to 1981 Greek Radio's 'Third Programme', and from 1975 to 1982 the State Orchestra. In 1985 and 1986 he edited and published *Tétarto*, a magazine that presented challenging and influential articles on Greek culture and society. In an effort to help protect Greek music from the vulgarities of Western commercial influences, in 1985 he set up a record company, *Sírius*, which continues to this day to release fine music. In 1989 he founded, and of course began to conduct, 'The Orchestra of Colours', a first-class 85-member orchestra that has garnered accolades across Europe for bringing into focus original music that usually goes ignored by other symphony orchestras.

Like many great composers Mános Hadjidákis was prolific in his output, and, while by no means does he rank amongst the world's great classical composers, he was certainly a towering Greek pioneer. For as he respected and revelled in Greek and world cultures, he was at the same time sufficiently nonconformist to produce a corpus of work which was astoundingly new and generally profound. In the sphere of music Mános Hadjidákis synthesized the East with the West. And so immediately following his death on the 15th of June 1994, aged 68 years, there appeared in almost all of the world's more serious newspapers lengthy obituaries in his honour.

Although my discovery of Hadjidákis's philosophy of song and my breakthrough in performing his music were of course inspiring, I ignored the call to greater action for eight more years. And then, after reading again my notes on his beliefs about the power and function of song one afternoon a few years ago, I determined to purchase a very fine Internet radio much lauded by lovers of classical music. I hoped it might 'let me in', further, into that world of pleasures and mysteries of which Hadjidákis had written. I tuned this astounding machine to the very best of the scores of stations that broadcast from within music-loving Greece, and from then on for several hours during and after dinner, almost every night of the week, Greece's finest music flooded the living-room of a house in a remote valley in the hills of South Shropshire. It quickly became apparent that the most irresistible of these many stations were those run by people as spell-bound as myself by the music of composers like Hadjidákis and Theodorákis. I also found that there was at least one Greek radio station which was able to broadcast an almost continuous stream of these composers' music without having to repeat anything within a 24-hour period. But again, although delighted and electrified by this experience, I took no further action. I merely continued to enjoy the intoxication. And so although at the same time I knew that I was getting closer to something, underlying discontent continued to niggle.

As I tried to understand why I felt as I did, the realisations to which I came only vexed me. But thankfully, in my determination to fathom things, I did eventually come to see how the discontent had arisen. Over the decades the stuff and substance of my life had simply become far removed from that which in reality I really needed, removed from that which has always most intrigued and excited me. There had been, and was still, a disparity and an incongruency between the actual focal points of my life and my real inclinations. So I eventually saw that I needed to be braver, that I needed to put aside all the 'important' projects and matters that filled my days, to let those real and very old desires breathe again. I had to go back, all the way, to revisit even those crucial first moments amongst the hibiscus and frangipani of Fiji, hearing for the first time those exotic sounds of the East. I had to attend to my attraction to that particular form of music, that stream of Eastern sound that rushed into my life all the way back then, almost fifty years earlier.

In particular, I had to get to the heart of the music of Mános Hadjidákis. I transferred my old and much-used LP of Mihális Theodórou to a computer disc (the album has never been released on CD), made three copies, popped them into different players around the house and in the car, and then, for the first time in years, let that sunny, glorious, and magical music lift me again, each day. I began to devour books about Greece and learn a little Greek. And soon it was obvious where all this was heading! But I still wavered. Then my partner, decisive and devoted as ever, delivered the needed nudge. One evening over dinner I was informed that a return flight to Athens had been booked for several months hence and that I had plenty of time to start preparing!

Millions visit Athens annually, and many at the drop of a hat. Some people just get up and go for the weekend. Off they trot to Greece, trundling their wheeled cases behind them, with almost as much ease and nonchalance as if off for the weekly 'shop'. But for me, Athens has always been something very much more, almost sacred. Going to Athens is like daring to approach 'the revered one' - daring, still as a person from right down there on the other side of the globe, to approach the far-away shrine that has for so long been held in awe. A few weeks in Athens would be a step right outside my comfort zone. But I had just read the advice of a psychologist that if someone tells you they'd really love to do something, and they haven't yet done it although they say they intend to and there's really been nothing to stop them getting on with it, then they're simply lying, lying to others and lying to themselves. So during the winter spanning 2009 and 2010 I finally stepped up to the obsession of my life.

I briefly passed through Athens in 1991, but as with most visitors to Greece the intention was simply to escape the cold of the north and enjoy a couple of weeks' respite in the warmth and relaxation of a sunny and tranquil Greek island. So, like most people, we passed just a couple of nights in Athens and then rushed to Piraeus, to its ferries and the beautiful Aegean. Now, looking back, I can remember hearing at that time, though ever so faintly, a voice within calling 'Stay! Don't go! This is where you need to be!' I didn't listen. But finally I am. At last I'm going to get to grips with Athens. I'm going to mine this city and find what it's really all about, and from where and from what the magic and allure of all its extraordinary music arises. The excitement, the reading, and all the intensive research and preparation in the months and weeks and days leading up to my departure, has almost killed me!

回 回 回 回

2

Genocide & Rebétika

Odós Ermoú & Psyrrí

Just after touch-down, in the large main hall of the wordily-titled 'Athens International Airport Elefthérios Venizélos' there's suddenly before me a CD shop selling hundreds and hundreds and hundreds of Greek recordings! Greek faces and Greek names of Greek singers line the shelves in profusion. Their presence is like the great welcoming clang of a gong, it's the finest of greetings. Furthermore, the shop's long back wall has been entirely coated with a giant poster promoting a new recording of songs by Mános Hadjidákis! What an embrace, what a welcome! I've clearly arrived where I've so long yearned to be. And perhaps I should snap up the new disc there and then? No, it can wait till later, for the chances are slim of any new recording outdoing my old Theodórou.

I want to really savour Athens as I enter it, and so, rather than the underground, I choose the bus, Coach X95. As soon as an energetic young man leaps into the driver's seat, tugs at the gears and turns the wheel wide, the X95 hurtles a dozen or so Greeks and me rapidly towards the city and Sýntagma Square. At first we fly past massive modern buildings surrounded by car-parks and colourful well-maintained gardens. Then we move on through fields of gnarled and twisted olive trees. The highway cuts right through them. Next we come upon a corrugated-iron and cardboard shanty-town, a reminder for me of the frightful slums I've seen in Mumbai and Kolkata, in India. It's right beside the impressive multi-laned motorway. Many of the cardboard shacks are protected from the rain by large thin sheets of clear plastic, wrapped over and around them like cling-film. And thrusting up here and there through the flat plastic-covered 'roofs', and seemingly in direct contact with the cardboard and the transparent plastic sheeting, are narrow metal drainpipes through which wisps of smoke escape, from stoves and fires inside the shacks of card. The poverty and the danger are startling.

The traffic moves at a noticeably fast pace; pauses at lights are few and brief. All manner of modern concrete buildings are soon flashing by, leaving me little time to decode their Greek signage. A vast and sleek supermarket of the French-owned Carrefour chain suddenly rushes past, as large and as long as the biggest supermarkets of the UK. Next come endless furniture shops with windows full of expensive and impressive furniture of the traditional gilt 'Versailles' variety, as well as tables, beds, sofas and chairs of the stark ultramodern kind. Then well before I expect it we're pulling up in Sýntagma Square, in the heart of Athens! I ask the driver, in my poor Greek, where Ermoú Street is, and at first he looks puzzled, but then his eyes sparkle, he grins with flashing white teeth and roars 'You mean, Odós AIR-rrrrrrrrr-MOO!' He delights in rolling the r and hitting me with a proud tsunami of Greek testosterone, for the street is named after the great messenger of the gods Hermés (pronounced rather like Air-MIS).

Hermés was also thought of as a god of persuasion, and perhaps it's because of this attribute that I discover pedestrianized Ermoú to have become extremely stylish. For from its high and wide windows there loudly reaches forth every manifestation of wealth and ostentatious luxury. Aided by all the tools of the persuasive arts, seductive Athenian mannequins show off the trendiest and most extravagant of Western fashions. And gazing at the displays, in states of desire and indecision, dawdling late-afternoon shoppers weave and mingle their way from one side of the street to the other, pausing to admire or to examine, bending to read the price tags. In 2006 a major firm of global analysts, headquartered in New York, ranked Ermoú Street as the 10th most expensive retail location in the world.

When I find my hotel, I'm warmly welcomed by a well-educated Greek woman called Roúla, who, she tells me, has ten years of experience as a receptionist in fine hotels in New York and Paris. She has the perfect room for me. It's spotlessly clean, filled with lots of old-fashioned and very comfortable dark wooden furniture, the paintwork is a gentle yellow, the fabrics dark green, the floor a greyish marble, and several fine Greek archaeological prints hang framed upon the walls. An enclosed little hallway and bathroom will buffer me well from any late-night noise in the corridor, and from the bed I have a wide and unobstructed view of the wooded spur of Philopáppou Hill and the fine Byzantine-style domes of both the National Observatory and the Church of Aghía Marína high upon its slopes. Beyond the hill, the trees, and the domes, the late afternoon sun has begun falling over the Saronic Gulf, the Pelopónnesos, and the Iónian Sea.

Unpacked by 7.30 and hungry, I venture out into the night for something to eat, but hopefully, better than that, for a little dinner in some wonderfully magical and musical place! I walk and walk, savouring the city by night and passing all sorts of restaurants in which Greek music springs from hidden sound systems. But I'm hoping for something authentic, something better than just recorded music. I make my way cautiously into Psyrrí - cautiously because while the name 'Psyrrí' is asserted by some to derive from the Greek slang for 'fleeced', due to the quarter's history of roughness, a considerable part of Psyrrí today is unpleasant and dilapidated, and home to junkies, destitutes, and illegal immigrants.

Near Plateía Iróon, the Square of Heroes, and amongst a string of restaurants and *ouzerí*, there comes into view a characterful *mousikó mezedopoleío*, a simple Greek restaurant specialising in live music. This one is decorated in traditional style with much colourful Greek bric-à-brac upon its walls. Through the glass of the front door, I make out four singer-musicians in the passionate and visceral throes of a *rebétiko*! I head in but find there are only two other diners: a couple of friends sitting at a table for four which is literally covered in various dishes of food and jugs and glasses filled with water and wine. And it's an astounding and a striking coincidence that on this my first night in Athens one of the two men looks just like the large and stately Hadjidákis in his later years! They eat and occasionally turn their heads to the musicians, to sing out loud along with the odd phrase or perhaps even for the duration of a whole verse or chorus. I order *oúzo* and water and a small plate of *bekrí mezé*, pieces of pork in a tasty red sauce, and then sit back to revel in the impassioned singing and the accompaniment flying from fingers moving frantically up and down the necks of the two *bouzoúkia*. Eventually I speak with the Hadjidákis look-alike, and he and his friend readily enthuse about the musicians, assuring me I've come upon a place where one only hears the original and authentic *rebétika*!

Each *rebétiko* brings into focus some aspect or concern of the subculture that existed almost a hundred years ago in the *hashish* dens of the port of Piraeus (properly spelt Peiraiás in Greek, and pronounced pee-ray-US). The singular subculture of the Piraeus *hashish* dens was generated by thousands upon thousands of Greek refugees from Asia Minor. These *mikrasiátes* were Greeks who had fled to Greece during the 'Asia Minor Disaster', of 1914 to 1923. The Disaster included the 'Great Fire of Smýrna', of 1922, and the enforced population exchange, or, more correctly, the ethnic cleansing, of 1923, which saw 1.3 million Christians forced to leave their ancient homeland in Asia Minor for the newly enlarged Greece, while most of the roughly 400,000 Muslims of Greece, regardless of the fact that many of them spoke only Greek, were required to move in the opposite direction. The countless refugees from Anatolía ('The East'), crammed inside their Piraeus slums in wretched dwellings which they put together from mud-bricks or sheets of old tin, sang of their sufferings, their exile, their poverty, drink, drugs, disease, crime, violence, death, prostitution, love and eroticism. But despite the horrendous experiences of these displaced people, not all of their songs were sad. Much *rebétika* is rousing and joyful, music that often inspires listeners to take to the floor and to lose themselves in slow, ecstatic, and concentrated dance. But whether sad or joyful, all *rebétika* come from a place that is raw and visceral.

The catastrophe of 1914 to 1923 is also known by some as the period of the Greek Genocide. The unbelievably tragic events of this time came about partly, and sadly, as a result of Greece's *Megáli Idéa* (The Great Idea), a nationalist dream and irredentist ambition which arose after the end of the Greek War of Independence, of 1821 to 1830. The Great Idea was desirous of eventually extending the new Greek borders of 1830 still further, so as to encompass all those ethnic Greeks who had been left living very close to the new Greek state but not, unfortunately, within it. These 'stranded' Greeks included the many Greek communities of the north, of Macedonía, and of Thrace; and all of those Greeks who lived on historically Greek islands that remained under Turkish occupation; but, most of all, the two million or so Greeks whose forebears had flourished on the coasts and many inland areas of Asia Minor for 3,000 years. In remote Cappadokía alone, in the mountainous south-east of Turkey, there lived an estimated 50,000 Turkish-speaking Greek Orthodox Christians. The *Megáli Idéa* sought to reach and embrace even these. In short, it sought extended and total Greek independence from *Tourkokratía* (as the Turkish domination had become known), with Constantinople (now Istanbul but once Constantinoúpoli, the centre of the Byzantine Empire) becoming again the city that all Greeks would look to as their capital.

The catastrophe came about because the Greeks' discontent, and their *Megáli Idéa*, engendered such fears amongst Turkish leaders that unfortunately their solution for dealing with those fears was, in the end, to choose to deliberately 'cleanse' Asia Minor of every one of its Greek Orthodox citizens. Following the War of Independence, Crete had been one of those islands that remained under Turkish control, but in January 1897 Cretans desiring union with Greece revolted against their Turkish occupiers and thereby sparked revolt elsewhere, culminating in the brief Greco-Turkish War that occurred three months later on the northern mainland, in an area that was eventually to be returned to Greek control. Although the Turks quickly forced a Greek retreat and won that brief war, such events naturally raised Turkish anxiety as to Greece's dream of liberating those several million Greeks who dwelt in Asia Minor. The Committee of Union and Progress, which formed the Turkish government of the time and which was inspired by the ideals of 'The Young Turks', could only perceive the Greek dream as a distinct and dangerous threat.

Thus in 1914 there began the most barbarous, cruel, and inhuman removal of all indigenous Christians from Asia Minor, notably from the areas of Thrace, Póntus, Constantinople, and Smýrna, but overall from roughly the entire western two thirds of what is now the Republic of Turkey. The 'cleansing' extended also to those nearby islands that were still under the control of the Ottoman dynasty though they were inhabited mostly by Greeks. By the end of 1914 the 'cleansing' had caused roughly 100,000 Greeks to flee their native Anatolía for Greece. At the same time the Turks employed horrific methods to remove Armenians from the region, for they too were Christian. Well over a million Armenians were thus deported, while about a further million and a half perished through slaughter or because they had been driven into the Syrian desert to be left to die of thirst and starvation. The European Parliament in Brussels has recognised the Armenian Genocide since the 18th of June 1987.

By 1918 questions had been raised in the Ottoman Parliament as to the murder of large numbers of Greeks, the expulsion to Greece of many others, and the deaths of thousands of Greek males who had been conscripted to brutal 'labour battalions' in the harsh Turkish interior. In 1922 the Ottoman Central Council of Póntus stated that in its area alone more than a million and a half Armenians and Greeks had been massacred by local agents. Despite these appalling and significant losses, however, the *Megáli Idéa* almost succeeded. Shortly after the end of the First World War, Greek forces crossed the high barren central plateau of Anatolía, driving the Turks ever backwards, towards Asia (from whence they had come, centuries earlier), but then, at the very last moment, due to utter exhaustion and weariness, to broken supply chains, and to their isolation on that high, dry, and barren plateau, the Greek army momentarily weakened. Suddenly the Turks got the upper hand, and the Hellenic army had no option but to flee. But as it retreated across the central plateau, towards the coast, its soldiers, bitterly disappointed and furious after having come so close to victory, torched many of the abandoned Greek villages and almost every inhabited Turkish hamlet or town upon which they came.

Such arson and vengeful acts of violence, all subsequently acknowledged by Greece's leader of that time, Elefthérios

Venizélos, were of course totally abhorrent and appalling. However, they unleashed the most monstrous reprisal from the other side, when the Turks, pursuing the fleeing Greeks, reached the towns of the coast and in particular the city of Smýrna. Greeks and Turks inflicted numerous atrocities upon each other in these final years of the Ottoman period, including extensive pillaging and indiscriminate massacres of entire towns and villages, but substantial documentation presents totally credible evidence that the Greeks' atrocities caused the unleashing of the greatest hellishness of all shortly after the Turks entered Smýrna. As thousands upon thousands of Greek inhabitants huddled along the city's harbour-front, desperate to be rescued, and Mustafá Kemál, the Turks' leader, lodged in comfort on the outskirts of the city, Turkish soldiers and irregulars massacred at least 30,000 Greeks and Armenians in cold blood and systematically plied petrol over every part of the city except its Turkish quarter, before setting the petrol alight and razing most of Smýrna to the ground. Many of those huddled on the quayside were killed by the scorching heat and flames, others hurled themselves to their deaths in the harbour, and rescue efforts came late.

In January 1923, the 'Convention Concerning the Exchange of Greek and Turkish Populations', later ratified shortly after the Treaty of Lausanne, set in motion the tragic population exchange that was intended to bring the disaster to an end. Even the 50,000 Turkish-speaking Greeks in the far south-east of Asia Minor were amongst those the treaty forced from their homeland and sent packing to Greece. Of the total 1.3 million Greeks who managed to escape death on the horrendous journey westwards, most entered Greek territory with diseases such as smallpox, typhus, and cholera. Many arrived in Greece bearing nothing more than the clothes they had fled in and maybe a few items they or a beast or two had been able to carry. All of their property and land in Turkey or on the islands had been confiscated. Efforts to compensate them for their losses were ragged and haphazard. Here is how Ernest Hemingway, in a cable he wired to an American paper in 1922, described just one scene he witnessed.

In a never-ending, staggering march the Christian population of Eastern Thrace is jamming the roads toward Macedonia. The main column crossing the Maritza River at Adrianople is twenty miles long. Twenty miles of carts drawn by cows, bullocks, and muddy-flanked water buffalo, with exhausted, staggering men, women and children, blankets over their heads, walking blindly in the rain beside their worldly goods.

This main stream is being swelled from all the back country. They don't know where they are going. They left their farms, villages, and ripe brown fields and joined the main stream of refugees when they heard the Turk was coming. Now they can only keep their places in the ghastly procession while mud-splashed Greek cavalry herd them along like cow-punchers driving steers.

It is a silent procession. Nobody even grunts. It is all they can do to keep moving. Their brilliant peasant costumes are soaked and draggled. Chickens dangle by their feet from the carts. Calves nuzzle at the draught cattle wherever a jam halts the stream. An old man marches bent under a young pig, a scythe and a gun, with a chicken tied to his scythe. A husband spreads a blanket over a woman in labor in one of the carts to keep off the driving rain. She is the only person making a sound. Her little daughter looks at her in horror and begins to cry. And the procession keeps moving.

All of these Greek Orthodox Christians of Anatolía, the Black Sea, the Caucasus, and Eastern Thrace, were then thrown together on pieces of Greek wasteland where all they could do was create shanty-towns consisting of acres of wretched and miserable hovels, filthy and infested with vermin and in which they dwelt sick and hungry. These 'camps' that were created were immediately slums, places of frightful overcrowding, abject poverty, and disease. Their inhabitants had lived through a nightmare that we can only imagine today by recalling television footage from the early 1990s showing something of the genocide committed by the Serbs against 200,000 Muslim civilians in Bosnia, or the plight of people resisting the régimes of Libya and Syria in 2011 and 2012. The situation of the refugees of the Asia Minor Disaster was so serious that the newly-born League of Nations became involved, although unfortunately only at the last and only to assist with resettlement.

The land that the refugees arrived in was as we find third world countries today, for Greece had entered the Great War in 1917 and soon after it ended the nation had plunged into and suffered from its long and disastrous campaign in Asia Minor. In 1922 Greece had a population of 4.5 million: a year later it had somehow to accommodate 1.3 million more. Conditions quickly became such that it was feared the state would collapse. The Greek outflow from Anatolía in 1922 and 1923 was at that time considered to be the most tragic *éxodus* in the history of humanity, only to be eclipsed by the Nazis' attempt 20 years later to exterminate all the Jews of Europe, and, 24 years later, by the 'partition' of India. And of course such monstrous efforts as these do not end once they have been officially completed: their tragic effects linger on. In 1930, seven years after the population exchange between Greece and Turkey, there were an estimated 30,000 refugee families still living in squalor in the slums of Piraeus and Thessaloníki, as well as in other parts of Greece. The condition of the Greek state remained so desperate that in 1930 the Greek prime minister, Elefthérios Venizélos, travelled to Turkey to discuss with Mustafá Kemál, 'Father of the Turks', amidst a series of lavish balls and glittering banquets, the possibility of a mutually beneficial working-partnership.

An excellent impression of the indescribable suffering endured during the long eight years of the Greek genocide is offered in the excellently translated novel 'Farewell Anatolía' by Didó Sotiríou, for many years a standard text (*Matoména Hómata*, literally 'The Bloodied Earth') in Greek schools. It's a harrowing read and at points one can hardly believe the clues it offers regarding the horrors of the period. However, Sotiríou's novel is based on well-documented facts and anyone wishing to read more deeply can consider the comprehensive bibliography at *www.greek-genocide.org*.

By enabling some understanding of the terror of the time, reports like Hemingway's and books like Sotiríou's also enable an understanding of the roots of *rebétika*, for they help us to appreciate the anguish and pain that existed in the slums and which thus gave birth to that unique form of Greek song which is still being performed throughout Greece today. For the horror of the Asia Minor catastrophe has most certainly not been forgotten. Only twelve years ago, in 1998, the Greek Parliament affirmed by decree the genocide of Greeks throughout Asia Minor, including the Póntus region, and designated the 14th of September as an annual 'Day of National Remembrance for the Genocide of the Asia Minor Greeks by the Turkish State'. Twenty-five other international states or authorities have formally recognised the Greek Genocide, the United States Senate, in 1921, having been the first. In 2007 the Greek Genocide was recognised by the International Association of Genocide Scholars. Unfortunately both the Armenian and Greek genocides continue to be denied by the Republic of Turkey.

The mourned East is so obviously perpetuated in the Eastern strains I'm hearing on this first night in Athens. For many of the Christians who fled Asia Minor spoke only Turkish, and, while they had sung in some of the musical modes that were used by the Greeks of the mainland, they contributed Eastern and Arabic modes and motifs to the creation of the new *rebétika*. Indeed, some early *rebétika* did not only sound musically like a mix of Greek and Eastern styles but the lyrics were sometimes sung not in Greek but in Turkish, Arabic, or Judezmo. Of the 50,000 Turkish-speaking Christian refugees from the Anatolian interior many could not speak, never mind sing, in Greek, hence the *rebétika* that exists in Turkish and in Arabic. *Rebétika* in Judezmo exists due to this Judeo-Spanish tongue having been the common language of Thessaloníki during the Ottoman occupation and having remained in substantial use in that city in the years following the population exchange. In fact, Judezmo remained prevalent in Thessaloníki right up until the Nazi's extermination of the city's massive Jewish population during the Second World War.

Although more and more people have gradually been entering this *mezedopoleío* while I've been sitting enraptured by the songs of the *rebétiko* players, the two women from the kitchen tell me, during one of their frequent cigarette breaks at the table beside mine (yes, Greece's recent cigarette ban is clearly being flouted!), that the place won't be full until two in the morning, and that the singers will continue not only until then but onwards until about four! I find this amazing, for since my arrival I've watched these men smoking and constantly sipping *oúzo* and wine or whisky between their songs, although never hitting wrong notes in the complicated melodies that they sing or the intricacies they pluck upon their strings! And to perform passionately and emotionally, song after song, for eight hours, with not a piece of sheet-music in sight, is also remarkable. Between each *rebétiko* they briefly discuss what they'll perform next. Usually this entails one of them singing a phrase or two, or picking out a melody on the strings to jog the memories of the others, then each person summons to mind the lyrics of the agreed piece and then off they go, like a bandwagon, the wheels grinding into motion and everyone rocking along in harmony behind the melody. The size of their repertoire is impressive, and there are just over twenty-four thousand *rebétiko* songs on record.

The musicians are fully aware of my delight tonight and so it isn't long before we get talking. Aristotéles and Nikólaos sing and play *bouzoúkia*, while the other two sing and handle a drum and tambourine. The four kindly oblige me with some Hadjidákis but it seems light stuff indeed compared with the raw and pure *rebétika* from which it's derived and which they've been playing and singing with such power and passion. As the hours pass we have further interaction: sometimes a few questions and answers are exchanged, and at others Áris simply calls out, over everybody in the restaurant and often in the middle of an instrumental section, '*Yeiá sou*, David!' In similar fashion he cries out to others whose names he knows and it creates great atmosphere and rapport, a wonderful warmth, familiarity, and intimacy. And over the music people call back to him '*Ópa! Ópa!*' - demanding of him and the others, and everyone present, even greater zest and zeal, even more zip and zing, in rousing and deliberate exclamations of sheer joy!

At one point Nikólaos beckons me over to where they're sitting and asks me what other Hadjidákis songs I know and I begin to sing for him one that I've been studying back in Shropshire. Suddenly everyone in the restaurant falls silent. (It's now about eleven and the place is roughly a third full!) In absolute stillness I hear a seemingly far-away and tiny voice, mine, singing the first four phrases of *I Pétra Eín' O Thánatos* (The Stone is Death). Unfortunately they don't recognise it but they do know something similar, and so off they go again, and it's thrilling! Yes, *Ópa! Ópa! Ópa!*

Well after midnight I know I must go, for my journey from London began at five in the morning and I'm tired. As I say farewell, it's clear the band has been pleased with my appreciation of their music and they've been impressed by the fact that I've been singing along, as best I can, nearly all of the time. 'David, you play an instrument?' asks Nikólaos. (He charmingly seems to mean that if I do, then I could join them!) When I tell him that unfortunately I only play the keyboard, he replies in all sincerity 'Then you can play the melodeon or the accordion!' Simple, he thinks, because the prodigious musicians of Greece often play more than just one or two instruments. Few play only one. I thank them all profusely and go to some lengths to make sure that they all fully understand as I tell them what extraordinary performers I believe they are.

I then go to my room on this first night in Athens totally elated. It seems almost foolish not to have foreseen it, but I had no inkling that on my very first evening I'd walk straight into the magic that's haunted me for decades. It's astonishing that I've begun my sixteen days and nights in the city of my dreams with such overwhelming satisfaction, plummeting right into the heart of live *rebétika*, actually speaking and interacting with the musicians themselves, and even, myself, singing for them and with them! I'm devastated. I never thought such a shaft of joy could be! The exhilaration experienced this evening in that *mezedepoleío* has me feeling, as I fall asleep, like someone who has fallen totally in love, as if up till now I've been completely wasting my life!

3

Edge of the East

Kapnikaréa; Kerameikós; Technópolis;
Hill of Nymphs; Karaghiózis; Athenian Operetta;
& Áno Petrálona.

A fter a rather amusing chat at reception with the very
theatrical Kiría Roúla (Madam Roúla), I strike out, on my
first Athenian morning, for a good bookshop, and am quickly
surprised to stumble upon nothing less than a FNAC! Yes, a
branch of the famous French retail chain *Fédération Nationale
d'Achats des Cadres* right here in the centre of Athens! And
what an impressive branch it is! Five spacious floors offer
all manner of modern entertainment-technology, to books,
recordings, and films. When a young assistant very kindly
comes to my aid with a mixture of learner's English and
simple Greek, specially dumbed-down for me, I can't recall
the last time I enjoyed such delightful interaction with a shop
assistant. With exceptional charm she helps me select a heavy
book-map of Athens and Piraeus which is entirely in Greek,
and which should, therefore, force me to become quicker at
using that difficult Greek alphabet! Though it costs just over
twenty euros it's a good investment, for during the next two
weeks I intend to pound the pavements of this city and to
never get lost.

In Ermoú Street (remember, AIR-rrrrrrrrrr-MOO!), I locate
the first gem on my itinerary, the little Church of Panaghía
Kapnikaréa, or simply 'Kapnikaréa', so named because it was
founded by an official who was responsible for collecting 'the
hearth tax', the Greek word for smoke which arises from any
hearth being *kapnós*, and a hearth-tax gatherer therefore being
known as a *kapnikaréas*. Thought to have been built in the 11th
century, Kapnikaréa is regarded as one of the oldest and most

interesting little churches in Athens. Its interior is all dark, warm in tone, and intimate. Its beautiful floor of coloured marble, its ancient icons, and its many frescoes glimmer in the light of scores of candles lit by a stream of devotees, by Greeks young and old, coming and going as they attend to their morning business. The atmosphere of this charming little church dedicated to the Virgin Mother of God is rich and theatrical but also humble. The frescoes that cover almost every square inch of its walls and ceilings are all 'fresh' but 'old', created in the 1950s by the artist Phótis Kóntoglou. Painted in the style and shades typical of the Byzantine period they enable us to envisage what the interior of many early Christian Eastern Orthodox Churches probably looked like centuries ago, before paint and plaster, blackened by the smoke of endless burning candles, began to age and flake. And although it is recent, this profusion of Byzantine-like frescoes here in Kapnikaréa is a reminder of what 'Byzantine' properly means: that which was produced within the civilization and empire which arose from the enforced fusion of Greek culture with Christianity. (Of course our common adjective 'byzantine' - without the capital letter - imputes a more specific quality. It arose from Western perceptions that the politics and bureaucracy typical of the Greek and Christian fusion were labyrinthine and inflexible, not to mention full of scheming, deviousness, corruption, and intrigue.)

The Greeks' love-affair with *eikónes* (icons) has been long and difficult. When worship of the gods of ancient Greece was finally suppressed by the emperor Justinian in 529 CE, the old gods were simply replaced in the people's devotions by images of the Christian saints. Shamed by the beliefs of Muslim neighbours with regard to idolatry and representations of the human figure, still forbidden in Islam to this very day, Byzantine emperor Leo III (c. 685 to 741 CE) then banned the adoration of even Christian images and icons. Later, Eiríni, widow of Leo IV, emperor from 775 to 780 CE, rescinded the ban and permitted them. In 815 CE Leo V banned them again, and then Theodóra, another widow, this time of Emperor Theóphilos (813 to 842 CE), allowed them! With iconoclasm thus banished once and for all, ever since then reverence towards *eikónes* and frescoes has been a hallmark of Greek Orthodoxy, in fact Byzantine architecture came to be chiefly all about creating magically decorated interiors beneath a series of domes. And so today the interior of little Kapnikaréa provides a wall-to-wall feast of sacred imagery beneath its domes. Stand very still in the semi-darkness, surrounded by the faces of the countless saints, smell the fragrance of the flickering candles and the remnants of incense, and then just listen and it's not too difficult to conjure up the beautiful echoing strains of the unaccompanied Eastern liturgy which has been sung within this little church for approximately a thousand years. Yet after the Greek War of Independence, in the early 1800s, when Athens was being rebuilt by its new Bavarian administrators, this charming church was scheduled for demolition. But thankfully, King Ludwig I of Bavaria, avid lover of Greek and Roman culture, sufficiently admired the little Church of Panaghía Kapnikaréa to insist of the city's new administrators that they show it mercy.

Then after all the hustle and bustle of the rest of Ermoú Street, right down at its western end there comes into view my first Athenian museum, the little Oberlaender, tucked into an elevated corner above all that has been exposed of Athens's ancient Kerameikós cemetery and therefore known to locals simply as the Kerameikós Museum. Many of the finds unearthed in this graveyard are displayed in the National Archaeological Museum, but those which were discovered by members of the German Archaeological Institute, after taking over the excavations in 1913, are presented here in the building named after the wealthy German-American textile magnate who funded the excavations and the erection of this museum during the 1930s. Athens currently offers its visitors just over a staggering total of 80 museums - and this sum does not include the many 'art galleries' where paintings and sculptures are displayed for purchase. Quite deliberately, I'm starting with possibly the smallest archaeological museum in the city, whereas most visitors head directly for either the Acrópolis Museum or the National Archaeological Museum. I prefer to start with exposure to smaller displays and then to work gradually towards grander exhibitions.

Before entering the Oberlaender, I pause and briefly look out over the ancient cemetery of 400 BCE. The entire site is all a luscious well-rained-upon green and the air is singing with delightful bird song, pleasantly audible despite the roar of the nearby Athens-Piraeus highway, the building of which, in 1861, led to the discovery of this long-lost *nekrotafeío*, or cemetery. The entire scene below the hillock upon which I stand is punctuated by creamy ruins overlooked by the stately Neo-Byzantine church of Aghía Triáda (The Holy Trinity). Beside a marshy brook that wanders almost undetectably through the site there arise a number of burial mounds, the Street of Tombs can be discerned, and the foundations of ancient towers and walls are visible, as are all manner of grave-markers. Places where people were laid to rest are distinguished by plain slabs or the remains of elaborately decorated *stéle*, or funerary urns, or columns topped with sculpted designs, or low table-monuments, or the remains of podia and bases of statues and sculpted reliefs. The luscious and vivid winter green of these cemetery grounds dotted with ceramics is thus named 'Kerameikós'. For this part of old Athens was named after Kéramos, a son of Diónysos and Ariádne, and hero of those potters who once settled along the nearby excellently clayish banks of the Iridanós brook - so that they might easily practise their craft and make a living in the service of the adjacent graveyard.

The rooms of the little Oberlaender Museum are packed with an impressive display of fine ancient artefacts that have been retrieved from the graveyard outside: warm sensuous funerary reliefs and sculptures, terracotta figurines, vases, urns, plaques and other ceramic pieces, often of exquisite delicacy. Archaeologists have discovered that in the oldest graves in Kerameikós, going back as far as the 12th century BCE, the dead were laid with a few small decorated ceramics in tombs that were lined with slabs. But from 1100 BCE cremation prevailed, and so special funeral pots, or urns, containing the ashes of the deceased, came to be laid within the tombs. Grave-offerings too were buried with these pots and urns, and they were usually placed inside variously shaped and highly decorated vases, the paintings upon which have related to us a great deal about life in ancient Athens. By 7 BCE the potters' craft had so developed that graves were also being surmounted by monumental funerary urns. And several centuries later, elaborate statuary was being added, either as luxurious reliefs in large stone panels or as complete figures in the round. However, in the 3rd century BCE, under the rule of Demétrios of Pháleron, all such monumental work at Kerameikós came to an end: Demétrios forbade anything other than small, plain, and modest columns. But at least he didn't destroy all the fine work that had already been created. So this morning, all these centuries later, one typically grand old Kerameikós sculpture, a magnificent stone lion, roughly a metre and a half in length, sits watchfully in the far corner of the museum's verandah, carefully eyeing everyone who comes and goes at the entrance. For over two thousand years he sat upon an Athenian's tomb in the *nekrotafeío* below. Now he guards the entire site, including all of those small dull columns that followed the edict of Demétrios.

Overhanging a hidden corner of the grounds is a vast and thriving lemon tree, bedecked prolifically with small fattened rugby-balls of brilliant sunny yellow, each fruit sparkling like a jewel against the rich dark green of the great tree itself. And beneath, but out of the way and not meant to be observed as part of the Kerameikós exhibition-trail, is an enormous terracotta pot, about half a metre wide and a whole metre high. It's just lying on its side, old, discarded, out of the way, with only a small part of its rim broken off and lost. Its fired clay is rich, ochre-coloured, warm and so marvellously Mediterranean. It sits in a splurge of leaping green winter weed, a kind of Greek nettle which is fuller, brighter, and more juicy-looking than the British variety, possibly due to its being watered by the marshy brook that passes through this cemetery's heart - the remains of the original Iridanós. And on the fringes of Kerameikós a great date-palm shoots up as if to reach the summit of Mount Lykavittós, towering in the distance. The palm's long verdant branches, thrown out as gracefully as a dancer's arms, transport me momentarily back to the vast date plantations of the wadis of Sa'udi Arabia. They, and the giant fruit-laden lemon tree, are reminders that Athens sits on the edge of 'The Orient', the exotic East.

Over the extremely busy and rather frightening multi-laned Athens-Piraeus highway, with its endless barrage of cars, trucks, and speeding motorbikes, and a safe pedestrian-crossing difficult to locate, there lies Technópolis, the large converted site of the old Athens gasworks, dedicated now, as an arts complex, to Mános Hadjidákis. Here, on my first morning in this long-dreamt-of city, I expect to locate details of concerts, exhibitions, and activities associated with the nation's great and lauded composer. But unfortunately, while there are now fine modern art galleries and several performance-spaces within the old gasworks buildings, there's not a trace of anything whatsoever to do with Mános Hadjidákis except for a small bronze plaque near the main gate, dedicating Technópolis to his memory. Oh, dear. How likely am I to discover anything of Hadjidákis anywhere in Athens if not here?

But what a fine job has been made of converting a dirty old gasworks, a place of grimy pipes, of corroded taps and ugly cylinders, into an arts centre! All the walls of the buildings have been thoroughly cleaned to reveal stonework of rocky creams, beautiful browns, reds and golds. The traditional pantile roofs of funnelled terracotta, all returned to states of good order, once more glow a happy orange against the clear and cloudless blue of the Attic sky. Complementary paintwork in a deep grey-blue and a warming ochre has here and there been introduced to very pleasing effect upon exterior doors, upon arches, and on outdoor partitions. Inside the metal web of one old gas-tank, a many-sided almost-circular galleried theatre and exhibition space has been erected. And just outside the same metal skeleton, all the old pipe-work that once conveyed gas to and from the vast tank that lay within remains in position, although the pipes are now painted in a warm mustard so as to blend with nearby modernist sculptures that are being encouraged to age towards rusted melancholia.

Unfortunately, I've arrived during the *ypnákos*, the Greek siesta, and all the exhibition halls are closed and locked. But in one courtyard at least, there's a small outdoor show. One life-size figure holds out to passers-by a bouquet of extremely fine and delicately filigreed metal flowers and it's astonishing that in this public place no one has yet reached forth to maliciously bend and vandalise them by just the press of a finger. Nearby, a classical life-sized winged-angel extends a flaming torch, all in bronze, as if she has just descended from amongst the gods of ancient Ólympus, to revitalise this site with spirit and life. She succeeds, for if the roar of the adjacent highway didn't echo so loudly within Technópolis's walls one could easily think oneself in some old village high in the mountains of Ípiros (Epirus) or the Pelopónnesos where the buildings are generally of a similar unpainted, natural, and glowing stone.

The adjacent Gázi area, so named because of the once-active gasworks, is mostly like some of the commercial back streets of Kuwait City - all oily metal-filled garages, wholesale suppliers of spare parts and catering equipment, pot-holes and dilapidation. Here in Gázi, however, many modern night-clubs sit strangely amidst the ugliness. These are bars which come alive only late at night, long after all the district's day-time workers are gone and the mantle of darkness masks everything that is unattractive. But for all who come here late at night, and who venture beyond the pleasant square that surrounds the shiny new Metró station, Gázi must be a tricky place to negotiate in the dark. The many uneven, broken, and interrupted pavements suggest a strong likelihood of tripping, or spraining an ankle, or even, by tempting people to walk much more easily down the very middle of the streets, of getting run over. Anyway, although there are apparently as many gay nightclubs in Gázi as there are square ones, I'm unlikely to be visiting here again, not so much because of fear of negotiating hellish footpaths but because I'm not partial to clubs which may only exist provided they're hidden away, in the abandoned areas of a city.

Safely back over the busy highway, a footbridge across the Monastiráki-Piraeus train line lets me head into the locality of Theseíon - where I'm immediately stopped in my tracks by a giant orange tree, shooting straight out of a gap in the pavement directly in front of me. And then I see another, and then another! Street after street is literally lined with trees that are thick with large bright oranges! They fill this neighbourhood with festivity, a sense of carnival, and they must surely be out like this in time for the celebrations of Christmas and New Year! They're a form of completely natural street-decoration. You walk beneath these trees, spaced just five or six metres from each other along both sides of the streets, and are amazed to have come from a horribly cold and snow-covered Britain to a land where, despite winter, apparently thousands of oranges just burst into colour like a myriad suns! It's almost ridiculous, each orange is an effervescence of joy, and the sight of hundreds of them can't but haul your damp wintry northern spirits high.

Several blocks of orange trees onwards, there's a long arcade of dark covered cafés backlit by thousands of tiny twinkling light-emitting diodes, or 'fairy lights'. And within these cafés, under gas-heaters that are pumping out quite unnecessary warmth this pleasantly mild and sunny afternoon, hundreds of young Greeks sit socialising over coffee and cigarettes. Books, papers, and sleek portable computers are parked about upon table-tops amidst cups, glasses, and ashtrays, largely, it seems, for academic effect. For nobody is doing any work here except the staff. I chat briefly to a waiter who saunters by with a tray laden with coffees and bottled water and learn that this arcade hardly ever closes, it's open well into the early hours of the morning. And scanning all of the tables that I pass this afternoon I see not a sign of alcohol. In each café modern trendy Eurobeats pulse quietly from hidden stereo-systems and the whole arcade rings merrily with the sounds of innocent chatter, gaiety, and laughter. There's not a single visual hint amongst the hundreds of people here that anything in Greece at this time is wrong.

Near the north-eastern tip of that large green central lung of Athens which is generally referred to as Philopáppou Hill, I pause at the foot of a tumbling white rocky slope which was once surmounted by the Sanctuary of Zeus. Towards the top of this cascade, which seems on first glance of raw marble though in fact it consists only of rock-hard limestone, an ancient chiselled inscription, dating from about 5 BCE, reads *Hóros Zéus*, indicating a shrine to the god. But higher up, beyond this cascading rock, there was once an earlier shrine, it too marked by a still discernible inscription chiselled in rock: *Hóros Nýmphai*. This rock-cut is now enclosed by the grounds of the Asteroskopeíon, which sits atop the north-eastern tip of Philopáppou Hill and looks for all the world like a large and handsome Byzantine church. It is instead an astronomical observatory, founded in 1842 by the wealthy banker Yeórghios Sínas but designed and built by Theophilus Hansen, the 19th century Danish architect responsible for so many of Athens's fine neo-classical constructions. The inscription in the Observatory garden indicates that this place was sacred to 'nymphs' and hence this point of the ridge is still referred to as The Hill of Nymphs. It's thought likely that the nymphs in question were the daughters of the divine hero Yákinthos, those daughters, or 'Yakinthídes', who, according to legend, were sacrificed for the good of the ancient city. Subsequently, because of their youth and the purpose behind their sacrifice, they became known as the *genéthliai*, a word which means 'concerned with childbirth', or successful regeneration. And so since that time when the *genéthliai* were sacrificed, in order that Athens might prosper, this hill has had a very long and strong relationship with procreation. Upon the grand tumbling cascade of the rough white terraces of its lower part, it's believed that for as long as two thousand years women of Athens partook in a bizarre ritual.

In the creation of Christianity, the first Christians were adept at adapting and christianising 'pagan' myths, sites, and symbols wherever they located them. Thus, certainly by the 13th century, but probably as early as the 5th or 6th centuries, zealous Christians in Athens had very cleverly commandeered the 'holiness' of both 'pagan' shrines upon the Hill of Nymphs by creating within an ancient cistern, dug within the rock adjacent to the shrine to Zeus, a small and simple chapel dedicated to that saint, St. Marína, who is throughout the Greek Orthodox Church a patron of childbirth and expectant mothers. The conical roof of the tiny chapel of Aghía Marína of Theseíon, as well as the upper portion of the narrow circular structure that supports it, looks today as if it has just popped out of the surrounding rock like a mushroom. It's a simple sight, but a charming and a singular one, and at some point after the christianization of the cave-cistern in and upon which the chapel was built this whole hillside came to be respected as The Hill of Aghía Marína. And concurrent with the christianization of the site, and probably as a natural way of making connection with the specific ancient 'holiness' of the place, women petitioned St. Marína by seeking to bring into dramatic contact with the ancient stone of this hillside the same part of their anatomy as is involved in conception and childbirth. Here, for possibly two thousand years but certainly since the practice was first documented by foreign visitors to the city in the 19th century, women of Athens have slid down a particular sloping rock known as the *Tsoulíthra*, meaning 'slide', in the hope of conceiving children or of having an easy labour. By the mid 19th century pregnant women had been observed at it too, believing that they could learn the sex of their unborn babies by the direction to which their bodies inclined, to the left or right, as they slid. Some Greek women were still slipping down *Tsoulíthra* as late as the 1920s. But with the arrival of more and more foreigners in Athens, from the mid 19th century onwards, the practice began to decline. And what slipping and sliding embarrassment failed to quell, church authorities put a decisive end to. The sliding rock was crowned with a concrete terrace which thwarted any woman from getting a good run at it!

The large five-domed church that now rises beside the ancient subterranean chapel of Aghía Marína possesses an interior that is at once clearly Greek Orthodox but also impressively glamorous, theatrical, and smart. It's an interior which sings of the antique past although the whole church was in fact completed only in 1931, to a design modified by the Greek architect Achilléas Yeorghiádis but initiated by Ernst Ziller, the Saxon responsible for so many of Greece's fine buildings. Several massive delicate cut-glass chandeliers, suspended from the high ceiling and bedecked with dozens of tiny candle-bulbs, hang so extremely low that they dominate and illuminate the central space of this church with sheer magnificence. A thick and extraordinarily deep-red carpet floods the floor beneath, as if seeking to rise up and greet the lavish and sparkling displays of cut glass. This afternoon's sun fills the central dome high above with a light that is literally golden, while beneath, here and there in the mysterious dark and upon the richly-stained wooden *eikonostásion* that closes off the sanctuary from the nave, are warming splashes of glittering lemony icons. Over in the dark south-eastern corner, hidden behind a row of columns and ecclesiastical furniture, I peer through a rough womb-like rocky opening into the tiny cave-like interior of the original little chapel that was created within the ancient water cistern at some point between the christianization of 'pagan' Athens and the 13th century. The chapel is now used as the *baptistírion* of the main church and at the centre of its rough floor there stands a huge, magnificent and beautifully decorated silver baptismal font. The greater structure of Aghía Marína possesses a recently-created antique atmosphere, a form of swish faux Byzantine, but surely no other church in Athens can match its rapturously gorgeous and theatrical interior while being connected umbilically to such a magical and historic little parent.

Above the tiny chapel and its larger sophisticated offspring, and beyond the cascade of ancient limestone which they both crown, the upper part of The Hill of Nymphs offers both astounding tranquillity and a splendid view of all that central part of Athens which lies between this spur and Mount Lykavittós. In the warm yellow of the late afternoon sun, as it drops slowly to the edge of the Saronic Gulf behind me, all the creamy buildings of the city below glow beautifully beyond the original Aghía Marína's conical little roof. The deep reddish-brown pantiles of the long Stoá of Áttalos, stretching from left to right on the eastern edge of the Ancient Agorá, seem to bake and glimmer in the final shafts of today's wintry but warm Athenian light.

Rounding, a little higher up The Hill of Nymphs, the handsome Byzantine-looking National Observatory, now home to Greece's environmental research and weather-forecasting operations, I locate to the south-west the ancient deme of Koíli (pronounced KEE-lee), a locality that was somewhat akin to a British country parish or local district. In ancient times the Attica region was dominated by four tribes and each of these was divided into three brotherhoods, or *phratríai*, resulting in a total of twelve *phratríai* which each consisted of a number of *démoi*, or demes. Each *démos* had its own authorities, religious festivals and so forth, and up until 4 BCE the *démos* of Koíli was one of the most densely populated areas of Athens. Today all one can see is where the homes of ancient Greek philosophers and others were cut into the hard white limestone rock: the absolute right-angles of their little rooms, often no bigger than three metres by two, still amazingly easy to make out after the passing of so many centuries.

And what a site for a miniature city! All around is a profusion of thriving growth: ranks of different trees, lush green grass, stalks of delicate pink flowers thrusting several feet high, and now and again a lashing great milky-grey-blue succulent, the *athánatos*, a kind of agave with long sharp spiky leaves erupting from its centre as if desperately seeking escape. At some point in recent months these plants have yielded their once-in-a-lifetime blossom, sending up just one giant flower-stalk each, fourteen to fifteen feet tall, though sometimes they can reach twice that height. Now, in winter, the stalks are dry and woody, suspended in the air like old, long, unbroken bones, still perfectly formed but bereft now of flowers.

Back over on the north side of the hill, the Pnýx, pronounced Pníks, the high 6 BCE location of the world's first ever democratic legislature, presents the most astounding view possible of the Acrópolis and its majestic structures. In Ancient Greece the word Pnýx meant 'a place where you must stand crowded tightly together' and indeed today people still crowd here, in the warm months of summer, to view performances of the Acrópolis *Son-et-Lumière*. The Pnýx itself is a large and almost level plateau set into the hillside but having about it something of the shape of a natural and gentle amphitheatre, so that in ancient times the assembled thousands could clearly hear those who addressed them from its focal point, the *víma*, a platform of stone still intact today and large enough for perhaps a dozen or so people to stand on in comfort. The *víma* is surrounded on three of its sides by three steps, raising it to a height of roughly a metre above the immediate ground. On its remaining side the platform is overlooked by a stone altar that rises some three metres above it. Upon this altar a ritual animal sacrifice marked the start of each of the meetings of the *Ekklesía*, the Assembly of Athens.

As orators like Periclés, Demosthénes, and Themistoclés addressed the citizens of the city from the *víma*, they benefited as they spoke from perhaps the most inspiring backdrop to be seen in any city on Earth. For behind their audience there swept a panorama that included, way out to the speaker's left, The Academy of Pláton, then from west to east every structure and roof-top of the ancient city, with Lykavittós gazing down upon them all, and then finally, over to the speaker's right, the most magnificent view that it's possible to enjoy of the Acrópolis and its crowning resplendence, the Parthenon. The ancient crowd however stood with their backs to this stunning vista and could focus on little more than the speaker and the rocky hillside and sky above him. This may slightly explain why many members of the popular Assembly had literally to be 'roped in'! A quorum of 6,000 citizens was required each day when the Assembly met - otherwise no decision that might be taken could be deemed legal. Thus before each Assembly officials first sent soldiers to the outskirts of the *agorá* below with a very long rope that had been smeared with red paint. Fear of having one's clothes blotched red as the rope was then dragged towards the hillside effectively hastened the city's citizens upwards to their duty, for any tardy souls who ascended to the Pnýx bearing the marks of the rope were further penalised by way of a fine.

As the sun sets pink over Piraeus and the far distant sea, casting the Acrópolis and its Parthenon in fabulous golden glory, I descend this legendary hill in the romantic tranquillity of twilight and suddenly spot on the path before me a perfect sheet of fresh white A4 paper. Upon it, in thick black marker-pen, has been drawn a cock and two balls, along with a mobile telephone number, all very clearly and quite stylishly indicated. A short distance onwards and to one side two figures embrace within a fairly dense cluster of trees. Whether male and female, or same-sex, I can't make out, although one of the two looks definitely middle-aged and feminine. As daylight dims the occasional man or woman walks a dog through the hill's labyrinth of paths, a number of runners flash hurriedly by, pairs of elderly ladies take a slow and gentle early-evening stroll, chatting and chuckling as they go, and young Athenian lovers begin to ascend, hand in hand or arm in arm, to sit and watch the sun depart. This ancient acclivity, this Hill of Nymphs, or Philopáppou Hill as it's generally now called, is clearly still pulsing with life.

At the base of Philopáppou I make my way to the 'Cultural Centre Melína Mercoúri', in Irakleidón Street. The ground floor of the Centre is occupied entirely by the Harídimos Shadow-Puppet Museum, as well as an associated workshop and theatre. The museum features the history of the famous Karaghiózis shadow-puppet, the main character in the traditional Greek shadow-theatre. This form of entertainment is thought to have arrived in Greece from Asia Minor in the early part of the 19th century while Greece was still beset by Ottoman occupation, and it's believed that the Turks acquired it from 14th century Arab travellers who had been entranced by the shadow-theatre of far-away Java. Karaghiózis, the name of the drama's main character, is actually a Turkish term meaning 'Black Eyes'. This figure is however more obviously distinguished by his enormously protuberant and upcurling nose, as well as a hunched back, an extremely long left arm, and a sadly receding hairline. In every show he appears barefoot, his clothes are patched and ragged, and poor Greek that he is he can only support his wife and three boys by endless and very entertaining mischief, aided or thwarted by a dozen or so other characters who populate the Karaghiózis plots. The wily Karaghiózis has shown generations of Greek children how to survive, and how to enjoy life through wit and cunning. The nine hundred or so items on display in this exhibition reveal the whole history of Karaghiózis from 1925 until about 1980 and include many of the hundreds of Karaghiózis scripts and designs that have delighted so many Greek children. The display also reveals the different materials and techniques that have been used by the masters of Greek shadow-puppetry, particularly those of the eponymous Sotíris Harídimos.

On the upper floor of the Cultural Centre Melína Mercoúri a late 19th century collection of Athenian shops has been recreated, revealing how stylish Athenians lived at that time in Greece's history when parts of Athens formed something of a Paris of the Eastern Mediterranean. Each shop has its name emblazoned, in Greek of course, over or upon its frontage, and each shop-window is full of old-fashioned goods and products, many of them bearing original Greek labels. I have an entertaining time making out the lettering, identifying the names of the shops and the hundreds of items in the windows. This fascinating recreation of a late 19th century Athenian *agorá* (a shopping area) takes you right to the heart and daily realities of a certain kind of Athenian life of the time. Clearly, for some people life in late 19th century Athens was not without its share of sophistication and elegance.

The little shops are all arranged as if around a tiny square and in the middle of this space are rows of comfortable seating arranged before a magnificent black grand piano. I'm so tempted to lift its lid and fill this 'city square' with music, for the whole museum is unfortunately completely silent, dead silent, and this exhibition on the upper floor pleads for some background music of the time - as well perhaps as for the occasional sound-effect, of old motor-cars and donkeys and carriages passing through, the chatter of people going about their business. The most suitable music for the scene presented here would be from Athenian operetta, operettas like those of Níkos Hadjiapostólou who was one of the most influential of Greek composers at the time that shops like this existed, and when Athenian operetta had actually reached its zenith.

Following the Greek War of Independence there had grown a public desire for Europeanization, as the very Western contents and preoccupations of this collection of shops clearly demonstrate. Such 'Europeanization' was a reaction against four centuries of Turkish or Muslim domination and by the 1870s many French and Italian operetta companies had visited Greece and created in Greeks a hunger for European melody. Greek composers thus created operettas in the European idiom but embellished them with motifs from traditional Greek and Eastern (or 'oriental') music. They produced works that sound something like the operettas of Franz Lehár but charmingly overlaid with the musical soundscape of Asia

Minor! Performed by a full orchestra and fine opera singers, the content was generally cheerful, often amusing, and always fairly easy to sing. The songs were published as sheet-music and sold in shops like these recreated here, to be played and sung in any Greek home that possessed a piano. Most importantly, it was through Greece's own form of operetta that the Greek public acquired a taste for new and original Greek music, an inclination which continues to this day.

I emerge into darkness and head south for Áno Petrálona - an ordinary working-class locality populated mainly by Greeks along with a small number of Albanians and Bulgarians. At this hour parts of Áno Petrálona remind me greatly of shopping streets in Kuwaiti, Sa'udi, and Egyptian districts where there are a wide range of basic shops and everyone comes out to pass the evening and to do a little business, nipping in and out of the stationery store, the hardware store, the pastry shop, and so forth. I enter an Áno Petrálona pharmacy to ask after a product no longer available in the UK. The assistant, another Greek beauty oozing charm, warmth, and helpfulness, tells me that unfortunately it's been 'de-listed' in Greece as well. 'EU regulations', she advises, with a shrug of the shoulders. I've had trouble texting home with my mobile, so I pop next into a phone shop. As a dozen Greeks are already inside, looking at the latest phones or seeing to their accounts, I have to wait. An attractive young female nevertheless calls over to kindly ask the nature of my need, before continuing, of course, to assist the customer with whom she's dealing. Ten minutes later I attract her attention just to say it really isn't all that important, not to worry, I'll leave it for now, but she's visibly distressed! Loudly she calls back 'Oh, but please, please, you can wait, surely? I want to help you! Just five minutes more, please?' Her concern is clearly genuine, and very winning, but I resist and leave, with all of the dozen customers, plus staff, turning to look at this odd English-speaking creature who can't be doing with waiting! Their expressions all seem to ask 'What on earth is your hurry?'

Shortly before eight, at the Oikonómou Tavérna on Tróon Street, I rendezvous with actor Pantelís, a friend of a Greek colleague in London. As Greeks don't normally venture out to eat before 10pm, we two are this evening's first customers. I've chosen the Oikonómou because it's a genuine old-fashioned working-class *tavérna* and I'd like my first proper eating experience in Athens to be a simple and authentic one. And given that only the most successful actors in any country can ever afford to fork out for meals in expensive restaurants, I hope that Pantelís will like this place as well. The Oikonómou's interior is plain and exceptionally clean; the walls are painted in light washable pastels, with barely any decoration on them; the furniture is traditional, simple, and charming; the atmosphere is somewhat austere, but not cold; and, most importantly, the warm kitchen is bubbling with enticing and mouth-watering smells.

I don't eat a great deal in the evening, or at any time for that matter, and I expect that due to Greece's poor economic situation Pantelís may well approve of our meeting over a wholesome but appropriately moderate meal. However, I've read a great deal about the generosity of Greek hospitality, and of how Greeks like to see a table laden with an abundance of food. So as we prepare to order, I believe myself successful in having Pantelís agree that one large single dish for each of us, plus plenty of wine and bread and water, ought to be sufficient. But when the owner of the *tavérna* comes to enquire what we'd like, it transpires he's not eager to engage in any difficult and torturously simplified Greek with the foreigner: instead, he defers entirely to Pantelís. With just a few seconds of rapid Greek, Pantelís thus tells him what we'd both like. Or so I think.

The wine arrives first, and then not long afterwards, despite my efforts to avoid it, there appear plates and plates of food! Pantelís has ignored my plea for restraint and has ordered just as Greeks like to do, that is, in the case of two people eating, to ask for a variety of at least four or five different dishes, in addition to a decent basket of bread, from all of which both people select during the course of the meal. Consequently, this evening food enough for six big hungry adults is being set out magnificently at our table for just the two of us. It's vexing and confusing: I find this display at once both generous and obscene. It puts me in mind of the many meals I've had with Arab colleagues in homes in Sa'udi and Kuwait, where Arab 'hospitality' and 'generosity' demand the presentation of an impressive array of distinct and harmonious dishes. 'You know,' Pantelís pleads, beguilingly, 'we like to do this, we need to do this, because for so much of our recent history life for we Greek people has been very very hard.' What can I do but acquiesce? We eat a fraction of the feast before us.

However we happily sink a litre and a half of the very good *híma* (wine purportedly from a barrel rather than a bottle) while talking animatedly for four splendid hours. Pantelís speaks good English and he's very giving, expressive, and highly informative. Most of all, he's genuine, and often as this Greek actor speaks I feel true pain or joy triggering the words that trip from his tongue. His father was a refugee from Smýrna (now Turkish Izmir) and his family has known great hardship. But somehow, despite the difficult years, the young Pantelís developed a soft spot for England and all things English, and he tells me that when he was a lad his parents often joked that he behaved like a little English Lord. Pantelís seems rather proud of this and I fear he's been exposed to rather too many English chocolate-box films of the Merchant-Ivory kind. I don't have the heart to ensure he understands that most of England isn't really as depicted in such films, and never has been. And at one point during our discussion of the Asia Minor Disaster I also don't have the heart to suggest to him that if Britain's prime minister Lloyd George, his head so full of schoolboy adulation of Greek myths and the history of Ancient Greece, had not so enthusiastically encouraged Elefthérios Venizélos to pursue the *Megáli Idéa* then Pantelis's father would not have been amongst those hundreds of thousands of unfortunate Greeks forced to flee Anatolía and suffer for years in the slums of Piraeus and Thessaloníki. Pantelís has a rosy image of Britain that it would be hurtful to deflate and I comfort myself with the thought that surely he knows that although the charismatic Venizélos was adored by many, and is still, others think less of him for his part in bringing about the tragic events that led to the horror of 1923.

Strolling back to my room at about 1.30 in the morning, I pass a restaurant where two *bouzoúki* players are singing another Hadjidákis melody I came to know so many years ago in New Zealand: *To Pélago Eínai Vathí* (How Deep The Sea!), a song that was popularised by the great Stélios Kazantzídis, a singer who, incidentally, like thousands of Greeks during the 1950s and 60s enjoyed the 'filmi' songs of Indian cinema, and who after seeing 'The Vagrant of Bombay' adapted a melody from that film into one of his most successful recordings, *Mantouvála*. Thus did Stélios Kazantzídis have all Greece humming along to intricate and enchanting tunes which though dressed in the swirling cascades of *bouzoúkia* actually originated from India. But Greeks have been enjoying Indian exoticism for over 2,000 years. For Greek traders were delighting in much of the magical colour and culture of India during the 300 years before the Common Era, the period of the Greek Ptolemaic dynasty. Then from the start of the Common Era the western coastal towns of the Indian subcontinent saw an even greater stream of Greek-speaking merchants. These were followed by traders of the Roman Empire, the Byzantines, and then the Ottomans. In exchange for cargoes of spices and fruit, silk, pearls and ebony, tigers, rhinoceroses, elephants, peafowl, and snakes, the traders of the Mediterranean gave the merchants of India gold and silver, wine and olive oil. And in all that time to the Balkan Peninsula and Asia Minor the occasional sailor no doubt returned with an Indian melody or two.

I stand at the window spellbound, looking in and soaking up the exoticism, until the many Greeks inside burst into applause and yet another stunning Hadjidákis melody commences: *T'Astéri Tou Voriá* (The Star of the North). I am transfixed until this too concludes, but then know I can't linger a moment longer, for this wonderful music will just go on and on and on, towards dawn. I ascend to my room reflecting that the two *bouzoúki* players in that one restaurant along with literally hundreds of others elsewhere in Greece have been playing and singing these entrancing melodies night in, night out, for decades, and all along I've been missing out! But at least I now know.

4

Cháos & Puppets

The 'Modern Greek State';
Ághioi Theódoroi;
Mihális Theodórou;
Odós Akadimías & Panepistimíou;
Exárcheia; Omónoia Square;
& laïká.

The modern *agorá*, or shopping area, of downtown Athens consists of a maze of little lanes that lie for the most part within a triangle that is bounded by Athinás, Stadíou, and Mitropóleos Streets. As I stride out on a perfect sky-blue winter's morning, this modern Athenian *agorá* teems and heaves with life. All of Athens seems to be coming and going, thousands and thousands of people, in some way or other, are all active, bursting with vigour. Cars, vans, buses, motorbikes and scooters buzz almost bumper to bumper up and down the streets, as I wind and turn through a labyrinth of lanes to the Museum of the City of Athens on Klafthmónos Square.

This museum occupies a fine old neo-classical building that was once home to the Bavarian King Otto of Greece, as well as his German wife, Princess Amelie of Oldenburg. Yes, the first royal couple of Greece didn't possess a drop of Greek blood between them, but here, on the edge of Klafthmónos Square, from 1836 to 1843 they established and were resident in a small and provisional palace. Today its ground floor houses an exhibition that reveals Athens as it was in the two hundred years prior to the arrival of these first royals, while the next floor gives an impression of how the German king and his queen actually lived in this building. Amelie, or Amalía as she was known in Greece, enjoyed a magnificent drawing room, and similarly well-appointed is Otto's Throne Room, overlooking the Square. The entire house was filled with furnishings and *objets d'art* typical of a fine house of Germany in the early 1800s. Yet there are some Greeks today who consider this house, also known as The Old Palace, a symbol of the beginning of the modern Greek state. However, this term 'the modern Greek state' is an enormous misnomer, and here at this early point in getting to grips with the reality of Athens, as well as the reality of Greece, it's important to recall, albeit by way of a necessarily and extremely brief history, why this term is so misleading.

It must firstly be understood that liberated Athens, following the Greek War of Independence, was only a small town, at that time having less than half the population of Salonica in the north (officially Thessaloníki), although Salonica's population was more Muslim and Jewish than Orthodox Christian. Additionally, the vast majority of Orthodox Christians in the region who identified as 'Greek' dwelt in Asia Minor. The newly liberated 'modern Greek state' was thus a very small one, most of its members living elsewhere. Furthermore, those members who did live in the liberated territory had never before co-operated with each other. The immediate problem of the new 'modern Greek state' was that Greece had never actually existed hitherto as a single unified nation. Instead, that geographic territory that we now term 'Greece' had been dominated by ancient and often warring city-states.

The first leader of this somewhat strange new nation was Ioánnis Kapodístrias. The newly formed Greek National Assembly chose Kapodístrias as Governor not only because he had been very active in support of independence from the Ottoman Turks for many years prior to the start of the war, but because, as a Greek from Kérkyra (Corfu) who was resident in Geneva, he had become an illustrious and truly European politician. From 1809 until 1822 Ioánnis Kapodístrias had worked as the Foreign Minister of Alexander I, Emperor of Russia. However, as the first Governor of Greece he ran into difficulties with those who had actually driven out the Turks: for Greece's chieftains were powerful, rebellious, freedom-loving mountain spirits who remained very much in fighting mode! Kapodístrias simply couldn't control them. He resorted to toughness, and to behaving like a despot. And soon he was hated. In 1831 he took a step too far and ordered the imprisonment of the chieftain of the ancient Mavromicháli family of the Máni Peninsula, at the southern end of the Pelopónnesos and one of the most spirited parts of all Greece. Consequently, the chieftain's brother, assisted by his son, then assassinated the Governor, just as he was entering a Náfplion church for a Sunday morning service. Ioánnis Kapodístrias was then succeeded by his younger brother Avgoustínos, but Avgoustínos 'ruled' for only six months, for Greece was in *cháos*. Amongst all those diverse clans which had successfully fought as one against the Ottomans, there was now rivalry and distrust: somewhat understandably, no single Greek was prepared to hand over to any other the hard-fought-for and long-fought-for liberty of the new nation! Thus, with the final ousting of the Turks following the Battle of Pétra in September 1829 but with the new nation's tribal leaders still distrustful of each other, the way was clear for the three 'Great Powers' of the time, Britain, France, and Russia, to step in and recommend an 'independent' 'unifying sovereign'. During this period in Europe's history, king-making and empire-building often walked hand-in-hand, and the empire-builders were regularly offering newly-created crowns around the palaces of Europe's royal families.

So, under the conditions of the Convention of London of 1832, Greece became a new and independent kingdom protected by Britain, France, and Russia, with Otto of Wittelsbach, a prince of Bavaria, as its first king. But Otto was just seventeen years old! And Greek opinion in this choice was simply never sought. Despite the decision that until Otto became of age the country would be administered by Bavarian regents, the appointment of a German lad to rule over a people who had battled for 9 long years to overthrow 377 years of almost uninterrupted Ottoman domination (Athens was very briefly captured by the Venetians in 1466 and in 1687) was surely an act of gross insensitivity and imperialist arrogance, an insult to the people of the newly-formed state. Worse still, when Otto duly arrived in Athens it was with a cohort of Bavarian advisors who immediately set up a bureaucracy under which Greeks found themselves more heavily taxed than they had ever been under the Turks! Naturally enough Greeks quickly came to despise the new Bavarian bureaucracy, the *Vavarokratía* as they came to call it, as much as they had done the Turkish tyranny, particularly as Otto at first showed little of the respect for classical Greece and the Greek culture that had so beguiled his father King Ludwig I, he who had insisted that the Church of Panaghía Kapnikaréa be saved from demolition. Young Otto's immediate wish for a location for a nice royal palace in Athens was atop the Acrópolis! Fortunately, however, archaeologists fought hard to protect *Ierós Vráchos* (the Sacred Rock) and its ruins, and the palace was built elsewhere. Nevertheless, such experiences of the *Vavarokratía* gave the people of Greece reason enough to continue the subtle ways of resisting imposed rule that they had developed under the *Tourkokratía*.

When King Otto decided upon a German wife, and in 1836 visited Germany with a view to marrying Princess Amelie of Oldenburg, the wedding did not even take place in Greece. On their return, however, the new Queen did at least seek to emulate Greek dress, by devising and wearing a romantic folksy court costume that was based upon traditional Greek styles. But her interference in the affairs of government made her unpopular. Thus, just as the King and Queen were settling into a much larger and finer palace to the south-east of Klafthmónos Square in 1843, public dissatisfaction with the inflicted royals reached such proportions that there arose demands for a constitution. The young German king refused outright. And thus, in September 1843, two Greek soldiers, Colonel Demétrios Kallérghis and Captain Ioánnis Makriyiánnis, led the infantry to assemble in the square in front of the new royal palace, where, supported by many of the Athenian population, they threatened a military *coup*. Otto relented and agreed not only to grant a constitution, and to convene a permanent national assembly that would include Greeks, but to dismiss all foreigners from his service, except for those who had assisted Greeks in the War of Independence. The square where this confrontation took place became known as Sýntagma Square, which translates as Constitution Square. It has been the heart of Athens ever since.

Twenty years later, in 1862, while Otto was visiting the Pelopónnesos, a further *coup* was threatened against him, and ambassadors of the three 'Great Powers' quickly urged Otto and his queen not to resist but to accept assisted escape to Bavaria by way of a foreign war-ship. Then, for a while, the 'Great Powers' considered ushering in as a new King of Greece, in Otto's place, the eighteen-year-old Prince Alfred, second son of England's Queen Victoria. In the end, however, they decided on another young continental: a seventeen-year-old lad from Denmark with German connections, Prince Christian Wilhelm Ferdinand Adolf Georg of Schleswig-Holstein-Sonderburg-Glücksburg - and the story goes that this prince, as a young naval cadet, learnt of his new position from the headlines on a sheet of newspaper that had been wrapped around his packed lunch.

The new Danish King adopted the Greek name Yeórghios I (George I), he learnt Greek, and when after five years as King of the Hellenes his first son was born he agreed that all of his boys should be raised as members of the Greek Orthodox Church. Meanwhile, as a reward to the Greeks for adopting a pro-British monarch, Britain handed Greece control of the Iónian Islands. When Yeórghios I was then assassinated by an anarchist in Thessaloníki in 1913, Yeórghios's son, Constantínos I, became the first Greek king who had been born in Greece and who was a member of the Greek Orthodox faith. Although of course his veins bore not a drop of local blood, there were demands from those who relished the *Megáli Idéa* that he be crowned not Constantínos I but Constantínos XII, to indicate continuity with the last emperor of Byzantium, Constantínos XI Palaiológos. This was a rather inappropriate desire given that the prince was married to the sister of Kaiser Wilhelm, German Emperor and King of Prussia. Partly because of this relationship Constantínos eventually came to be considered rather too pro-German, and so, very generally, the country fell into division, into Nationalists and Royalists. During the First World War the Nationalists supported the Allies, while Constantínos and his Royalists wished the country to remain neutral. Thus in 1916 the French occupied Piraeus, bombarded Athens, forced the Greek fleet to surrender, and made Constantínos accept an Allied ultimatum whereby he would leave the country, without actually abdicating, and his twenty-three-year-old son, Aléxandros, would become 'acting King' of Greece.

Four years later, in 1920, while Aléxandros was trying one day to save his dog from the attack of two pet monkeys, the monkeys bit him viciously, the bites gave rise to septicaemia, and he died. A few days after his death, the Nationalists, led by Elefthérios Venizélos, lost the elections and this allowed Demétrios Rállis, a well-known Royalist, to become Prime Minister. Twenty days later, after a disputed plebiscite, Constantínos I was returned to the throne. However, in the year of the Great Fire of Smýrna, 1922, when hundreds of thousands of Greek refugees from Asia Minor fled for their lives to Athens and other parts of Greece, Constantínos, who had thrown all his weight behind the ill-fated surge across Anatolía in pursuit of the *Megáli Idéa*, was forced to abdicate, and his son Yeórghios II succeeded him. But the Greeks blamed the monarchy for all the bloodshed and horror that had occurred in Asia Minor during the campaign for their ancient homeland, and particularly for the tragic events of the Smýrna Disaster, and so at the 1923 elections Venizélos's Liberal Party was swept to victory. After an astonishing total of ten changes of government since 1920, Greece was proclaimed a republic on the 25th of March, 1924. And so today a significant number of Greeks believe that this moment, in 1924, rather than 1832 and the arrival of the imposed young Otto, more accurately describes the beginning of 'the modern Greek state'.

But the proclamation of a republic did not see the end of Greece's Danish royal family. In 1933 a pro-monarchist government revoked the republican constitution of 1924 and two years later brought back to the throne Yeórghios II, despite an attempted *coup* in March 1935 by Venizelist officers who feared such a royalist restoration. Venizélos, himself proven to have been involved in the *coup*, was forced into exile in France, where he died shortly afterwards. In 1936 Yeórghios II appointed General Ioánnis Metaxás as Prime Minister, and Metaxás, believing war with Italy was inevitable, persuaded

Yeórghios that only an authoritarian government could prevent internal conflict and prepare Greece for the battles that lay ahead. The king thus agreed to support a dictatorship: the rule that is referred to as the Metaxás Régime.

In 1940, his troops in position on the Albanian border, Italy's Mussolini presented Greece with a humiliating ultimatum. Metaxás is celebrated as having immediately responded with a one-word telegram saying *'Óchi!'* ('No!'), pronounced like a guttural 'rocky' but without the r and the k - although in truth Metaxás's actual reply was *'Alors, c'est la guerre'* ('Then, it is war') and it was the Greek people who generated the famed *'Óχι!'*, as they took to the streets in defiant support of Metaxás's refusal. The Italians still invaded but the Greek army, despite Metaxás's unfortunate death in January 1941, managed to drive them back, over the Albanian border. But Hitler, sadly, then came to Mussolini's rescue, and by June of the same year Germany had seized control of most of Greece. By the time the Nazis had withdrawn from the country in October 1944, no less than 300,000 Greeks had died due to the German occupation. Of this number about 21,000 had been members of the Greek military; 71,000 had been Greek-resident Jews exterminated by the Nazis as part of the Holocaust; and 209,000 had been civilians, roughly 140,000 of whom died of starvation.

Following the German withdrawal, Yeórghios II and his government returned to Athens from Egypt, where for the period of the war they had sought safety in exile. But in 1946 tensions in Greece led to the outbreak of civil war. By the time this civil war had ended, in 1949, a further 100,000 Greeks had died. Of course, there are many older Greek people today who remember this entire period and all that followed it.

For almost the next twenty years Greece was ruled by a succession of unstable coalition governments, until in 1967, just prior to elections, Colonel Yeórghios Papadópoulos and a clutch of other right-wing colonels seized power in a *coup d'état*, claiming that their action was vital to save Greece from Communism. Their real motive, however, lay in the fact that for several years, since Constantínos II had become king, Greece had once again been in a state of governmental turmoil:

relations between Constantínos and the Prime Minister, Yeórghios Papandréou (grandfather of the Prime Minister of 2009 to 2011) had deteriorated badly, with the monarch determined to impose his will. Although Constantínos was surprised by the *coup*, it was noted that he took no massive action against it, and, in the weeks which followed, that he was even photographed smiling and consorting with the colonels. However, after eight months he and his family fled the country. While actress and singer Melína Mercoúri and others had immediately put their lives and careers on hold and embarked upon a fiery campaign of protest against the *coup* all over Europe, the king, in exile, continued to demonstrate no inspiring resistance. For the people of Greece, life under the Júnta was harsh. Many democratic rights were withdrawn. In special 'centres' an estimated 3,500 people were tortured by procedures which were unimaginably painful, degrading, and humiliating. One such building, not far from the heart of Athens, preserved to this day as the 'Museum of the Antidictatorial Democratic Resistance' offers a grim reminder of life under the colonels. Today many Westerners are surprised when they learn that the Júnta was supported by the United States, that in 1947 (as part of 'The Truman Doctrine') the United States actively began to support authoritarian régimes in Turkey, Iran, and Greece, simply to ensure that such countries did not fall under Soviet influence. Some of the Anti-Americanism that thus arose during the period of the Júnta continues in Greece to this day - despite President Clinton's 1999 apology to the Greek people for America's having intentionally supported the colonels as part of its 'Cold War strategies'.

When in 1974 Kýpros (Cyprus) was invaded by Turkey, senior Greek military officers withdrew their support from the Júnta and it collapsed. Constantínos Karamanlís was then encouraged to return from exile in France to establish a government of national unity. A referendum in the same year led to the abolition of the monarchy, the creation of a new constitution, and the election of Greece's first President. Today the ex-king, Constantínos II of the Danish line and second cousin of Charles Windsor, Prince of Wales, stripped of his

Greek citizenship and a resident of Hampstead, London, must use a Danish passport whenever he visits Greece. So there are some who see 1974 as the true beginning of 'the modern Greek state', superseding the earlier 'beginnings' of 1832 and 1924. Since 1974 the politics of the Third Hellenic Republic have swung between the Panhellenic Socialist Movement (Panellínio Sosialistikó Kínima, or PASOK) and the New Democracy party (Néa Dimokratía, or ND).

Thus the so-called 'modern Greek state', so hopefully established on the edge of Klafthmónos Square by young puppets Otto and Amalía, has been through a most turbulent history since the termination of nearly four hundred years of *Tourkokratía* (and almost five hundred years in the case of northern Greece). All the delicate decorative silverware, glassware, porcelain, fine wooden furniture and art from Germany, France, and England that fills their first Athenian palace has survived a century and a half of tumult, often horrendous and often bloody. It's little wonder that the music Greece has produced during this period often aches with anguish and yearns for freedom.

But the sad thing is that this very difficult history is by no means over! We are hearing at this time that Greece's coffers are currently empty although this land of just over 11 million people is continuing to spend more, per head of population, on protecting itself from possible attack than any other state in the entire European Union. In fact, Greece is NATO's second-largest spender on defence after the USA. Greek army, navy and air force personnel number approximately 100,000. The massive expenditure and the vast personnel of the three forces are simply deemed vital for the nation's safety.

And Greece can point to a number of incidents, all of them having occurred within living memory, which suggest that such deep and continuing concern is fully justified. For example, although in 1923, under the Lausanne convention, 120,000 Greeks (and 65,000 Armenians) had been allowed to remain in Istanbul, a law passed in the Turkish parliament in 1932 barred all Greek citizens resident within Turkey from employment in thirty different trades and professions, ranging from carpentry through to careers in law and medicine. Then during the Second World War, Greeks resident in Turkey, along with Armenians and Jews, were subjected to arbitrary detention in labour camps, as well as to a considerable range of penal laws. In 1942 the authoritarian Turkish government of that time levied an exorbitant 'wealth tax' against Istanbul's hard-working and generally prosperous Christian population, transparently using them as scapegoats for Turkey's economic ills. Although this tax was abolished after two years, due to international pressure, it crippled many of those Greeks and Armenians who were still living in Istanbul. And then on the 6th and 7th of September 1955, as a response to the demands of the historic Greek majority of Cyprus for political union with mainland Greece, the Turkish government implemented a systematic pogrom in Istanbul, a premeditated infliction of violence upon the 80,000 who constituted the Greek community of the city at that time. Five hundred or so specifically enlisted Turkish factory-workers were transported under police supervision into the heart of Istanbul to implement and lead the attack. A dozen or so Greeks were killed, about 30 were severely wounded, and scores of Greeks of both sexes were either sexually assaulted or raped. Serious damage, and in some cases total destruction, was wrought upon roughly 4,000 Greek-owned businesses and homes, 73 Greek churches, and 52 Greek schools. The World Council of Churches estimated the cost of the damage to have been in the region of at least a hundred million pounds. Naturally, as was the intention, this pogrom caused a sudden acceleration in Greek emigration. In 1991 a Human Rights Watch report observed that the number of Greeks in Turkey had been reduced to about 2,500, over half of whom were over 60 years of age.

And to this day Turkey continues to intimidate Greece. Despite being a fellow member of NATO, as well as an applicant for membership of the European Union, Turkey regularly exercises its warplanes just several hundred metres above the heads of the inhabitants of Aegean islands. Ignoring the Helsinki agreement of 1975, and seemingly desirous of acquiring more than Asia Minor, Turks pay rather too much attention to Greek territory. Turkey eyes adjacent Greek islands, it seeks greater use of the Aegean Sea, and in Greek waters not far from the Turkish coast Turkey appears intent upon drilling for oil in what it claims to be its 'continental shelf'. Thus, sitting so vulnerably down in the extreme south-eastern corner of Europe, it's little wonder that Greece continues to feel the need to keep itself armed to the teeth.

From Klafthmónos I move to the small square of Aghíon Theódoroi, just to the south-west, and to the little church within it of Ághioi Theódoroi. This small place of worship has seen a great deal more of local history, and at first-hand, than the so-called 'Old Palace' in nearby Klafthmónos Square, for a marble plate on its western wall is inscribed with a date believed to read 1065 CE. While the exterior, consisting of elaborate stone and brickwork beneath a high octagonal dome, is generally solid and substantial in appearance, there are in this church's small cross-shaped interior a number of unusual and interesting details. Just enough flickering light within the mysterious and very 'holy' 'gloom' enables one to make out attractive brick arches and dentils adorning the windows; a terracotta frieze, all around the walls, of small plates featuring animals and plants; and here and there exotic calligraphic patterns that speak of Arabia. An exceptionally beautiful Greek woman of about thirty-five, clad in tight-fitting denim jeans, a breast-hugging black top, and knee-high tan boots, long lustrously dark hair falling about her shoulders, moves elegantly from icon to icon while lighting candles and moving her lips in silent and fervent prayer. Despite her very deliberately chosen designer-gear, she is totally engrossed in her religious preoccupations. She seems completely unaware of everyone and everything else. Earlier this morning she has clearly paid considerable attention to preparing herself for a stylish and stunning presence upon the streets of central Athens, but at this point she is immersed entirely in piety.

My next call is to a small music-shop off Stadíou Street, where I succeed in finding a collection of piano transcriptions of the beautiful *Methisména Tragoúthia* (Drunk Songs) composed by Chrístos Nikolópoulos and made famous by the singer Yiórgos Daláras. Next door in a very fine CD shop, stylishly packed with hundreds of recordings of Greek 𝚛 I meet the widow of Níkos Xiloúris, a famous Cretan ꜱ and Greek popular hero. She is in deep conversation with two music-loving friends and I introduce the three women to the recording that so inspired me in sunny Sydney thirty-five years ago, a personal copy of Mihális Theodórou that I've brought with me from England. It intrigues them enough to want to hear the disc played over the shop's sound-system, and, as I expected, it turns out that they've never before heard this singer. They've not even heard of his name, or the name he used to go by in Germany. They know nothing about him. I'm pleased to note, however, that they're sufficiently intrigued by the voice and accompaniment to ask for the volume to be turned right up, so that this Greek music-shop becomes filled, loudly, with the lavish swirling sounds of Theodórou's glorious tenor voice which I have transported all the way here from Australia.

Yet it's disappointing to observe that these three lovers of Greek music are clearly not knocked over by what they hear - although one of them does remark, 'This voice, it reminds me of Mario Lanza. Possibly even Caruso.' Instead, they seem perplexed by what they hear, even slightly vexed. They gaze around the shop, looking upwards, as if its air has been invaded by something foreign! They know they're listening to Greek lyrics, and expertly delivered by a Greek voice, but it suddenly dawns on me that they're either consciously or subconsciously aware that the accompaniment features not a single Greek instrument! Furthermore, it's symphonic and lavish, the melodies having been arranged for a large German symphony orchestra by the three German music arrangers, Schmid, Barthel, and Pleva, all of whom were active in arranging and recording German operetta and orchestral music in Germany during the 1970s. The record that I have treasured for so long has Greek foundations but suddenly I perceive that it is, in fact, a magnificently souped-up German production, that it's been saturated with all the grandeur and majesty of romantic German or even romantic Russian symphonic orchestrations! No wonder that when Theodorákis heard this recording he said that he had been totally surprised to listen to a large German orchestra and a superb tenor voice perform his 'simple melodies'! I've never really understood what he meant. Now I see that he wasn't just referring to the pleasure of hearing his songs played by a large orchestra, for Greece has several and Theodorákis has written much for large orchestras: no, he was referring to the distinctly Germanic treatment. So often the West has taken elements of Greece and run away with them, whipped them up into something even more magnificent. One has only to look at Western architecture to see how components of classical Greek design have been elaborated and celebrated in much grander forms throughout all the capitals of Europe, across North America, and right down to the fine stonework of Oamaru and Dunedin in the south of New Zealand. I never suspected that my cherished recording was produced by much the same process and that it's clearly as much German as it is Greek!

I tell the ladies of Theodórou's sensational success in Germany during the seventies and of his many recordings, and that he then suddenly withdrew from singing in 1982 aged only forty-three, for reasons unknown, and that it's thought that he now quietly divides his time between the city of his birth, Thessaloníki, and a leafy suburb of Munich. One of the women then suggests I should ask a Greek friend to share my disc with Greek radio stations 'because wouldn't it be nice for that singer, particularly if maybe he is now old and not so well, to have a surprise when he returns here from Germany, to hear his voice on the radio?' The spontaneous compassion of this kindly thought is coupled with a certain coolness and detachment, a strange treating of this son of Greece as being almost 'other'. I suddenly find myself considering that Greece may not have been greatly interested in Theodórou on account of his glittering career having occurred in Germany. After all, at the time of his success in Germany in the late sixties and early seventies memories of the horrors of the Nazi occupation of Greece had not faded, and, additionally, the Germans had fallen in love with Theodórou during that period when Greeks in Greece were suffering under the dictatorship.

Because of the Nazi occupation over 300,000 Greeks had died, thousands having been killed in Nazi atrocities and approximately 140,000 having perished in the agonies of starvation. It takes generations for the pain of such events to dissipate, but in 1957, only thirteen years after the Nazis' departure, memories of Nazi horrors were suddenly returned to full and widespread consciousness throughout Greece. The Nazi administrator Dr. Maximilian Merten who had been in charge of operations in Northern Greece from 1942, and who was alleged to have been involved in the deportation of roughly 46,000 of Thessaloníki's Jews to the death camps as well as the killing of just under 700 Greek citizens, had dared to return to Greece on business. He was promptly arrested, thrown into jail, and only released after a highly-publicised trial and a full two years' of intense bargaining between Greece and Germany. Then later, during the dictatorship of 1967 to 1974 the Greek people had seen their royals of Danish blood and German connections flee Greece and abandon them to the harsh rule of the colonels. Thus there obviously remained considerable anti-German hostility in Greece from the time of the Nazi's departure at the end of the war right through to the 1970s. Indeed, it is still evident today, though mainly amongst the older generation. And so I suspect that this hostility may account for the fact that although a number of Greeks have enjoyed great popularity in Germany in the decades since the end of the Second World War, their German triumphs haven't been mirrored, or repeated to anywhere near the same extent, in their homeland. Anyway, I don't leave this temple of Greek music empty-handed: the ladies greatly approve of my purchase of Yiórgos Daláras's seminal 'Fifty Years of Rebétiko', a double-album which since 1975 has sold over half a million copies, an unprecedented and unsurpassed achievement in the world of Greek *rebétika*.

Eleftheroudákis Bookshop on Panepistimíou Street (officially Odós Eleftheríou Venizélou) offers eight spacious floors of books, and I'm bowled over by the realisation that the greater number of them are of course in Greek: the shelves of Eleftheroudákis are crammed with books of the ancients right through to the works of contemporary Greek writers in every genre. It's overwhelming, and perhaps my surprise stems from my years in the nearby Middle East where books and ng are certainly not a significant feature of daily life and erage Arab home has not a shelf of books in sight, apart from a copy or two of works like the Qur'an. I've assumed that modern Greeks, likewise living under a scorching sun for much of the year and in much the same geographical region, similarly don't read a great deal, and, certainly, writers travelling through Greece as recently as the 1960s noted that Greeks generally preferred to debate and talk rather than read. But things have progressed and literacy in Greece has clearly leapt forward.

All of these books that are now before me, smelling new and fresh, sporting beautiful and stylish covers, and emblazoned with magical titles in Greek that say I-do-not-know-what, are like treasures found in the deep recesses of some newly discovered cave. I feel a tremendous urge to take a little part of this experience away with me. But what? There's even a vast range of fiction in Greek for young adults and I'm tempted to buy a teenagers' novel as a surely easier method of unlocking the Greeks' fascinating and mystifying language. And then I think I'd be better off looking at Greek language-learning materials, and so find my way to an enormous section of language-learning books in all the major European languages - for despite its small population, Greece is intensely involved in language-learning. Sales of English language-learning books represent roughly a fifth of total sales of books in the entire country! But young Greeks are not only hungry for English: a considerable number of them become fluent in two, three, or more, other European languages. Languages are considered requisites for success. In the end I decide to hold fire, and am soon passing at least a dozen other enticing bookshops on Akadimías Street. With a name like that I should have expected them - similarly, on Panepistimíou Street, for that translates as 'University Street'.

Both Akadimías and Panepistimíou Streets run north towards Exárcheia, and as I enter Exárcheia I wonder what all the fuss has been about. Many sources, including travel-guides and local people, warn you to steer clear of this area, saying it's ridden with dangers, that it's full of wild-eyed anarchists, indeed that it's often been called *Anárcheia*, and that at any moment someone may rush up behind and mug you! But in fact Exárcheia seems no more threatening than Psyrrí or Gázi.

It seems simply a small downtown area of Athens that brims with student life such as is to be found in university cities everywhere. Yes, it's tatty and ragged but it's also clearly an artistic, a bohemian, and an intellectual enclave. Anarchism and left-wing extremism have, however, turned Exárcheia into an area in which the police are vigilant, and highly wary while in uniform. When in December 2008, after an altercation with two armed policemen, the teenager Aléxandros Grigorópoulos was shot in the street here by one of the two men, witnesses claimed that once the boy had fallen to the ground, clearly very seriously wounded, the policemen simply walked off, leaving the boy where he lay. So just recently, in December 2009, on the anniversary of the murder, Exárcheia erupted into a week of fearful riots. Barricades were set alight, rocks were hurled, the police were forced to retreat, and angry protesters occupied the rector's offices at the university, lowering the Greek flag and replacing it with a black one. Other protesters got through to Omónoia Square where there were further violent clashes: shop-fronts were beaten in, and one store was completely consumed in flames. At Sýntagma Square the protesters were met by motorised police forces that came charging unexpectedly at them from Odós Ermoú.

Amongst the scruffiness of Exárcheia on this particular day, there's little evidence of the recent violence. Life is simply ticking along quite normally. Although a large navy-blue police-bus stands right outside the offices of PASOK and its cargo of young policemen patrols the adjacent pavement, it seems that in the rest of this locality the police are keeping a low profile. They're focussed more on central Athens, where there's been a string of attacks on businesses and government departments since the 2008 shooting of the teenager. But here in Exárcheia hundreds of people, including lots of single females, are strolling the streets as if nothing dangerous is likely to happen. There's activity in many little computer-shops, stationery stores, and yet more bookshops. There are cafés too, packed with students sitting at tables with coffee and cake, engrossed in laptops. Some of these cafés offer free wi-fi, as does a lot of central Athens. Since 2006, in Sýntagma Square, and in Kotziá Square (in front of the imposing Athens City

Hall), and in the café area of Theseíon (in those cafés twinkling with little lights), free wi-fi has been available for some time as part of the service known as 'Public Wireless Internet Access in Athens'. In these areas you just visit any café or sit down on any park bench, get out your laptop or other digital assistant, double-click 'athenswifi', enter the given code, and you're instantly connected to the Web.

In the central small square of Exárcheia a great many dishevelled and radical-looking sorts stand around quietly talking. There are sixty or seventy of them, they're mostly men, generally in their twenties or thirties, and it seems that they've just had some kind of meeting. I wander amongst them, frequently catching the smell of cannabis and the occasional questioning eye. Many are clutching notices or pamphlets in Greek. Maybe another demonstration is in the offing, shortly to launch out for the city centre. Just a short distance away, in Spirídonos Trikoúpi Street, in glass cases on the walls of the Néo Ellinikó Théatro enticingly colourful stills advertise a production of Pirandello's 'Man, Beast, and Virtue'. The foyer of this Exárcheia theatre is spacious, modern, and stylish, suggesting a professional company and a professional production, even if luridly costumed and garishly lit. But will I have the energy and nerve to push myself to a performance in the heart of this reputedly dangerous part of the city when evening shows are not scheduled to commence, as is fairly typical in Athens, until shortly after 9.15pm?

Leaving Exárcheia, I pass through the similarly maligned Omónoia Square, which translates as Concord or Harmony Square, and find that it's as busy as Piccadilly Circus and hardly much scruffier. Omónoia Square has always been surrounded by a nearly unbroken line of fairly tall buildings, only these days they're also all very ugly buildings. And unfortunately the space that they surround consists of a large and very bare pedestrian area lacking any satisfying focus - there is nothing here, like Piccadilly's statue of winged Antéros, to give this busy fume-filled intersection any degree of style. But this was not always so, for a hundred years ago Omónoia Square was full of large elegant palm trees, flower beds, and a high and beautiful fountain. The arrangement was then varied over the decades until in 1988 the artist Cóstas Varótsos, having been commissioned to create a modern centre-piece, produced a giant sculpture made of thousands of large shards of glass, stacked one on top of the other, to give the impression of a runner flashing through the middle of the square. Varótsos had meant his *Droméas* (meaning 'Runner') to contrast dynamically with the tall buildings all around, as if the figure had suddenly darted out from one of the six canyon-like avenues that converge upon Omónoia in order to cut through and rapidly exit the square via some other passage. As a flash of vital freedom, the 26-foot-high *Droméas* apparently worked very well, although its brutal modernism caused much debate in Athens at the time. However, only a few years later, it was seen that the great weight of the glass would pose a danger to the new Omónoia Metró station below, and so the concept was removed to another location. Unfortunately today's square remains the poorer for the loss of a strong central point of interest.

At 5.30 I meet a new friend, Andréas, in Sýntagma Square and he suggests a nearby *ouzerí*. Andréas responded to a political statement I ventured some months ago in the online edition of the influential centre-left Athenian paper *To Víma* and it turned out he's a great Hadjidákis fan, fluent in English, with lots of experience abroad. I expect an ordinary and simple *ouzerí*, but Andréas clearly has a taste for style and the *ouzerí* towards which he leads us is a rather swanky affair, where we're immediately swooped upon by a very pretty young waitress. Her looks are like those on the front of the many Greek women's magazines which are displayed alongside the drinks, snacks, cigarettes, and so forth at every *períptero*, or kiosk, in town. She's a beauty and a delight and we're immediately engulfed in her Mediterranean warmth. She banters with Andréas in a joshing and flirtatious manner that suggests they've surely met before, and Andréas rises to the play though he assures me once she's gone that he's never clapped eyes on her before in his life! 'Ah, we Greeks, we just love to flirt!' he says. 'Don't you know we're the greatest flirts in the world?' I had no idea. I thought that maybe the super-confident and out-going warmth I'd experienced from nearly everybody about town so far was partly an after-effect of the highly successful staging in Athens of the 2004 Olympics, combined perhaps with Greece's having pulled off a totally unexpected victory when it won the UEFA European Football Championship earlier the same year. Anyway, remembering last night's tableful of largely uneaten dishes with Pantelís, I convince Andréas that we needn't wastefully plaster our table-top with food which we do not want, and, due probably to his considerable experience outside Greece, fortunately he agrees. The waitress then re-appears, coquettish and radiant with smiles, just as before, and Andréas tells her very pleasantly and in Greek of the little we would like. Instantly the warmth is withdrawn, her face goes blank, almost accusatory, and after quickly writing down our order she turns abruptly and is gone! However, the one large dish and carafe of wine placed in front of us several minutes later prove delicious and ample and at half-seven Andréas and I proceed to the Metró.

We head south on the Ághios Demétrios line to a concert in homage of the famous lyricist Pythagóras Papastamatíou. His *Mikrá Asía* recording of 1972, with music by Apóstolos Kaldáras, helped launch the careers of two of Greece's most respected singers, Yiórgos Daláras and Háris Alexíou. It's tough locating the venue and although I make good use of my fine new map, I notice that every time I open it Andréas prefers to very obviously dart off, to stop somebody, and to chance their knowledge of this vast and chaotic city. Although he's a university-educated professional he seems to have no faith in my map whatsoever, despite my relating to him over dinner what a splendid book it is, and, so far, how it has proven absolutely accurate.

Cháos to Greeks is not the frightful lack of order that we Westerners consider it to be. To Greeks, it is, from mythology, simply that initial state of pregnant being from which all life arose. For Isíodos (Hesiod), in 7 BCE, *Cháos* was the origin of the gods. First came Earth, then Éros, the god of love, followed by Erebus and his sister Night, and from these were produced the children Aethér, Heméra, Némesis and the rest. For Pláton all the elements of the universe were first set out and put in order within *cháos*, before being propelled out of the void and into being. So for Greeks, familiar as they are with ancient mythology, from school and home, *cháos* is a fruitful state! From it came this Earth and all its wonders, and, most importantly, from *cháos* came love! To put it simply: for Greeks if there is no *cháos*, no randomness, no serendipitous chance, no unexpected possibilities, then there is no excitement, and there is little to live for. *Cháos* is good!

By a mixture of my determinedly avoiding *cháos*, by map-reading, and by Andréas's capitulation to *cháos*, through his hit-and-miss dependency upon passers-by, we eventually make it to the theatre, though rather flustered and with just minutes to spare before the performance begins. As we follow an usherette down an aisle of the stalls, she overhears a few words of mine to Andréas and suddenly turns to say 'So tonight we have here someone all the way from England?' I nod, and she continues 'Well, for you two gentlemen there are two very special seats!' She then guides us to the middle of the second row from the front! Superb. The Greeks all around us are friendly, warm, and welcoming, and soon we are settled and ready for the feast to commence.

Each performer excels. Vassilikí Papaconstantínou, a tall, beautiful, and slender young woman in her twenties, dazzles as she sings! In the broadness of her voice tonight there is raw and expressive intensity. She wears a simple white long-sleeved blouse and thin black leather drainpipe trousers atop patent ebony high-heeled shoes, her long lustrous dark hair is swept back tightly into a tail, and her bright red spectacles marry gorgeously with the rich red and mother-of-pearl casing of the accordion upon her lap. Behind her is a very talented and handsome young Greek at the piano, two others send their *bouzoúkia* into raptures, and a drummer delights in providing a vast and impressive palette of percussive colour. The main vocalist is the very pleasant young Cóstas Triantafyllídis, who occasionally accompanies himself on the guitar. He's extraordinarily relaxed and affable and his rapport with the audience is touching. Now and then, between songs, he banters with the crowd before him and when a chorus approaches he encourages us to sing it instead of himself, stepping deliberately back from the microphone so that the members of the audience are flattered by the sound of their own voices. Greek concerts like this often have an element of ritual about them. People don't attend only to watch and enjoy the performers, but to actively participate in the event.

The evening offers no interval. For just two whole hours the singers and musicians perform without break. Although everyone observes an etiquette and keeps silent during verses which are profound, and when the heart-felt expressions of the soloist need to be respected, many members of the audience, including Andréas, at various points sing robustly along with the lyrics. Then about halfway through, a young woman in the first row, immediately in front of us, becomes so transported that she lifts her arms above her head to follow the intricacies of the singer's melody with curling and fluttering fingers, her whole upper body becoming involved in a kind of meandering Eastern dance. This is the *tsiftetéli*, brought to Greece by refugees from Asia Minor and which involves movements much like those of Persian belly-dancing, further demonstration of Greece's bond with the Middle East. Very soon a few other women in the stalls have been set off by the twirling and encircling *tsiftetéli* before us, and then throughout the theatre men begin to call 'Bravo! Bravo!' to both the 'dancing' women and the performers upon the stage. The level of satisfaction, expectation, and excitement increases palpably.   *Lye - ee- KAH*

The programme of music we are being treated to tonight is drawn from early *laïká* (pronounced 'like-AH'), the mainstream popular music of Greece which emerged during the 1950s as the commercial evolution of popularized *rebétika*. Since then *laïká* has grown to refer to Greek ballads of a wide variety of styles, from folk to rock, and which may feature a range of instruments, from those of Greece to those of Western pop, though of course the instrument most associated with this genre is the *bouzoúki*. By the 1960s *laïká* had developed several distinct sub-genres. *Elafrolaïká* is a light and innocuous form, created to please those who wished for a somewhat more refined style of popular song, a kind that was easier upon the ear. But *éntechno*, or 'art song', as developed by Hadjidákis and Theodorákis, in particular, is more refined still. Often involving as many characteristics of *dimotiká*, the age-old music of Greece's many mainland regions and islands, and elements of *rebétika*, as it does characteristics of Western classical music, *éntechno* can be as profoundly serious as rapturously joyful. *Éntechno* remains the most sophisticated form of *laïká*. Also to be acknowledged, although thankfully it's making no appearance here at this concert tonight, is the *laïká* family's crude and decadent member *skyládika*, a term translating literally as 'doggy music'. Stemming from the early 1960s *skyládika* has a number of colourful explanations for how it got its name. One is that in an effort to boost takings, certain open-air summer music-clubs in Greece began offering their guests food in addition to the usual range of soft and alcoholic drinks, but one of the meats that was prepared, boiled veal, so the story goes, was often so unpalatable that guests flung it with disdain beyond their tables to the local dogs, attendant upon the periphery. Word then naturally spread within the canine community so that it wasn't long before the music and singing in such clubs was being accompanied by a chorus of many highly excited and very noisy dogs! Another and perhaps a more plausible explanation holds that the term arose when a certain stratum of rather unsophisticated singers began trying to enliven their performances by greatly speeding up the *tempi* of their songs, with the result that their delivery sounded breathless, rasping, mangled, and so departed from the traditional polished delivery of Greek artists that it was said to resemble the whining of dogs. But whatever the true explanation, as Greece's form of hip Arab and Balkan pop, it's *skyládika* that now gets most young Greeks dancing on the table-tops at three in the morning.

Many different composers have written the music that we enjoy this evening, but the words of all the songs performed here tonight were written by the noted Greek lyricist Pythagóras Papastamatíou, referred to simply and respect-fully in Greece as *Pythagóras*. He was born in 1930 and not only became a songwriter, but an actor, a screenwriter and a playwright. In all he is said to have written about four thousand songs, many of them still loved and sung to this day. He died in 1979, aged only forty-nine. Those who set his lyrics to music created songs that seem to step straight from the heart and flow with the blood. An evening of such music simply cannot be equalled. Each song we hear is a jewel. There is pain, there is longing, and the groan of a people that has suffered for centuries, but there is also compassion and great joy. The songs are thrilling and deeply satisfying.

Andréas and I part at Sýntagma Square and despite the late light rain I walk home buoyant, threads of melody and sounds of *bouzoúkia* still weaving and winding deliciously through my brain. Although 'the rain' tonight is nothing more than the lightest drizzle, successive young black hawkers reach out urgently to me as I pass, seeking to sell me an umbrella, or, since I'm not interested in an umbrella, some cannabis, which they offer to me as *hashish* and *ganjha*. Everyone who is out and about on the streets seems to be treating this gentle shower as if it were a deluge, a reason for panic! Figures scurry urgently, with newspapers or plastic bags held closely over their heads, though I note that apart from myself, the hawkers, and the occasional prostitute sheltering in a doorway, there are actually remarkably few people around. All the way from the theatre to the Metró station, Andréas held his scarf over his head and several times warned me, with deathly seriousness, that in conditions like this we could both catch pneumonia! I just smiled, and nodded, and remembered being out on our hillside in Wales during a cloud-burst, when all the waterfalls of our stream were pounding violently from pool to pool, and I was soaked to the skin whilst trying to clear runnels to stop parts of our up-hill track to the house being once again washed away! I never caught anything remotely like pneumonia in those storms of West Wales but I'd certainly be very wary of suffering from heat-stroke during the height of a Grecian summer! Perhaps we all just fear that which is rare in our experience.

On reaching the hotel, the night porter who unlocks the front door for me erupts immediately and unaccountably into an explanation of why the area just south of Omónoia Square is full of so many empty buildings. I haven't met or seen this man before. Has he confused me with another guest? Or has he simply been simmering away for days, weeks, or even months, and now, tonight, at my arrival, suddenly come to the boil, having had more than he can stand? Or does he regularly apprise guests in this manner? Breathlessly he tells me that Greeks won't live south of Omónoia any longer because Pakistanis, Chinese, and Africans have rented practically all of the spaces that are available, whether business or domestic. Still streaming forth in wild and broken English, he then sails outdoors and firmly beckons me to follow him! Here's a Greek who's not afraid of the drizzle, at least.

He takes me half a street away and points across to a very fine large neo-classical home which he says has recently been fully restored. 'You can have it for 50% of its fair price!' he announces. 'Because of all these Pakistanis, no Greeks will buy!' I suggest to him that, in truth, surely it's not the Pakistanis who are putting people off, but more likely the many Arabs and Africans standing around on the street-corners, idling in the doorways, drinking and smoking while accosting passers-by with urgings to buy drugs? The few Pakistanis I've so far seen here in Athens have all been busy in their little shops, rather like the many Chinese, who to me seem to outnumber all of the other immigrants in the area. He shrugs. 'What can we do? It's terrible! But 50% of the fair price and it's yours, my friend!' I'm so overcome by this outburst that I fail to enquire what the 'fair price' of the fine neo-classical building opposite us actually is! Maybe the man was making me an exceptionally good offer.

This final episode in the rain provides an extraordinary end to an extraordinary day and I can't sleep for all the excitement that has occurred. My head is so full of Greek history and Greek music and all the sights that I've seen that nearly a whole hour passes before I finally manage to nod off.

阅 阅 阅 阅

5

Streets of Dreams

Varvákeios Agorá;
Nákas; Kolonáki;
Benáki Museum;
Panathenean Stadium;
Mets & Pangráti.

This city invites and encourages spontaneity. It offers so many chances for off-the-cuff conversations and impulsive spur-of-the-moment decisions. If only I were fluent in the language, rather than being confined to just giving off, like a parrot, phrases of rather useless Survivor's Greek. Perhaps I should simply 'force' English on the people I meet so that I may enjoy even more interaction than has exhilarated me so far, for many Greeks speak a very reasonable degree of English and they're generally delighted to practise it. All the indications are that the people of this city, the Athenians, as frenetically busy as they may be on their daily treadmills, very much welcome interaction with other human beings. In fact, I'd say they thrive on it. So I start this day resolving to be more assertive and I feel sure that greater openness on my part will at least provide amusement, if not welcome distraction, to those I encounter.

The Athens Varvákeios Agorá, the city's Central Market, is spectacular and astounding. It possesses all the elements of the Middle Eastern *souk* or *bazaar*. How could I have forgotten my very brief experience of it here in Athens in 1991, for surely there is no sensuous immersion on the face of this earth which is more truly 'visceral'. In the meat section there is flesh, red and raw, set out in great quantities on all sides, with long shining steel cleavers slamming through the air to slice it up, hands and fingers perilously close to the butchers' blades. It's almost a circus act! My own fingers shrink with sympathetic horror as knives hurtle down all about, causing fibres torn apart to almost screech in one's ears, while blades hit with a thump the wooden slabs beneath the flesh.

In all the many different stalls of the fish section there are such plenteous and teeming arrays of seafood that you momentarily stop and challenge all you've read about the Mediterranean having been over-fished, how Greece has failed to carefully conserve its fish stocks, and how this country's many polluted rivers are decimating the life in its seas. I've read reports that there has been concern in Brussels regarding research carried out by an interdisciplinary committee of the Agricultural University of Athens, published in September 2009, proving that some of Greece's waterways are seriously poisoned, with concentrations of toxins far exceeding limits set by the EU. Much of the contamination is due to the inappropriate or illegal dumping of trash and waste materials by individuals, private companies, and, worst of all, by local authorities. In Greek lakes and subterranean water-tables high concentrations have been found of dangerous elements from pesticides and fertilisers, as well as from inappropriately dumped waste materials. But here, today, in Athens's Central Market, it seems that this cannot be, as before one's eyes there's such rich abundance. However, an examination of the prices of the fish reveals that what used to be the cheapest staple food of Greece is now very expensive indeed. All the more reason, perhaps, for displaying it in the most tempting manner possible. This morning some of the market's fishmongers have created resplendent eye-catching exhibits of their produce by placing amongst splurges of fish and crustacea of a reddish and orangey hue handfuls of flame-coloured chillies and slices of brilliant red peppers, accentuating and complementing the shades and tints of the seafood. You can imagine the delicious aroma of the whole lot, fish, crabs, lobsters, prawns and peppers, all simmering together in a creamy *thalassiná katsarólas*, a seafood casserole.

Nearby are shops full of spices, stores with glass cases crammed full of local cheeses, speciality butchers' offering tasty and colourful sausages, short, fat, long, or u-shaped, while all of these merchants offer additional curiosities seldom found in the West. Adorning the exteriors of the spice merchants' are two-foot necklaces of orange and dark russet chillies, plaited chains of white garlic-bulbs, garlands of one aromatic herb and wreathes of another. In one old shop, its walls lined with dark wooden drawers and glass cases, a queue of Greek women wait to purchase scoops of loose and ground spices from dozens of large containers all huddled together in the middle of the floor. The air is heady and intoxicating with the scents of cardamom, cumin, cinnamon, cloves, rosemary, oregano, and literally dozens of other herbs and spices. Assistants run back and forth from counter to container, cupping out the required amounts, and packing them all up in little transparent cellophane bags. Hanging from the walls and ceiling of the shop next door is a similarly enticing profusion, this time of still more sausages, in all shades of red, brown, and black. The beauty and the busyness of all these merchants inspires joy! It's exhilarating! The senses are bombarded and they rejoice in the stimulation.

In Athinás Street, brimming with pedestrians, and traffic that jolts along in fast-moving fits-and-starts, with the lights seeming to change three times as quickly as they do in Britain, there are lots of little rabbits, uncaged on part of the pavement, but huddled together on pans of litter. Just inches away streams of people pass by, and a few feet beyond them are the cars, the buses, motorbikes, and scooters, all loudly roaring past! Don't these little creatures ever bolt? Or are they simply too frightened? Within the adjacent pet-shop there are cages of all sorts of colourful and exotic birds, from large flamboyant pheasants through to little budgies in an array of vivid and saturated colours. Their feathers have surely been dyed: in deep apricot-pinks through to a ridiculously but fabulously bright orangey-yellow which shrieks of artificial food-colouring or cochineal. Perhaps these birds are all well-fed and cared for, but one can't help feel for their imprisonment. In transparent perspex pens, deep with bunched-up narrow strips of torn newspaper, are many adorable little puppies. Some are active, but several are strangely and suspiciously still. If these poor animals can hope, surely it must be for quieter captivity way up in some fourth or fifth floor Athenian apartment.

After a lot of leg-work and questioning of passers-by and assistants in several shops, Athens's main music store is at last located. The ground-floor and mezzanine are entirely devoted to sheet-music (Greek song and Greek instrumental, classical, and world pop, though mostly classical), while from some upper floor there come the sounds of virtuosic Liszt-like brilliance from a number of different pianos. Unfortunately for me, most of the collections of Greek music are prepared not for keyboard but for *bouzoúki* and guitar, so that only the melody and chord indications are provided, with perhaps a little vocal harmony here and there. But given how difficult this style of music is to play on any instrument, I find more than enough piano arrangements to keep me occupied for many months to come. Although it's only late morning and mid-week the store is busy, as were all the other music-shops I passed on the way here. For music is very important to Greeks. A steady stream of men come in to buy little packets of replacement strings, usually for *bouzoúki* or guitar, and much discussion is had as to quality and length of string. I slip upstairs past a floor of orchestral instruments to the clavinovas, and then higher still to the piano showroom. Two young Greeks sit at gleaming black grands, with brand new Bluthners, Steinways, and Yamahas sparkling all about. The two pianists flash up and down their keyboards with astonishing confidence and skill, totally unperturbed it seems by the dissonance of their combined musics! I ask permission of an assistant to play through my handful of simple *laïká* and he suggests, mercifully, that I go and use a digital clavinova in a corner of the much quieter floor below.

I've long dreamt of entering such a store in Athens, plucking from the racks a selection of music, and then sitting down at a keyboard to throw off Greek song after Greek song, effortlessly! This morning the actuality is that the music is so 'foreign', so damned difficult, with its strange harmonies and exotic time-signatures, like five crotchets or nine quavers to the bar, that before commencing I turn down the volume-control on the digital piano that I've chosen as low as possible so that others won't hear me, particularly as they're likely to recognise every piece through which I'm about to stumble!

I recall how proficiency in the playing of such songs took me months of anguish and perseverance at home in Wales and Shropshire, so why on earth did I imagine that my comprehension and sight-reading would be magically enhanced upon taking to a keyboard in an Athens showroom? Once I'm done, the assistants downstairs are clearly surprised that this English-speaker purchases several books of music by Greek composers other than the famous Hadjidákis and Theodorákis and who are completely unknown outside Greek communities. The two women make something of a kindly fuss and present me with a special cotton shoulder-bag in which they have placed the volumes, a catalogue, and the receipt. The Greek music world is vast, highly developed and very professional, and I leave the country's premier music-store rather humbled.

I loll awhile for lunch in a small green square where all about are many more of those trees laden with gorgeous glowing oranges. But only a little of the fruit lies on the ground beneath the trees, and although I've met these specimens almost everywhere I've been in Athens so far, I've seen no one actually reach up to pluck an orange. Is taking them illegal? Are they strictly for ornamental purposes? Is clearing up fallen oranges a night-time activity conducted by some army of designated 'orange-collectors'? Was the orange I had with my breakfast at the hotel this morning one that was taken from trees like these in the dead of night? I think it could've been, as the oranges presented in my hotel are not at all like the fine pristine assortments displayed in British supermarkets: they're all rather rough-looking, although they're sweet and taste utterly delicious.

Walking through Kolonáki to find the Benáki Museum, I come across even more bookshops! Their windows are filled with Greek texts, softbacks and hard, all bearing colourful and exquisitely-designed covers, and all titled of course with the letters of that strange and magical alphabet. They exert a curious power. They seem to reach out and offer all the secrets of the universe, or at least all the secrets of Greek life and Greek culture. Kolonáki is named after the small ancient column that stands in the centre of what's now referred to as Kolonáki Square, although the square's proper title is Plateía Filikís Etaireías, after the society that spurred the fight for Greek independence in the 1800s. Kolonáki consists of a standard grid of streets, half of which run parallel to those main thoroughfares which fly north from Sýntagma towards Omónoia, while the other half rush uphill to halt at the forest that fringes the summit of Mount Lykavittós. Stand in any one of the latter streets and gaze upwards and you may well glimpse the little 19th century Chapel of St. Yeórghios that looks down upon Athens from the very tip of Lykavittós. To do so though, you may have to negotiate a battalion of big flashy parked motorbikes, their long sleek seats of *faux* leather bare to the air and quite unconcerned about vandalism, as Athens has long been regarded as one of the safest cities in Europe. The apartments above are all meticulously well-maintained, their wide balconies streamlined, smart, and uncluttered. Here and there are a tasteful decorative pot, an elegant ornamental shrub, and pieces of outdoor furniture that are distinctly upmarket.

Below Kolonáki's apartments, at street level, are endless smart boutiques selling flash jewellery, antiques, and luxury clothing, the sort of shops you expect to find in the smart areas of Paris and the most expensive streets of central and west London. Some of the window displays are dazzling, highly inventive, put together with a good deal of theatrical style and flair. And amazingly I haven't seen a spare or empty shop-space in such streets yet, although back in Britain, in some of my nearest big towns, 10 to 15% of spaces in most of the main streets are currently empty due to the recession. Why are the Greeks immune, when it's just been announced that the country's financial deficit is massive, the largest in Europe in fact? How do they keep going? How is Greece managing to keep such a good face? European analysts at this time are saying on the news that they fear the Greeks will rely on Brussels to bail them out. Well, if that's the case, from what I see here if the EU does bail Greece out they could simply be enabling its people to continue with what appears to be a splendid fiesta - unless there's some grim desperation going on behind the scenes, miseries which I haven't yet detected!

The cafés and restaurants are full, often overflowing onto adjacent pavements with people eating and drinking beneath outdoor gas-heaters, and in Kolonáki, and all of downtown Athens, the streets are currently awash with well-heeled Greeks carrying home bags and bags of designer-shopping. It's all rather puzzling.

The Benáki Museum is beautiful in itself. The building's fine neo-classical portico and white marble steps rise from a fanfare of brilliant red hibiscus, the flowers of my Fijian childhood, while directly opposite lie the forty lush green acres of Athens's National Gardens, all a world away from the completely snow-covered Britain I left just a few days ago. Within the Benáki Museum are breathtaking treasures, mostly Greek, all laid out with exquisite taste and a wealth of illuminating written information. For me, the most astounding exhibit is an example of the intricate filigree jewellery that was created on the island of Pátmos, in the Dodecánese, in the 1600s. From one elaborate precious gold and enamel necklace there hangs, as if the necklace itself were not gorgeous enough, a minutely detailed three- or four-inch-high gold, pearl, and multi-coloured enamel pendant shaped as a replica of a ship with ten sails all a-billowing in the breeze. Two six-inch-long intricate matching ear-rings also bear beautifully-worked replicas of similar caravels at sail. The overall effect of the detail and the craftsmanship is breathtaking. Only one thing is missing: one should be seeing this jewellery next to the 'olive' skin and shining long dark hair of a ravishing Greek beauty.

Elsewhere there are hoards of treasure from Éuvoia, Thébes, and Thessalía; vast ancient Greek pots that stand some six feet tall; pieces of sizeable, very early, crude domestic earthenware of such burnished surfaces that they gleam a deep golden honey; Byzantine *eikónes* that are vivid and dazzling with detail in vibrant reds, greens, and blues; and two fully reconstructed rooms from a wealthy merchant's home in Kozáni, northern Greece, in the mid-eighteenth century. These two beautiful salons feature vaulted ceilings, ornate built-in cupboards, lattice-work, and intricate wall-decorations that include scores of small highly-worked inset panels. All of the salons' surfaces are composed of carved, painted, or gilded wood in a style born of both Greek Byzantine and European influences. I'm struck particularly by the low seating, complete with opulent Persian-style rugs and numerous cushions placed around low coffee tables such as one often sees in traditionally furnished homes throughout Arabia today. All that are naturally missing from this static display are the sugared fruits, the sweetmeats, the little coffee cups, and the brightly coloured and intricately cut little drinking glasses of the Arabian *milieu*. But above and high on a shelf that passes around the edge of the vaulted ceiling are all the highly decorated brass plates that are a feature of the Middle East. These rooms combine elements of both the Arab *diwaniya* (receiving room), and the elegant European drawing-room. They're a magnificent synthesis of Arabia and Europe.

On the top floor of the Benáki I find a special one-room temporary exhibition reviewing the Greece of the 1960s - that magical Greece to which I had been serendipitously introduced by way of a documentary at school in New Zealand. All I remember of that film now is a positive, sunny, and developing country wrapped in the cascading sounds of *bouzoúkia*, so it's quite amazing that, as if prepared specially for me, this exhibition illustrates the individual years of the Greek sixties by way of a stall for each. And it's thrilling to find too that Hadjidákis and Theodorákis, and the poets Elýtis, Rítsos, and Seféris, are featured prominently in each year and are clearly now regarded as Greece's most significant artists of the period. Indeed in 1963 and 1979, respectively, Elýtis and Seféris won the Nobel Prize in Literature, and in 1977 Rítsos was awarded the Lenin Peace Prize. I learn that when Theodorákis's music was banned by the dictatorship, Hadjidákis and about twenty other Greek composers and poets immediately retaliated, in support of Theodorákis, by requiring that their works too should not be played on Greek national radio. Because Theodorákis had been banned, in solidarity with him they all banned themselves! Theodorákis was even placed under house arrest until such time as his captors permitted him to go into exile, in Paris, where other Greek activists greeted him rapturously and supported his continued work against the dictatorship.

The most dramatic exhibit in this temporary exhibition is a huge sepia enlargement of a photograph of a handsome young man standing vulnerable in T-shirt and trousers while handcuffed to a policeman and surrounded by determined-looking men in suits. The young man, Aléxandros Panagoúlis, had just tried to assassinate Yeórghios Papadópoulos, the Second World War Nazi collaborator who had led the military *coup* of 1967 and become the nation's dictator, by seeking to ignite a bomb beneath the tyrant's limousine. Panagoúlis was the founder of the National Resistance and he fought hard for a return to democracy. For seeking to assassinate the dictator he was sentenced to death, but because of his popularity the régime didn't dare carry out the sentence. In prison Panagoúlis was subjected to horrific physical and mental tortures, yet, nevertheless, he passed the time by writing powerful poetry, sometimes famously using his own blood as ink.

Because of international pressure Panagoúlis was eventually released, but like Theodorákis he went immediately into self-exile. In nearby Italy, he engulfed himself in the important work of resistance. With the eventual restoration of democracy Aléxandros Panagoúlis was elected to the new Greek parliament, however he died two years later in a mysterious car crash, aged just thirty-eight. As a total of five noteworthy 'undesirables' had died during the Júnta in 'traffic accidents', there was much speculation in the Greek press of the time that Panagoúlis's accident too had been staged, to halt his plan to release several days later documents which named certain individuals who had collaborated with the dictatorship. Theodorákis set some of Panagoúlis's poems to music and in 1997 the people's hero was commemorated by the issue of a postage stamp bearing his face, name, dates of birth and death, and the words 'Greek Democracy'. So far, over twenty streets in Athens and one Metró station have been named in Aléxandros Panagoúlis's honour.

The exhibition ends with a celebration of the singer Níkos Xiloúris, 'The Archangel of Crete', who came to national prominence towards the end of the decade. Yesterday in the small city-centre CD shop where I introduced the voice of Mihális Theodórou, I met Xiloúris's widow, Ouranía, but not until today, at this exhibition, do I realise how great an honour that meeting was. In 1941 when Xiloúris was just five years old his mountain village, Anógheia, was razed to the ground by the invading Nazis and like many other Cretans he and his family were forced to hide high in the island's mountains, where the young Xiloúris soon began to show uncommon talent at playing the *lýra* and singing. At the age of seventeen he left the mountains and despite the preference of the people of Irákleion for the modern tango, waltz, and rumba, by way of his exceptional musicianship Xiloúris rekindled their love of their own ancient music. Later, during the dictatorship, he inspired hope and resistance throughout Greece with songs that strengthened public resolve for the restitution of democracy. In 1980, aged only forty-four, Níkos Xiloúris lost his battle with cancer.

As I leave the Benáki, my head filled again with thoughts of the nobility and determination of these people who have for so long been downtrodden, I'm struck by the power of a large oil-painting of a 19th century Greek warrior whose rich and sumptuous apparel suggests a leader of considerable importance. A voluminous loosely-pleated *foustanéla* (a tough kind of white pleated kilt, of ancient origin) hangs from his waist; he carries no less than four swords, all of different sizes, two strapped into his waistbelt, one held as if ready for action in his left hand, while a fourth, bowed, black and bronze, hangs ceremonially from his belt; a kind of supple white *flokáti* rug is slung over one shoulder; his black jacket is richly embroidered in gold; and he wears a vibrant ochreous headscarf bearing bands of brilliant blue and red. A finger of the right hand points defiantly downwards, towards the ground, as if this chieftain is declaring '*Óchi!* No! Never! Not over our dead bodies!' The image is thought to depict either Theódoros Kolokotrónis or his nephew Nikitarás Stamatelópoulos, two revolutionaries who fought to free Greece from Turkish domination during the War of Independence. Stamatelópoulos was such a fierce fighter that he became known as 'The Turk-Eater'.

Returning to the Benáki's foyer you notice several imposing full-length portraits in colourful modern style on the walls above and around the information desk. You may not see them when you arrive, seeking the glories of Greece's past, but as you prepare to leave the building, quite appropriately they arrest you. The tall elegant gentleman with the very wide dash of moustache, wearing a simple open-necked shirt, jumper, and trousers, is Antónis Benákis, the man who brought together most of the wonders of this outstanding museum and for whose father the architect Anastásios Metaxás built this mansion. Antónis Benákis was born in Alexándreia, in 1873, the son of the politician and magnate Emmanuél Benákis, and he started his collecting in Egypt, at the beginning of the 20th century. After settling in Athens in 1926 Antónis made real his dream of donating his collections to the Greek state, to which, in 1931, he also gave his father's mansion. For the remaining 23 years of his life, Antónis then organised, administered, and augmented the collection which is named in his honour. He had long been familiar with the principles of generosity and nobility, for his father, a close friend of prime minister Elefthérios Venizélos, had already contributed much of his fortune to numerous charitable causes, including the settlement of refugees from Asia Minor. And on the day that the Nazis marched into Athens in 1941, Antónis's sister, Penelópe Délta, Greece's first truly successful children's novelist, took poison and died.

The Benáki Museum is so fascinating that, emerging hours later than planned and finding darkness has descended, I must abandon my plan to see the fifteen remaining columns of Emperor Hadrian's greatest gift to Athens, the largest Greek temple ever built, the magnificent Temple of Olympian Zeus, erected between 125 and 132 CE. Thankfully, however, most of the temple's highly decorated Corinthian columns, colossal in size, are clearly visible despite the lines of trees which now enclose them, thanks to powerful spotlighting. And also regardless of the hour, one can still go right up to the gates of the nearby vast Panathenean Stadium, the only such stadium on the planet built completely of white marble, and which is therefore also referred to by Greeks as the *Kallimármaro*, the 'beautifully marbled'.

In 330 BCE the precursor of this stadium was laid out by the orator and rhetorician Lykúrgos (390 to 323 BCE) to seat

50,000 spectators. However, the massive arena that Lykúrgos created was very simple, for between two hills, the southern one of which, Ardittós Hill, is still clearly visible today to one side of the present stadium, he just levelled and shaped the ground so that people might sit on it and comfortably view the spectacle below. Only for important guests in the area of 'the front row' did he create some marble seating. However, at the Panathenaic Games of 140 CE the wealthy Athenian Iródis Attikós was inspired by the potential of the site and thus for the games of 144 CE he transformed the simple 'stadium' of Lykúrgos into a magnificent sea of white Pentelic marble. For this and many other outstanding acts of generosity, including the building of a great marble theatre on the south side of the Acrópolis, when Iródis died, about 177 CE, this renowned benefactor, scholar, and writer was honoured with a tomb adjacent to the eastern wall of the *Kallimármaro* and the remains of his elegant sarcophagus are visible still.

With the sacking of Athens by invaders in the early centuries of the Common Era, as well as Christianity's outlawing of all competitions of pagan origin, Iródis's magnificent Panathenean Stadium fell into disrepair and became hardly recognisable. Only when the young French aristocrat Baron Pierre de Coubertin succeeded in 1894 in arousing the interest of a handful of nations in reviving the Olympic Games did serious attention fall once again upon this ancient Athenian site. Then like Iródis Attikós almost 2,000 years earlier, another wealthy Greek, Yeórghios Avéroff of Alexándreia, stepped up to the challenge and financed all the work that de Coubertin's dream required. Ernst Ziller produced the plans. The same kind of marble and the same design, a long horseshoe left completely open at one end, as had been used before, were employed again. Sufficient progress was made for the first modern Olympiád to be held on the site in 1896. But it was not until 1906 that this second *Kallimármaro* was completed, at which time, as had been effected by Lykúrgos, and then by Iródis Attikós, Avéroff's recreated stadium, 83 metres wide and 204 metres long, once again provided accommodation for 50,000 spectators. The benefactor's generosity is honoured by a sculpture of him set high upon a pyramidal plinth just to the side of the stadium's entrance. Viewing Avéroff's great gift now in its flood-lit magnificence, the marble all very white in the strong illuminations, I can imagine how magical must be the musical concerts that are occasionally given here, though surely the wide adjacent Vasiléos Konstantínou Avenue must first be cleared for the night of its many lanes of roaring and incessant traffic.

Escaping the noise, I wander past Ardittós Hill and into Odós Márkou Moussoúrou and the quiet and pleasant area of Mets. Although its narrow hilly streets are packed with serried *polykatoikíes* (apartment blocks) and cars parked bumper to bumper upon pavements, Mets is a residential locality popular with artistic folk. It has a naturalness and an intimacy about it, with here and there a *tavérna*, a bakery, or a café, and in one little street I chance upon a shop window which is like a theatrical production. I've only ever before seen shop windows like it in Venice, Paris, and Amsterdam, and even there only occasionally. Delicate sheer curtains embroidered with elaborate gold ornamentation frame the entire window as if it were the stage-set of an elaborate Victorian theatre. The composition is comprised of elements of a 19th century childhood, the most dominant being beautifully painted porcelain faces of large dolls in rich costumes. The Red Queen, or the Queen of Hearts, arrayed in a luxurious multi-coloured tunic with a gold crown upon flaming red hair, reigns over all from up-stage centre. The rest of the display consists of highly decorated masks and small antique ornaments, frayed but beautiful old cushions and wraps, bronze statuettes, glowing lamps upon burnished brass, all positioned on or about pieces of fine old furniture in highly polished dark woods.

Just to the north-east of Mets lies the adjacent locality of Pangráti, and though it's dark and cold I'm so delighted and charmed by the stage-set window of the antique store that I'm spurred to go an extra mile! Wending my way in and out between block after block of apartments, a brisk twenty-minute walk delivers me to a very ordinary and rather grubby-looking older *polykatoikía*, of only a few floors, just off bustling café-lined Ymittoú Avenue, at 3 Mánou Konstantínou Street. From 1936 to 1962 this building was home to Mános

Hadjidákis, his mother, Alíki, and his sister, Miránda. It's a basic block, very vaguely and modestly Art Deco in style, with a slightly grand front entrance at the centre of the ground-floor, two large windows with doors in them to each side, and just a couple of shuttered windows on the simple balconied floors above. The two ground-floor windows are boarded-up, and the one on the left has been defaced with graffiti. But to the side of the window on the right, a sizeable white marble plaque has been affixed to the concrete casting of the wall. Upon it, beside a monotint image of Mános in his final years, are words commemorating the composer who gave us the music-theatre piece *Odós Oneíron* (The Street of Dreams) and all its wonderful songs, including the extremely touching *Manoúla Mou* (My Little Mother).

This humble Mánou Konstantínou Street was Mános Hadjidákis's very own *Odós Oneíron*, his very own street of dreams. It was his home from when he was 11 until he was almost 40. And it was in this very ordinary street, in a little flat down in the basement that he shared with his mother and sister, that the internationally famous composer stored his Oscar. And now I understand why when Theodorákis was on the run from the secret police in December 1947, for having addressed a conference of the Greek Resistance Movement and for having led a huge protest-parade singing songs of rebellion through central Athens, and he had turned to his old friend from the Greek Resistance Movement for a bolt-hole, Mános was unable to offer him shelter here at 3 Mánou Konstantínou. But Mános was already successful at the Art Theatre, writing for Károlos Koun, as well as composing for films, so he was a popular man about town. He thus took Míkis along to parties, introducing him as being other than who he actually was, just so that Míkis could eat. And then at the end of such evenings, before Hadjidákis returned home to this little flat in Pangráti, he would let Míkis into the Art Theatre to sleep. Most of the time though, Theodorákis spent his nights among the rocks at Piraeus or hiding in building sites. Then in June 1948 the authorities captured him, and he was returned to Ikaría, a prison-island not far from the coast of Turkey where during the period of the Civil War roughly 13,000 left-wing intellectuals and communists were held in concentration camps. In January 1949 Theodorákis was transferred to a 'Re-Education Centre' on Makrónisos, a similar island holding 30,000 political prisoners and where he was beaten and tortured and several times left for dead. It's little wonder then when Greeks compare Theodorákis with Hadjidákis, why it's the former whom they view as 'the great political hero'. But you only have to visit humble Odós Mánou Konstantínou to see that Hadjidákis, who incidentally was born in the very same year as his friend, also lived with simplicity and integrity.

Turning back for the night, I hurry by the new Acrópolis Museum, closed now and dark, and then take a short detour in the direction of the great arched windows of the theatre built by Iródis Attikós in the period 161 to 174 CE, in memory of his wife Ríghilla. It too is of course closed and dark, and at this hour of night and in winter there is absolutely no one within earshot. The area is deserted. And I find I am able to walk very close to an up-stage central arch behind the performance area, to peer through the gate there and see the marble horse-shoe of the steeply sloped ancient amphitheatre directly in front of me, as if I were an artist about to walk through the arch and into the spotlight to sing. The acoustics of this Roman theatre are said to be perfect, so I venture into the night air, up towards the glowing Parthenon above, a few phrases of Hadjidákis. But my voice is completely lost! The great rake of white Pentelic marble returns not a sound, not a single echo, no resonance of any kind. I really need to get beyond the railings and through the arch, but all I can do is try to sing louder and more boldly from where I am. But, sadly, to no avail. If the theatre were full, with a capacity audience of 5,000 soft and sound-absorbing human bodies, as it was built to accommodate, what hope then? But no, this is one of those amazing Greek amphitheatres where members of the audience are able to hear the quietest of sounds, and where even the slightest noise is carried undistorted to the highest reaches of the auditorium but in some spaces like this, the performers, however, hear no echo and must trust entirely in their projection. So much then for hearing my own impromptu midnight recital at *To Iródio*.

After a rather rich *keftedákia Anatolís*, a traditional Greek dish from Asia Minor consisting of meatballs in a deliciously peppery tomato and cheese sauce, I could do with a strong drink to help settle my stomach. So in a little lane not far from the hotel, I step into a late-night liquor shop to buy some *oúzo*. Though the Greek owner fully understands and helps me select a good bottle from the many different brands he has available, he then calls a young Bangladeshi man from somewhere at the back to speak with me in English and to see to the taking of the money. When the Bangladeshi appears he firstly talks in seemingly fluent Greek to the owner, so in English I ask him where he's from and how long he's been in Greece. 'Ten years!' he answers chirpily. So here's clearly one way of doing it. Arrive in Greece without a word of Greek, eke out a living in some small backstreet store, and after ten years it'll have happened: you'll have mastered the impenetrable and frightening mysteries of the Greek language. Like this young man from Bangladesh, you'll be fluent.

As I dart along to the hotel with my little bottle of *oúzo*, a dark female leaning in the shadow of a doorway makes long squeaky sucked-in kissing sounds at me, like lots of creaky doors opening one after the other. Her suggestive squeakings and suckings are all very off-putting - they sound more insulting than they do alluring - but she doesn't fail to advertise the nature of her services with absolute clarity.

🜂 🜂 🜂 🜂

6

Artefacts & Legacies

Centre for Folk Art and Tradition;
Museum of Greek Popular Musical Instruments;
Oi Aérides;
Hammám Abid Efendi;
Anafiótika;
& The National Gardens.

In a beautiful mansion in the old Pláka neighbourhood, nestled at the foot of the northern side of the Acrópolis, an extremely mindful assistant follows me unnervingly from room to room within the Centre for Folk Art and Tradition, as if absolutely sure I intend to pocket something! No amount of charm will shake her off. Early on this gloriously crisp and sunny morning I'm the only visitor present, and so I'm the sole focus of her attention. No poses I strike or expressions I wear, to demonstrate that I'm a mature and respectable individual, will convince her to leave me alone! Maybe in the past they've had some very shrewd thieves through this museum, people who look like the most honourable souls under the sun but who are quite otherwise. From room to room she follows me, never more than about six feet away, her eyes fixed upon my movements at every moment. She doesn't speak any English so there's nothing for it but for me to try to imagine she isn't there.

The interior of this mansion bears something of a resemblance to the two reconstructed Kozáni rooms in the Benáki Museum, in that it's a synthesis of fine old European design and the best of the East. There are old houses in Cairo which are similar, most notably because of the airiness and the internal interest which are created by apertures in the walls of upper rooms opening onto the upper spaces of larger chambers which are adjacent but beneath. Such arrangements allow someone in a higher room to move aside a screen or open an internal window to observe someone who may have just arrived in one of the grand reception chambers below. The Centre for Folk Art and Tradition is interesting mainly because of this very Arabic interior, otherwise it's largely bare, although there is on display a reasonable number of genuine Greek folkish objects, ranging from about the mid 17th century to the present day: costumes, embroideries, pottery, and musical instruments - items which are all surely too large for anyone to pocket! When done, I turn and cheerily tell my diligent Greek minder, 'Αυτό το σπίτι είναι θαυμάσιο!' (This house is marvellous!) and her whole demeanour instantly transforms. She relaxes and beams and suddenly becomes very beautiful, and for several moments we grin at each other like love-struck teenagers.

Not far away, at the Museum of Greek Popular Musical Instruments, I spend just over an hour listening to recordings of all the ethnic instruments of Greece and am struck again by how strongly the country has been influenced by Arabia, by how the traditional music of Greece has so much in common with the music I came to know and love during my years in the Middle East. I find the most arresting exhibit in this museum to be a very large colour photograph of Theodore Leblanc's mid-nineteenth century painting of three Greeks in song, titled 'Chanteurs Grecs'. One of the singers wears a *foustanéla*, while the other two are dressed in loose knee-length pantaloons; each man bears a colourful waistband below his vest, little jacket, or waistcoat; and two wear a richly decorative cloth about the head while the other sports a small deep-red Turkish *fez* cap. Their faces are rugged, all wear moustaches, two have their heads thrown back in passionate song, and their instruments are a *tambourás* and a lute shaped like an Arabic oud. Tucked into their waistbands are daggers in highly decorated silver sheaths, such as are still worn on ceremonial occasions by modern Gulf Arabs. Beside the obvious Eastern characteristics of these three singing Greeks, I'm tickled by seeming to almost hear their voices. They are all older men and the central figure, who is both singing and playing an instrument, is clearly producing his song from a place of passion and pain. His eyebrows are angled downwards and knitted, and it's clear his song involves assertion, possibly defiance. Two even older faces, beneath elaborate Turkish-style head-dresses, peer from over his left shoulder. They listen with serious and intense concentration. One can perceive the link between such musicians and the raw, potent, and piquant works of *rebétika*.

The exhibition at the Museum of Greek Popular Musical Instruments is largely the result of forty years of research by the ethnomusicologist Phoébus Anoghiannákis, from whose collection of over 1,200 Greek musical instruments, dating from the 1700s through to the present day, the displays here are drawn. The beautiful three-storey 1840s Pláka mansion in which the exhibition is housed bears a strong similarity to the house visited earlier, the Centre for Folk Art and Tradition. Not surprisingly, it was built by a writer, playwright, and teacher from the Kozáni region, a Yeórghios Lassánis, who played an active role in the Greek revolution. Painted now a soft warm yellow with grey-green shutters, the mansion is set around a small tranquil lawned courtyard overhung by graceful palms. Spread out over three floors within the house, the exhibition of musical instruments is divided into four categories: *aeróphona* (wind instruments including *flogéres, souraúli, mandoúres, tsaboúnes, gáides,* and *zournádes*); *chordófona* (stringed instruments including *tambourádes, laghoúta, bouzoúkia, violóliras, kmanés, lýres,* mandolins, dulcimers, and guitars); percussion (*toumbelékia, daoúlia, défia,* and suchlike); and *idiófona* (instruments like bells and cymbals that produce their sounds by their own vibration, without strings or membranes, examples being *koudoúnia, masiés,* and *símandro*). It's from this unique heritage of instruments that the magical sounds of Greece have arisen, so for the lover of traditional Greek music this collection is a delight.

Just a few steps away from the Museum of Greek Popular Musical Instruments is the Roman Agorá, sometimes referred to as the Agorá of Caesar and Augustus, and within it stands the Tower of the Winds, or *Oi Aérides* ('the windy ones'), as the locals call it. This octagonal building with a conical marble top, known to archaeologists as the Horológion, is deceptive in its appearance. It looks quite short and squat, but it's actually just under 12 metres high. Although big enough to have once been used as a place of worship, it was erected as a water- and clock-tower in the 1st century BCE by the astronomer Andrónicus Kyrrhéstes, a street in whose honour lies immediately to the east.

The tower's eight façades bear a well-preserved frieze representing the eight 'windy ones': Voréas (from the north) driving down the cold north wind through a large shell, Kaikías (the north-east wind) thrusting down a basketful of hailstones on unfortunate beings below, and so forth, each relief including an inscription stating the mythological name of the wind depicted. The time of day used to be indicated by a sundial on each of the eight façades, and the direction of the prevailing wind by a bronze statue of a *tríton*, a mythological merman with the upper body of a human and the tail of a fish. An early observer, the Roman architect Marcus Vitruvius, described this *tríton* as a weather vane high on the summit of the tower, the *tríton* turning with the wind and always facing directly into it, so that the rod in his right hand would always point over the depiction on the frieze below of whichever of the eight winds was blowing at the time. The clock, or Klepsýdra, that once graced the structure, driven by water from the Spring of Klepsýdra close to the Beulé Gate on the Acrópolis above, has unfortunately long since disappeared. It, of course, enabled passers-by to tell the time during the hours of darkness, when the sundials were of no use. And this tower even had a fourth function, as perhaps the earliest known forerunner of the modern planetarium. Andrónicus Kyrrhéstes, being an astronomer, designed the interior to feature a mechanical device, perhaps the very first kind of 'computer', that followed the path of the sun in relation to the moon and the visible planets, as is believed to have been possessed by Archimédes 200 years earlier. A further but unintended function of *Oi Aérides* must also be noted. During the Ottoman occupation this exotic tower attracted the attention of a school of Mevlevi dervishes and many foreign visitors to Athens during the 18th century described a rather theatrical scene taking place inside the building after Islamic prayers on Fridays. With quotations from the Qur'an decorating all of the interior walls, and following a leader dressed all in green, the sacred colour of Islam, the dervishes whirled round and round and cried aloud until such time as, exhausted, they fell seemingly unconscious into the arms of their spectators!

Today the main interest of this tower, apart from its octagonal shape, lies in its external frieze, and it's anomalous that two thousand years down the centuries the reliefs are all still largely intact and discernible. However, on each of the eight walls strong ochre stains stretch down from the roof as a result of rain and local pollution. Truly this dear and characterful little building ought to be protected for posterity, but if one were to encase this gem within a large glass structure where would preservation in Athens end? All of the Roman Agorá, as well as the Ancient Agorá, and the entire Acrópolis would surely deserve similar treatment. Athens's numerous monuments have withstood the blistering sun of the Attic summer and the cold of its mid-winters for over two thousand years, and they must simply continue to do so, each year decaying just a little more.

A few buildings along Kyrrístou Street, leading off from one side of the little square in which *Oi Aérides* stands, lies the old Hammám Abid Efendi, now referred to as The Bath-House of the Winds on account of its proximity to 'the windy ones'. Enclosed behind the plain façade of the street this unusually fine relic of Greece's four centuries of Turkish occupation is easily missed. Although the Hammám Abid Efendi is now managed very professionally by the nearby Museum of Greek Folk Art, surprisingly few Athenians or visitors appear to be aware of it. The low profile could well be due to the structure's Ottoman roots and a tendency for Greeks to blot out that unfortunate period of their history so closely linked with the Muslim world. This part of Pláka used to be known as the Turkish Quarter and the shops nearby were as much referred to as the *bazaar* as the *agorá*. Half a dozen mosques were once sited in this locality and, of course, dervishes occupied *Oi Aérides* nearby. When the great Turkish traveller and prolific writer Evliya Çelebi visited Athens in 1667 he noted three fine Turkish *hammáms* in the city, one of which he declared to be this bath-house of Abid Efendi. Another, the Hammám of Oula Bey, was also in this same Turkish Quarter. So we know that the Hammám Abid Efendi must have been constructed some time between the start of the occupation, in 1453, and 1667. We also know that despite the Turks being ousted in 1829, this bath-house continued to provide Athenian men and women with a place of cleanliness, relaxation, and bodily beautification right through until 1965, when it was closed.

Today The Bath-House of the Winds is no longer an operating *hammám*, in fact no water or steam is now to be seen anywhere within it, but it is, however, a very fine restoration of the surviving structure. To the left and right of the front entrance, two disrobing areas with little changing rooms feature elegant painted wooden panelling; exquisitely decorated, high, canopy-style ceilings; and floors superbly decorated with tiles featuring intricate Islamic designs. All the chambers beyond the two grand and galleried changing areas are separated by exotic rounded arches and linked by a maze-like labyrinth of atmospheric tunnel-like hallways. In the bathing rooms themselves, long white marble benches and elegant low marble basins, with hot and cold bronze taps, contrast stylishly and dramatically with the deep reddish-ochre of the surrounding walls. In the floors several glass panels have recently been inserted, to reveal the furnaces that supplied the *hammám* with its steam and hot water, as well as the hypocaust that with its hot smoke warmed the marble beneath the bathers' feet. High above, in the thick red walls of the tepidarium and caldarium, are small round holes in domes and barrel vaults that are typical of the ceilings of antique Turkish, Moroccan, and Egyptian *hammáms*. These charming little apertures, glazed in clear glass, drop magical shafts of bright daylight into the chambers below. Unlike the thermae and balneae of the Romans, the Athenian *hammám* did not include a frigidarium. This was due to the Qur'anic injunction that the body be cleansed only by cool running water - not still.

Overlooking the elegant panelling and tiling of the separate male and female disrobing areas, the airy galleries and rows of further small cubicles on the upper floor of this bath-house probably helped to engender amongst all those who came here a most delicious feeling of well-being, communality, and privacy. Indeed, during the Ottoman occupation *hammáms* afforded the women of Athens gathering places where they could socialise intimately and in complete comfort, for men and women were never permitted to use a *hammám* at the same time. In fact, in 1638 Evliya Çelebi had written of Athens that by day no one ever saw any women in the city, neither Muslim nor Christian, neither in the market nor passing along the streets. However, he wrote, come the night thousands of women proceeded outdoors with lanterns either to visit other homes or to amuse themselves in the *hammáms*.

Quite refreshed by the magic of the Hammám Abid Efendi, I head uphill, above Pláka, to find Anafiótika, the shambolic little shanty-town that hugs part of the north-eastern face of the great rock on which sits the Acrópolis. It's astonishing that at such an elevated height, and in such a prestigious location, there still remains a ramshackle community adjacent to the very heart of Athens, directly beside the Sacred Rock. For over a hundred years the élite of the capital have tried hard to have this 'illegal blot' removed, no doubt imagining themselves ensconced instead on this prime piece of land, but the community here has always fought back, and thankfully it has always won. In the 1860s, following the Greek War of Independence, this small neighbourhood of tiny houses was thrown together by immigrant workers who had been brought in from the remote island of Anáfi, just east of the island of Thíra (Santoríni), to help build Greece's fine new capital according to the grand desires and designs of its new Bavarian bureaucrats. Anafiótika today is thus simply what remains of that collection of humble lodgings in which Anafiot labourers dwelt when not hard at work upon the construction of the new Athens. Most of the houses of Anafiótika consist of just a few rooms that are no bigger than those of the ancient quarters that were once spliced into the rocks just below the Parthenon, or in the region of the two demes on Philopáppou Hill, rooms rarely larger than just five or six square metres.

Today the better-maintained lanes of Anafiótika are similar to those of the little stepped whitewashed communities to be found on many of the Greek islands. There are points at which you could easily think yourself in some of the quiet back-streets of the Chóra, on the islands of Náxos, Amorgós, or Astypálaia. The tiny white houses are arranged higgledy-piggledy, little doors and windows contrasting strongly in vibrant dark colours against all of the white. Each year the concrete filling between the large grey stones in the pavements and steps are also painted white, so that every stone before you assumes the shape of a gentle round. On either side of each narrow lane a row of verdant pot-plants lines the wall. Anafiótika's little alleys are charming, quaint, and proud, the antithesis of the vast sprawl of the city below. Some corners of the community, however, have been abandoned and these are both strewn with rubbish and 'decorated' in a riot of disordered but colourful graffiti, applied nocturnally by high-climbing youths with spray-cans and gas-masks. But without these bright anarchic scrawls and drawings the derelict corners of Anafiótika would look even sadder.

Leaving Anafiótika, I descend through Pláka, also referred to as '*the* Pláka', scores of souvenir shops to the left and right of my path, to visit the lush forty acres of the National Gardens. Sponsored in the mid-19th century by Queen Amalía, and therefore originally known as The Royal Gardens, the landscaping here is rather formal but nevertheless attractive. Amalía had the botanist Karl Froos fill this royal park with 15,000 rooted plants and trees of over 500 different species, all imported from Genoa. For years afterwards they were cared for by Amalía's court gardener, Frederick Schmidt. A century and a half later, however, the cultivations in these gardens are not outstanding. This isn't due to a lack of pride in botanical exhibition, for clearly the gardens are subject to consider-able maintenance, but rather to the fact that it's simply very difficult to develop and maintain an impressive garden in a city that gets as frightfully hot at the height of summer as it does in Athens. Unfortunately, despite Schmidt's best efforts, many of the specimens that were imported from Italy failed to survive the harsh dryness of the Balkan Peninsula, threshold of the boiling East. Thus these gardens remind me of many Kuwaiti, Sa'udi, and Egyptian attempts to create and maintain similar gardens, although nowhere in Arabia have I seen such a green, well-populated, and well-laid out park as this. However, a plethora of tall trees, paths, and concrete ponds, snaked about by endless miles of visible black rubberlike irrigation-tubing, does not make for the most satisfying botanical experience. So, somewhat disappointed in Athens's National Gardens, I find myself fondly recalling the magnificent Botanic Gardens of Christchurch, New Zealand, set in a very large loop of the beautiful and meandering River Avon. Upon its banks, the city of Christchurch offers a large and magical daffodil wood, two rose gardens, a rock garden, a herb garden, a heather garden, a primula garden, an azalea and magnolia garden, a wide and long herbaceous border, an extensive water garden set around three large and winding lakes, six conservatories, a bonsai house, and a pinetum and conifer wood, not to mention half a dozen lawns overhung by massive trees, indigenous and exotic. But one must also recall that sedate Christchurch has practically none of the exhilarating buzz, energy, life, and stimulating *cháos* which is offered by the city of Athens.

In the early evening I meet Andréas again, to have dinner and see a film. He assures me that the restaurant will not be expensive or flash, but as we walk along Panepistimíou Street, past expensive boutiques crammed with sparkling jewellery and glamorous watches, I'm intrigued as to how he may suddenly pull something economical from his sleeve. And indeed, for there's no deterring him, once inside Andréas's restaurant of choice it's clear that this is going to be a costly meal. However, it promises to be also a very stylish one. The décor is lavish imitation *art-nouveau* and, as before, the professionalism of the waiters is astounding. When the food arrives it is equally impressive. I never realised that livers can be enormous, never mind that slices of them could be so tender! My two large grilled slabs of liver almost fall apart at the gentlest touch of the knife, and they're absolutely delicious. When it's time to start thinking of moving towards the cinema, I insist on paying the bill and hand the waiter notes totalling six euros more than the amount required to be paid. Although Andréas and I then linger in conversation for another twenty minutes or so, no change is returned to the table! For Andréas's sake I make no fuss and treat the pocketed amount as a tip given. As we leave the waiter is all smiles and obsequious gestures as if farewelling dear old friends. It's very flattering but I would have preferred to have freely given a tip rather than to have had it taken without consent.

At the theatre a few doors along, the mature Greek lady behind the counter takes one look at me (I haven't said a word - Andréas seeing to the purchase of the tickets) and then informs my friend that I should be made aware that the film's dialogue is 'half English, half French, with only Greek subtitles'. Andréas explains 'the problem' to me and I then thank the lady for her concern and tell her that I'm looking forward to the experience. But what's so startling and significant is the woman's almost totally correct perception, drawn entirely from my silent visage, that I'm an English-speaker and therefore unable to speak or read Greek and most probably will be unable to understand any of the French either! Linguistically, and quite rightly, Greeks don't appear to think very highly of we native English-speakers. As it was, however, when utterances in the film were made in French, my limited knowledge of that language was a help, and when it was not then my even more limited Greek came sufficiently to the rescue.

Over drinks after the film I tackle Andréas on how it can be that Greece is said to be in dire financial straits when the people of Athens are swanning about looking utterly glamorous and seeming to sup never-endingly in hundreds of city-centre cafés and restaurants, with not an empty shop-space to be seen. He advises there's a saying of Greece that is of great truth: 'As a nation we are poor, but as a people we are rich!' I then gather that what this maxim is meant to indicate is nothing sentimental. Instead, it refers to the fact that although the nation's coffers may be empty, the people are artfully avoiding the payment of taxes! Andréas explains that the first 12,000 euros that a Greek earns annually have been tax-free - and therefore few have declared for years that they earn anything or much beyond that figure! The government believes that nearly five million of Greece's current population of roughly eleven million have been declaring an annual income below the threshold! Before I left Britain I read one report of a hardworking Greek taxi-driver telling a journalist that he'd earned roughly 72,000 euros in the previous financial year, but that he'd only declared 12,000 - which sounds, on the face of it, a more reasonable income for a taxi-driver. So it's no wonder then that despite a special Greek tax exemption on cars intended to be used as taxis, some of the sleek canary-yellow cabs of Athens are Mercedes Benzes and BMWs, while the remainder are at least all very smart and new! Apparently flash taxis have been something of a feature of the Greek capital for many years, stemming back to decades when the city's cabs were nearly all of those American brands of elegant limousines that used to be featured in glamorous full-page advertisements in the National Geographic magazine: expensive Cadillacs, Buicks, and Oldsmobiles. When I was a youngster in New Zealand it was always thought that earning a living by ferrying other people round in a taxi was a rather unfortunate career. Your average New Zealand taxi-driver was usually someone who could not, or would not, acquire a position more demanding of skills than simply driving a car, and New Zealand cities were not, and still aren't, large enough to require taxi-drivers to be people with excellent memories for street names. Consequently taxi-drivers would generally own and use the cheapest car they could get away with. So I was astounded by the high quality of vehicles I saw being used as taxis in Sa'udi Arabia, but even in that incredibly oil-rich state one never saw a Mercedes-Benz or BMW being put to use as an everyday cab, as one sees here, in Athens.

Back at the hotel, Kiría Roúla is again on duty and when I dare to quiz her on how Athenians can possibly afford all the lavish consumption that I've been witnessing, she immediately flies on the defensive. Roúla has really got it in for Brits and Americans. She says that all this excessive consumerism has been thrust upon Greeks, that they've been exploited, that multinational companies have simply wished to exhaust and take possession of Greece for their own gains and profits, just as the British, the French, the Russians, and the Americans have all sought over the centuries to control a country that they've viewed largely as the last stop before the Islamic world! Roúla has a good grasp of her nation's history. And she's proud of it. With total conviction she pours forth her belief that Greece has yet again been shafted.

I fall asleep pondering that beneath all the gloss and all the relaxed easiness of this entrancing city there may lurk a seething anger.

回 回 回 回

7

Over the Moon

The next day reveals a dull and uniformly grey sky, streets thoroughly wet, and drizzling rain. So I head up Odós Athinás towards Omónoia Square to find a large store called NotosHome: half a dozen floors consisting entirely of homeware. I want a duvet-cover of some uplifting Greek design, to jolly up the cold winter of our Shropshire valley, something sunny that speaks stylishly of warm leisure-filled days in the Greek islands. Each level of Notos is linked by sparkling silvery lifts and escalators, the homeware all set out upon gleaming modern fixtures, and the place is packed with Greek shoppers, mostly women. The few men there are in the store, all accompanying wives or girlfriends or mothers, eye me with either interest or suspicion! Maybe Greek men aren't seen dead in a shop like this unless 'dragged' there by a female?

The first floor is devoted entirely to bed linen, and half of it has been produced in Greece; the rest consists of luxury brand names from the West, like Ralph Lauren, Lacoste, Calvin Klein, and Versace. But unfortunately it appears that in Greece duvets are not particularly popular: most people just buy sets of sheets and pillow-cases and supplement them for warmth, in the middle of winter, with a blanket or two, or a particular kind of thin modern roll-up eiderdown. I'm also out of luck with regard to size: it seems that Greek companies don't make their duvet-covers in measurements that are standard in Britain. Sizes are all indicated in metric measurements and a Greek cover for a double bed is over a foot larger one way and almost two feet longer the other way than a British one. Regardless of sizes, I can't find a single cover on the entire floor sporting a Greek design or motif, so I'm saved from fretting over appropriate colours. But as few of the assistants, all of them women, speak English, this morning does at least provide me with a good opportunity to practise Greek - except that I possess absolutely none of the vocabulary of the bedding and linen departments! After protracted though abortive 'conversation' with a helpful young fellow-customer we part, but five minutes later, in another section of the store, she suddenly re-appears, holding before me a glittering new iPhone, its display flickering away like a miniature television. She has kindly gone off, scoured her clever little machine for a conversion program, entered the relevant figures, and has now tracked me down to show me precisely how big Greek duvets are in imperial measurements! The helpfulness of the average Greek is overwhelming. You leave the UK and arrive in Athens and you're overcome. Kiwis and Aussies surprised me similarly when I returned down-under in 2001. So how come aggressive, 'reserved', 'independent' unhelpfulness remains such a general trait in Britain? What good does it do? Why do we in the UK put up with it? It only keeps folk apart, each of us 'safe' within a series of anonymous non-communicating bubbles.

After depositing one very generously-sized Greek-cotton duvet-cover back in my hotel room, not exactly the design I was hoping for but it'll do nicely all the same, a visit to Mitropóleos Square unfortunately reveals that Athens's largest Orthodox Church, the *Mitrópoli* (the Metropolitan Cathedral), is currently filled with and covered by a great deal of metal scaffolding. Large-scale restoration appears to be underway and, both inside and out, the cathedral's domes are completely hidden from view. The lower areas of the church however are still visible and a small number of locals and tourists are quietly and respectfully moving around the interior.

The *Mitrópoli* is yet another building of 19th century Athens that was designed by Theophilus Hansen, although in this case the work was also influenced by the Greeks Demétrios Zézos and Panaghiótis Kálkos, as well as by the French architect François Boulanger. Although this team produced a lavishly and colourfully decorated blend of Byzantine and neo-classical elements, which regularly provide an impressive backdrop for important state and ceremonial occasions, sadly a total of seventy-two Athenian churches were demolished to provide all of the marble, and some of the finance, that was needed in order to erect it. Despite all the rather ostentatious and glittering furnishings of the interior, the profusion of ugly scaffolding at this time suggests that up-at-the-crack-of-dawn mass tomorrow morning, as I have been planning, is likely to mainly offer me an hour or so of sung liturgy such as I've already experienced in the orthodox churches of Cairo. So, tonight need not be early-to-bed!

However, three shrines at the *Mitrópoli* cannot go unvisited. Just inside the entrance of the church, in an unmissable elaborate marble sarcophagus, heavily decorated with blue and gold, there lie the remains of Patriarch Grigórios V of Constantinople. When the Greeks rose in revolt against the Turks in 1821, Sultan Mahmud II was enraged by Grigórios's inability to suppress the movement, even though Grigórios did indeed do his best to quell it. Therefore, directly after the Patriarch had celebrated the Easter Liturgy in the Patriarchal Cathedral in Constantinople in 1821, Mahmud ordered Grigórios to be hung, in full Patriarchal vestments, from the main gate of the Patriarchate compound, and, furthermore, to be then left on view there for three full days. Grigórios was 80 years old, but it's said that his executioners needed to pull hard on his legs in order to achieve their end. His body was eventually given to a mob so that they might drag it through the streets before throwing it into the waters of the Bosphorus. The body was subsequently recovered by a Greek sailor, Nikólaos Sklávos, who secreted it to Odessa where it was buried in the Orthodox Church of the Holy Trinity. After the liberation of Greece and the completion of the *Mitrópoli* the Patriarch's remains were transferred here to Athens.

In a highly decorated gilt case in a side chapel rest the relics of Saint Philothéi, a Greek nun of wealthy background and good works who is particularly remembered for ransoming Greek women who were enslaved in Turkish harems during the Ottoman occupation. By 1589 her conduct in this regard had so vexed Turkish commanders in Athens that they dragged her, and several other nuns, by force from within the Church of Saint Andrew so that they might then beat her with clubs and stones. Her injuries were such that several days later she died.

Outside, in the grounds of the cathedral, there stands a shrine to the last Byzantine Emperor, Constantínos XI Palaiológos, revered by some as an 'ethnomartyr' and an uncanonized saint. Standing before a large marble *stéle*, the emperor is depicted magnificently in bronze, wearing full imperial regalia, and cast every inch in the image of the noble Greek warrior. Constantínos resisted the Ottoman siege of his city, Constantinople, for a full six months, from the winter of 1452, but while leading his soldiers in a final charge against the Turks on the 29th of May 1453 he was killed, and the day of his death marked the fall of Constantinople. As his body was never identified from those of the many dead soldiers who lay all around him, there arose a myth that the Emperor Constantínos still lives, that he was rescued by an angel who transformed him temporarily into a marble statue (*Marmaroménos Vasiliás* - Marble King), and that the angel then stowed him safely in a cavern beneath the earth, where, still, the last Byzantine Emperor awaits the day when all of Asia Minor, including Constantinoúpoli (officially renamed Istanbul by the Turks in 1930), is returned to Greece. During the Greco-Turkish War of 1897, the two Balkan Wars of 1912 and 1913, and the Asia Minor Campaign of 1919 to 1922, all of which were driven by the *Megáli Idéa* (that Anatolía and Constantinople could be regained), he who was either Commander-in-Chief of the Hellenic Army during these episodes, or Greek king (King Constantínos I, as it happened), was associated by the people with the *Marmaroménos Vasiliás* and the prophecy that the Emperor of 1453, or at least his resuscitated spirit, would return to liberate the lost Empire. The lyricist Pythagóras and the composer Apóstolos Kaldáras enshrined this myth in a song entitled *Marmaroménos Vasiliás*, which has been recorded by many major Greek stars, including Daláras, Glikería, and Alexíou. Composer Stamátis Spanoudákis recently wove the tale into a powerful work for choir and orchestra.

Late morning, on the edge of a wet and windy Kolonáki, with Mount Lykavittós towering above, what, I wonder, am I to do next? The magnificent collection of Byzantine art in the Byzantine Museum is unfortunately inaccessible until the museum has been fully remodelled and the whole complex in which it is housed, the Vílla Ilíssia, is re-opened in the spring. I can however peer through the grand arched doorway of the gatehouse, and there before me, but quite some distance away on the other side of a broad and gravelled forecourt, stands an imposing two-storey Italianate mansion, flanked at a respectful distance by two long low-lying stone buildings that reach forward and connect to the length of the gatehouse. The face of the mansion looks up to Mount Lykavittós but the building is happily saved from the din of the adjacent and very busy Vasilíssis Sofías Avenue by both the large and elegant courtyard, with its cypress and plane trees and tinkling fountain, and the solid two-storey stone gatehouse.

The Vílla Ilíssia was commissioned in 1837 by the American eccentric Sophie Barbé de Marbois, Duchess of Plaisance, who wintered here from the Villa's completion in 1848 until her death in 1854, at which time the property came into the possession of the Greek State and subsequently housed various military authorities, until in 1926 it became the home of the Byzantine Museum. Since 1930, when the doors first opened, exhibits have been displayed in the central mansion, but from Spring 2010 this museum's rich collection of ceramics, mosaics, frescoes, *eikónes*, sculptures, jewellery, and ecclesiastical textiles are to be laid out partly in the two lateral wings that stand either side of the Vílla (buildings originally intended for ancillary purposes) and in a continuous series of lavish subterranean galleries, commencing beneath the wing on the left, continuing under the courtyard, travelling into the basement of the mansion, then under the courtyard again, before finally emerging into the wing that lies to the Vílla's right. This new state-of-the-art accommodation has been designed to impressively display over 1200 artefacts from the Byzantine era (roughly 313 CE to 1453 CE) and over 1500 artworks from the 15th century to the present day. The handsome old marbled and porticoed mansion, in the centre of the courtyard, is to house a shop and a café. I'm sure the new museum will be an unmissable treat, however, in relaxed and laid-back Greece little effort has been made to ensure visitors are forewarned that until next spring this site is entirely inaccessible, so how am I to fill in the greater part of this afternoon?

The answer is staring me in the face. And so I make my way back through Kolonáki to the foot of the mountain that towers above, and begin to climb. Half-way up Lykavittós's steep though helpfully zigzagging footpath, I take to a bench for a breather. With one hand clutching an umbrella that's constantly snatched at by an insistent wind, I eat sandwiches and fruit while gazing down upon the south end of the city. I'm caught in this odd state by a young, well-built, dark-headed Swede in his twenties and I'm glad to note he's as exhausted by the steep ascent as I am. He says he's 'doing' every country in the European Union within four months and entirely by himself. He's perplexed as to my accent: he tells me I'm not English, not American, and not Antipodean. He's young, confident, and cocky, but he's also wary, in that Northern European way that's common in Britain too. I give him every opportunity to push on uphill ahead of me, but strangely he hangs on, and unfortunately not in any endearing manner. There's little charm in his swaggering self-assertive and belligerent attitude of 'I'm-all-man, I am!' After having been in Athens for nearly a week, I note now in this fairly average Northern European little of that accepting and embracing warmth and openness which is generally typical of Greeks and Arabs, and which is always so pleasant to experience.

The view from the top of Mount Lykavittós is the most spectacular to be had from on high in all of Athens. For the tip of Lykavittós, 910 feet above sea-level, lies far above the height of the Acrópolis - a substantial 420 feet higher, in fact. And somehow, despite all its chaotic city-planning, Athens has managed to avoid the erection of anything offering a rival viewpoint. No building in Athens remotely approaches the height of a normal high-rise except just one now-well-disguised eye-sore far away on the Piraeus harbour-front. In this complete absence of towering buildings this ancient city is blessed. From the top of Lykavittós the uniformity of the sea of structures below adds to the profundity of standing just in front of little St. Yeórghios's Chapel and understanding that as you look down on the Acrópolis, down onto the 'top of the city', and down upon all of central Athens set out in front of you, you are actually gazing upon a community with a recorded continuous living history of around 3,400 years. Athens is thus the oldest living city in Europe. Furthermore, if that's not impressive enough, it's been established that human beings known as the Pelasgians once dwelt upon the north-western slope of the Acrópolis, just to the west of Pláka, during the Neolithic period, or Late Stone Age, 7,000 years ago.

From the top of Mount Lykavittós you also perceive the preciousness of Pláka, as well as little Anafiótika nestling just above it. A hundred years ago Athens was a small and beautiful city, not at all the great sprawl it is nowadays. Much of it consisted of charming neo-classical buildings, as well as other structures of humble and simple charm, surrounded by open fields. Some of the older buildings remain today, the odd one here or there, dotted about within the dense cubic jungle of the modern city, but in all of Athens the only coherent and largely well-maintained collection of old buildings that remains is that which now sits just below the northern edge of the Acrópolis, in Pláka. And from this vantage point one can appreciate the unsettled debate concerning the etymology of the area's name, for in Greek *pláka* means flat, while in Albanian it means old. Both describe the district below the Acrópolis perfectly, and it's feasible that Albanian immigrants brought the term with them when they settled in Athens in considerable numbers during the 16th century. Looking down from Lykavittós the charming red pantiled roofs of old Pláka, and Anafiótika, are unmissable. However, as you scan the city skyline left and right, you note that sadly there are few pantiled roofs to be seen anywhere else. Those that do exist in other places, are generally hidden by the countless concrete and concrete-topped *polykatoikíes*.

From the top of Mount Lykavittós you can also view, lying just above the distant shoal of old roofs, Athens's other precious jewel: its major central lung, that large green wooded park which extends from the east side of the Acrópolis and along the full extent of Philopáppou Hill. The guerrilla gardeners of Athens are convinced that the city authorities have decided that this greenery that is Philopáppou should slowly die. For in late 2010 concerned residents observed that since 2007 the municipal authority had added few new plants to this hill. Furthermore, in 2008 the entire elevation was declared an archaeological site, hours of permitted entrance were planned, and this precious lung was fenced off. The guerrillas maintain that this was because of 'Olympic Games Fever' up to, during, and following 2004, that the authorities considered the tourist potential of Athens's largest stretch of central green and the considerable revenue they might acquire by removing the wood and uncovering yet more archaeological treasures. And without doubt, there's no telling what wonders might be found beneath the hill's crust and which could then be mounted in yet another Athenian museum, to net further tourist income.

However, in recent years the oasis that is Philopáppou has also been threatened by another force: climate-change. One environmental-impact study has shown that since the droughts of the 1990s about 20% of the biomass of the hill has diminished. Mature trees on Philopáppou have died. Even saplings that were planted about the time of the 2004 Olympics have perished. Significant plant-life, young and old, has not been saved by the hill's artificial water-supply because the watering system is no longer being properly maintained. Furthermore, trees found to be suffering from diseases haven't been given the treatment that could have rescued them. Thus, due to both the behaviour of the authorities and the effects of climate-change, this one sizeable lung adjacent to the historic heart of Athens is very much under threat. Local Athenians, however, determined not to have to live out their lives in endless concrete apartment blocks and cafés, have removed the fences that were erected by the authorities, and, for the time being at least, Athenians and visitors can still enjoy free access to Philopáppou at any time of the day or night.

Inside Mount Lykavittós's little funicular railway station, I thankfully lose the company of the swaggering Swede. He opts to let the railway slide him rapidly down to Ploutárchou Street, while I take another footpath, a gentler one, down the other side of the hill, towards the artificial, raised, and largely plastic amphitheatre that nestles further along the ridge, between the tip of Lykavittós and its smaller north-eastern promontory. The modern Lykavittós Amphitheatre, though in itself ugly in comparison to the Iródis Attikós theatre, is no doubt a splendid venue for evening concerts on warm summer nights. As well as great Greek stars, many international artists and performance companies appear here. And the theatre's brightly-coloured plastic bucket-seats are no doubt a great deal more comfortable than the flat marble benches of the Iródis Attikós, cushion or no cushion.

The 'great forest of Lykavittós' surrounding the theatre and this double-peaked hill, and often referred to in travel literature, has proved this afternoon to be little more than a planting of uniform conifers, with bushes and grass below. The pine trees which are solely responsible for any semblance of 'forest' around this mountain have been deliberately planted here since 1882. However, the trees do provide Athens with another sizeable lung and a buffer against the unceasing noise of the city below, no doubt providential for concerts in the Lykavittós Amphitheatre. And at least at this time of year the grass is a deliciously vivid green and plentiful, so that the scene is quite unlike the barren and rocky landscape that Xenophón and Pláton described as existing on this mountain-side. Due to maintenance and conservation, a walk through the 'forest' of Lykavittós today, well above the densely-packed dwellings which have encroached all around the mountain's base, enables one to imagine that wild and deserted mountain-side that caused Lykavittós to be named as it was: 'the hill walked by *lýkoi*' (wolves).

Back in Kolonáki, immediately below Lykavittós, I'm astounded this late Saturday afternoon by the enormous number of glamorous men and women sauntering the streets with large box-type paper bags at their sides, every capacious carrier emblazoned with a famous brand name from the international arenas of fashion. One Kolonáki Parisian-style boutique brazenly announces in large lettering, right in the very middle of both its two front windows, that it sells clothes by Alexander McQueen, Dries van Noten, John Galliano, Dolce and Gabbana, Miu Miu, Yohji Yamamoto, and half a dozen other 'important names'. The interior of the little shop is packed with people. Further down the hill, the more ordinary downtown part of Athens is similarly thronging with shoppers. The cafés are full and it seems that while I've spent most of the day up on the mountain, in the wind and the rain, Athens below has been celebrating some sort of carnival! I really can't make it out. Have I misunderstood? How many billion euros did they say this country is in debt? Surely, as Greece has little oil, in global terms, it must have large quantities of some other valuable resource that I've heard absolutely nothing about?

This afternoon the very stylish people of Kolonáki and central Athens remind one that the Greeks have always worshipped natural and physical beauty, and that since ancient times this land has produced exceptionally handsome men and remarkably beautiful women. It seems as if nothing has changed, for despite all the turbulence of the centuries, with the comings and goings of many different peoples, the stunning faces and physiques of classical Greek statuary are still to be occasionally spotted, here and there, on the capital's streets. Nearly every young Athenian male today enhances his presence with studiously-attended designer-stubble, and almost every young woman to be seen in the city-centre on any day of the week could grace the front of any one of the nation's slew of glossy magazines. The Greeks even invented a goddess to protect and personalize their beauty: Aphrodíte, the goddess of love, of eternal beauty, and of sexual healing. In classical painting and sculpture Aphrodíte was a figure for whom nudity was natural. It was said that she could make any man fall in love with her the moment he first saw her. Nowadays Greece combines this adoration of bodily beauty with its history as a birthplace of medicine by providing the people of other nations with 'Medical Tourism'. Greece is now home to private cosmetic, dental, and *in vitro* fertilization clinics which offer some of the most modern state-of-the-art medical facilities in the world. The nation's private surgeons, generally trained either in the UK or the US, are such leaders in their field that Greece has now become a significant destination for 'Medical Tourists'. It's been estimated that each year just under 10% of all foreign arrivals here in Greece enter the country specifically for some form of medical, dental, or cosmetic treatment. Prices are appealing, with many procedures being offered at a saving of up to 40% against what is charged in the US, the UK and in some other EU countries. And the suffering involved in receiving such treatment is of course combined with a degree of pleasant vacationing. Some Athens surgeries not only arrange attractive accommodation for their patients, but will even organise private chauffeurs for transfers to and from the airport, the hotel, and the clinic, as well as around the city's many attractions.

Wandering into the touristy lanes of the Pláka to locate a few Greek bits and pieces for the kitchen back home, it very quickly becomes apparent that that which is not tat is rather expensive. Neither is the tat particularly cheap! Small three-inch-high impressions of ancient Greek vases are priced at about ten euros, while a seven- or eight-inch-high mass-produced replica of an ancient Greek urn appears never to sell for less than thirty. Retracing my steps to buy something I realise was quite competitively priced, in a shop that I've only just exited, I discover that in the space of no more than five minutes the store has been shuttered, locked, and abandoned! It's 5.30 and all about me stall-holders are suddenly and frantically packing away, metal shutters clattering down noisily on all sides. I head for home and find that all the shops of central Athens have now closed, and that the streets have suddenly become almost deserted but for straggling clusters of Greeks laden with shopping at bus-stops. Clearly, come 5.30 on a winter's Saturday in Athens, nearly everything commercial comes to a grinding halt - no doubt for the relaxation and entertainments of Saturday night and Sunday morning.

Roúla's again on duty in reception and I relate to her my puzzlement regarding this afternoon's Athenian spending-spree, in the light of the massive national deficit. She advises that central Athens is no gauge of what's going on elsewhere and that if I travel way out into the suburbs, to the fringes of the city, I'll find empty shops and evidence of many businesses having gone 'bust'. She also tells me that most of those to be seen buying so ostentatiously in central Athens are buying on credit. She says that in Greece all you have to worry about if you ever go over your borrowing limit and fail to repay is that you'll be blacklisted, for no legal moves will be taken against you, and five years after you've repaid your debts you can start anew with a completely clean record. So, she says with a shrug, Greeks simply have no great fear of being in debt; they feel they can live with it and deal with it. It all sounds rather precarious, never mind irresponsible. And the news at this time is full of suggestions that Greece may ask other Eurozone states to bail it out of its financial predicament with a massive loan, totalling billions of euros!

I opt for dinner in a brightly-lit working-class restaurant between Psyrrí and Omónoia, well away from all the stylish eating-places of Psyrrí and Pláka. Inside, the walls and ceiling are all gloss-painted surgical white and are spotless; the tables and chairs are of the simplest old-fashioned wooden variety; and nothing else is on view except a couple of small mirrors on the walls, paper tablecloths, staff and clientele, the food and the drink, and several blazingly bright white strip-lights up on the ceiling, illuminating everything beneath and banishing any possibility of privacy. I could so easily be in a typical working-men's restaurant in Sa'udi, Kuwait, or Egypt, except that here there are as many women eating in public as men, and at the same tables as the men, and that these women have on display a very un-Islamic quantity of glorious locks and cleavage.

Ordering is difficult because there's no written menu, even in Greek, and no one in this out-of-the way *estiatório* (restaurant) speaks English. But in the end I manage to order meat, salad, and *retsína*, and all arrive in copious quantities, though, for the simplest of meals in the simplest of restaurants, at a relatively pricey fourteen euros. The 'Greek salad' consists 'only' of tomato, red pepper, and onion, all chopped and mixed and surmounted by a considerable slab of *féta* with olive oil poured over it, and then the whole dish hit with a handful of mixed green herbs. The 'meat' is five or six sizeable pieces of grilled pork piled upon a bed of thin and greasy chips. Bread comes too, and I'm supplied with a traditional aluminium carafe of *retsína* - a full litre of it! It's all enough for two people really, and after reflecting upon the indigestion that consumption of even half of the very fatty meat and fried chips is likely to produce within my particular stomach, I guzzle down a good measure of the cool and delicious *retsína*.

Over at a table in the rear of the restaurant I note that the Greek-looking middle-aged foursome sitting there, three men and one woman, issue the odd *'Nai!'* and *'Óchi!'* (Yes! and No!) and interact in Greek with the waiter, but that most of the time they talk boisterously amongst themselves in another language. I ask the waiter where they're from and he winks and then quietly tells me they're *Kýprioi*, which means 'from Cyprus'. They're visiting Turks, long-settled in the northern part of the island, and who, since the Turkish invasion and occupation of Cyprus in 1974, have come to know and use Greek in their interaction with Greek Cypriots. Outside, four young black men, 'economic migrants', probably homeless and almost certainly illegal, stop at different times in front of the window to stare stilly and intensely into the kitchen area. On each occasion the waiter then goes out to them, engages in a little conversation, and then returns inside to receive from the cook a paper-napkin filled with a meal such as mine, fresh from the grill and salad bowls. The immigrant then accepts the bundle with barely more than a word and a nod, without any noticeable display of gratitude or recognition of the generosity involved. Maybe he doesn't want to attract attention. He then quietly disappears, slipping away in the direction of Koumoundoúrou Square, where many such migrants sleep rough on cardboard or grass, or in the abandoned buildings nearby that they've turned into squats. The waiter tells me that the proprietor gives the food free, as charity, and I note that all the Greeks eating around me watch the interaction between the waiter and the migrants pleading for food very closely, but not, apparently, at all unkindly.

Across from my table sits a swarthy, well-built, and very handsome Greek of about thirty-five. In his conversation with the two younger Greeks to whom he seems to be performing, he is all *machismo* and dramatic masculine gestures. Several times, and I think without his knowing, I catch him stealing admiring glimpses of himself in an adjacent mirror. He's playing a very Greek role: something akin to Zorbá, in fact. He may also be performing for me, because suddenly he turns his head in my direction, fixes his eyes upon mine and fires off a very long line of affable Greek that ends with a clearly upturned inflection. Some word in his utterance causes me to know that whatever it all meant it has ended with an enquiry as to my country of origin. Despite his not having heard me utter a word, and regardless of my being dressed much as he is, quite like the average Greek in winter, it seems clear to him that I'm not one, and that I hail from some indiscernible country. I answer; he nods and smiles; and then he immediately resumes his performance before his two friends. The three of them soon order another large bottle of beer, they each take a long swig of it, they pay the waitress, and then suddenly they're gone, swaggering off into the dark with deliberately exaggerated masculinity.

I drop my old friend Kríton, from my acting days in London, a text to ask whether I'm to just crawl into my bed this Saturday night, or to meet up with a dear old friend 'and even possibly LIVE!' I add that I'm going to the 9.15 Pirandello performance at the Néo Ellinikó Théatro and at midnight to a *rebétiko* club in Exárcheia. Then, after a twenty-minute stride to the theatre, I'm informed, forty-five minutes before the curtain goes up, that there aren't any seats left! The foyer is already filled with stylish intellectual-looking Greeks of all ages, all plushly dressed. But I was led to believe by one of the receptionists at the hotel that as there are so many theatres in Athens (the *Athinórama* listings magazine tallies one hundred and forty!) getting a seat would not be a problem, particularly on a cold winter's night! However, after a tense twenty-minute wait, the ticket-seller beckons me over and advises that somebody has just rung in and cancelled. And so, for twenty euros, one seat to 'Man, Beast, and Virtue' becomes mine.

The play is wildly and chaotically presented, but flawlessly. Countless and constant entrances and exits, as well as changes in music and lighting, all occur absolutely on cue and with total assurance. 'Man, Beast, and Virtue', a tragi-comedy, was written as a biting satire, a grotesque caricature, of how we human beings live much of our lives behind masks, or, in other words, how we exist in states of hypocrisy. This no doubt accounts for every character in this production appearing as an exaggeration of some particular manner or mode of human self-presentation. Each preposterous portrayal is aided by make-up, lighting, and a variety of costumes, all in colours which are glaringly bright and showy, as in the peculiar photographs which attracted me to this production while passing by several days ago.

One of the female characters is played by a man and as a figure-of-fun, as a somewhat neurotically effeminate middle-aged transvestite. I hope the intention behind this unusual casting is only to generate laughter, but if that is the objective then the actor succeeds only in bringing forth the odd chuckle. The audience is clearly uncomfortable with the caricature. As the plot unfolds, my total incomprehension of the Greek dialogue enables me to focus and perceive an energetic male actor working extremely hard at portraying either an embarrassingly camp transvestite or a neurotic Greek woman imprisoned by exaggeratedly feminine mannerisms, distinctly feminine women's wear, and an excessive use of cosmetics. But unfortunately whichever is the intention, the few laughs that this character raises are *at* her, rather than *with* her. The audience's discomfort is palpable.

The lead, on stage for nearly two and three quarter hours, is played by a man of about sixty-five who fires out his lines and chunks of text with never a moment's hesitation and who is all the while constantly in motion, often leaping, jumping, or rolling about on the floor. Physically and verbally his performance is virtuosic. On London's Southbank antics like his would earn some aged knight a five-minute standing ovation, at least.

When the lights come up at the interval, waving in my direction from the other rake, I spot Kríton. I never dreamt he'd appear and somehow he too has managed to get a seat. With great enthusiasm we renew our acquaintance on the edge of the stage, and Kríton relates how he arrived just two minutes before the start, only seconds before we all witnessed an angry couple storming out of the theatre. Apparently they were unhappy with their seats, and so Kríton was in luck. When the play ends we prepare to make our way to the *rebétiko* club, and as soon as we step out onto the street I produce my map. Then whilst I'm standing there quite efficiently working out the route we must take, Kríton seems unable to bear it! He has exactly the same reaction to my use of a map as Andréas, a few nights earlier! And so, as it appears Greeks simply must do, he hops rapidly back into the theatre to ask people for directions. A minute later he emerges excitedly to announce that he's just bumped into the lead actor and director, and would I not like to meet him? Would I not? Indeed I would!

Yiórgos Arménis is charm personified. He's sitting on a sofa in the foyer and relaxing with a drink. He offers us both a glass of wine. 'Oh, no, we can't possibly . . . ', but he insists and calls to one of the barmen to bring over a bottle of good Greek. The three of us are then joined by a trainee-director of about twenty-five, bearded, tobacco-pipe in hand, Brechtian-looking, pleasant, and possessing good English. This student of the master tells us how Arménis created the Néo Ellinikó Théatro to continue the tradition and legacy of the famous Greek theatre-director Károlos Koun. Born in 1908 in Asia Minor of a Greek mother and a German-Polish-Jewish father, Koun came to Athens when he was very young and slowly rose to be lauded all over Europe for his bawdy and colourful stagings of the 5 BCE political comedies of Aristophánes. Later, during the Nazi occupation of Greece, and following his establishment in 1942 of the experimental and historic 'Károlos Koun Art Theatre', he introduced Greek audiences to Bertolt Brecht and Luigi Pirandello. His Art Theatre continues in Athens to this day, in Pesmatzóglou Street beside the *Stoá Tou Vivlíou* (a wondrous long dog-legged arcade consisting entirely of bookshops). In 1967, Koun became one of only a dozen or so non-British directors who have been invited to direct a play at the Royal Shakespeare Company in Stratford-upon-Avon, Franco Zeffirelli having been another. Although one English critic described Koun's Stratford production of 'Romeo and Juliet' as being of 'unrelieved gloom', it seems that his devoted followers today in Athens would most probably not have agreed. The memory of Károlos Koun is almost sacred.

Yiórgos Arménis is faithful to Koun's legacy, and tonight's production of one of Koun's favourite plays was certainly bawdy, colourful, and not in the least gloomy. We learn that Arménis not only directs, runs the theatre, and takes on demanding acting roles in the company's productions, but in conjunction with the nearby university he also runs a drama-school on the site. He explains that one afternoon next week about twenty-five second-year drama students will be presenting scenes: would I like to come and see them, and meet the students? I would indeed! Kríton then twinkles from the other side of the table: 'So you see, David, why we Greeks don't use maps, yes? We wouldn't be here now, if we had used your map, now would we?' He's being playfully mischievous, and he has a point. In this chaotic city all is talk and interaction, a bit of chat here and a bit of bargaining there, everyone making the most of the moment, being spontaneous. This is how most Greeks prefer it. I am made to feel ridiculously, even stupidly, efficient, as the Germans are sometimes viewed by people from the UK! After warm farewells, and a repeated translation from Kríton of my congratulations to Yiórgos for his sustained and energetic performance in the play, we depart. And Kríton is having none of my map, nor any walking. He assertively hails a yellow cab.

For just a couple of euros we're dropped several minutes later outside a large neo-classical building that appears, unfortunately, to be deserted. There's not a soul in sight. And strangely for Athens, neither is there barely a sound in the air. All is very quiet. However, we spot an open doorway, lit, although Kríton thinks I've got it all wrong, and that there's either nothing happening here tonight or I've made a mistake with the address. Oh dear, all the excitement and expectation may have been for nothing. But we enter the building anyway, and walk along a hallway. We follow the light and go down some stairs. There's still nothing but silence. This appears to be a building abandoned. We descend another flight of stairs, and then all at once hear the distant hubbub of dozens of voices. Further on, and through a door, we enter a large low-ceilinged room, rather dark, but beneath us at the foot of yet a further flight of steps we come upon a sea of little night-lights on tables, over which there are scores of Greeks drinking, laughing, smoking, and talking. It's after midnight and the place is about half full.

Arrayed on a narrow dais against one far wall, in a kind of red-curtained alcove, are two rows of singers and musicians. There are eight of them in all: six men who play bass, accordion, guitar, *bouzoúki*, *baglamá*, and oud, and two young women who sit in the front row without instruments. All are bathed in just a couple of simple soft red spotlights, so that with only the tiny candle on each table, there is in this place the delicious feeling of a forbidden subterranean night-time rendezvous.

The band appears to be between songs; the musicians and singers are smoking and drinking. On the other hand, it may be that the evening's music has not yet begun. Kríton and I wonder if our delight at finding this very special club open is writ large upon our faces because the performers all follow us with their eyes as we weave our way through the crowd to a small table for two right over on the other side of the room. Even as we settle into our seats the members of the band still watch us, each of them grinning. Why? Are they expecting some impresarios in this evening? Who are they mistaking us for? Or is it simply that Kríton and I are beaming so broadly ourselves that we're giving off some sort of unusually positive energy? Anyway, only a couple of minutes after we both sit down, a dramatic rippling of the *bouzoúki* begins. It's the long and elaborated flourish, known as a *taxími*, that heralds the start of a song! And then the whole band swings into a rhythm behind it, that rhythm is engulfing and very soon the entire room becomes transported with it. A *rebétiko* has just been launched!

We order a bottle of red wine and it arrives with a jug of water and a large silver platter of fruit, consisting of many thin slices of apple, orange, banana, and kiwi-fruit, in the centre of which burns our own little night-light. Over the course of the next hour every seat in this cavern is taken, so that by half-one in the morning the club is packed with Greeks. It appears that I am the only non-Greek in the room. The music is amplified but only enough to ensure that every sung word and every note can be heard amongst the sea of bodies; people can still comfortably talk. A flower-girl circulates slowly amongst the tables, in her arms a tall pile of little wooden trays, full of paper petals. A few people hand her money to go up to the stage on their behalf and gently flutter the red 'petals' over the head of whichever performer they particularly admire and want to congratulate. The singing is either in unison, with men and women singing the same melody together, though with a little part-singing in places, or the two women take turns in singing solos. Every song is so emotionally laden and powerful; quite unlike anything western. It is genuine old *rebétika*! You can hear where Hadjidákis, Theodorákis, and many other Greek composers found much of their source material.

Just after two in the morning a woman rises from one of the tables in the middle of the room and begins to make her way to the small floor-space directly in front of the band. She begins to dance. All alone! However, as she starts, and as she continues, I see that she's keeping her eyes fixed on someone back at the table from which she's come. It's as if she's casting a spell on him, willing him in some way. Then after a minute or so, while she continues to dance, she beckons him, with twirling movements of her fingers, to follow, to come to her. He complies, making his way amongst the tables to the edge of the space. There he drops upon one knee, looks up into her eyes, begins to clap with the rhythm of the song, and gives support to she who has so bravely taken to the floor before anyone else in the room has dared. Her dance is the famous *zeïbékiko*, a slow improvised solo of seriousness, intensity, and introspection, and which is nearly always supported by a companion who on one knee claps to the rhythm of the music and who, more importantly, is just 'there' for the person lost in the magic of the moment.

A very handsome well-built young man with dense black hair is next to bravely command the floor. At first he confines his movements close to the stage-side table from which the beautiful young woman with whom he's been sitting now follows his every gesture. He struts flirtatiously before her, then while looking intensely into her eyes he holds against his thigh one hand with fingers outspread as if to frame his virility! This statement made, he then spins off into the middle of the space before suddenly seeming to lose balance, 'falling' to the ground on one knee. There he stays, upright while moving only his arms, as if broken or helpless, as if mourning or contemplating some tragic fall from grace. And then, as his torso writhes and heaves from side to side, he seems to struggle against forces beneath him, till, resolutely, he bends forward and slaps the ground as if to defy it. No longer dispirited, he rises, lifts a thigh, slaps it too, as if to show determination, and then, gazing upwards, his arms raised, he begins to glide, like an eagle dignified and free upon the winds, maintaining balance while invincibly swooping and swirling above all the challenges of life. Moving now in long, calculated, and graceful sweeps, his arms still flung wide, he seems beyond all turbulence - though occasionally he almost fails and falls again! But each time he regains himself so that by the end of this stunning *zeïbékiko* the entire room is behind this 'Greek god', this young hero who has inspired us with his beauty, his grace, his power, and his determination!

During the course of subsequent songs, several different pairs of people begin dancing in the same way. Sometimes it's two men, sometimes two women, or a mixed couple; the pairing doesn't matter. What seems extraordinary to the Westerner looking on, is the seeming open sensuality in the relationship between the members of each pair, regardless of their gender. They appear to share an intensely intimate moment knowingly and willingly in public! The eyes of the dancer and the supporter lock in a kind of profound visual embrace, broken only when the dancer has received sufficient reinforcing strength from the supporter to be able to spin off into a few moments, or even several minutes, of lone and ecstatic communion with the music.

As a new song begins and Kríton recognises the tune, and the floor has not yet been taken, he quickly rises, without warning, and makes his way through the crowd, all the while turning back, gazing directly at me, and beckoning with his hands for me to follow! In front of at least two hundred people! Couldn't he at least have talked about this first? Couldn't you have warned me, Kríton! I'm stricken with fear. And excitement. He won't stop signalling. He's determined. His beckoning is commanding, and, of course, totally public! People are beginning to turn their heads towards the corner where I'm still sitting! It's not honourable of me to resist. The power of their eyes, their staring smiling faces, coerce me to action. It's a moment of moral compulsion. You cannot betray your friend! I can feel them all thinking it, the will of the audience. And so I rise and make my way between the tables. On the edge of the little space I fall to one knee, as I've seen the others doing, and then look up at Kríton and clap him onwards. As he descends into a transported state and his movements become more dramatic and intricate, there in front of all, for everyone to see, he smiles down at me, and I must return the feeling likewise. It really feels like making love in public! It's so unnerving! And, for sure, this is no gay venue! There's absolutely nothing whatsoever gay about this lark at all! It's not even sexual. It's simply fabulously Greek!

As the evening continues, the glorious rippling *bouzoúkia* play on; the voices of the singers rise and fall, sometimes in anguish, sometimes in joy; and as the music swirls around the room to the repeated and rousing cry of '*Ópa! Ópa!*', each song takes us on a magic carpet-ride to the exotic. It's irresistible. This music, the atmosphere, and of course the wine, all make for an unsurpassable mix. And so the inebriating concoction brings pair after pair to the floor. Soon after two new women have taken the spotlight, the supporter begins dancing as well, so that both persons in a pair dance equally with each other. Though they seldom ever touch, to me they seem almost to be making love. Pairs of men then do exactly the same. Mixed couples likewise. To support is now clearly also to dance! Just kneeling on the edge, and giving every ounce of moral affirmation you can, is no longer enough! The night has moved on! Inhibitions are now cast to the wind. And there's absolutely no embarrassment whatsoever about same-sex warmth. It's utterly astounding. As the instruments and voices whirl ever onward, this night, or rather this morning, has turned into the thrill of a lifetime.

I hadn't thought that there was such a transporting and ecstatic experience left in this world for me to enjoy. I have, in my nearly sixty years, experienced some wonderful highs, and I didn't think before I arrived in Athens just days ago that they'd ever be bettered. But this fabulous Athenian morning I am consumed by *rebétiko* after *rebétiko*, by intoxicating musical jewels, one after the other. The people at the adjacent table have been raising their glasses and chinking them together frequently for three hours! They order bottle after bottle of white wine. They appear to be a party of six, but after Kríton has chatted with one of the women in Greek he reports that before tonight three of them didn't know the rest! You would never have thought it. They've been carousing, and singing, and dancing with each other like long-term friends. By 3.30 Kríton has risen to dance about four or five times and it seems he has impressed our neighbours: he reports that he and I have just been invited to join them all in a village high in the mountains of the Pelopónnesos in late July, when most Athenians escape Athens's intolerably hot August for the big annual holiday. Imagine enjoying *rebétika* like this every night, to have this evening again, not just for one night but for many, soaring in the Greek mountains with all this scintillating music, in the embracing warmth of high summer! No wonder Greeks don't take seriously our Western efficiency, our willingness to suffer, and our adherence to unending toil. They're so right! There's so much more to life than system, red tape, and everything being always orderly, correct, and proper!

At four o'clock I lean over and suggest to Kríton that even the most wonderful things must come to an end, and he calls for the bill. Then all at once the liveliest of the women at the adjacent table is up and protesting, and in English, to me!

'But this is only the beginning! This is only the beginning of the evening!' She repeats it over and over, rather like a child who's been told the birthday party has come to an end. I think she must surely be jesting, until Kríton explains that in fact the evening is now only reaching its peak, its *tsakír kéfi* as the Greeks call it, that point in the night's revelry when people become transported, over the moon with joy and distraction. It usually occurs around four in the morning and then the merriment in no wise draws to an end until sunrise! Only two other people have left so far, and there's no sign of anybody else preparing to go. But we placate our neighbour, thank her for all the fun and amusement that she and the others at her table have given us, and say that for us it has been so wonderful we can't possibly last any longer, that we are unfortunately 'old men', and will they please forgive us? A waiter then hands Kríton the bill and fearing that my friend may attempt to pay it entirely himself I reach over and nip it from his fingers.

'Eighty-nine euros?' I blurt. (Roughly eighty pounds in sterling.)

'Yes. It's reasonable, don't you think?' ventures Kríton. I'm speechless. 'We'll go Dutch, yes?' he adds.

I don't answer. I'm stunned. We ordered no expensive petals to be emptied over dancers, singers, or musicians; we had only one bottle of red between the two of us all night; and the only other things we had were the one jug of tap water and the very simple platter of very ordinary sliced fruit!

'So, you can't be doing this every weekend?' I suggest.

'Oh, no', says Kríton, 'not every weekend!'

In hindsight, for such an extraordinary night forty-five euros from each of us was perfectly reasonable. I can only imagine I reacted as I did because of the informality, the simplicity, and the venue's café-like atmosphere. In London I could pay much the same amount for a good seat in some theatre and never be anywhere remotely so moved and transported as I've been tonight in a very special *rebétiko* club in Athens.

After an engulfing flurry of farewells, kisses on cheeks, and handshakes all round with those at the adjacent table, we leave. Kríton hails a cab for his north-east Athens apartment and I walk the thirty minutes back to my hotel. At about four-thirty I have my first real encounter with a beautiful black prostitute - this one being a great deal more forward than the young lady who threw sucking noises at me the other night! I was warned about Athens's 'beautiful black prostitutes' before I left England. Now six of them appear, all at once, and seemingly from nowhere. None of them is more than about twenty years old. Shortish girls, in tiny skirts or hot-pants, they're all otherwise very natural-looking; they have dark faces, they wear little make-up, and every one of them has frizzy gleaming black hair, carefully oiled. One of them launches out of their huddle and comes to my side in the middle of the street, where I've been walking so as to avoid the approaches of the many drug-pushers on the pavements. And although I'm striding meaningfully she locks onto me and slips an arm firmly around mine, so that we stride on interlinked, like a couple of lovers hurrying home just before daybreak.

'You and me, we go and have really good, good sex!' she coos seductively, softly, while coping admirably with my brisk step. 'Really really, good good, lovely sex! Long time! You and me, yes?'

She won't let go, despite many a firm '*Óchi, efcharistó!*' (No, thank you!) as I try to give the impression I'm totally familiar with this lark and am genuinely not interested. In the end, with her friends all giggling and calling out behind us, and more groups of young migrant drug-pushers coming up at the intersection ahead, I begin to panic a little. I start to chant, playfully, quietly, and unthreateningly, '*Óchi, óchi, ÓCHI! Óchi, óchi, ÓCHI! Óchi, óchi, ÓCHI!*' Eventually, and thankfully, she disengages, and breaking off like a refuelling plane that has just mated with a bomber high in the stratosphere, she then curls around and glides smoothly back to her kin, tittering and chuckling as she goes.

In my bed, as I sink into sleep, I marvel at the totally fantastic night I've had. Thank you, Kríton! And thank you, Athens.

8

Scents & Sparkle

Mégaron Mousikís;
Záppeion;
& Greek Television.

Waking just before noon with a sudden startled jolt, I sense immediately that I'm back in my apartment in downtown Al Khobar, in Sa'udi Arabia! Before going to bed, for a little fresh air I left the window open, and so now, at midday, this 5th floor room is full of dazzling sunlight and the pungent and hunger-inducing aromas of sizzling *souvláki*: grilled pork, grilled lamb, roast chicken and beef, and even, possibly, from one little place on Odós Mitropóleos, *souvláki strewthokámilou* (ostrich souvláki)! This Sunday noon in Athens smells just like midday Friday in a Muslim town. But whereas Arab cities are generally quiet on their day of rest, the downtown streets below me are alive and roaring as usual, though not quite so loudly as on other mornings. If it weren't for the sound of the interminable traffic and the sight of the Acrópolis and Philopáppou, then from here in my eyrie Athens this lunch-time might easily be mistaken for any highly-populated city of Arabia. It looks much the same. It's bathed in similarly glorious light, it's beautifully warm, its sky is clear and blue, and its air is heady with the delicious aromas of hot meats and herbs.

I know that after last night, and nearly one full week in this city, my mind is full and intoxicated. Like Níkos Kazantzákis's hero Zorbá, many Greeks have a belief that one who accepts death, who expects death, and who waits for death, will lose, in everything. But he or she who acts as if there will never be death, who lives with optimism, energy, and expectation of immortality, who believes in the possibility of being able to enjoy everything and forever, that person will win, and in everything. This practical simple Greek philosophy makes good sense, and I think it explains much of the busyness of this city. It may well be a rather superficial impression, but from the perspective of someone walking round this *metrópolis*, as I've been doing, long-term objectives are not greatly apparent here. Yes, there are some, such as, for example, that demonstrated by the cranes that each day slowly lift vast pieces of marble up on the Acrópolis, as part of the ongoing restoration project there, and the gleaming Athens Metró is most certainly evidence of a long-term ambition which is being completed to seeming perfection, the envy of every capital in Europe. But short-term objectives in Athens would appear to reign supreme. Hence thousands of people are constantly expending energy in shuttling back and forth, between one place and another; doing something here and another thing there; then after a few items bought, or a few words had, they're busily back on their way, attending to other things, elsewhere. Greeks are most certainly not lazy.

The people of Athens are engulfed in an active and tireless way of living which is substantially communal. Greeks really do seem to need to be close to one another, constantly interacting. Or rather, perhaps they know the great power of such interaction. It fires them up, it inspires them, and they thrive on it. The energy of one is derived from the energy perceived in another. It's a chain reaction. They're like bees in a hive. This doesn't necessarily mean though that they all love each other. Greeks are known to be litigious, and lawsuits are often filed for the most trivial of reasons. This readiness to appeal to the law is fired by the same spirit that lies behind Greeks' fierce discussions and debates, as demonstrated every day in hundreds of cafés and on a number of Greek television channels. But it's odd that a people who choose to live so communally can also take against each other so easily.

I'm tempted to think that not as many people are lonely or solitary in a Greek community as in towns and cities in the West, but I know that in the week I've been here, endlessly out and about, day and night, I've not seen anyone in a wheelchair or on a mobility scooter. Not a single individual. They exist though; they must do. Neither have I caught sight of even one blind person with a stick! And come to think of it,

I've not seen a pram either. I expect it's partly the city-centre pavements that are to blame. They're often a nightmare. Even able-bodied folk must at all times keep an eye out for the next sudden drop, the unexpected steps upward, the next unfilled or uncovered hole, the badly-placed lamp-post, or the solid trunk of some lovely ornamental tree which springs straight up in the centre of your path! Athens's municipal authorities often replace pavements unnecessarily and at great expense, regardless of the fact that pedestrians will still have to take to the road because of all the cars and motorcycles which are habitually left mounted on the pavements. But where are this city's old and infirm, its young mothers with prams? I must keep my eyes peeled when I get away from the city-centre.

Just like an Athenian, I've been constantly engaged and busy in the course of the last week, but possibly unlike most Athenians I desperately need more sleep! Even if one's pocket were able to afford a night of *rebétika* every weekend, one's health certainly couldn't! But having revived somewhat after last night's mind-blowing experience, I set out late afternoon this Sunday to purchase the odd small item and then to take a good long walk before returning early for bed. But as I recover from last night's merriment, I find on passing through Psyrrí and Pláka that another *rebétiko* 'shift' has begun. Many of the restaurants are packed with Greeks and are in full song. Each place has two or three *bouzoúki* players singing *laïká* or much the same sort of *rebétika* as Kríton and I enjoyed in the early hours. Tables are covered in dishes of food and there are glasses, bottles, and carafes of wine and *retsína* aplenty. So it seems you can do it almost any early morning of the week or you can make merry all of Sunday afternoon! I wonder if there are some Greeks who have such great expectations of immortality that they occasionally do both?

This afternoon the door of the tiny Byzantine church 'Panaghía Gorgoepíkoos and Ághios Eleanthérios', just to the side of the Metropolitan Cathedral, is wide open and welcoming. During the 18th century this church, *Mikrí Mitrópoli* (Little Metropolis), as tiny as it is, at just 7.6 metres long and 12.2 metres wide, served as the metropolitan church of the Archbishopric of Athens. It does have grandeur however: into its exterior walls are incorporated assorted 'pagan', Roman, early Christian, and Byzantine marbles, many of which bear interesting reliefs and inscriptions. Though the building's construction was completed by the 13th century, if not the 12th, unlike other Byzantine churches I've seen so far in Athens the interior of this little gem has been totally 'cleaned'. It once featured numerous frescoes, but after crumbling and being damaged over the course of the centuries they're now gone and the plaster has been completely removed, so that the walls are now all naked honey-gold stone, adorned very sparingly by a small number of large glitteringly gilt mosaics in frames.

A young Greek, clad tightly in black, the silver metal zips and buttons of his patent leather jacket gleaming in the soft interior lighting, steals little glances at me from one of the few pews that are wedged within the tiny interior. Another man, tall and much older, leans somewhat nonchalantly against a pillar - though fully alert, as if on the lookout for the arrival of the next train. A young girl of about sixteen, long stockinged legs very noticeably on display, sits in another corner looking very concerned, distressed even. In fact, all three are palpable embodiments of anxiety. And then all at once an old priest enters through the front door behind me, a round black hat on his head and his black skirt flowing full-length to just above the ground. I turn and he whispers 'Kalispéra!' (Good evening!) to me, and then quickly he whispers the same to the man, and then the girl. She then rises and nips quickly to his side, where she grasps at his hands while dropping her head in respect, almost as if she's desperate for forgiveness, or for the granting of some favour. Stopping no longer than three or four seconds for her, but not replying, the priest then steps into the little sanctuary, and then beyond it into some tinier chamber, presumably to change into liturgical vestments.

From behind his column, the tightly-clad young man takes another peep at me. As I move to admire another of the glittering eikónes, he then steals quietly to my side, smiles with beguiling innocence, as well as with much respect, whispers 'Kalispéra!', and then asks if I am Orthódoxos. I swallow all my atheistic pride and quietly say that I am Catholikós! I figure this should cause as little offence as possible, and indeed it appears to please him a little. He then asks, nervously, where I'm from, but still detecting in him some kind of internal anxiety I softly say, 'You are having liturgy now, and so I should go?' He almost collapses with relief, and while smiling and quietly sputtering *'Efcharistó! Efcharistó!'* (Thank you! Thank you!) he hurries back to his pew.

The 'Panaghía Gorgoepíkoos' element of this church's name translates as 'The Virgin Who Answers Prayers Quickly' and I'd love to know what each of the three attendees this afternoon so desperately wants of her! The nervous young lady with the long legs: some favour to do with love, or sex, or a baby, wanted or unwanted? The tall middle-aged man: some wish for the success of a business venture, a happier marriage, or the health of a relative? But the fresh-faced, dark-haired, handsome young hunk, dressed all in patent black leather with gleaming silver studs: what on earth could he have been so wanting of the Blessed Virgin, I wonder?

All I want now is to see the Mégaron Mousikís (The Palace of Music), the massive Athens entertainment complex that was opened in 1991, the splendid main hall of which, horse-shoed with jutting balconies all around, has been highly praised by renowned international conductors for its perfect acoustics and pleasing aesthetics. My route to the Mégaron is via the very fine and broad Vasilíssis Sofías Avenue, which, though streaming with Athens's fast-moving vehicles, passes through an area of considerable grandeur. Lining both sides of Leofóros Vasilíssis Sofías are fine well-spaced buildings, often with impressive front gardens. Some of the architecture here is grand, intricate, and delicate. Here for sure is a tiny touch of Paris in the East, though many a Greek would be angered by the suggestion, since, for many Greeks, Greece is and always has been 'The Centre', neither East nor West.

The exterior of the Mégaron Mousikís gives little indication of the magnificent modern concert hall which is cradled within. You approach a large white marble-faced cube that has all along its frontage a series of impressive and massive rectangular columns which fly up past all seven floors of the interior. The entrance-level foyer stretches impressively almost the entire width of the building but sadly it is cuboid, low-ceilinged, and mostly a sterile white. It has much the same blandness as the concourse of a large modern railway-station. At the ticket-counter a beautifully-mannered young Greek woman informs me that at 8.30 tonight there is to be a classical concert featuring orchestral works by Weber and Mendelssohn, performed by the City of Athens Orchestra, the cheapest seats being twenty euros. Unfortunately I see from the programme that there's to be nothing particularly Greek performed in the complex for the rest of my time in Athens, although a great many of the performers in each night's events are talented Greeks with international experience. Most of their fellow performers are Italians or Eastern Europeans of similarly high standing.

A visit to the Mégaron reminds one of the excellence that Greece has attained in classical music. For it was the internationally renowned Greek conductor and pianist Dimítris Mitrópoulos, along with a Greek soprano, a local publisher, and an art-collector, who triggered and launched the early stages of this complex. Born in 1886, Mitrópoulos conducted the Boston, Minneapolis, and Philadelphia symphony orchestras, the Berlin and New York Philharmonics, and the Concertgebouw Royal, amongst many others. Gay, he is said to have enjoyed a close relationship with Leonard Bernstein while working with the orchestra in New York. Mitrópoulos was a lion in the sphere of classical music, but particularly so in the championing of new modern music. Though warned by doctors in 1959 that his heart could no longer stand the strains of conducting, he continued regardless, and a year later collapsed from a heart attack and died while rehearsing Mahler's demanding Third Symphony with La Scala Opera House Orchestra in Milan.

Although the ticket-office assistant speaks good English she's quite unable to elaborate on the content or the nature of a number of concerts that are rather tantalisingly but too simply and obliquely described in the programme. My efforts to draw forth a little more information only cause her discomfort. It seems, from her performance, and possibly also from her attire, that she may not be greatly interested in classical music. On one of her wrists she sports an enormous gold watch the face of which must be nearly two inches in diameter. Beneath the glass lies a sea of glittering tiny gold chips, all irregularly packed in, and inset in this ocean of glitter are two large letters in sparkling and contrasting fragments of silver: 'D & G', the initials of the Italian fashion designers Dolce and Gabbana. And somewhere on that dial, though I can't immediately distinguish them, there are also presumably the twelve hours of the day and a pair of hands. The boutiques of Kolonáki are as full of this ostentatious form of time-piece as the almost countless watch-shops of the oil-rich states of the Arabian Gulf. The girl's other arm sports five or six golden wristlets, each one nearly an inch wide and creating, *en masse,* an armour which stretches from her wrist to just short of her elbow. I tell her I need to go for a wander and give the Weber and Mendelssohn a little thought. I have two hours to decide.

Despite the solitary guard watching my every movement in this vast and empty foyer, I dare to descend an unlit marble staircase in a far corner and find a similarly-sized sterile white foyer immediately below, along one side of which is a bookshop all aglow, open, but empty except for one other middle-aged visitor - an eccentric chap who is dribbling a little and dressed like a tramp. Avant-garde piano music tinkles softly from hidden speakers as I discover to my surprise a considerable number of Greek classical CDs, recordings of Western-style classical music composed or performed entirely by Greeks, with all of the titling and text on their covers being, of course, in Greek. These discs are obviously produced entirely for the home market. So I spend an hour practising Greek transliteration again, familiarising myself with a whole new field of classical performers, musicians, and composers. It's a most interesting exercise but it's so annoying that after a whole week I still get words wrong because it takes me so long to realise I've completely forgotten that the sound, for example, of what looks like a P is actually the sound of an R ! And all the while I'm wondering whether to shell out twenty euros largely to see the interior of what some have described as Europe's finest concert hall.

Back upstairs, and a full hour before the concert begins, many members of the audience have already arrived. Of course I noticed the same early swarming only last night over in liberal Exárcheia. Greeks seem to enjoy the anticipation, the expectation, the chances of social interaction before such events. Few turn up ten minutes prior, as we Westerners tend to do. I catch two older women, settled side by side on a nearby bench and comfortably sitting back, making whispered comments while staring in my direction. They're clearly not impressed. I expect it's my casual black cargo pants and my brown leather jacket, for they are adorned in glittering, elegant, and undoubtedly expensive evening-wear! They're both clothed in seeming 'acres' of fashionable greys and blacks that are shot through with metallic filaments that catch the light and glitter. They're also bedecked with much jewellery and a considerable amount of make-up. And, of course, they're magnificently coiffured and lacquered. So, as in any Western capital it seems the Athenian classical music scene is just as much about wealth, élitism, and the coming together of the establishment. Although there are also a few modestly-dressed folk beginning to arrive for the evening's concert, my mind is now made up: I'll stick to my plan for a long night's sleep.

As I cut through the park that is adjacent to the Záppeion and just south of the National Gardens, a great fountain suddenly awakes and erupts into an impressive display of dancing waters blazoned by a fine array of lights. The gloom that was all about has been instantly transformed and this part of Athens is made all at once very grand and fine. Also floodlit is the nearby Záppeion Palace, a fine and imposing horseshoe-shaped neo-classical building which is now used as a conference- and exhibition-centre. It was funded by a legacy of Evághelos Záppas, sponsor of the 1859 Olympic Games, and benefactor of the 1870 and 1875 Olympics, as well as of the first truly international Olympiád of 1896. However, the Záppeion is named not only in honour of Evághelos, but in honour too of his cousin Constantínos Záppas, who also played an essential role in the revival of the Olympics. Life-size sculptures of the two men stand clearly lit to either side of the Záppeion's handsome portico. Unfortunately at this late hour I can spot no memorial in the vicinity recording the fact that through this very fine and stately entrance in 1922 there streamed a ragged and utterly pathetic procession of hundreds of Greek and Armenian children, all made homeless and parentless by the horrors of the Asia Minor Disaster. The Záppeion was just one of many Greek public buildings that were turned into children's homes, providing temporary accommodation for the thousands of little *orfaná* that Greece's Anatolian disaster left in its wake.

Over the busy Amalías Avenue now, past the imposing but rather lost-looking Arch of Hadrian of 2 CE, erected by Athenians as a token of their gratitude to the Roman Emperor, the Pláka is very quiet this wintry evening though many of its bars and restaurants are open for business. As I hurry by, waiters eagerly try to lure me in. One restaurant is projecting into the street, via its music system, the voice of the great Yiórgos Daláras singing *rebétika*, and I find it very tempting. But I know I must sleep. So on the edge of Monastiráki I opt instead for a Greek form of filled roll, for just three and a half euros, from a *fastfoudádiko*, a Greek version of an American-style sandwich chain. It's got to be one of the cheapest meals to be had anywhere in Athens. But though I carefully choose the least fatty of all the fillings that are available, the large hot roll that I'm finally handed oozes with molten cheese and great chunks of oily meat. This sort of stuff no doubt contributed to the general aroma that so entranced my nostrils upon waking at noon, but it's a calorific and digestive nightmare.

So, to hopefully obviate an agonising case of nocturnal indigestion, throughout a night when I really must get quality kip, I pour a strong *oúzo* back at the hotel and settle down to have a closer look at what's on offer on Greek television. I'm quickly amazed to discover that there are several dozen different Greek channels available to my room. And then a glance at a local newspaper reveals so many more! Greece runs seven different state-owned national networks (four analogue and three digital), as well as one state-owned satellite network, several private networks that run nationally, and in the wake of all these there are a further 150 regional or local channels throughout the country! All these in a land of just eleven million people, while New Zealand, with its population of roughly four million, runs just eight channels (plus a few satellite, cable, and regional options).

Flicking through the several dozen Greek stations available in this particular hotel, I find that they offer mainly entertainment, either home-grown, American, or British, with a smattering of French and German films. There seems to be an unfortunate quantity of low-grade material from the USA, all of it subtitled in Greek for local consumption. The most serious Greek TV programmes appear to be those few that consist of a panel of four or five people, usually men in suits, discussing national issues with a great deal of theatrical colour and interjection. When on one Greek channel I find the UK TV chef Gordon Ramsay in full flow, it's clearly time to reach for the remote, turn off the light, and put my head to the pillow, for Ramsay is uttering his usual torrents of the foulest Anglo-Saxon expletives - unedited, unbleeped, and with Greek subtitles.

回 回 回 回

9

Unexpected Creatures

Attica Zoological Park;
Ianós Bookshop;
activists & police;
& Cretan estiatório.

Sotíris, on duty this morning at reception, informs me that the Greek subtitles on Gordon Ramsay's cooking programme last night were all very carefully cleaned up. Apparently, when Ramsay curses someone with one of his customary obscenities the subtitle that appears on Greek televisions is far less inflammatory, sanitised to something as gently chiding as 'Don't be silly!' So Ramsay's constant use of vulgarities is only perceived by Greeks who are fully familiar with colloquial English. Sotíris thinks it's a shame such programmes are now being fed non-stop to the Greek public, and he tells me they're all being chosen by certain individuals inside Greek broadcasting companies who just accept the notion that every import is automatically and unquestionably 'cool'.

Amidst all the excitement of Athens's *Kentrikí Agorá*, its Central Market, I learn to my cost that buying an item on Athinás Street can involve paying twice as much as what's required for exactly the same thing just a few steps away, down a side street. It seems there are enough Greeks who don't, or won't, walk that little bit further in order to buy at half the price, to save 50% of the cost of a packet of herbs or spices or a good many other everyday household items. Anyway, from Monastiráki, at the southern end of Athinás Street, I catch the Metró way out into the suburbs, in order to connect with a bus that should take me to the Attica Zoological

Park, today's main destination. But when the bus deposits me in the middle of Spáta, a suburb not far from Athens's new airport, I can't locate anyone in the little collection of shops there who knows of the further bus that I need in order to get to the park. Several shop assistants are even surprised to learn from me that there is actually a major zoo nearby. There's nothing for it but to walk.

The only other people I encounter, face-to-face, during my forty-minute march through the suburb of Spáta, are a couple of Pakistanis. The Greeks are all flashing by in cars. Once again, I could be back in any town or city in the Arabian Gulf, where the only people ever seen walking alongside roads are Indian, Pakistani, Bangladeshi and Filipino servants or labourers. Occasionally in Arabia you may spot the odd Westerner power-walking in smart gym kit, or taking a serious jog, but for Gulf Arabs, and even reasonably well-paid foreigners, it's become a matter of style and pride not to be seen walking along the sides of roads. Furthermore, the appearance of this outer suburb of Athens is nearly identical to that of many areas of Kuwait City, Dhahran, or Riyadh, except that instead of garish signage in Arabic lettering, the similarly garish signage here is all in Greek. Where there are not houses in Spáta, there are either open plots of land or large modern Sa'udi-style showrooms, with parking spaces for customers set directly in front. You want some home or office furniture? Then drive right up to the showroom door. You want to take home some pastries and cakes? Hop back in your car and just drive along to the spaces directly in front of the large *zacharoplasteío* (a Greek sweet shop), sitting all by itself in a weedy wasteland just fifty metres further up the road. You don't walk. It's like an unwritten rule. Often in the Gulf you see Sa'udis going from shop to shop along an avenue by hopping in and out of luxurious limousines and if there are no car-parking spaces provided they'll simply drive right up onto the pavement, so that their vehicles are as close as possible to the front door and they'll need to do a minimum of walking. The strange thing though, is that while in these and certain other respects Greece bears surprising similarities to Arabia, it's also a nation with marked Western characteristics.

Prostitution is legal and long-established, there are Mr Greece pageants, annual gay pride parades have recently begun, nude beaches abound, and Greece's birth-rate is considerably lower than that of Arab states.

But the existence of such liberal qualities in Greece doesn't alleviate this afternoon's depressing experience of Spáta. Tossed carelessly or contemptuously out of vehicle windows, a great deal of litter hangs tangled in bushes beside the road and deteriorating upon the verges. There are no proper footpaths in outer areas like this probably because they're simply not needed or wanted by Greek citizens, who all appear to be wedded to wheels and petrol. Where beside the road or along the central reservation there's been an attempt at landscaping, miles of ugly black irrigation tubing snakes in and out of the ground. I just don't understand it, for watering ornamental growth in a dry and hot country is expensive, not to mention wasteful, and if not closely monitored and maintained such systems result in the kind of sad and neglected displays which are to be seen here in Spáta: exposed ugly tubing being more noticeable than verdant growth. Roadside greenery is maintained very impressively in cities all over the Arabian Gulf, but to my knowledge Greece, unlike Gulf states, doesn't have the wealth necessary to fund such a luxury.

So where on earth are the Greeks getting their money from? Agriculture can't be making them rich, as roughly 70% of Greek land simply can't be cultivated, most of it being covered with forests or scrub. Much of Greece is stony, the soil is poor, and 80% of the total terrain is mountainous and heavily dissected. Greece is a significant producer of cotton, tobacco, olive oil, and fruit, like grapes, peaches, oranges, melons, and tomatoes, but certainly not in quantities that can account for an affluent lifestyle. In 2009 Greek agriculture was responsible for just under 4% of Gross Domestic Product. The country possesses mineral resources, particularly manganese, lignite, and bauxite, but the Greek mining industry is tiny, accounting for little more than 1% of today's GDP. The country does have some reserves of natural gas and oil, but when compared to global quantities Greece's reserves are small and production is limited. As for the nation's seas, well, they've been so polluted and over-fished that in recent years revenues from them have diminished considerably so that fish in Greece is currently a luxury and a single plate of it for just one person at a good Athens fish restaurant at this time can cost between 45 and 70 euros, depending upon the particular fish ordered.

Industry and construction only accounts for about 20% of Greek Gross Domestic Product and both have been largely dependent upon infrastructure projects that have been financed by money from the EU. Among these are the Athens Metró, new roadways, railroads, bridges, and the fine new Athens International Airport, 45% of which, in the winter of 2009 and 2010, was owned by a company in Germany. The EU requirement that with regard to major projects Greece must be open to international bidding has confronted the Greek construction industry with tough professional competition from elsewhere. Meanwhile, manufacturing industries remain modest, the most significant being those producing foodstuffs, textiles, chemicals, and metal goods.

It is Greece's service sector that contributes the most to the national economy. In 2009 it delivered about 75% of total GDP. And although this sector includes vendors, public administration, banking, communications, and defence, it is tourist-related services and transport services (mainly shipping) which contribute the most to the nation's economy. It's estimated that on average tourism provides roughly 15% of Greek GDP, while the Greek commercial shipping fleet provides roughly 7%. (Greece's shipping fleet is the largest on earth, followed by Japan's, then Norway's, and then the USA's at roughly half the size of Greece's.) So can these two main earners in this land account for all the affluence which I'm seeing about me at this time? Surely not, because even these contributors are known to be under threat. Greek tourism faces tough competition from Turkey and Egypt, both of which offer cheaper holidays in similarly pleasant climates. And the global recession that has set in since 2008 has literally slashed demand for the shipping of commodities to the developing nations of China and India. Furthermore, Greek shipping and tourism are dominated by tightly-knit families who tend to keep their income to themselves.

So is there, I wonder, simply an unfathomable willingness on the part of Greeks to live the high-life on money that they don't actually have?

The road that leads directly to the Attica Zoological Park doesn't help to raise my spirits, or my hopes for the zoo ahead. Although the park is located in the very centre of a large shallow basin of countryside and is well away from busy roads, the roar of traffic can still be heard as I approach it, and, this afternoon at least, the air in this basin absolutely reeks of industrial pollution. What kind of hideous environment is this for a collection of animals, I wonder. When I arrive at the front entrance, three beautiful young Greek women greet me warmly, furnish me with a glossy plan of the park, and then request a whopping fifteen euros! After the depressing experience of getting all the way here, it's surely an excessively high tariff. However, I am to slowly discover over the course of the next three hours that this zoo houses one of the finest collections of birds to be seen anywhere, as well as a great menagerie of other creatures, including Barbary macaques, black-capped capuchins, white-cheeked tauracos, crowned gouras, Patagonian maras, Gila monsters, African penguins, sitatungas, and servals, as well as all the other cats, bears, giraffes and so forth that one expects to find in any decent zoo.

The Attica Zoological Park is enormous and although there are certainly more impressive-looking zoos around the world, zoos in which animals reside against lavish backdrops, imaginative landscaping, or authentically recreated natural environments, the creatures here in Spáta at least have plenty of space in which to move - even though the big cats, like the white lion, the leopard, and the cheetah, sometimes pace about as if lost in remembrance of roaming free. The so-called 'Monkey Forest' is astounding. Through a series of gates and hanging chains, designed to keep the 'monkeys' from escaping, you emerge into a vast 'cage' which is completely open to the sky and maybe several hundred metres square. Within this 'cage' are a good number of large mature trees, and within them is a population of about twenty orange-eyed, highly intelligent, black and white ring-tailed lemurs, leaping about or just lolling quietly on the branches. I walk beneath them, stop, look up, and then down they all rush! In seconds I'm met by a welcoming committee: they're immediately before me, all around me, and directly above, stretching out towards me tiny tentative hand-like paws. One of them licks my fingers where I'd been eating an orange and his tiny tongue feels utterly soft and gentle. Then several of these charming creatures reach out in curiosity for my arms. They begin to hop onto my leather jacket, to perch on my shoulders. I feel them fingering and playing with my hair. One keeps his balance by gently holding my right ear. Two more climb up my legs until we're face-to-face, their eyes poring directly over my features, their little heads swivelling with intense interest from my nose to my mouth, to my eyes, and then back again. These are the most trusting and intelligent non-human creatures I've ever met. With their panda-like dark rings around orange-button eyes, black snouts, black caps on white faces and gecko-like hands and feet, they're also the most adorable creatures I've ever encountered. For just this experience alone, the zoo's fifteen euro entrance fee is more than worth it.

Later, I discover several long avenues of large cages housing absolutely magnificent parrots from different parts of the exotic world. There are parrots of vivid green with patches of bright sky-blue and flaming orange; parrots that are nearly all a rich deep navy, except for heads of red, orange, and brilliant yellow; and parrots bloody-crimson, with green wings and a cap of iridescent ultramarine. Their colours are breathtaking. One bright lime-green species has a disconcerting call that sounds up and down the avenue of cages like an effect from a horror film: like the sound of some lost and abandoned soul lingering long on her vowels and repeatedly and softly calling into the night 'Mommm-eee! Mommm-eee!' Most stunning of all are the Sun Conure parrots from South America, each a foot's length of flaming beauty and hysterical activity. These have to be the darlings of all parrots! Their plumage is mostly a vivid saturated yellow, but around the eyes a thin ring of violet is followed by a wider outer circle of fiery red, before giving way to a head and neck of vivid egg-yolk. Their chests are of tropical orange, their wings of emerald-green, with touches of dark cobalt, and their beaks are jet-black. They're magnificent. They're also birds with big personalities and considerable intelligence: they screech and fly *en masse* to the netting before you, like a frantic and impulsive mob of worshipping young pop fans, greeting their idol at an airport.

This entire zoo is surely superb - for at closing time there are still some distant parts of it that I haven't yet seen despite already having roamed the site for just over three hours. And as I begin the long walk back to a bus-stop in Spáta, it's good to note that the noxious vapours that were streaming through the basin when I arrived here have entirely gone and the air is suitably clean and fresh. The sad thing though is that I've observed that many Athenians have no idea that this magnificent attraction exists. And of course for those who are aware of it, the entrance fee may be prohibitive: this afternoon I've encountered only five other visitors.

Of all the bookshops that are full of texts in Greek, and mainly by Greek writers, one in particular has enthralled me: Ianós, on Stadíou Street. Its shelves and tables are packed with beautifully-printed and well-designed titles. As a book-lover, I feel I want to possess every one of them! A fever grips me: which to purchase? But why bother when I'm still stumbling over the correct pronunciation of just their titles! It's silly. But in Ianós, after surveying hundreds of Greek novels and books of Greek poetry, I'm especially drawn to a soft-backed, but lusciously bound, and beautifully illustrated edition of poems by the Greek Nobel prize-winner Odysséus Elýtis. It's a fairly slim soft-back that costs an outrageous and a ridiculous fifty-five euros. And it's not entirely an exception: there are quite a lot of other titles at roughly the same price. Who can afford such books? Furthermore, of this particular title there's a pile of about thirty copies, just sitting here in the open alongside cheaper volumes. Books aren't subsidised in Greece as they are in the UK, and the two-for-one or three-for-two offers constantly available now in British bookshops, not to forget the slashed prices of books in UK supermarkets, don't occur at this end of the Mediterranean. In Greece the book remains tremendously prized, and often excessively expensive.

So obvious is my delight in Ianós that an assertive young assistant strides over to the table where I'm standing, and almost drooling, and offers me a *'Voétheia!'* (Help!), not exactly as a question but in empathic and friendly understanding that I could probably do with some assistance. I try to answer in Greek, enough at least to show my fondness for Greece, but must then continue in English to explain that it's occurred to me that once back in the UK, and eventually getting down to seriously studying Modern Greek, it'd be nice to close the textbooks now and again and just try to read a 'real Greek book', but which one? My helper, intense and perceptive, and used to all sorts of nutters, as shop-assistants generally are, immediately understands. She leads me a short distance to shelves that are packed with thin 'readers' - for Greek children! They're all graded according to reading ability and she drops to her knees to search the lower shelves, explaining that I shouldn't try anything beyond ages five to six. She then presents me with a twenty-page volume full of colour illustrations and very large text. It has all the hallmarks of a kiddies' picture-book. But, of course, she's right. Kindly, however, she then helps me locate a title which is at the same ability-level as the picture-book but not so affronting to my adult pride: an extremely simplified re-telling in Greek of Shakespeare's 'Romeo and Juliet'.

Early evening, in front of the main university building on Panepistimíou Street, beside the Valliános National Library, a group of about twenty young activists have set up a table from which to offer leaflets and pamphlets to passers-by while one of their number calls rousingly and urgently into a handheld megaphone. His voice reverberates throughout the square and adjacent streets and I ask a young Greek passer-by what it's all about. She speaks no English but kindly glances round the faces of the activists before calling over a woman whom she presumably thinks looks appropriate or sympathetic. That person comes over, learns what I want but then calls over another person whom she assures me speaks much better English. Woman No. 3 never gets round to telling me what the stall is all about because she and I immediately establish rapport. While four or five other activists stand close by and dozens of Athenians in business clothes stream homewards along Panepistimíou Street, Woman No. 3 and I fall into intense conversation regarding the news of Greece's dire financial straits.

Her name is Phaédra, she's a teacher, was once a drama student, and she's been an activist for ten years. She tells me her life is now lived according to the estimable motto 'You are what you *do*! - not what you think, or what you say, or what you dream, or what you write, but what you actually do!' Phaédra goes on to relate passionately her belief that over the last 30 years Greece has been exploited by outside interests. Then I notice how, while subtly eyeing the small group of activists behind me, she moves slightly to one side, as if seeking to hide her face. Without moving an inch myself, I quietly ask why she's frightened of being overheard. She pauses, seems pleased by my observation, and then very quietly says 'I trust you, I know you are only a curious visitor, but them I am not sure. I have been talking with them for half an hour, as if they were activists, but I think they might be undercover. Secret police.' I'm amazed. She says that activists believe that Greek security is currently wary of a surge in public discontent; that in the past few weeks, since Greek debt has become an international news item, the number of police on the streets of central Athens has risen noticeably.

When Phaédra then apologises that she must leave with a friend for an important appointment, it emerges they're heading in the same direction as me, so after being introduced to her friend Ártemis, who unfortunately for me speaks little English, the three of us set off together towards Sýntagma. As we walk Phaédra relates that activists are also alarmed that the Greek government has recently been promoting nationalism and patriotism, particularly in schools, the motive, the activists believe, being to ensure that the population supports the government, that they will not object, but stick together 'for the sake of Greece'. She says that most of the Greek media are in collusion with the government, that Greek journalists rarely dare to truly grill the politicians, and that they basically print whatever they're given. Although Phaédra gives every impression of being a sound, healthy, and well-balanced young woman, I find much of this hard to believe and so suggest that the situation she's describing actually sounds more like the days of the Júnta, whereupon she instantly and very matter-of-factly replies 'But what we have now feels not so different from the Júnta, it is like a hidden dictatorship, everything is controlled here in Greece, and we know there are spies.'

As we move down Stadíou Street I ask for more about these 'spies' and Phaédra says they're to be found wherever there are activists, that they're watching all the time. At some point in the five or so minutes of conversation that follows this statement, a man in his mid-thirties, dressed in blue jeans, casual shirt and an ordinary navy blue jumper, has appeared on my right side. I only slowly become aware of this totally ordinary-looking Greek - slightly plump, not exactly fetching, simply walking along on my right and never progressing beyond us nor ever falling a little behind. After a further few minutes Phaédra, on my left, appears to have also become aware of him, but she seems to have reached some conclusion, for suddenly she engages boldly with this total stranger, across me! His unfriendliness towards her is unmistakable. I note that Phaédra's friend, Ártemis, is now showing transparent alarm, childlike fear. But Phaédra speaks volubly, cheerfully, and without concern to this man; and both she and he continue to speak as if I wasn't walking between them. After a while I interrupt and ask Phaédra who he is. She responds 'He's been listening and he wants to know who you are.' I'm shocked. Worse still, I'm shocked to note that I have no reaction beyond speechlessness. This is real-life drama and I'm unused to it.

Phaédra and the stranger continue their exchanges, she speaking loudly, without fear, and cheerfully, and he quietly answering her back with short curt statements which never manifest a morsel of warmth or humour. Then Phaédra tells me 'He wants to speak to you!' and a further pang of shock shoots through me. But I'm still numb with fear, not knowing how to react. But I know it is such shock that lets aggressors get the upper hand and take advantage of you, so while Phaédra and the stranger continue exchanging for a minute or so I decide upon a response, for surely I must assert myself!

I interrupt again and ask Phaédra 'Well, will you tell him, please, that I don't wish to talk to him!' She immediately conveys my message in Greek and the man then turns his head, for the first time, to look me full in the face. His cold expression seems to say 'How dare you!' But we all keep walking, close to Sýntagma now, and Phaédra and he keep talking, although she seems now to be taunting him. Then all at once he halts us, produces his wallet, holds it up before us, right in front of our eyes, and shows us the card that sits in its little plastic window. It's some kind of official identification, in Greek. 'What's that?' I ask Phaédra. 'He's police', she answers.

Fear rattles through me like machine-gun fire! I'm 'under surveillance'! I immediately see myself imprisoned in some horrid stinking cell! Or worse: I recall Ann Chapman, the British reporter found murdered in Athens, bound with wire and strangled, in 1971, during the Júnta, when thousands whom the régime didn't like were arrested, often tortured, then imprisoned or exiled. Chapman was visiting Athens in the hope of getting information about the Greek resistance movement. Is Greece a police state still, I wonder? Well, they're obviously watching! This foreigner, me, simply got into conversation with a known activist at a city-centre protest and now one of the other people who were there has turned out to be an undercover cop - and he's after me! My heart thuds. Should I quietly drop back, then quickly turn and make a run for it? No, maybe he's got backup behind him. I keep walking, thinking, fearing, planning, the adrenaline pumping.

But several minutes later as we enter Sýntagma Square, the man just breaks off and curls away, without any final word or gesture. He just goes and is gone, thankfully. He's completely gone! Ártemis and I are greatly relieved, but Phaédra's response is to start calling out loudly and generally to everyone passing by. They hear her, they look blankly in her direction, but they show no reaction, they just keep walking. It's as if they're used to it. When eventually she pauses I ask what she's been saying and she says 'Oh, wherever we go now, we just react, immediately, we speak out, we don't care anymore, it's the only means we have to ensure the truth is heard.' She means that while on an escalator, or in a supermarket, or on a busy pavement, or standing in a moving train, she and fellow activists will suddenly break from their thoughts and begin speaking aloud, perhaps only for a minute or two, but so that everyone around will hear their concerns. They simply speak out what apparently doesn't appear in the papers, things like 'The police are watching us! They trying to intimidate us! The government isn't on our side! Greece is a puppet state! Our country has been taken from us!' It's bold behaviour, but it's desperate.

A short distance down Ermoú Street, we must say goodbye and part, but not before I share with Phaédra a few details regarding Ann Chapman. The truth of Chapman's murder has yet to emerge, but just before she left London in October 1971, for a ten-day travel-rep junket, she apparently told her parents she wouldn't only be reporting back on holiday options available in Greece but that she also hoped to collect two scoops. She was excited about the possibility of interviewing the celebrated World War II Greek Resistance member Amalía Fleming, Greek widow of Sir Alexander, the Nobel prize-winner. For Lady Fleming had just been released from jail on health grounds, after having been imprisoned for assisting an aborted plot to spring from prison Aléxandros Panagoúlis, the hero who had tried to assassinate Colonel Papadópoulos, the leader of the Júnta, in 1968. And it's believed that Chapman also hoped for some other even more dramatic story. However, she didn't return to the UK with either. Instead she was found battered, bound, and strangled in wasteland not far from her beach hotel, roughly 11 miles south of central Athens. Phaédra shrugs and says it doesn't surprise her, that during the Júnta there were hundreds of such cases and that since the end of the Júnta the terrorist organization N17, also known as *Orgánosi Phántasma*, has murdered at least two dozen, including a British military attaché! She says I must try to enjoy my time here in Greece and she urges me not to stay in Athens, but to go to the islands. She wants me to see the other side of Greece, its clean and sparkling beaches, or the greenery of the forested north, all far from the general *cháos* of the capital. Clearly, she'd prefer me to associate her country with pleasant postcard impressions.

To this day it's not generally known whether Ann Chapman was simply the victim of a random attack as she waited for a bus, or if there's a much darker explanation. What is sure, however, is that the circumstances of her murder were referred to in both the House of Lords and the House of Commons in 1978 and 1979, respectively, but the British government has always refused to investigate the matter, maintaining it to be entirely the concern of the judicial authorities of Greece; that Turkey's Deputy Prime Minister at the time of the murder stated in 1978 in his memoirs that Chapman was found in possession of USA intelligence documents and that she was killed by the Greek secret service on the instructions of the CIA; that in the same year, 1978, the Soviet diplomat, Arkady Shevchenko, who defected to the USA while Under-Secretary General of the United Nations, indicated while being de-briefed that the circumstances of Chapman's death were sinister; and that in 1983 the Greek government released from jail the 46-year-old Greek voyeur who had been convicted of the murder, declaring him an innocent man. Theories which have been put forward as possible explanations for the killing include the Júnta fearing what Chapman would share with the world's press about its brutal treatment of political prisoners; Chapman actually being a British spy who got into difficulty while trying to uncover a Soviet agent; and, most dramatic of all, Chapman being compromised by coming to learn of a Resistance plot to crash a helicopter carrying United States Vice-President Spiro Agnew whose discussions with the Júnta concerning the heated issue of the Turkish invasion of Cyprus coincided with Chapman's stay in Greece. When the truth emerges it could be most interesting, but for the moment I'm just glad that this evening's undercover cop seems to have decided to abandon his interest in me.

At about eight, I meet actor Pantelís again and I'm dying to tell him of my real-life drama, but I barely know him, or his true politics, and so decide to hold back, till later. This time we go to an *estiatório* of his choice and proceed to Koukáki, the district where Míkis Theodorákis resides, on the south side of Philopáppou Hill, to a Cretan restaurant where the décor is delightfully simple and clean, with pale lemon walls, pale blue closed shutters on the insides of the windows, plain old-fashioned wooden chairs and tables, and with traditional Cretan mountain music emanating unobtrusively from hidden speakers. In this placid oasis, far from the eyes of any undercover cops, it feels as if there's been a total change of scenery in the highly theatrical drama that is Athens.

Once again I urge Pantelís not to order excessively and although he agrees, very willingly, the table is nevertheless soon covered with four large platters of food, a dish of grated cheese, a plate of quartered lemons, a big basket of fresh bread, a great jug of water, and a very large carafe of *kókkino krasí* (red wine). As before, just one of the main dishes alone, like the pile of *hoiriná païdákia* (pork chops) that is set before us, would provide enough meat for half a dozen adults. Pantelís is an ordinary jobbing actor, he's far from wealthy, and he has every reason to be as careful in his spending as most British actors need to be, but it seems that in Greece one must generously and lavishly coat the table-top with every sign of abundance and good living, despite knowing that you'll consume only a small portion of it and that the rest will be returned to the kitchen.

Pantelís and I eat and drink and talk about everything under the moon and stars, until half-one in the morning, until a solid five and a half hours of intense interaction has just flashed by. Such is the delight and pleasure of a Greek meal with a Greek person in Greece, and I wonder if we would've so enjoyed ourselves this evening if there hadn't been the sense of occasion created by that impressive display laid out upon the table. Several junctures in our conversation have offered perfect opportunities for me to grandstand with a dramatic account of the encounter with the undercover cop, but other moments have warned that Pantelís might simply not believe me, or that his great pride in Greece would be hurt. For it's now clear that Pantelís's magical wrap-around world of theatre, music, and literature lies quite apart from the world of grass-roots activism, protests, and politics.

Heading for my hotel via a string of residential streets near the southern base of the Acrópolis, each street absolutely crammed with parked cars, it's good to observe that there are parts of this seemingly indefatigable city which come to an absolute standstill late at night, that while people sleep there's barely the slightest sound to be heard. Ascending the steps at the end of Drákou Street, knowing that the great Míkis is probably slumbering in one of the apartments above, I'm inspired by the pleasant night, not at all cold, to abandon making for central Athens by the pedestrian way between the Acrópolis and Philopáppou and to return instead by climbing over Philopáppou itself, for a hilltop view of the city by night. The scramble up the bush-clad hillside is well worth it, for the top of Philopáppou at this hour offers the most wonderful feelings of peace, purity, and solitude. The horns of cars on the city's main thoroughfares, far below, are reduced to mere squeaks, barely to be heard. The night is dark, the air is clear, and the lights of Athens twinkle magnificently all about. The only other people up here at this hour appear to be a group of five young Greeks sitting upon a rug on the grass, quietly eating, drinking, and chatting in the gentle breeze.

But then in trying to get down the other side of this hill, I chance upon the most unexpected and romantic delight! In a dark wooded area that no locals would go near because, as I unfortunately find, there's no exit from it and I must turn back in order to find a way out, there comes a magical soft tinkling, gentle music, perhaps delicate glasslike chimes suspended from branches. I creep through the trees to try to make out the source, probably some fifty or so feet away, deep in the mass of foliage beneath a rocky escarpment. There's someone there, with some kind of instrument, some kind of *lýre*, some kind of magical plucking thing. In the dark I can't make out whoever's playing it, but there's clearly a melody involved. But it's vague and odd and seems to go round and round, sometimes slowly, sometimes fast, as if somebody's turning a handle on a barrel, plucking a pre-set melody from strings, perhaps from something like a music-box. I stop still, and listen. The effect is fantastical. It may be a homeless person, an illegal immigrant lulling himself to sleep upon a sheet of cardboard, or, on the other hand, it may be a dreamer, a poet! Whoever, I prefer to interpret this as a moment from Ancient Greece, from over

2,000 years ago: a chance encounter with Orphéas and his *lýre* on a wooded hillside in the heart of Athens!

▢ ▢ ▢ ▢

10

Rules & Rebellion

Pallás Theatre;
Athens Theatre Museum;
Exárcheia;
Drama School;
& Greek Orthodoxy.

I wake at 7.30 eager as ever to embrace the *metrópolis* again, and find my mind fixed on the notion of purchasing one of those alluring and beautiful Greek books I was leafing through yesterday, even if it's only to be a treasure, a jewel-like thing to sit upon a coffee-table back home, to look through now and again and to be inspired by. And then suddenly I see I've left the main door of my room open by six inches all night! I could've been burgled, murdered even; Greek secret service police could have rifled through all my things! In the early hours of this morning I obviously swept into my room totally preoccupied with the day's events and rather careless from all that delicious *híma* consumed with Pantelís. Now my head's caught somewhere between the ache of a hangover and buzzing intoxication. Never mind satisfying the obsession with Greek books, how on earth am I going to make it through this day? Well, like the average Greek, I suppose: with a strong injection of caffeine!

Athens beckons again. Athens powers you up. My head's spinning with thoughts and feelings and joys but above all with excitement and inspiration. I possessed nothing remotely approaching any kind of death-wish before I arrived here, but this city so very clearly provokes the opposite: it makes one want to LIVE! Yes 'LIVE!', in capital letters. Dionysian exuberance is intrinsic to this place, and Athens somehow gives one the feeling that there is vast possibility, that all good things *could* happen. But I'm also aware that some of the people who reside here, day-in day-out, like Phaédra, feel trapped and yearn to escape. They very clearly see the problems of Athens, as well as its merits. But not so much that between each year's *éxodus* to the islands or other holiday places, they can't forget their cares every once in a while at some *tavérna, bouzoúkia, rebétiko* club, and lots of other places of distraction or escape in this *metrópolis*. This city's tight communal living and all of its associated problems are partly the cause of that perpetual eruption which is Athens's delicious banquet of happenings.

My head is so jangling with different thoughts and leads this morning that I'm frightened I won't remember them all. One thing I mustn't forget to do is locate a public library! I haven't seen any. Do they exist in Athens? What are they like? Books, while certainly plentiful, are expensive here, at least they seem so in comparison with the UK, but maybe they're not too costly if somehow Greeks are all earning so much more than I imagine? I still haven't cracked this one. Buyers can easily hand over credit cards at tills, but where does all the money come from to support the thousands of sellers, in all those glittering boutiques, shops, and showrooms, street after street? Are they also reliant upon borrowing?

The morning begins with my first visit to an Athenian Internet café. It's 'hip', very modern, well set-up, and the computers are dazzlingly rapid - at least, in comparison to the very reasonable broadband we enjoy in our little valley near the Welsh border. Two young Greek men with long pony-tails fly around the room attending to users with all the splendid aplomb of seasoned Greek waiters: a successful case of 'cross-over', the transference of skills from restaurant to digital enterprise. Unfortunately, however, both young men also sail around with lit cigarettes and the room is dense with stench and fog. They could increase their revenue by advertising this place as a 'Surf 'n Smoke'! I quickly type in the address of my ISP, and bang, there instantly appears a massive week's worth of email from home.

Voukourestíou Street fails to yield the traditional Greek craft-shop which an enthusiastic waiter told me the other night I simply mustn't miss - it seems that unknown to him it's long ago packed up and moved elsewhere - but Odós Voukourestíou does reveal the recently refurbished Pallás Theatre. In its opulently marbled foyer an absolutely charming and beautiful young woman (yes, Athens is full of them!) indicates that if I wish to see a Greek diva who is to open here next week, then I could be in with a chance! I've been noticing this diva's young face on billboards all over Athens since my arrival, her thick black hair tumbling to the sides of delicate elfin features and the beatific smile of a young angel. I've heard many of her recordings on Internet radio and although her songs are very often expressions of pain or assertion, cries from the heart, the voice is quite agile, but, most alluringly, the music that she sings is nearly always highly Eastern, harkening of Smýrna and Asia Minor. So to imbue my penultimate night in this fabulous city with a touch of Eastern rapture, I very willingly hand over twenty-five euros for one of the last remaining seats, albeit a seat that is way up in the circle. Seats in the stalls, ranging downwards from just under 100 euros each, have completely sold out.

Just before stepping back out into the street, I turn and raise my camera to take a picture of the foyer's splendidly marbled interior, its walls, floor, and elegant staircase, but I suddenly find myself being barked at, by a young blonde Greek in suit and tie. 'Pictures are forbidden! Pictures are FORBIDDEN!' he shouts, while striding towards me. Thankfully, although the picture has been taken, I didn't use the flash so he's not to know he hasn't managed to stop me. I look at my camera and shrug my shoulders and he appears to think he's halted me in time. 'Forbidden?' I repeat, incredulous at the use of this fascist-like term, and I'm on the verge of adding, *'Verboten?* Ah, Heil Hitler!' but I think better of it. 'You may not take photographs!' he answers. This situation instantly thrusts me back to Sa'udi Arabia, where, officially, one may not take photographs anywhere in public, and where once during a sports day event at a college I was teaching at, students getting into position on a starting line became irate and frighteningly aggressive towards me when I raised a camera. I had a number of other similar photographic experiences in Sa'udi. I want to say to this young Greek 'Look, this place may be called The Palace Theatre but it's only a souped-up cinema, you know!' but I confess I swing instead into my Arab mode, play the penitent, and conform to exotic local requirements.

Several blocks away in the foyer of the Athens Theatre Museum I meet yet more choking cigarette smoke. When I arrived the front door wouldn't open. Only after my rattling it, quite vigorously and for some time, did the reception-ist release it electronically, from where she was sitting - and smoking. What are they exhibiting in this theatre museum to warrant such security, I wonder? The intact skulls of Aristophánes, Sophoclés, and Evripídis? And then I notice that nowhere in the vicinity of the receptionist is there a cigarette visible, or an ashtray. So perhaps she keeps the door locked to give her time to spirit her gear out of sight. And perhaps she also hopes that if she's slow enough to release the door, the visitor may simply give up, move on, and so cause her no bother at all. For she can't unfortunately do much to hide her noxious fumes: by the density of the fog in here this morning it would appear she's been solidly burning her way through cigarettes since taking to her desk. So much for Greece's ban on smoking in public places.

The foyer is full of old framed photographs of scenes from classical productions at Epídavros, as well as aged framed portraits of notable Greek actors, actresses, directors, and designers. Entrance is free, and as I move off into the body of the museum, my camera totally concealed in an inside pocket, the secret smoker has the nerve to call after me very firmly 'No photographs, thank you very much! With or without flash. Photographs are strictly forbidden!' Here we go again: this extreme inclination to privacy, which I've only ever encountered before in certain Islamic countries, and a good many years ago at that. The Hellenic Data Protection Authority recently prohibited all vehicles operated by Google's 'Street View' drivers, from cars to specially adapted tricycles for penetrating narrow alleys, from touring and photographing any public way within Greece. Google's 'Street

View' facility, allowing 360-degree views along all public ways in North America, Australia, New Zealand, Japan, Brazil, South Africa, and much of western and northern Europe (including the UK, France, Germany, Spain, and Italy) thus remains unavailable on any of its online maps of Greece. Like China, Russia, the Middle East, and all of North Africa, Greece is very concerned about 'the threat' of 'invasive technologies'. With regard to privacy, all of these countries are of a common mind-set. A limited number of CCTV cameras were introduced above Athens's main roads shortly before the 2004 Olympics, to help regulate the flow of traffic, but it took the city-centre riots of 2009 to persuade the Greek parliament to pass legislation allowing the use of surveillance cameras in the city-centre.

Despite being housed within a very fine neo-classical building, the entire Athens Theatre Museum is shabby. It's comprised of three or four windowless rooms, along with several offices, in the basement of 'The Cultural Centre of the Municipality of Athens'. It accommodates photographs, old theatrical posters, some set-designs, costumes worn in various productions, and a series of seven mocked-up dressing-rooms as may have been inhabited by famous Greek performers like Melína Mercoúri and María Cállas. The display featuring the latter, in particular, demonstrates that this entire exhibition desperately needs re-homing: the international legend *La Divina* is represented here only by a gown that she once wore, a number of large old photographs, and half a dozen of her LPs just left propped against various vertical surfaces. So if the impressions created by this exhibition are anything to go by, it appears that the Athens Theatre Museum is as impoverished as most Greek actors and actresses appear to be, for the objects in the displays, particularly within the little mocked-up dressing rooms, suggest lives lived tenuously upon shoe-strings. Nevertheless, this museum is certainly testament to Greece's great theatrical past. It also reveals how its theatre history has been punctuated at points by a considerable sense of adventure. One of the highlights of the exhibition is a depiction of a beautiful young woman, voluptuous and naked, lying on her back, her long tresses spread out behind her, while with one hand she cups a breast and caresses its nipple, and with the other holds a grinning human skull between both breasts.

While moving on to the acting class in Exárcheia which the director of the Néo Ellinikó Théatro so kindly invited me to observe, both doors of the Nákas music store on Navarínou Street swing suddenly open and two young men roll out a full-sized, brand spanking new, beautiful black Steinway grand, on a tiny wooden trolley. They negotiate the curb, squeeze the great instrument between parked cars, and then proceed right down the centre of the street, even though it's full of moving vehicles! I follow their progress with amazement. Soon we're in the heart of colourful Exárcheia, and the beautiful concert grand suddenly darts inside a small dim lobby. At ground-level the area is alive with Greek businesses of every kind, small shop-fronts and cafés following one after the other, while above there are the usual four or five floors of apartments, one of which is presumably shortly to become home to a fine new Steinway. But the street below has a deliberately scruffy and student appearance. There are posters or graffiti on every spare area of wall, no matter how small: 'The Future is Now', 'Fuck the Police!', 'Change The System!' and hundreds of messages in Greek. Few walls are left untouched. Those that are are usually only those walls that are inaccessible. The frontage of a bookshop offers two windows full of expensive academic texts and the shop's interior is meticulously well-ordered, but all of the surface around and above the outside of the windows and the door is absolutely dense with the mayhem of graffiti! It's a riot of wordage and symbolism in brilliant reds, yellows, blues, and blacks, and some of the messages have been painted in stylish and quite complicated fonts. Much of it is, of course, messy, but here and there can be seen some quite well-executed icons or motifs. And high above it all, painted rather beautifully, are a pair of placid birds. One suspects the proprietors of this bookshop may quite like having their shop-front covered permanently in calligraphic *cháos*. Or have they simply given up trying to paint it all away?

As the police have tended to avoid entering Exárcheia for months now, for fear of infuriating student activists and of triggering yet another expensive city-centre riot, involving yet more broken windows and burning cars, Exárcheia's graffitists can 'work' without interruption or fear! Several times during the past week, I've seen large dark buses parked at intersections in the adjacent area of Kolonáki and they're there again today. These coaches provide bases for the young policemen in navy blue uniforms who stand around on street corners keeping guard, the machine guns in their hands frighteningly and always at the ready. There are a number of important governmental buildings in neighbour-ing Kolonáki and it's feared that at any moment activists may charge out of *Anárcheia*, as Exárcheia is sometimes now humorously referred to, and cause disruption.

In October 2009, directly after the election of Yiórgos Papandréou (Junior), the new government decided to show its strength and bring the police stand-off with Exárcheia to an end. So, shortly after the conclusion of a book-reading in the café of the historic Blue Building on Exárcheia's main square, the police arrived and randomly arrested several of those who had attended the event. But locals in the vicinity, young and old, were quickly alerted and descended to the street where they surrounded the police to give them stick. The police had gone in heavy, fully-armoured and wearing those large spherical white helmets that give them the intimidating appearance of invaders from outer space. The locals wanted to talk, but of course the policemen were all ordinary young Greek men just acting on orders and unable to deal with the challenging questions and views being put to them. Some of the locals tried to remove the policemen's helmets, to establish normal human interaction, but of course they were physically rebuffed. However, in the end it was the police who retreated, cowed and intimidated by the locals. They are wary of returning (at least in uniform), and Exárcheia is once again largely 'no-go'. But unfortunately, a consequence of the residents' victory is that now whenever there's an emergency in the locality, or a crime is reported, the police remain reluctant to attend.

A little further along, at the Néo Ellinikó Théatro, Yiórgos Arménis greets me warmly. However, as I don't speak anywhere near enough Greek, and he speaks only a little English, further communication between us is difficult. But luckily one of the students who also works at the theatre is fluent in English and I'm placed in his care. This young man tells me it feels to him like almost everyone in Greece wants to be a singer or an actor. By 'everyone' he means, of course, everyone who's young and aspiring. He confirms that Athens possesses well over a hundred small theatres or theatre-groups, and that so many young people dream of their faces being up on a theatre billboard or on the front of a CD, or on television or in the newspapers, that competition between performers in Athens is intense. And although this rivalry produces considerable artistic creativity, Greek performers often carry a strong sense of inferiority, despite their belief that it was in their land, Greece, that theatre first came into existence, and then blossomed into works which are still performed on every continent. I find it interesting to note that this young actor goes on to explain the absence of Greek equivalents of the great European masters, like Bach and Beethoven, Shakespeare and Goethe, with the spirited defence 'You see at that time we were under the Turks! We were suffering and resisting the Turks while Europe was having the Renaissance!' And Greece has indeed long been immersed in a deeply troubled history that must have diverted or even quashed a great deal of its creative potential, while the lands of the West were engulfed in, or closely witnessed, the Renaissance, the Reformation, the Enlightenment, the French Revolution, and the Industrial Revolution.

We descend to a spacious studio in the basement and I'm introduced to a well-known theatre and opera director who, it quickly emerges, once collaborated with Mános Hadjidákis! Luckily for me he speaks a little English and soon he's introducing me to his students: and twenty fresh young faces beam in my direction, teeth glistening from each! They're a charming-looking bunch and I talk for several minutes. But detecting that they would happily listen for much longer, I then urge them to forget my presence and conduct their session as normal, without anyone feeling any need to interrupt and translate just for my benefit. With their teacher sitting behind a small table to one side, the performances then begin with two young men presenting a scene from a play by Sam Sheppard. Once finished, they remain on stage and the famous director gives them feedback. He then encourages reflections from the audience. The nature of the subsequent discussion is a delight! Frequently the students interrupt each other, and their teacher, with strongly-felt points of view. The teacher fires questions back at them and answers come from all sides, so that the whole process appears to be considerably Socratic. These students are clearly not the slightest bit shackled, controlled, or held in subjugation. Their tutor is not on any student-strangling self-adulatory power-trip. They're free to let their creative impulses take wing and fly. The only ones who don't contribute are the very few, amongst the young women, who have come along to this actors' workshop done up like Hollywood starlets attending a première: who wear smart frocks, lengthy and extraordinarily well-conditioned hair, and rather too much make-up.

Unable to understand the students' rapid Greek, it's fascinating to find myself focusing strongly and solely upon their acting, judging the extent to which they're performing truthfully and how well they're faking the underlying motivations. Several fail and impose unnecessary burdens and heaviness upon the text, so that their performances appear false and laboured. In such cases the director has them repeat their scenes in a simpler manner, with the result that their work improves considerably. Then one young man, with a large silver ring in his left ear and a black and white Palestinian *keffiyeh*, or *Arafát* as such scarves are often referred to in Greece, arranged in stylish bohemian fashion upon his shoulders and chest, takes to the stage to deliver Tom's monologue from the end of 'The Glass Menagerie', by Tennessee Williams. He's about nineteen, black-haired, and classically good-looking. He takes a seat, places it centre-stage, and sits. For a long minute or so, he says and does nothing. Then slowly he raises his head to look into the audience. At first his face is completely still. But you can tell the character is thinking. And very quickly you can also see that he is feeling. The actor is taking himself into the character's heart and mind. He continues to take his time. And then very quietly he begins to speak of Laura. He moves his head just a little, and his hands barely at all, but we are all there with him, in his quiet confidence and his stillness, as he progresses through the speech. Emotion begins to pour forth, though subtly, because he's doing so little. The feeling is indicated by filling eyes, an occasional microscopic wobble of the chin, a slight faltering over a word, a barely perceptible choke in the throat. In Greek he comes to those gut-wrenching lines where Tom says, 'I pass the lighted window of a shop where perfume is sold. The window is filled with pieces of coloured glass, tiny transparent bottles in delicate colours, like bits of a shattered rainbow. Then all at once my sister touches my shoulder. I turn around and look into her eyes. Oh, Laura, Laura, I tried to leave you behind me, but I am more faithful than I intended to be!'

He fakes it brilliantly. Every one of us present is inclined to believe the scene real. When he ends, he deserves applause and I wait to see if the students will give it. They don't. But in lieu of audible acclaim his performance is followed by a noticeable stretch of utterly silent seconds, the affirming quiescence of respect and approval. The tutor too has been moved, and is slow to initiate discussion. When he does, he speaks in low and measured phrases, in tribute towards what we've all just witnessed. The student says almost nothing while his piece is then discussed. He seems to know that success in acting is quite distinct from the ability to hold forth in debate *about* acting, or about any other matter.

After one and a half hours of fascinating scenes and discussions I take my leave and say goodbye to a handful of the students on the theatre's front steps. For ten minutes or so I answer questions and try to give them something in return for what they've given me. As I look from face to face I catch such intense eyes, so wide open, so hungry! As soon as each sees that I've noted his or her keenness, they each pull back a little and deliberately narrow their eyes to hide their hunger. I impress upon them how lucky they are to have tutors who let their students' impulses soar, and as I leave them I rejoice in the certainty that this afternoon I've truly been in touch with the hearts and minds of aspiring and inspiring young Athenians.

Making my way through the centre of this busy city at about seven in the evening, I'm forcibly reminded of the years of political turbulence to which the young actor at the theatre referred earlier and also of my unnerving encounter at roughly the same time the previous night. All of the rushing traffic of Panepistimíou Street suddenly ceases to be, for somewhere, further back, vehicles have either been brought to a halt or been diverted. All the lanes of this busy wide street are suddenly empty and quiet. And then slowly, from afar, there comes the sound of a loud amplified chorus of male voices united in a marching song. Then, in the gloom of the distant road, several dozen strong lights appear. These prove to come from an array of policemen on motorbikes, heralding a large truck on which there are loud-speakers and an enormous structure that bears a message in Greek lettering to both sides of the road. The truck is in turn followed by forty or fifty large motorcycles which all sport massive identical flags, flying from rods that shoot from the rear of each bike to a height of some six or seven feet above their seats.

As this phalanx of motorbikes passes along the road, the riders or those sitting immediately behind them hurl handfuls of leaflets onto the tarmac. The papers land in thick bunches of twenty or thirty sheets, most of them being caught by the wind to blow all over the road and pavements and into the gutters. None of the hundreds of shoppers and passers-by who are all around reaches down to pick them up, though many have stopped to watch the spectacle. I toss a *'Yiatí?'* (Why?) to a young Greek beside me and he indicates that it's just something to do with the endless to-ings and fro-ings between Greece's two main political parties. 'Papandréou and Karamanlís! Just the usual! What can we do!' he shrugs. He really means to indicate to me the constant debate that there has been in Greece between PASOK and Néa Dimokratía, PASOK being headed at the time by Yiórgos Papandréou, and Constantínos Karamanlís having founded ND in 1974 (with his nephew Kóstas Karamanlís later being its leader until Antónis Samarás took the reigns of Néa Dimokratía in late 2009).

A varied route through the colourful maze of little back-streets which make up Athens's central shopping area takes me past three or four entirely separate ecclesiastical supply shops. I've already seen similar stores for the faithful in other areas of the city and am surprised to be finding yet more. The walls of each are covered with jigsaw-like arrangements of scores of *eikónes* (mostly modern reproductions), the air in each shop is heavy with the rich perfumes of fragrant candles, and suspended from the ceilings are dozens of little incense-burners in imitation gold or silver or bright shades of glass. All this ecclesiastical ornamentation lends mystery, magic, and theatricality to those devotional little corners, or *eikonostásia*, which many Greeks like to set up inside their homes. Unlike Christian or Catholic religious supplies stores in the West, the Greek Orthodox equivalents stock nothing for the faithful that we associate with sentimentality: no comforting religious frippery in shades of baby-blue and gentle pink, no soft soppy pastel pictures of saints holding to their breasts snow-white lambs or bunches of perfect roses or lilies. There's not a sign of juvenile kitsch in sight. Instead, the merchandise of the Greek ecclesiastical store has a scholastic and antique quality, an edge which is hard and firm, more masculine than feminine. And although much of it's mass-produced it doesn't seem so: these goods appear to have an authentic archaeological aspect, as if they've been taken from ancient and humble shrines high in the mountains. But close to the Metropolitan Cathedral there are a score of completely different ecclesiastical suppliers: small but very upmarket stores which stock a glittering array of highly expensive trappings not for the faithful but for churches and exclusive chapels. The shelves and windows of these shops sparkle with magnificent gold-embroidered liturgical vestments for the clergy, beautiful and finely-worked pieces of silver and gold altar ware, and even grand and colossal candelabras in silver, gold, or crystalline glass, to be suspended from church ceilings and Orthodox domes.

Like the black-clad Orthodox priests frequently seen walking Athens's streets, their salaries paid to them by the state, this city's many and varied church stores are an indication of how very strongly the Greek Orthodox religion is meshed with the nation's life. The Orthodox Church is the largest single land-owner in Greece, and many of its individual churches and monasteries are extremely wealthy, particularly the twenty communities of the large Mount Áthos peninsula, south-east of the city of Thessaloníki, all of which participate in an antique and cultish form of extreme Christianity that's existed on that peninsula since the 4th century CE. Despite objections from the EU and various women's groups, the monasteries of the 'Holy Mountain' continue to violate the universally recognised principle of gender equality and to strictly permit only men (and animals that are male!) to step foot anywhere upon their territory. In 2008 the bank accounts of the richest of these monasteries, Moní Vatopedíou, were found to contain in excess of two hundred million euros. Thought to be worth even more is the monastery's fortune in real estate. Experts in Greek property and finance have been reported as considering that Vatopedíou's total assets lie somewhere between 1,000 and 2,000 million US dollars, or, in other terms, between 1 and 2 *billion* dollars or between 700 million and 1,400 million euros. The wealth of this particular monastery was revealed when in 2008 Vatopedíou was found to have traded low-value land for valuable state property in a deal with Néa Dimokratía, a deal that is believed to have lost the Greek state at least 100 million euros. Two ND MPs subsequently resigned over the scandal and, as of mid 2013, the abbot of Vatopedíou, released on bail to Mount Áthos after three months in jail, awaits trial on charges of having incited officials to acts of perjury, fraud, and money-laundering.

The Orthodox Church is thus proven to hold and wield a great deal of power within Greece. Its wealth assures its control of the nation's moral compass. And the Orthodox Church is of course a strong force amongst those opposed to gay and lesbian rights. Its influence hinders gay men and lesbians from being out and open in the Greek military. And when on the island of Tílos in June 2008 a gay couple and a lesbian couple were married by the island's mayor, under the law of 1982 that introduced civil marriages but which didn't specify which sexes could be civilly married, the church was believed instrumental when in May 2009 the mayor was charged with breach of duty, and the marriages were later annulled by judicial authority. Furthermore, until 1982 the only marriages that were permitted in Greece (religious marriages) had to be conducted in religious forums.

It's estimated that about 98% of the population of Greece is of Greek descent and that roughly the same percentage of the population consider themselves Orthodox Christians. In other words, most people in Greece who are of Greek descent identify as members of the Christian Eastern Orthodox Church. Of the 2% of the population who do not think of themselves as Orthodox Christians, just over half identify as Muslim, and live mostly in the Greek part of Thrace, adjacent to Turkey; and just under a half belong to that mixed minority which is composed of Old Calendar Orthodox, of Jews, of Catholics, of Protestants, Mormons, Jehovah's Witnesses, and so on. However, regardless of what Greek citizens state when asked about their religion, a European Commission 'Eurobarometer Poll' in 2005 revealed that only 81% of Greeks actually believed there is a 'God', with 16% saying they believed in some sort of general spirit or life-force. Unfortunately only 3% of Greek citizens stated that they did not believe there is any sort of supernatural being or spirit-like life-force whatsoever. But Orthodoxy is such an integral part of Greek identity and traditional culture that heterosexual Greek atheists, who make up most of the non-believing 3%, think twice before breaking with religious tradition and marrying by way of a civil ceremony rather than in a church. The Eurobarometer Poll of 2012 showed that in the UK believers numbered 64% of the UK population. So why the near invisibility of ecclesiastical suppliers on British city streets, compared to the great number of them to be seen here in Athens? The answer is largely that Greeks have a far greater liking for objects of religious devotion, and that after the Poles, the Romanians, and the Portuguese, they're the most religiously observant people in the whole of Europe.

This intense religiosity is odd, however, existing as it generally does alongside the Greeks' enormous pride in their glorious classical past, the age of Ancient Greece. For it was this very form of religion, Christianity, that literally annihilated all of Greece's ancient gods and goddesses - Cháos, Zeus, Apóllon, Diónysos, Aphrodíte, Athená, and the whole colourful legion of them, along with every ancient semi-god and spirit - thus terminating Greece's classical era and plunging Athens into a darkness that lasted some 700 years. In 353 CE Roman Emperor Constantius II ordered the death penalty for anyone involved in sacrifices and the worship of 'idols', and the following year he began executing Hellenic priests. Two years later he ordered the destruction of all functioning Hellenic temples and the execution of all 'idolaters'. Throughout the following twenty years such brutal edicts and actions were repeated in different forms every few years or so, showing that Constantius clearly found it extremely difficult to stamp out Hellenic Polytheism, Greek 'paganism', belief in the many ancient Hellenic gods.

In 380 CE Theodósios I decreed Christianity to be the exclusive religion of the Roman Empire. But Hellenic Polytheism obviously still refused to go, because in 391 CE Theodósios was driven to prohibit anyone from even *looking* at *vandalised* statues of Greek gods! Two years later he banned the Olympic, Pythian, and Aktian games because of their traditional connection with the forbidden 'idolatry'. But despite such determined persecution, people would simply not relinquish their Hellenic gods, for, forty years later, in 435 CE, Theodósios II issued a further decree forbidding all 'pagan' worship. Two years later he ordered the 'purification' of the Parthenon, dedicating it to *Aghía Sofía* (Holy Wisdom) and transforming it in terms of function into a Christian church. Then during the following one hundred years Christianity finally succeeded in extinguishing Hellenic Polytheism. In 529 CE, Christianity drove the final nail into the coffin of Ancient Greece's religion when the Emperor Justinian ordered the closure of Athens's ancient Academy of Pláton, thereby stripping the city of even the study of Greek philosophy and thus severing the Greeks' final living link with their glorious past. Beset by self-righteous Christianity in this manner, Athens then all but disappeared from the pages of history.

In 1205 Athens's generally 'Frankish Period' began. The previous year the Latin knights of the Fourth Crusade (Venetians and French Franks) viciously and outrageously ransacked Constantinople, thereby completing the schism between the Catholic West and Orthodox East, splintering the Byzantine Empire and subsequently giving Athens (in 1205) to the Bergundian (Frankish) knights Othon de la Roche, succeeded by his brother Guy de la Roche, followed by Walter de Brienne and his descendants. When the Catalans seized power in 1311, under the protection of the Aragonese king Frederick II of Sicily, control passed to Roger Deslaur and then to Frederick's sons and other descendants. In 1388 control passed to the Florentine aristocrat Nerio Acciajuoli and descendants. When the Ottoman Turk Turahanoğlu Ömer Bey captured Athens in 1456, the ancient 'pagan' temple of *Athená Parthénos*, the Virgin Goddess, atop the Acrópolis, was at last relieved of its function as a Catholic cathedral. However, the Turkish occupiers very soon converted it into an Islamic mosque - although to their credit they did at least permit the Greeks to practise their Christian faith in churches elsewhere in the city.

The Hellenic uprising which eventually ousted the Turks from the Balkan Peninsula almost 400 years later was in character, inspiration, and intention substantially Eastern Christian Orthodox (or, specifically, 'Greek Orthodox'). And so once the peninsula had been reclaimed from Muslim control, Orthodoxy was severe in immediately making itself intrinsic to the life of the newly emerged nation. Even before young Otto arrived to take up his position as King, the Orthodox clerics of Athens had become inflamed by the efforts of missionaries of the nascent Greek Evangelical Church, initiated by one Jonas King, an American Presbyterian, to convert Greek schoolchildren from their Orthodox beliefs. Consequently, when Greece's first Constitution was drawn up in 1844, determined Orthodox clerics ensured the inclusion of a clause forbidding 'proselytism' and any other action against the country's official religion.

By 'proselytism' was meant, in essence, any attempt, direct or indirect, to intrude upon, undermine, or alter the religious beliefs of Orthodox Christians. Only proselytising on behalf of the national religion was to be permitted. The revised constitutions of 1864, 1911, and 1952, simply reproduced the clause of 1844, but during the Metaxás Régime (1936 to 1940) the rule was considerably hardened. From 1939 onwards anyone found 'proselytising' became liable to imprisonment, a fine of between 1,000 and 50,000 *drachmés*, and to police supervision lasting from six to twelve months. To encourage Greeks towards any belief system other than Orthodox Christianity had thus become a criminal offence. So, from the Metaxás Régime onwards, fear of being seen to draw people away from the official faith became a part of Greece's national *psyché*.

Following the end of the Júnta, the revised Constitution of 1975 (by which Greece is currently regulated) also prohibited 'proselytism' but defined it more generally and sat it alongside recognition of the inviolability of freedom of conscience and the right of citizens to practice any religion they might choose. Nevertheless, over a century of ingrained dread of supporting any belief system other than that of the dominant religion naturally continued on into the life of the republic. However, the Church's grip was seriously challenged when in 1993 a Greek Jehovah's Witness dared take his country to the European Court of Human Rights, in Strasbourg, claiming that his right to religious freedom had been violated. The Court heard that from 1936, when Mínos Kokkinákis had become a Jehovah's Witness, Greek police had arrested him for proselytism just over sixty times and on three occasions he had been jailed. The Court also observed that since 1975 a total of 4,400 Jehovah's Witnesses had been arrested in Greece, of whom 208 had been convicted. Furthermore, it was learnt that over the decades courts in Greece had found people guilty for such actions as having described Orthodox saints as only 'figures adorning the wall', for likening the Orthodox Church to 'a theatre, a market, or a cinema', and for having been so bold as to dare to give Orthodox priests certain printed materials along with recommendations that they should study and apply them!

Kokkinákis won his court case, the Greek government was required to pay him considerable costs and damages, and prosecutions for proselytising have dropped considerably since 1993. Nevertheless, Greece remains the only member of the European Union where proselytism is a criminal offence. And although since the EU ruling Greece's working definition of proselytism has been watered down in interpretation to mean affronting the dignity of others while introducing the content of another religion, there remains a strong feeling that any belief system other than that of the Orthodox Church bears the suspicion of being illegal.

In spite of early Christianity's success in stamping out the 'paganism' of ancient Greece and recent Christianity's retention of its grip upon the nation's beliefs, the old polytheism of ancient times has nevertheless remained to this day something of an inspiration to most Greek people. Greek children, like children all over the world, are fascinated by the heroes and characters of Greek legends - who are very often the gods and goddesses of Hellenic Polytheism. And every year thousands of visitors from other cultures pour over Greece's landscape to locate at almost every turn rocks, plains, valleys, mountains, and endless ruins connected with the land's colourful mythology. Meanwhile, academics from every corner of the globe continue to muse upon the beliefs of the ancients and to produce further learned theses. Thus the gods of ancient Greece live on, and, furthermore, despite the law against proselytism, in the course of the past 25 years their forbidden worship has been revived. The most significant revival occurred in 2005 when a group of 34 Athenian academics, writers, lawyers and other professionals formed *Ellínon Archeothrískon Ierón Somateíon* (The Holy Association of Greek Ancient Religion Believers), known in the West by the simplified acronym *Éllinais*. Remarkably, in 2006 this group, headed by three 'high priests', persuaded a Greek court to recognise *Éllinais* as a cultural association with a religious goal, a judgement which some have interpreted as having endorsed *Éllinais* as an official religion of Greece. Other groups of Hellenic Polytheists in Greece are The Supreme Council of Gentile Hellenes, he Greek Society of Attic Friends, The House of Thýrsos,

Dodecátheon, The Return to the Hellenes Movement, *Lávrys*, and The Apollonian Society. Hellenic Polytheist groups abroad are to be found as far afield as Australia.

In January 2007, at the Temple of Olympian Zeus, and in defiance of a government ban, *Éllinais* staged the first known polytheistic ceremony to be held publicly in Athens in 1,572 years - the first such ceremony since Theodósios banned 'pagan' worship in 435 CE. Beneath the soaring Corinthian columns of the Temple of Olympian Zeus the high priests of *Éllinais*, bearing flaming torches and dressed in ancient costumes, led a rite of hymns, dancing, and invocations lasting an hour and a half as they called on Olympian Zeus to bring peace to our planet. Then a year and a half later, atop the Acrópolis on a free-entrance Sunday in August 2008, *Éllinais* again hit international headlines when its members suddenly transformed themselves from seeming tourists into white-robed worshippers and before the Parthenon called upon the goddess Athená to protect the ancient sculptures that were shortly to be taken from the old Acrópolis museum to the sparkling new complex below. The fifteen-minute ceremony also involved an appropriately contemporary creed of world peace, ecological awareness, and the universal right to education. There was no ritual slaughter of animals, as practised in ancient times.

The President of the Society of Greek Clergymen has publicly dismissed all *dodecatheistés*, worshippers of the *Dodecátheon* (the twelve Olympian gods of ancient Greece), as 'ludicrous adherents of a dark religious past', 'a handful of miserable resuscitators of the old religious decadence' who 'try in obvious frivolity to reinstate the ancient delusion of the idols of darkness, that morbid myth of the pagan worship of the Twelve Olympians'. The observation that Orthodox priests have a strongly vested interest in other beliefs has often accompanied a simplified version of the above statement on its migration from a BBC webpage to over 7,000 other websites worldwide. But despite such pompous denunciations, Hellenic Polytheism in Greece continues to grow. In 2009 the first modern Hellenic temple, surrounded by statues of the gods of Ancient Greece, opened in verdant grounds beneath the Oraiókastro Forest, eight miles north of the city of Thessaloníki, and every year now in various parts of the Greek countryside hundreds gather with offerings of honey, milk, wine, and flowers to celebrate the Spring, the Harvest, traditional Hellenic weddings, the Equinox and Solstice, and rites and ceremonies, like the *Anthestéria*, in honour of the god Diónysos. Meanwhile Greek polytheists continue their call for the removal of all Christian churches which have been erected over or adjacent to ancient temples. They ask for a return to the ancient Olympiád calendar, so that years are not dated according to the Incarnation of Christ but with reference once again to the first Olympiád (776 BCE). And, more importantly, polytheists continue to call for the separation of the Orthodox church from the Greek state, so as to end the performance of Orthodox rites within state ceremonies, to end the payrolling of Orthodox clergy by the Greek state, and to bring to an end the inclusion of Christian indoctrination in the Hellenic education system.

Late this evening up against the little wall that surrounds the 11th century Byzantine church of Kapnikaréa in Ermoú Street, about a hundred young African men, presumably the very same ones who hawk handbags and counterfeit DVDs illegally on Athens's pavements every day of the week, and who sometimes appear at restaurant windows begging for food, have gathered with a large banner and a ghetto-blaster that's pumping out a very jolly form of indigenous African music. To these sounds some of the men are dancing, in a style involving traditional African tribal movements. Not a single one of the hundreds of Greeks out shopping tonight in busy Odós Ermoú pauses to watch the spectacle. The only ones who have stopped to enjoy it are a few winter tourists: three well-to-do middle-aged Chinese, bedecked in authentic-looking Burberry, avidly taking photographs of the men, half a dozen cheerful youngsters bubbling away in Spanish, and me.

The reason why no Greeks have stopped to watch could be that Africans have been an accepted and an ordinary part of the Greek scene for centuries. The memoirs of Panaghís Skouzés, recalling the period 1772 to 1796, tell of the many

'Ethiopian' workers who were to be seen in and around Athens in the decades preceding the War of Independence. On the Balkan Peninsula people of African origin had for long been referred to as *Aithíopes* (ay-THEE-o-pess), Ethiopians. The earliest record of this usage occurs in the Iliad and the Odyssey of Homer (c. 800 BCE) where Homer described the *Aithíopes* as a loyal and lordly people living worlds away, at the farthest limits of mankind, meaning all over the African continent. Later, Xenophánes (c. 570 to c. 475 BCE), Aeschýlos (c. 525 to c. 456 BCE), Iródotos (c. 484 to 425 BCE), Aristotéles (384 to 322 BCE), Ploútarchos (c. 46 to 120 CE), Philóstratos (c. 170 to c. 250 CE), and others wrote of the *Aithíopes* who lived amongst them, in the many towns and cities of Ancient Greece.

It's believed Africans began arriving in increasing numbers on the Balkan peninsula and on some of the Greek islands after Alexander the Great founded the city of Alexándreia, on Africa's northern coast, in 331 BCE. Africans crossed the Mediterranean usually as slaves, but some worked amongst the Greeks as 'freed-men', as soldiers, athletes, diplomats, acrobats and actors. Iródis Attikós (101 to 177 CE), the richest and most powerful man of Ancient Greece, cared for a young African named Mémnon in addition to his own children. Of his three foster-sons Mémnon is thought to have been his favourite and a handsome marble sculpture of his head, clearly African in appearance and created sometime between 150 and 160 CE, can be seen in the Altes Museum in Berlin. Other Ancient Greek depictions of *Aithíopes*, all clearly modelled upon living subjects, are to be found today in collections like those of the Musée du Louvre, the British Museum, and the Bibliothèque Nationale. And in a fragment of monologue, possibly from one of his comedies, the Greek dramatist Ménandros (c. 342 to c. 292 BCE) had one of his characters argue by reference to an African that a person's racial origin, or 'pedigree', or whatever fine monuments they might create, are irrelevant, and that when it comes to determining a person's true worth all that matters is whether or not that person is of a good nature. Assertively, and clearly very vexed, Ménandros's character declares to his mother:

This 'pedigree' will kill me, Mother! Don't insist
if you love me, on 'pedigree' at every word!
Whoever by inherent nature have no worth
these all in this take refuge: in their monuments,
and pedigrees . . . [But] the man whose natural bent is good,
he, Mother, he, though Aethiop, is nobly born!

回 回 回 回

11

Chasms, Canyons, & Strata

National Archaeological Museum;
Colourful Planet;
Kypséli;
Exárcheia;
Sýntagma Metró;
& The Academy.

It seems the average Greek wakes hungry for words. Each morning during breakfast television the front pages of no less than about twenty different daily newspapers are briefly presented to the eyes of the nation. And then pegged up on lines around the *períptera* (street kiosks), one sees even more newspapers than the main twenty. It's quite out of the ordinary that each day, in a country with a population of only just over eleven million people, Athens produces 21 political newspapers, 5 financial newspapers, and 15 sports papers - a total daily crop of 41! In addition, the capital churns out 9 weeklies, along with a smaller number of monthlies and semi-monthlies. Thessaloníki, Greece's second city, produces a further 10 dailies, 2 weeklies, and 3 monthlies, while various other towns, all over the country, also roll out their own newsprint! And this morning, in a little park off Panepistimíou Street, in three long white tents, which have been set up in the shape of the Greek letter Π (Pi), three rows of wide trestle tables running through each tent are laden with remaindered books. They're on sale at considerably reduced prices and the tents are literally packed with early morning shoppers, such that I can barely move for the number of people jostling to get close to the tables. This obvious reverence and hunger for the written word ought not to have surprised me, for Greeks were avidly carving epigrams, inscriptions, statements, and verses into all sorts of stones and other solid objects several thousand years ago.

The moment you enter the first room of the National Archaeological Museum, just north of Omónoia Square, you're presented with a breathtaking display of some of the finest pieces of Greece's ancient past: treasures excavated by Heinrich Schliemann between 1874 and 1876 from the tombs of Mycénae, gifts that were placed in Mycenaean graves as symbols of the high status of the deceased, and which today confirm to us the truth of Homer's description of Mycénae, in his *Iliáda*, as being 'rich in gold'. For most of the pieces that Schliemann unearthed range in date from 1600 to 1200 BCE: years approximately concurrent with that time during which it is believed Homer lived and worked.

As you stand at the entrance to the first gallery of the National Archaeological Museum you're arrested by the dramatic sight of a piece of spot-lit metal, gleaming brightly against a background of black velvet. It's a fine, thin, beaten sheet of gold, only slightly three-dimensional, depicting the sleeping face of a moustached older man with small but prominent jug-handle ears: it's the famous so-called 'Mask of Agamémnon', a death-mask, and 'so-called' because modern archaeological research suggests that this mask dates from 1550 to 1500 BCE which is earlier than the time during which it is thought Agamémnon lived. The Mycenaean exhibition which then immediately follows this initial presentation includes fine signet-rings, ceremonial vessels and other precious pieces of tableware, and daggers with elaborate handles made from gold, ivory, bone, and stone, with astounding inlaid decorations of gold, silver, and niello. These possessions of the ancient lords of Mycénae mark the beginning of a grand exhibition of sublime antiquity, for nearly everything in Greece's National Archaeological Museum is extraordinary. As you wander, overwhelmed, through over fifty different rooms, you gaze upon products of unbelievable workmanship created as long ago as six thousand years.

Because the ancient Greeks made many things out of materials that were simply imperishable, we thus have them with us today and may enjoy an inheritance that consists

of a vast array of all kinds of antique and classical earthenware, jewellery, armour, and statuary. In this museum there
are many pieces likenesses of which I've not seen in any
of the museums of Paris, London, Rome or Berlin. Four
reconstructed ancient vessels, in different shades of earthenware, stand like plump alert ducks, their spouts formed as
of curious face-like structures with ears. Thousands of years
old they're extremely beautiful and were clearly useful,
probably functioning like large gravy boats. A limestone
vase, possibly ritual and probably sculpted in Minoan Crete,
bears three big handles, one on each side and one at the
rear, that are are so beautifully curling, tapering, volute,
and delicate that they seem to have come to rest like large
and lissom sea-horses upon the vase's lip. Another curious
vessel, rather like an intricate candelabra, consists of a kind
of elegant and beautifully decorated upturned bowl from
which seventeen flutes or funnels rise up like muscular but
graceful arms to then gently open like flowers, perhaps to
receive candles, or oil for burning, though the actual purpose
of this abnormous piece remains unsure. There are several
magnificently decorated and burnished ceramic pots which
are as high as a tall man and very rotund. The kilns inside
which they were fired must have been immense! One of
them, a funerary urn dated at around 750 BCE and retrieved
from Kerameikós cemetery, is banded with grazing fawns
and images of the laying out of the dead, as well as various
intricate geometric designs including the famous 'Greek fret'
or *méandros* pattern, the thick black line that travels along
in a repeated motif of right-angles, named after the path
of the River Méandros in Asia Minor and known in every
land as 'the Greek motif'. The life-size or larger-than-life-
size statuary and votive and funerary reliefs that conclude
the tour of this museum astound with their almost living,
seemingly animated and natural workmanship. The faces,
limbs, and bodies of the *koúroi* and *kórai* (male and female
sculptures), are sensuous, ravishing, and exquisite, as are
the myriad gentle folds of the gowns and garments draped
delicately upon them, appearing almost not to have been
carved from hard stone. This is the original genius! Here is

the gifted work that so inspired all the sculptors of Italy and the Renaissance and so much of the rest of the world.

I'm largely alone in this vast treasure-house of Greek antiquities but for two parties of young Greek school-children, several other individual visitors, and a large and annoying party of Chinese 'suits'! These 'suits' are businessmen on an organised trip, probably taking a morning off from some conference. They all seem nearly identical: dark suits, white shirts, dark ties, black hair all trimmed short and parted on one side, with most of them wearing barely-noticeable pairs of spectacles with thin gold, titanium, or rimless frames. One of their number carries on his shoulder a very large and sophisticated video camera. Footage is clearly being taken for the records, perhaps for some in-house documentary or television report. But above all of these gentlemen, I am pleased to note, there towers an impressive and handsome Greek of about forty years of age, and who is also in a suit. As the group moves from one room to another, this Greek guide delivers information confidently and rapidly to one short and plump member of the Chinese party who stands by his side, but who stares into infinity as he listens, looking for all the world like a terrified schoolboy whose brain is about to pop. The moment the stream of Greek ceases, a stream of Chinese begins. Surveying his party, the plump little interpreter flows in Chinese as rapidly as has the guide! It would seem that this gentleman from the People's Republic of China possesses superb abilities in comprehending and translating Modern Greek. Apparently the Chinese, Japanese, and Koreans adore Greece, in recent years they have 'discovered' it, and they are now as infatuated with its ancient history as European scholars have been ever since the Renaissance. I wonder if it could possibly be that some strange and ironic need to be linked with the birthplace of democracy is what has triggered all the recent exchanges of contracts and trade that there have been between China and Greece, and which, in turn, have led to a considerable influx of Chinese immigrant-workers to Athens.

In a quiet upstairs gallery I fall into conversation with a studious-looking Greek woman from Thessaloníki, probably in her forties, and like me enjoying a rather 'academic' sojourn in the capital. I eventually steer our delightful conversation towards the puzzling economic situation and learn that on her wage she can only afford to eat at some inexpensive café, *estiatório*, or *tavérna* three or four times a month, at the most, and that more than once a week would be impossible. However, she adds that a considerable number of her friends go out many more times than she does. She tells me that use of the *pistotikí kárta* (the credit card) is widespread and many of her friends have simply chosen to live on credit, or, more correctly, in debt. When I express concern she simply smiles and shrugs: 'It's what they choose to do. It's their choice. What can you do?' Unfortunately, our conversation is then rather gracelessly ended by a request for silence from a museum attendant whose expressions during my quiet discussion with the lady from Thessaloníki have suggested that he has not enjoyed overhearing much of what has been said: for during the last half hour, on this quiet winter's morning, there has been absolutely no one else in this upper area of the building for us to disturb! There has been only himself, me, and the one other visitor.

After lunch in the museum's peaceful courtyard garden, filled with trees and further ancient gold-stone statuary, positioned against the enlivening crimson paintwork of a cloister-like arcade, it's time to leave Ancient Greece and to return to the reality of modern Athens. As I emerge from the National Archaeological Museum and step again into the sunlight, there appear between Ernst Ziller's soaring great portico columns perhaps some of the ugliest and grimiest multi-storey *polykatoikíes* (apartment blocks) in the entire city. The contrast between the two worlds couldn't be more harsh or more unfortunate.

I head north to the poor district of Victória, home to an estimated 30,000 economic migrants, to visit *Polýchromos Planítis* (Colourful Planet), Athens's sole gay and lesbian bookshop. Online I've seen photographs of their showroom, and of considerable gatherings of writers and readers on their premises, but in little Antoniádou Street there's no immediate sign of any bookshop at all. The usual Athenian splatterings of graffiti have occurred on various vulnerable walls up and down the street, but there's no great out-and-proud sign to be seen directing people to a gay and lesbian bookstore. This may be because the road is largely residential. It's very plain, not too untidy, and apart from a couple of photocopying and printing offices the frontages at ground level are nearly all closed and shuttered. But persistence at every entrance eventually brings me to a little button labelled *Polýchromos Planítis*, sitting on an intercom board in one of the porches of the apartment blocks. At least when I press it, the adjacent lock immediately clicks open. And then up in the foyer one of the doors to the ground-floor flats has the shop's name upon it. I enter, find there are no other customers, and see that the books are set out in the large front room, overlooking the street - in the room which if this apartment weren't being used as a shop would most probably be its living-room.

Colourful Planet stocks hundreds of different titles and nearly all of them are in Greek, a sizeable number being translations from originals written in English and other languages. Spotting a beautifully bound Greek translation of E. M. Forster's 'Maurice', I ask the assistant if he could possibly direct me to novels of comparable quality by Greek writers. He doesn't point instantly to a particular section, nor does he quickly pluck out half a dozen titles from here and there, but instead he slowly and very carefully scans the many shelves, clearly cogitating and considering, until after several minutes he produces a book which I notice has been published by Colourful Planet. I congratulate him on the impressive quality of its printing and binding, and then ask if he could possibly recommend a second Greek gay novel of similarly high literary quality. He raises his eyebrows and seems amused. No doubt, as I'm asking him in English, he's wondering how on earth this visitor is going to decipher these works. But after a couple of minutes of further perusal, he hands me another. In the end I purchase both his second offering, 'Something Very Personal' by Iosíf Alygizákis, and the translation of 'Maurice', in the great hope that one day my Greek will allow me to read both.

A little more conversation reveals that Colourful Planet is seldom busy and that they don't actually need the locked door or the safety provided by the intercom, but by being tucked out of the way as they are the monthly rental can be kept low. I learn that this collection of gay and lesbian literature is the largest in all of Greece, and people access it from all over the country, mostly via its Internet site, not that the eleven million Greeks in Greece, of course, are all craving gay and lesbian reading material. In 2005 the UK Treasury and the Department of Trade and Industry completed a survey to allow the British government to consider the financial implications of the Civil Partnerships Act. It was concluded that there were approximately just over three and a half million gay and lesbian people in the United Kingdom, roughly 6% of the entire population. So, because of the domination of the Orthodox Church within Greece, as well as the prevalence of very tight familial and traditional constraints, it's reasonable to assume that the number of gays or lesbians willing and able to be who they are in this land is probably considerably less than 6%. A good number no doubt forsake their innate homosexual reality to adopt an inauthentic heterosexual lifestyle, for the convenience of it. But even if the officially estimated figure is halved, to as little as just 3% of the Greek population, that's still a lot of Greek gays and lesbians who would benefit from access to supportive literature. As the entire population of Athens, including the outer suburbs, is currently just under four million, it follows that there are likely to be between 120,000 and 240,000 gay men and lesbians resident in this city. Unfortunately, most of them are 'invisible', or 'in the closet', fearful of the repercussions of being honest about their sexuality. It's for this reason that the organisers of the annual Athens Pride celebrations have acknowledged, or possibly warned, in their literature, that 'We live in Athens, Thessaloníki, Pátra and Irákleion, but we also live in Métsovo, Souflí, Istiéa and Ierápetra. We are teenagers and adolescents, and we are retired. We belong to all social classes. We are communists, right-wingers, anarchists, liberals, and socialists. We are as often artists, teachers, policewomen, and soldiers, as we are hairdressers and truck drivers. We are workers, we are employers, and we are amongst the unemployed. We are by your side, because we are everywhere.'

In all the many mainstream bookshops which delight me here in Athens, I haven't found any sections headed 'Gender', 'Sexualities', 'Gay and Lesbian', nor even, so far, just 'Erotic' - although a good number of the many street kiosks sport soft-porn magazines with sexual images upon their covers. The gay liberation movement in Greece is in its infancy. It also strikes me, as I head further north towards the Kypséli district, that in nine days of walking the streets of Athens I haven't yet noticed a single obvious gay man or overt lesbian, although there must be some somewhere. By and large and during working hours it appears that Greek gays and lesbians generally dress and behave in a way which makes them indistinguishable, 'invisible' - to the new arrival at least. Do Greek lesbians ever divert from the long glamorous tresses that help make the thousands of Athenian women on the streets so very attractive? There must be some women somewhere here who prefer short no-nonsense haircuts. And certainly, few men in Athens wear their hair beyond the traditional and masculine short-back-and-sides. Similarly, it would seem that homosexual people in Greece choose not to show obvious affection towards one another in public areas. However, photographs of the Athens Pride events, which have been held each June in recent years, show that for a few hours each year minority sexualities become unmistakably visible in the heart of the capital as thousands of Greek gay men and lesbians, as well as many heterosexual supporters, parade directly in front of the Greek parliament building.

Kypséli's Fokíonos Négri is the first street in Athens in which I discover a few empty spaces where fairly recently there were clearly shops or cafés, and of those businesses in this vicinity remaining active most are largely empty at three o'clock this afternoon. No doubt they'll be busier in the evening, but it's good to see that clearly not everyone in Greece at this time is choosing to live on credit or in debt. And this locality surely provides a good measure of average Athenian behaviour because the population here is both great in density and considerably mixed in ethnicity. Kypséli is certainly the most thickly populated municipal district in all of Greece, and some Greeks claim it's one of the most densely populated districts on Earth. In Greek the name Kypséli means 'beehive', although it can't have been foreseen before the 1950s, when Kypséli still consisted of well-spaced one- to three-storey detached homes in quiet leafy streets, that by the late 70s this district would indeed have been transformed into something very closely resembling a human beehive, with thousands of people stacked cheek-by-jowl in almost endless concrete *polykatoikíes* as high as seven storeys and seldom less than five.

Fokíonos Négri is a long wide dog-leg of an avenue that now has a grassed area running down its centre where once a stream flowed from the nearby hills of *Tourkovoúnia* (The Turkish Mountains). The stream is now underground and the grass, trees, and park benches in the centre of the avenue are bounded on both sides firstly by wide pavements and then by the fringes of cafés and restaurants, along with occasional shops and other businesses. Fokíonos Négri thus has something of the feel of a pedestrianized Parisian boulevard, although unfortunately it's now become a rather jaded one. But although on this beautiful sunny winter's afternoon this street is almost deserted and lifeless, Fokíonos Négri provides another rare and valuable oasis for the people of Athens: a quiet and peaceful avenue so wide that, today, the cafés and restaurants along its northern side luxuriate in late-afternoon sunshine, while nearly all the places on its cold and dark side are empty.

At this hour of the afternoon most of the shops in the vicinity are closed and all the balconied canyons north and south of Fokíonos Négri are largely empty. So one is left noticing only the 'architecture' and the strong element of scruffiness and carelessness that lies all about Kypséli's streets. Its buildings appear to have been rammed together in *cháos*, so that there's hardly a hint of the elegance that can still be found in some other parts of the city. The deeper I penetrate into the area's back streets, the narrower the roads become, the greater the litter that's strewn about, and the more broken or unnavigable are the pavements. Above these streets, however, life appears to be going on happily enough. Balconies are crammed with flourishing plants and shrubs, and gigantic awnings protect people within the apartments both from the heat and, presumably, from the gazes of their neighbours, for the awnings are now all fully drawn even though it's the middle of winter.

But even Kypséli brings joy. While heading back through side streets to Fokíonos Négri, I come upon a small and rare corner of unused land, a patch where either nothing has been built, rather amazingly, or something has long since been removed and not yet been replaced. The ground is ablaze with lantana! Four or five bushes are afire with hundreds of hemispherical clusters of tiny brightly-coloured florets ranging from brilliant yellow, through orange, to crimson; or from white, through brilliant saffron, to purple; and regardless of the combination, every floret of every flower has an inner well of deep and gorgeous orange. When I was six and growing up in Fiji, I used to walk home from school through hills that were often cloaked in lantana and their mosaic-like composite flowers always brought me to a halt. I'd stand there beholding them with wonder. Where there was lantana there was something of 'heaven': for lantana brought bees, birds, and butterflies in profusion. And perhaps, as for these creatures, it was not just the appearance of the tiny florets that was so attractive, but also under strong sun the heady bergamot- or citrus-like fragrance of both the lantana's leaves and its flowers. I used to pick a leaf, tear it in two, lift the parts to my nose, and become intoxicated! The smell was enchanting, exquisite, but pungent, and even slightly repellent. Little did I know then what a beautiful evil I was fiddling with! Lantana is native to the American tropics but over the last four centuries it's been introduced as the gorgeous ornamental plant that it is to similarly warm climates all over the Earth - and hence its thriving here on a scraggy abandoned corner in deepest Kypséli. I never knew way back then in Fiji that every part of this alluring plant is poisonous to animals and humans. But here it is, on this scruffy little Athenian street corner, glittering orange, yellow, crimson, white, and purple in a shaft of golden late afternoon sunlight and filling the air with its intoxicating aroma. Even the ugliest back-streets of Athens offer touches of exotica.

Resting for half an hour on a park bench in Fokíonos Négri, I try to guess the languages being spoken by those passing by: Pakistanis; Turks; Arabs; Africans from Senegal, Nigeria, Cameroon, and Eritrea; Albanians; Poles; Bulgarians; and of course Greeks. When the communist and officially atheist régime in Albania began to lose power in 1991, Greece suddenly experienced a massive influx of immigrants from its north-western neighbour, as well as from Bulgaria and other Balkan states. About three-quarters of these immigrants were young male workers who, owing to their willingness to work longer hours and for less pay, were more attractive to employers in Greece than native workers, while at the same time, Greek workers were unwilling to do poorly-paid temporary jobs or to hold positions that didn't conform to standard working hours or come with social security. However, although everyone in Greece knows that most immigrants are Albanian, sitting here on Fokíonos Négri it seems otherwise. Africans, for example, appear to be numerous, because the extreme darkness of their skin really makes them stand out against the rest. The perception then that Greece has been somewhat flooded by Africans has caused alarm. But statistics on children in Greek primary schools indicate that the real proportions of immigrants in Greece at this time are otherwise. Non-Greek primary school-children are chiefly Albanian (there are over 100,000 Albanian primary school-children in total), followed by roughly 7,000 Bulgarian children, 5,000 Romanians, 2,000 Georgians, and then roughly a thousand each of Russians, Poles, Indians, Pakistanis, Armenians, Egyptians, Syrians, Moldavians, Ukrainians, and Filipino children. No doubt, if the young African men and women who are to be seen on Athens's streets today remain in Greece and have families, then their African offspring will begin to feature in the statistics too, but for the moment Africans barely have a presence.

Moving south from Kypséli, toward towering Lykavittós and into the northern fringe of Exárcheia, my spirits begin to lift. Yes, here in Exárcheia there's even worse scruffiness than in Kypséli, and a great deal more graffiti, but there's also an abundance of obvious creativity and a wealth of pleasing stimuli. Along the way, in different parts, I discover three separate *bouzoúki*-makers in dusty little workshops; each surrounded by an array of different woods, knives, brushes, various other tools, and all sorts of bottles of resins and spirits. These little shops have clearly been here for two or three decades, maybe longer. I stop at one and watch an old craftsman at work, holding the long neck of a *bouzoúki* upwards while he hunches over to scrape at its little belly with a tiny manual plane, all the while intently monitoring and controlling his movements with the help of a large lighted magnifying visor, strapped to his head. His studio is silent. I'd have expected it to be full of the music produced by his magnificent instruments, a little radio or CD-player sounding from some corner, but all that can be heard are the people and cars passing along the street outside. He lifts his head and greets me. He's probably in his sixties. I ask how many instruments, roughly, he's made in his life-time. He shrugs his shoulders, he has no idea. 'Ah, many, many!' he replies, pointing round the walls at the dozen or so completed instruments on display. There are *bouzoúkia*, ouds, *baglamádes*, *lýres*, violins, and he introduces me to two I don't recognise, a *tzourás* and a *sázi*. I note that in none of these workshops that I've come across in Exárcheia have I seen an apprentice, or any instrument-maker younger than half a century. Let's hope they exist somewhere in this city, and that Greeks won't soon be entirely reliant on the *bouzoúkia* that have Japanese and Chinese brand names emblazoned on their little bellies, even though they're said to be instruments of considerable quality.

A rather odd 'square' comes into view. It looks like one large vacant lot, a demolition site in an unusual state of transition. It's all reddish earth which has been very simply landscaped into rounded areas that are separated by winding shingle paths. In the reddish soil there are small trees, no more than three or four feet high, all carefully tied to an odd assortment of different stakes, rods, and poles. In one corner of this nascent park there's a makeshift shed, painted in bright colours like a roadside café in Cuba. I've stumbled upon one of those few 'squares' in Athens which defiant Athenians have wrested from the control of the authorities.

In trying to lessen the number of cars parked on the streets of this city, the planners have demolished small pockets of adjacent buildings with the intention of erecting multi-storey car-parks, but many of the city's citizens will have no truck with such schemes. They argue, with considerable sense, that the provision of such multi-storey car-parks will only magnify the influx of vehicles into an already choked and strangulated city-centre. So instead they wish for green spaces and trees, verdant health-giving 'lungs', where people can escape the confines of little else except cafés and apartments. This *Párko Navarínou* is a disused car-park that's been hijacked by determined activists and amateur gardeners, and the 'Cuban shed' over in the corner acts partly as their watch-tower, enabling them to be ever on-site and to instantly summon the support of fellow residents should bulldozers, council workers, or the police dare to try to take the ground back.

Just feet away from this inspiring communal endeavour is yet another fabulous Greek bookshop, 'Saválas'. It's laid out on several levels and in an open area at the back of the ground floor, in a part presumably used for recitals, there stands a lustrous and resplendent grand piano, in rich mahogany. Then as I move closer to the heart of town, I find yet even more fine bookshops. Just inside the front door of 'Papasotiríou' is a magnificent and immense mural, covering the entire wall behind the row of tills. It's about seven metres in width and it arches to a height of roughly five. It's a massive and splendid reproduction, in vivid colours, of Raphael's 'School of Athens', from the Vatican Museum. Here, in the land that fathered them, are depicted Pláton, Aristotéles, Pythagóras, Dioghénis Sinopéfs (Sinopeus), Efklídis (Euclid), Irákleitos, Epíkouros, and others. How apposite and fitting that this bookshop has 'requisitioned' Raphael's famous painting of many of Ancient Greece's finest thinkers. The centre of the store is an ocean of books, all in Greek, with many in high piles laid out on wide low parallel tables running all the way down to the back of the shop. All around are floor-to-ceiling bays of shelves packed with further titles. And this, as in a good number of other such bookshops here in Athens, is only one worth. Upstairs there's more.

At 7.30 I rendezvous with Andréas inside Sýntagma Station, to see the exhibition there of some of the many artefacts exhumed during the laying down of the Metró through this part of the ancient city. The boring of the Metró tunnels in the years leading up to the Athens Olympics of 2004 was subject to continuous archaeological monitoring and as a result a great many treasures were excavated. Within Sýntagma Station the initial floor below street-level comprises a wide and spacious exhibition hall, at the centre of which escalators connect with the platforms and trains beneath. The full length and nearly the entire height of one wall of this exhibition space reveals the strata of the ancient city, exactly as the tunnellers found it. Today this stratified wall, displayed behind floor-to-ceiling glass, looks as if a giant knife has been drawn cleanly through the earth, with all the soil and its contents that lay to one side of the great cut having been removed to allow the creation of the multi-floor chamber that is now Sýntagma Station. Thus here, in this great cross-section of Athenian earth, is now displayed evidence of an ancient sculpture foundry; a *nekrotafeío* dating back to sub-Mycenaean and Byzantine times, including a rectangular grave, sliced in half by the tunnellers; a baths complex dating back to Roman times; a part of the Peisistranian Aqueduct; the bed of the lost Iridanós River; and an ancient road that led from the gates of Athens to Messogaía. And standing proud in fine glass cabinets on the marble floor of this hall are majestic antique pots and other ceramics discovered during the digging. Thus today's Athenians, passing up and down via the escalators of Sýntagma Station, literally and daily ascend and descend through the stratified remains of 3,000 years of their city's history.

Emerging back into Sýntagma Square and the Athens of the 3rd millennium, Andréas and I pause before the stern-faced pair of *évzones* who stand guard at the Tomb of the Unknown Soldier, in the forecourt of Greece's 'Parliament of the Hellenes', or the *Voulí*, as it's known, the building that has featured regularly in news bulletins all around the globe since Greece's financial troubles were announced. The two young guards are dressed in an impressive uniform derived from that of *kléftes* (brigands) and mountain fighters of the Greek War of Independence. This uniform features pomponed red-leather shoes called *tsaroúhia* (pronounced *charoúkia*), white tights with black garters, a high-collared dark-blue jacket that tapers into a very simple kilt, a large scarlet cap with a long black tassel, and a lethally bayoneted rifle. This is the *évzones'* winter uniform: in summer the thick dark-blue jacket is replaced by a lighter one, of khaki. On ceremonial occasions they wear the famous white *foustanéla* of 400 pleats, one for each year of the Turkish Occupation. This evening, as darkness descends, the impressive height and handsome looks of these two surely hand-picked young men are enhanced by the fine *Voulí* illuminated and glowing gold behind them.

Designed by the Bavarian Friedrich von Gärtner, architect to Ludwig I of Bavaria, who also designed the Royal Palace in Bad Reichenhall and the Bavarian State Library in Munich, amongst others, the *Voulí* was originally the palace of young Otto and Amalía. Construction began in 1836 and was completed in 1847, although if those who thankfully knew better had not very firmly denied Otto his wishes, then something akin to this structure would unfortunately have been erected for the young king and his queen directly upon the Acrópolis. In 1909, long after Otto and Amalía fled from Greece, this palace suffered a serious fire and the royal family of that time moved to what later became the residence of today's largely ceremonial President of the Hellenic Republic, one block away, on Heródou Attikoú Street. In 1934, fully restored, the palace overlooking Sýntagma Square (Constitution Square) appropriately became the seat of the Greek parliament, and thereafter the object and destination of almost every protest march and demonstration in Athens.

We hurry in the diminishing light of early evening past the imposing and exquisite Academy of Athens, one third of 'The Athenian Trilogy', sometimes known as 'The Neo-Classical Trilogy', those three imposing buildings of Athens University which were designed by Theophilus Hansen and his brother Christian over the course of the mid to late 19th century. While fine statues of Athená and Apóllon surmount two high and free-standing columns in front of the Academy, and on either side of the main entrance there sit sculptures of Socrátes and Pláton, on each of the six great Ionic columns of the Academy's majestic central portico we note single letters writ large in black spray-paint, creating the exhortation 'R-E-S-I-S-T'. Students regularly occupy and protest within Athens's central university buildings and Andréas informs me that the word R-E-S-I-S-T has been on the Academy's columns now for some considerable period of time. Although this building is one of the great sights of Athens, and right in the heart of the working city, the authorities have clearly let the injunction remain. Above the columns, on the pediment over the entrance to the Academy, is a stunning multi-figured sculptural decoration similar to that which 2,000 years ago decorated the pediment of the Parthenon. It includes a representation of the birth of Athená, sculpted meticulously in the round despite the fact that high up on the pediment no one can view it from behind. In the mid 1800s the building's architects thus respected the ancient Greek belief that pedemental figures should appear as perfect from the unviewed rear as from the front: for humanity may only gaze up and see the outward surfaces of such sculptures, but the gods can see everything! Today graffiti like the call to R-E-S-I-S-T remain fully viewable upon even Athens's finest landmarks due to a similar form of respect: modern Greek regard towards the free expression of popular ideas in the public arena.

We press on to a little *ouzerí* in Exárcheia, where, *ouzerí* generally being simple restaurants serving *oúzo* and so forth along with fairly basic dishes, Andréas direct from work in his smart suit, striped shirt and tie, with fine leather satchel in hand, looks distinctly out of place - a seeming profit-driven capitalist about to dine amongst the likes of socialists, communists, and anarchists! All the men seated about us are casually if not scruffily dressed and are either bearded or stubbled. The women sitting amongst them are just as relaxed and without pretension in self-presentation. And so this liberal company galvanizes my determination to seek from Andréas this evening further answers to my vexing questions regarding Greece's economy, and where all the apparent wealth is coming from.

But very soon we are unfortunately hurtling headlong towards a heated debate about gay liberation! I was aware from the outset that Andréas was divorced but not that he was gay. When now he confides to me his sexuality, I wrongly assume he supports gay rights, and very soon he's telling me categorically that 'Gay liberation will never happen!' and not just in Athens but anywhere on earth! To my simple statement that it's happened already, and substantially, in certain countries, he asks why then in those countries has he never seen a significant number of gays and lesbians walking around the streets holding hands or snogging in public 'just like heterosexuals do'! He suggests that if there had been any real progress in gay liberation in any country at all, then one would constantly see gays and lesbians being intimate with one another in public! My blood begins to boil. I can't believe the nonsense I'm hearing. But my highly educated and very articulate Greek friend rolls on! His next argument is that homosexuality will never be accepted 'in any civilised society on earth' because nudity isn't! For nudity, he reminds me, has usually to be practised in hidden places, on certain beaches or in certain woods or in the privacy of people's homes or special hotels. It will forever be thus, he exclaims, and therefore homosexuality can similarly never expect widespread public acceptance. The strange processes of 'logic' behind this thinking irk me intensely, and I wonder to what extent Andréas is taking advantage of my polite wish not to allow this meal to turn into a full-blooded row and the end of our acquaintance.

When I learn not only that my Greek dinner-companion, previously married to a Greek woman, is gay but that he has opted for a long-distance relationship with a Frenchman who lives and works in France, I choose not to point out to him that he has not, instead, embraced a real, dynamic, day-to-day relationship with a gay person within his own country, nor even a non-Greek member of the same sex who resides on his own doorstep, here in Athens. I choose also not to dwell on the fact that his ex-wife, and his two sons, both of whom are now grown-up, apparently have no idea at all that their ex-husband and father is gay - because Andréas has deliberately chosen not to declare! Instead he has opted to keep it all a secret. And I suspect that when his French boyfriend visits Athens occasionally, at which time I understand he stays in a city-centre hotel where Andréas joins him, the two most certainly do not walk around Andréas's hometown by day or night holding hands, gazing into each other's eyes, and indicating to all and sundry, dangerous bigots included, that they're a gay couple!

I choose instead to keep my powder dry, for tonight at least, and my contributions to the rather heated debate that we have prove sufficiently restrained for Andréas to feel comfortable enough as the evening draws to a close to produce from his fine leather satchel an envelope of photographs which he says he would very much like to share with me. Perhaps this is his way of trying to smooth over the tension that has arisen during the course of the meal. The photographs are all shots of a recent wedding in a local Orthodox Church in which Andréas is clearly extremely proud to have played the role of *koumbáros*, best man to the groom. As he innocently and enthusiastically explains to me some of the charming customs of the colourful Orthodox wedding rite, Andréas clearly has no conception whatsoever of the shameful and glaring incongruence of his delight in his closeted participation in such a ceremony alongside his personal sexual behaviour! I also understand why this man has never dared set foot inside the Colourful Planet Bookshop and why when I showed him my copy of 'Something Very Personal', a gay novel of which he knows nothing of course, he only sneered.

So at the end of my day's wanderings in the canyons of Kypséli and my subsequent witnessing of the strange thought-processes of one highly intelligent gay professional, I return to my hotel-room rather dejected. I'm quite sure that not all gay Greeks are closeted, or as closeted, but in terms of sexual politics and liberation it's pretty obvious that Greece lies only a few rungs above its Middle Eastern neighbours.

▨ ▨ ▨ ▨

12

Identity

National Historical Museum,
Hellenism & the Greek language;
the 'collared dogs';
the Sírios;
Voúla & Vouliagméni;
Eléni Péta & Thodorís Oikonómou.

O n my way to the National Historical Museum, I pause in
the long white tents in the small square off Panepistimíou
Street and find that this morning they're at least three times as
packed with Greeks hungry for cut-price books as they were at
the same time yesterday. Twenty-four hours ago the tables were
all piled high: this morning three quarters of those books have
gone and lots of empty spaces indicate that some have sold out.
The crowd jostles desperately for those that remain. All along
the edges of the trestle tables mainly older Greeks stand three or
four deep, reaching forward, grasping, reading, turning pages
this way and that. I manage to edge my way in, only about ten
feet or so but just enough to see that the queue of those waiting
before the cashiers stretches the entire length of the other side of
the tent, some thirty metres or so in length, and almost everyone
in the line is holding an armful of books. So rather than getting
stuck in that queue for half an hour or even longer, I turn and
force myself against the incoming tide. But battling hard against
the contagion and pressing on up Panepistimíou Street, regret
almost tugs me back. For I've thrown aside the chance to
purchase an impressive hard-back book on Theodorákis, a
volume featuring descriptions of all his works to date, dozens
of interesting photographs, and all of the poetry that he's set to
music - all going for only five euros.

Greece's National Historical Museum is housed in the old parliament building, the *Palaiá Voulí*, a stately neo-classical Bavarian structure designed by François Boulanger and erected in 1858 in Kolokotróni Square. Previously on this site, but burnt down in 1854, stood a grand mansion which provided temporary accommodation for young King Otto, before he moved to the even grander provisional quarters in Klafthmónos Square. Today in front of the National Historical Museum there stands a fine bronze equestrian statue of Theódoros Kolokotrónis, Greek general and significant liberator in the war against the Turks. Inside the museum a considerable array of exhibits illustrates the extraordinarily chequered and dramatic history that Greece has endured since the Frankish rule of the 13th, 14th and 15th centuries, particularly the long centuries of domination by the Ottoman Turks; the Greek War of Independence, of 1821 to 1829; the resulting imposition of Bavarian and Danish kings; the Greco-Turkish war of 1897, in which Greece lost territory south of Thessalía; the surge of 1912 in which the city of Salonica (Thessaloníki) and much of western Macedonía was liberated from Ottoman occupation; the subsequent alignment in 1913 with other Balkan states against fellow-Balkan Bulgaria; the First World War; the catastrophic Asia Minor Campaign, of 1919 to 1922; the 1940 battle against the Italians on the Albanian border; and, from 1941 to 1945, Greece's horrendous occupation by Nazi Germany. The museum is thus rich in grand paintings and mementoes of this nation in conflict.

Many of the images on display feature those warriors of earlier times who dressed comfortably and casually in loose open-necked blouses and *foustanélas*, while others depict more recent soldiers in khaki jackets and breeches, on their heads French-style *képis*, each with a plume of feathery tassel, and upon their feet red *tsaroúhi* leather clogs, bearing the large black pompons that were so very handy for cleaning off mud and filth. And like some of their predecessors these more recent soldiers are often shown brandishing rifles, with knives tucked into their belts. Of particular interest to some visitors are George Byron's sword and helmet, mementoes of his presence in Messolónghi in 1824, only months after the famous

English poet had travelled to the Balkan Peninsula with the specific intention of becoming actively involved in the Greek fight for independence, a plan he was prevented from realising by his unfortunate illness and death. Sadly, I can find no great mention here of the hundreds of other Western Philhellenes, the many ordinary young men from all over Europe, who were also inspired by the revolt and who in the early days of the war travelled to the peninsula and joined the fight against the Turks.

The museum's final gallery features traditional Greek civilian clothing from the 15th century onwards, of which the most noteworthy aspect is the elaborate and very beautiful silverwork that often decorated female attire. The finest examples of this craft emerged in the 19th century in the Roumloúki region of Macedonía, in the vicinity of the modern municipality of Paionía, north of Thessaloníki. Beside fine ear-rings and bracelets, unusually prominent and elaborate silverwork was created for wearing around the neck and waist. These significant silver necklaces and 'belts' from Roumloúki are almost indistinguishable from corresponding traditional silverwork produced in Syria, Jordan, and Palestine and which is still worn on ceremonial occasions by Bedouin women in the Arabian peninsula, particularly in the Yemen and the mountainous Abha region of Sa'udi Arabia.

The Roumloúki costume jewellery in the National Historical Museum provides clear evidence of Greece's close and centuries-old cultural relationship with the adjacent Middle East. But this relationship isn't surprising because the Ottoman Empire of the early 1800s, of which Greece was a part, used to be synonymous with 'The Near East', a term which encompassed the empire that reached from the Balkans, around the Mediterranean, down the sides of the Red Sea, and then along the coast of North Africa, as far as the western border of modern Algeria. By the late 1890s the term 'Near East' had come to indicate the Balkans (including Greece), the Levant (countries at the eastern end of the Mediterranean), Egypt, all of the Arabian Peninsula, and the west of modern Iran. However, in the course of the Second World War use of the term 'The Near East' was dropped in favour of 'The

Middle East', referring to Turkey, Syria, Lebanon, Cyprus, Palestine, Jordan, Iraq, Iran, all the Arabian Peninsula, and, in North Africa, Egypt, Sudan, and Libya. And since the Second World War, Tunisia, Algeria, and Morocco have also been associated with the Middle East, as have Afghanistan, Pakistan, and, occasionally, Greece - although modern Greeks generally tend not to approve of any association of themselves with their Middle Eastern neighbours, despite Greece so obviously sitting on the Middle East's very doorstep.

Although Greece's geographical and cultural proximity to the Middle East is inarguable, Greek cultural pride today holds instead that as Greeks were the founders of 'western civilisation' Greece must therefore be considered a Western country. But Greeks with a greater sense of realism tend to acknowledge the nation's strong affinity and relationship with the east and so prefer for Greece to be considered neither of the west nor of the east, but rather as the Centre of the civilised world. The simple truth, however, is that when Greece joined the European Community in 1981, and then the European Union in 1994, it was the first country to do so with a long political and cultural heritage that was derived from Turkish rule and a religious heritage that stems from Istanbul. Indeed prior to the Greek War of Independence the Ottoman-controlled peninsula that is now modern Greece had generally been recognised, together with Asia Minor, as constituting 'Turkey', and on maps of the period that is how the peninsula was indicated. For example, in John Adams's 'The Young Lady's and Gentleman's Atlas for Assisting Them in the Knowledge of Geography' of 1805, reprinted in 1822, the one name, 'Turkey', is stamped over the Balkan Peninsula, the Aegean, and Asia Minor, the 'T' set down upon what is now Bosnia Herzegovina, just short of Hungary, and the final letter, 'y', falling just short of Syria. In his excellent history of Greece prior to the revolution David Brewer cites several references that prove the distinction between this Turkey and Europe. Firstly, in 1506 Terence Spencer, an English chaplain, wrote that 'all the country of Troy is the Turk's own country by inheritance, and that country is properly called now Turkey, and none other'. Then, in 1581 Elizabeth I gave an exclusive royal charter to 'The Turkey Company' to trade in that entire area of the Middle East that was under Ottoman control and known as 'Turkey'. Lastly, in the early 1800s, in the lead-up to the Greek War of Independence, Athanásios Psalídas, an Enlightenment thinker and educator who studied in Russia and in Vienna, exhorted all Greeks living outside Greece to 'imitate the Europeans', thereby acknowledging that at that time Greeks themselves did not view their Balkan Peninsula home as being a part of Europe. Such evidence helps explain why when throughout the 1700s and early 1800s the western well-to-do undertook their 'Grand Tour of Europe' their route did not usually extend beyond Italy. For that which lay beyond Italy was not 'Europe' but the Near East, the most western peninsula of which (modern Greece) had been so long under Turkish domination that it was considered a part of the Orient.

While Greece's membership of the European Union has greatly helped to create an impression of it as being a European country, the exhibits of the National Historical Museum very clearly suggest otherwise: that today's Greeks have emerged from a mixture of peoples who have lived upon and around the busy cross-roads between Europe and the Middle East, and that today's Greeks are an intermingled people who at such an intersection, on the threshold of the Middle East, have long had to struggle and fight to retain a unique and unifying identity. To this day the Greek battle for the retention of Hellenic selfhood and individuality continues, for there are valid reasons for Greece's abiding feelings of vulnerability: Greece has Muslim neighbours; it's the first port of call for economic migrants from all parts of Asia and Africa; and since Greece joined the European Union, the country has been flooded by commercial and financial interests which are more concerned with profits than what is best for Greece.

As a large class of Greek teenagers follows me around the rooms of this museum under the guidance of a couple of teachers and a museum official, I'm reminded that some Greeks are concerned that a culture of consumerism has quite markedly infected and diminished the mentality of the nation's young. The girls amongst this group of students, all about fifteen years of age, are simply far too made-up for school children. They have a sexualized and slightly corrupted look about them. Their eyebrows are all too obviously, unnecessarily, and studiously plucked; and the clothes they're wearing are generally inappropriately tight-fitting and body-hugging. I observe that they only show interest in cabinets displaying old Greek jewellery. The boys seem similarly reluctant to learn about their nation's history; for if, as they enter a new room, they spot a few chairs, they race each other to sit on them and fool and loll until such time as their teachers arrive, order them to their feet, and force them to give some semblance of respectful attention to the commentary being uttered by the guide. But as soon as the official turns her back and moves slowly off to a new room, rather than read the informative paragraphs which are mounted beside the many exhibits being passed on all sides, both girls and boys saunter on together, eyes downwards, in chattering threes or fours as if enduring a boring lunch-hour in the school-yard. Their hearts are so clearly not in this morning's journey through Greece's extraordinarily dramatic history. They appear to find their history a bore.

While these students may well not be typical of Greek teenagers, and disaffected youngsters can be observed all over the world, I wonder if there's any possibility that these students have been touched by the notion that Greece needs to look forwards more than it does. For some Greeks do admit that Greece has a considerable pride problem, that it looks too much at its glorious past, that it's too taken up with its ancient history and its more recent battles against aggressors. However, if Greece looks forward at all it appears to be mainly towards a future of glamour, of film-star lifestyles, towards flash marinas and yachts and high-end tourism, towards enjoyment of all the unnecessary and luxurious trappings of fashion and modern technology. Maybe this morning's disinterested students simply exemplify a national dilemma. It's perfectly reasonable to expect that some of them are members of the many friendship groups that now exist, particularly on the Internet, between young Greeks, young Turks, young Albanians, and young Bulgarians. I suspect that some of the students here today consider that Hellenism and excessive patriotism actually divides them from their true heritage, that it obstructs fruitful co-existence with Greece's Middle Eastern and Balkan neighbours.

No Greek would dispute that Greece is Mediterranean, or that its people are 'Mediterranean' in nature, but there are some Greeks who flare at the suggestion that they're as Eastern as they are European. The truth, however, is that they're all three: Mediterranean, Eastern, and European, in varying degrees. Also disputed in discussions of how Greece is aligned in the modern world is the strength of the nation's link with its ancient past. Regardless, Greeks are the only people on the planet who are regularly and commonly referred to as being of two sets: Modern and Ancient. There is the Modern Greek language, and there is Ancient Greek, obviously related; today's Greece is Modern Greece, as opposed to Ancient Greece, while both share much the same geography; and today's citizens are termed Modern Greeks, not Ancient Greeks, even though it's generally accepted nowadays (including by many Greeks themselves, although more privately than publicly) that Modern Greeks are not strictly Greek at all but largely though not entirely, a mixture of Balkan peoples, of Slavs, Vlachs, Bulgars, Turks, Arabs, as well as others, following the invasions of the Heruli, the Goths, the Avars, and the Huns. The relatively few Ancient Greeks who survived the successive invasions that followed the classical era were those who dwelt in isolated and forbidding mountainous areas of the peninsula, such as the Máni region in the Pelopónnesos or the heights of Macedonía. No doubt some amount of Ancient Greek blood survives in Modern Greeks but the general consensus of impartial international historians is that there isn't a great deal of it - for the tribes of Ancient Greece were largely thinned by the invaders. Genetic research could shed considerable light on this issue.

Although the youngsters being escorted around the National Historical Museum this morning aren't showing it, Greeks generally treasure the notion of unbroken continuity between 'their' Ancient past and their Modern present. Whether the heritage that this asserted continuity bestows is actually to the Greeks' advantage or not is a serious question, for this heritage forms an important aspect of the average Greek's self-image: at one extreme it's sensed as reason for pride and responsibility and at the other end of the spectrum it's perceived as a burden, or debilitating 'baggage'. However, regardless of how the individual Greek sees such heritage, there exists a living mechanism for its maintenance. It's called 'Hellenism'.

Hellenism, beside offering Greeks a great sense of pride and self-worth, has also given them much grief. It explains many of the disturbing exhibits that are on display here in the National Historical Museum. For Hellenism caused many 19th-century Greeks to think that they had a right to 'regain' and rule Anatolía, when, in fact, Greeks had never been the only people living there. Modern Hellenism (or, more properly, 'Neo-Hellenism') holds that Asia Minor was Greek since antiquity, that Greece and Byzantium were one and the same, and that prior to the agreed population exchange of 1923 Greeks were the dominant population of the neighbouring land mass of Anatolía. Many Greeks still deeply regret that the nation's bid to regain that land mass after the end of the First World War ended in failure. So, to understand Hellenism, this force which has been so instrumental in the development of Modern Greece, and which is responsible for most of the exhibits here in this museum as well as in many other museums throughout Greece, it's worth examining the history of Asia Minor, reviewing the actual numbers of Greeks who were settled there, and understanding how the force of Hellenism came to cause, amongst other things, the emergence of the Greece that exists today. One cannot get to grips with the truth of modern Athens without getting to grips with Hellenism.

回 回 回 回

Asia Minor, also referred to as Anatolía ('The East'), was originally settled by the Hittites, around 1950 BCE. Parts of it were then conquered by various others, including, around 1200 BCE, Greeks who settled along Anatolía's western coast, overlooking the Aegean. After the Macedonian 'Alexander the Great', as he's called in the West, inherited control of Greece from his father Phílip, he invaded Anatolía in 334 BCE and brought considerable though short-lived security to those Greeks who had settled along Anatolía's coasts. For when Aléxandros died, the Ptolemies of Egypt and the Celts of Europe invaded and settled, and then in 190 BCE the Romans arrived, ending the Hellenistic Period. In 330 CE the Roman Emperor Constantínos the Great founded his 'new Rome', the city of Constantinople, on the site of that Greek settlement of about 660 BCE known as Byzantium, on the western side of the Bosphorus. The old name lived on however, and from it emerged the term 'Byzantine' to describe the eastern Roman empire and all its aspects, centred around Constantinople. Already then, we see that the claim that Asia Minor 'was Greek', solely, since antiquity is absolutely disproved.

In 395 CE the Byzantine Emperor Theodósios I divided the Roman Empire between his two sons, and each half began to take on its own characteristics. Although the eastern realm, centred around Constantinople, contained Middle Eastern and Greek elements, its succeeding emperors thought of themselves as Romans and dreamt of reuniting the eastern empire with the west. However, as a number of Byzantine emperors, along with various subordinates, had been raised and educated in regions like Syria and Cappadokía, the Christianity that developed in the east took on liturgical, musical, and other oriental characteristics that began to distinguish it markedly from western Christianity. And although from the outset the official language of the government of the Byzantine Empire had, of course, been Latin, by the reign of Irákleios (610 to 641 CE) it had been replaced by Greek. However, despite such evolution in Constantinople, the long-established ethnicities of Anatolía lived on, side by side, and caused, overall, a disunity and weakness that was unable to withstand various invasions into parts of the region.

The first of the new wave of invaders of Asia Minor were the Persians, around 616 CE. They were driven out, but then, shortly after the death of Mohammed in 632 CE, Arabs invaded. Then the Caliphs of Baghdad arrived, besieging

Constantinoúpoli in 668. In 867 a Macedonian named Vasílios murdered his way to the Byzantine throne and so installed a Macedonian dynasty which set about Hellenizing the civil law of the eastern empire. However, the developing Greekness of the realm didn't enable it to withstand further invasions. In 1067 the Seljuq Turks swept in from Central Asia and by the 12th century they had come to dominate several parts of eastern Anatolía. In 1204 Venetians and crusaders attacked, and a line of Latin emperors was once again established in Constantinople. In 1243 the Mongols entered the picture, causing further skirmishes in various regions of Asia Minor. Byzantine exiles recaptured Constantinople in 1261 but from that point onwards the Empire, under the Palaiológos dynasty, was little more than a large city-state besieged on every side. So again we see that at this point in history too Asia Minor was certainly not simply Greek.

Up until the 1300s the Turko-Persian Seljuq empire, on Anatolía's eastern borders, had been the Byzantine Empire's greatest threat from the east, but during the 1300s one Osman (or Uthman), a prince of Bithynía, in Anatolía's north-west, led his fellow Turks, long settled in the region but derived from nomadic peoples of northern Mongolia and Central Asia, to enter and conquer neighbouring regions within Anatolía. The family of rulers that descended from Uthman the Turk became known as the Ottoman Dynasty, and in 1395 the Ottomans set siege to the near-impregnable Constantinople. It eventually fell to them, in 1453. By then the Ottomans had already taken the northern Balkan Peninsula, in 1430; they captured Athens in 1456; the Pelopónnesos in 1460; and in 1461 they took the final stronghold of Greek power, Trapezús (modern day Trabzon), on the Black Sea. From then on the Ottomans controlled nearly every part of Anatolía, imposing the use of Turkish and the Arabic script upon all the various ethnicities whom they conquered there and encouraging long-established peoples of different belief systems to convert to Islam. However, the Ottoman Turks were prepared to tolerate other religions, allowing the adherents of other faiths to maintain their beliefs and continue with their own spiritual practices and rituals. And so the Orthodox Christians of Anatolía chose to accept

Ottoman domination and to decline the offers of Western Christendom to oust the Turks in exchange for all Orthodox Christians surrendering to the Catholic papacy of Rome. From the 15th century onwards then, Asia Minor was dominated and ruled by the Turks.

A hundred years after Constantinoúpoli had fallen to the Turks, there emerged in this same city a class of wealthy ethnically Greek merchants known as the Phanariótes, so called because they chose to dwell in the city's Phanári area where the Ecumenical Patriarch of Constantinople had for long kept his court. Showing a degree of tolerance that was very unusual for invaders to demonstrate at that time in human history, the Ottomans had permitted the Patriarch to act as both the spiritual and secular head of all of the Empire's Orthodox subjects. Included among the secular responsibilities with which the Turks invested the Patriarch were the administration, the exercising of justice, and the levying of tax with regard to every Christian within the Empire, whether in Anatolía or elsewhere in the Ottoman realm, including, of course, upon the Balkan Peninsula (the later Greece). Thus the power of the Patriarch of Constantinople became considerably political, and soon the Patriarch was perceived by Greeks all over the Empire to function as the successor of the Byzantine emperors, despite Constantinople having fallen to the Turks and being under the rule of the Sultan! And so as the Phanariótes generally claimed noble Byzantine descent and identified as Hellenic, meaning simply originally ethnically Greek, they thus clustered tightly about their Patriarch, as a quiet self-supporting network of Hellenists.

By the 18th century the Phanariótes had succeeded in rising to positions of considerable influence in the administration of the Ottomans' Balkan domains. Furthermore, they developed educational and cultural programmes, using Orthodox churches and Orthodox schools throughout the Ottoman Empire, whereby they instilled the notion that to be a Greek was to be a member of the Orthodox faithful administered by the Patriarch of Constantinople. Greeks on the Balkan Peninsula, who may not previously have been heavily religious, obviously saw the benefit of joining with the powerful Christian Patriarchate and in accepting and promoting that synthesis which today's historians refer to as Neo-Hellenism. The Patriarchate also unified nearly all of the Christians of the Balkan Peninsula, the Balkans, and Anatolía (except for the Armenians of north-eastern Anatolía). Despite the fact that the Phanariótes and the Patriarchate were completely subject to the Turks, they thus succeeded in encouraging the ultimate spiritual and secular loyalty of a vast number of non-Turks to themselves. They Hellenized all of these people. Christians became more Greek and Greeks became more Christian. Diverse peoples were made to feel as one, as members of a secular and religious group that was without a state of its own. Thus it was that a unifying Greek Orthodox desire to possess a Greek Orthodox state gradually began to emerge.

In time the conviction amongst all of these homogenised 'Hellenes' that they had a right to live as a free people in one Hellenic nation grew strong. Furthermore, once the Greeks and Christians living under Turkish Muslim rule had been bound together, the Patriarchate integrated into its educational and cultural programmes a deliberate and intended identification with the glories of classical Greece - despite the glaringly incongruent fact that classical Greece had been polytheist, of an era that had been rapturously in awe of its 'pagan' gods! Similarly glossed over or omitted from this recourse to Greece's 'glorious past' was that sadistic horror, the totalitarian war-machine that had been the city-state of Spárta, of the 6th to 2nd centuries BCE. Spárta, a major player in the Ancient Greek world, had had such distaste for culture and all manifestations of humanity that it exposed babies deemed likely to be weak upon a mountainside to die, and then 'educated' all those who survived this sorting process to thieve, to lie, and to dissimulate for the 'good' of the state.

Thus the unique rising national consciousness of the Hellenes of the 18th century was intentionally rooted in, and deliberately attached to, selected notions of descent from grand antiquity. The artificial construct that was Hellenism imbued all those who identified with the Patriarchate with a profound sense of validity, as well as an energised inspiration and considerable feelings of unity and power. To be a member of the network of Hellenic Christians was now to claim that one was also a descendant of those who had built that spell-binding building which dominated the Athenian skyline, the majestic Parthenon, as well as a descendant of all those who had created the many similarly inspiring classical ruins and artefacts dotted visibly all over the Balkan Peninsula and parts of Asia Minor. Everywhere Hellenic Christians now looked they saw 'evidence' in the form of ancient stone of what they claimed to be their original ownership of the land upon which such antiquities stood.

In the years leading up to the Greek War of Independence a significant player in the continued development of this Hellenistic revival was Adamántios Koraïs, a native of Anatolía who studied in France, settled in Paris, observed the French Revolution, and became one of Europe's foremost scholars in the study of classical literature. Although working from France, Koraïs sought to inspire the Hellenes of the Ottoman Empire with further empowering notions of classical ancestry. He published a series of editions of classical Greek authors for Greek readership and prefaced each with persuasive paragraphs exhorting Hellenists everywhere to imitate the French, to throw off those who had 'enslaved' them, and to take inspiration from those whom he declared were without any doubt their classical forebears, their predecessors by blood: the heroes of Ancient Greece.

Under the influence of Koraïs, Neo-Hellenism thus became propagandist: it openly and fully asserted that there was a direct continuity between the Hellenes of the Ottoman Empire, combined as one under the Patriarchate of Constantinople, and those Greeks who had written plays for the theatres of ancient Athens and discussed philosophy in the Ancient Agorá. Now, Christianity in the region, the Byzantine era, the Patriarchate of Constantinople, and the heroes of Ancient Greece all became dynamically fused. Additionally, the Hellenist conviction was not only promoted amongst all Orthodox Christians in the Ottoman Empire, by priests, teachers, and anti-Ottoman insurgents, but also amongst the Orthodox *diasporá* in Europe and America, the latter, in particular, eagerly translating their enthusiasm into the raising of funds to support the uprising against the Turks in 1821. Hellenism became an all-consuming cause. It stoked the blood with all the elements of religious fervour, nationalism, patriotism, and the exceptionally dramatic history and mythology of Ancient Greece.

Along with this rising new form of Hellenism, the movement towards Greek revolt was also inspired by the European Enlightenment. In 1771 Voltaire, fired and fascinated by the glories of Ancient Greece, called upon Europe's dominant powers to liberate the subjected Greeks. Then in 1793 'The Rights of Man' enshrined in the constitution of the American Republic of 1787 were seen by all the nations of Europe and beyond to generate the ideals of the new French constitution. Then in 1797, moved equally by his association in Istanbul with the Phanariótes, and his observation of the Enlightenment and the French Revolution, Rígas Feraíos, thought now to actually have been a heavily Hellenized Vlach, published from Vienna his 'New Political Administration', a pamphlet containing a rousing revolutionary proclamation, a declaration of human rights, a constitution for a Hellenic Republic, and his famous *O Thoúrios*, an anthem or 'War Song' which declared that 'Better is one hour of free life, Than forty years of slavery and prison!' In 1814, in Odessa, the highly secretive and determined Society of Friends (Filikí Etaireía) was formed, its central objective being the liberation of Greece. In April 1820 Aléxandros Ypsilántis, a Greek prince and a major in the Russian army was appointed the Society's leader and Ypsilántis then spent much of the rest of that year and early 1821 preparing for the first days of the uprising.

At this point the part played by 'The Orlov Revolt' in the rise towards revolution deserves recall. 'The Orlov Revolt' of 1770 was an attempt by the Russian Orlov brothers, Theodore and Alexis, to serve their country, Russia, by liberating the Greeks. The two brothers were disposed to such a project partly due to Turkey's declaration of war against Russia in 1768, following a request for help to Turkey from Polish nobles whose homeland Russia had recently invaded. The

Orlovs were also encouraged by the suggestion of Yeórghios Papazólis, a Greek officer in the Russian army, that a Russian attack against Greece's occupiers could be combined with the might of a Greek revolt. Thus in 1770 Theodore Orlov and his troops invaded the Pelopónnesos, teamed up with Yeórghios Papazólis, and after initial success in the Pelopónnesos saw the setting up of a provisional Greek government. But two months later the Turks drove the Russians out and remaining Greeks either disbanded or were slaughtered. The Orlov Revolt was poorly planned, the Pelopónnesos became a scene of bloodshed and thousands died, but the attempt was of great importance for it left seeds of inspiration in the imaginations of both the Greeks and the Great Powers. The Greeks saw that a better-planned revolt could actually work, and the Great Powers considered that a little support given by themselves could ensure Greek victory.

It is popularly held in Greece that the revolution began on the 25th of March 1821 at the monastery of Aghía Lávra in the north of the Pelopónnesos under the authority of the bishop of Old Pátras, Yeórghios Ghermanós, as depicted in the famous painting by Theódoros Vryzákis. In fact, in late March 1821 revolt broke out sporadically in the Pelopónnesos and had become widespread by the end of the month, with Theódoros Kolokotrónis becoming recognised as its leader. Once a provisional national government was set up in 1822, Aléxandros Mavrokordátos took control, despite a period of rivalry with Kolokotrónis. On the 8th of March 1823, followers of the philosopher Jeremy Bentham, a considerable number of British MPs, activists, and reformers, and Philhellenes including George Byron, as well as some leading members of the London Greek community, had formed 'The London Greek Committee' to raise funds in Great Britain to support the War of Independence. Leaders of the Committee toured British towns and cities raising donations, large and small, from the British public, but as Professor Rosen has written, in the Oxford Dictionary of National Biography, 'in the end the funds that were raised were sent to Greece without safeguards in place and largely squandered.' The same went for two loans that should have granted their British lenders considerable profits. So the London Greek Committee disbanded in 1826 and in the following year, the Turks succeeded in taking back Athens. (The Greeks had ousted the Turks from the city in June 1822.) However, in that same year, 1827, the war took a major turn towards victory when in October at the Battle of Navaríno, on the west coast of the Pelopónnesos, British, French, and Russian ships sank 60 enemy vessels manned by Turks, Egyptians, and Tunisians and put to rout a further 29.

By 1830, after a decade spent in determined revolt against the Ottoman Turks, Hellenism had triumphed. It had produced an independent state. However, the little nation that emerged from the Greek War of Independence held within its borders only about a third of those people throughout the Middle East and the Balkans who had come to identify, in the preceding build-up, as Hellenes. A great victory had been won but for staunch Hellenists the battle wasn't over. In the many debates that occurred between the end of the War of Independence and the promulgation of the constitution of 1844 a most ambitious plan was thus conceived.

The term *Megáli Idéa* (the Big Idea) was coined by Ioánnis Koléttis, one of the new state's first ministers and Prime Minister of Greece from 1834 to 1835 and then from 1844 to 1847. In essence, the *Megáli Idéa* held that all of those people who identified as Hellenes but who were 'stranded' outside the borders of the new state must one day be rescued. Thus this Big Idea envisaged the eventual restoration of a totally Hellenized Christian Orthodox Byzantine Empire, with its capital once again at Constantinople, and the enlarged state encompassing whatever territory needed to be taken to embrace all those Hellenes who dwelt in the surrounding territories.

This extraordinarily ambitious task was to reach out from the southern Balkan Peninsula to incorporate Hellenes as far east as the southern shores of the Black Sea, Hellenes along the coast of the Sea of Marmarás (including all of those who dwelt in Constantinople), Hellenes who dwelt in considerable numbers along the Anatolian shores of the eastern Aegean, and all of those Hellenes who dwelt between all three of the above coasts along with those communities that resided in Cappadokía, in central Anatolía. The countless residents of other ethnicities who had dwelt throughout this region for centuries were also to be incorporated within the enlarged Greek state. The Bavarian administration's very impressive implementation of their own grand idea that Greece should be dramatically upgraded and reconstructed in the style of the finest architecture of the new nation's classical era bolstered the Hellenists' plan. The handsome neo-classical buildings which the Bavarian administration erected in Athens and elsewhere in Greece throughout the second half of the 19th century thus served to provide Hellenists with visible confirmation of their perceived right to reclaim the ruins of all their ancient dwelling places. The Greeks' Neo-Hellenism and the Bavarians' liking for neo-classical architecture thus fed and nourished one another.

It wasn't until 1919 and the end of the First World War that an opportunity arose for this enormous dream to finally become a reality. At the end of the war it was proposed under the Treaty of Sèvres that the Turks, who had been allies of defeated Germany, should lose control of about two thirds of Anatolía. These two thirds would be controlled thenceforward, in different parts, by the French, Italians, British, Armenians, and Greeks. However, Mustafá Kemál, a Turkish military hero despite the Turks' defeat, would not accept this humiliation that was to come with having lost the war. Refusing the terms of the Treaty, Kemál rallied his army in the Anatolian interior and rebelled. The Hellenic Christian communities of Anatolía were thus immediately in danger, there being no sizeable military force on hand to protect them. Additionally, there were no Allied forces in the vicinity to protect the proposed interests of the major powers. The nearest sympathetic army was that of the Greeks, on the Balkan Peninsula. So Britain's Prime Minister, Lloyd George, encouraged Greece's Prime Minister, Elefthérios Venizélos, to assist. Mr. Venizélos was of course delighted, for here, at last, was an opportunity to implement the *Megáli Idéa*. And Lloyd George, a long-time romantic admirer of the mythology and notions of Ancient Greece, was content to support the thrilling idea that if the Greek Army succeeded all by itself in resisting the Turkish rebellion then Greece might be rewarded with control of all of Anatolía.

After the Greek troops landed at Smýrna in May 1919, as has been described earlier, they succeeded in eventually driving the Turks right over to the eastern edge of the Anatolian plateau where, amazingly, they came within a hair's breadth of defeating Kemál's forces and actually controlling all of central Asia Minor. Acquisition of more than just those coastal areas proposed as theirs under the Treaty of Sèvres became almost a reality. But the Greek army had chased the Turks over a vast, harsh, and parched plateau, and the Greeks were very weary. Their supply lines from the Aegean coast, stretching across the desolate and exposed plateau, were long and insecure and provisions of all forms repeatedly failed to get through to them. Thus the Turks suddenly got the upper hand and the Greek army was left with no alternative but to flee, back to the coast. There then followed the atrocities on both sides and the indescribable vengeance of the Turks. The Big Idea had completely failed. In 1923, under the Treaty of Lausanne, all of ancient Anatolía became the new Republic of Turkey, and the tragic population exchange between it and Greece was set in motion.

▣ ▣ ▣ ▣

In considering whether or not Asia Minor, or any part of that land mass, was in fact overridingly 'Greek' prior to the campaign of 1919 to 1922, we can also examine records which indicate the numbers of Hellenes who dwelt in the area shortly before the campaign. The Ottoman census of 1893 allows a general picture of the ethnic make-up of Asia Minor in the decades before the *Megáli Idéa* took its chance. However, before one considers its figures, it needs to be borne in mind that of the 33 Ottoman areas counted during the 1893 census there were several regions, like northern Greece, which were not within Asia Minor. Additionally, we can't take for granted that everyone whom the census counted as Muslim was actually so, for the Ottoman Empire encouraged, and oftentimes forced, large numbers of Christians to convert to Islam. A considerable number of such 'Muslims' were, in fact, *kryptochristianoí* (Crypto-Christians) who continued to practise their Orthodox faith in secret while at the same time living as Turks and speaking the Turkish language. Also, despite Ottoman tolerance of Orthodox practices within the Empire, Christian families of the Balkans were often required to provide a proportion of their most handsome and intelligent offspring for conversion, after which such young men would then be employed in the Ottoman apparatus, in either administrative roles or as élite members of the military. This enlistment of Greek boys, known as the *devşirme* (or the *paedomázoma*, in Greek) was imposed by the Turks for the first 250 years of the occupation. The practice ended in the early 18th century. The figures are distorted even further due to Muslim families having sometimes presented their finest sons as Christians so that they too might be 'converted', and so increase their prospects and rise to greater heights. Practices such as these during the centuries of the Ottoman Empire partly explain why today it's sometimes difficult to distinguish visually between Greeks and Turks, and partly why some Greeks of Anatolian heritage retain surnames ending with the Turkish suffix *oglou*, as with Kátia Margarítoglou, the Μις Ελλάς (Miss Greece) of 1998. Incidentally, close association with Turkish Muslims explains why other Greeks today have surnames beginning with *Hadji*, as in Mános Hadjidákis. For *Hadji* was an honorific taken from the Arabic word *Hadj,* meaning 'pilgrimage'. So just as Turkish Muslims who had performed 'the Hadj' and worshipped in Mecca were recognised after so doing by their surnames having taken the prefix *Hadji,* so could their Greek neighbours be distinguished after they had made the pilgrimage to the Christian shrines of Jerusalem and the Holy Land. And today's Athens phone book suggests that during those many centuries when Greeks and Turks lived side by side many a Dákis made such a pilgrimage.

The figures of the 1893 Ottoman census reveal a total population within the entire Ottoman Empire of 17.4 million, of whom the overwhelming majority, 12.5 million (72%), were counted as Muslim. Only 2.3 million citizens of the

Empire (13%) were counted as Greek. The census of 1893 also revealed the presence of 1 million Armenians, 817,000 Bulgarians, 149,000 Catholics, 183,000 Jews, 35,000 Protestants, 18,200 Latins, 22,000 Monophysites (Eastern Christians of a form separate from the Orthodox faith), 3,100 non-Muslim gypsies, and 235,000 'Foreigners'. In 1893 then, Hellenic Orthodox Christians counted as only a little over a tenth of the population that resided on territory controlled by Turks beyond the borders of the new Greek state.

Only in three regions of the Empire of 1893 did Greeks significantly outnumber Muslims or any other group of citizens. In Cezaryir-i Bahr-i Sefit (the islands of the eastern Aegean and Cyprus) there were 226,819 Greeks and just 27,481 Muslims; in Catalca (the peninsula west of and adjacent to the Bosphorus) there were 35,848 Greeks and only 15,091 Muslims; while in Yanya (in the region spanning southern Albania) there were 286,304 Orthodox living alongside 225,415 Muslims. However, most notably, in Istanbul, where dwelt the Ecumenical Patriarch of Constantinople, and to which city Hellenes felt a long historical and religious affiliation, the census revealed there resided actually 384,910 Muslims and only 152,741 Greeks, well under half of the celebrated city's Islamic population. Thus it seems clear that 26 years later, in 1919, when the Greek army landed in Smýrna, Greece had no right based upon population figures to any major region of the Anatolian mainland.

However, it should also be considered whether the figures of 1893 might possibly have changed with any significance by the time the Greek army was launched into the Asia Minor Campaign. By 1914, despite the Turks' recent loss of northern Greece, and although the total population of the Ottoman Empire had risen to approximately 25 million, reliable estimates provided by Western embassies suggested that 17.5 million (70%) of the population of the Empire consisted then of Turks (10 million), Arabs (6 million), and Kurds (1.5 million). So roughly then, that section of the population identifying itself as Islamic (although it may not have been entirely so, for much the same distorting reasons as in the earlier figures) remained of much the same proportion around 1914 as had been revealed by the census of 1893. Greeks still constituted much the same minority within the overall population.

In fact in 1914 Asia Minor was thought to be home to roughly 1.5 million Greeks (6% of the total population), along with a similar number of Armenians. Although the drop of Greeks from 13%, in 1893, to 6%, in 1914, is considerable, a 1914 figure somewhere between the two percentages is likely due to the shrinkage of Turkish territory, the Turks having lost control of Crete and all of their Balkan territories except Eastern Thrace. Additionally, many Greeks had already begun to quit Asia Minor because of mounting hostility. However, in view of both sets of figures, for 1893 and 1914, it's clear that Greeks in Asia Minor did not number more than 13% of the population just prior to the Asia Minor Campaign, the implementation of the *Megáli Idéa*.

Furthermore, the compulsory exchange of Christian and Muslim populations that occurred in 1923 was fairly well documented by officials on both sides and the estimates of 1.3 million Christians leaving Turkey and 400,000 Muslims being forced to quit Greece are generally accepted as true. So if there were only roughly 1.5 million Greeks in Asia Minor in 1914 and 1.3 million were forced to relocate to Greece in 1923, then it follows that the number of those Greeks 'lost' between 1914 and 1922 must have been approximately 200,000 in number. And in fact this figure accords with the estimates that have been given of those who either died, perished, or were killed amidst the fighting of 1919 to 1922, as well as those who had abandoned Asia Minor voluntarily.

回 回 回 回

Having thus examined the origin and rise of Hellenism, and having considered the figures for the populations of Asia Minor prior to the great disaster of the early 20th century, it's important now to recognise that when Greek troops landed at Smýrna in May 1919 they didn't do so solely in pursuit of any gross notions, such as the belief that Greece had a historical right to control of all of Asia Minor. It has to be remembered that the Turks, who as allies of Germany had lost the First World War, were clearly not prepared to accept the Treaty of Sèvres, and thus Greece was very strongly encouraged, by powers led by Britain, to effectively and justifiably force the defeated enemy to accept the terms being placed upon them. That was the Greek Army's immediate task upon landing on the shores of Asia Minor. Had the Greek troops succeeded, as they almost did, in forcing the defeated enemy to accept the considerable loss of territory as laid out in the terms of the Treaty, we obviously cannot know whether or not Greece would then actually have been more greatly rewarded, whether or not the Great Powers would then have agreed to Greece being given control of their own proposed slices of Asia Minor.

As things turned out, in terms of territory Greece acquired none of Asia Minor but it was left with all of the Balkan Peninsula and over 6,000 islands. And of course it was also left with its Hellenism, which, although it was now a greatly wounded and hurt Hellenism, remained constructed of a strong identification with nearly all of the finest aspects of Ancient Greece, of the Byzantine Empire, and of Eastern Orthodox Christianity. The Balkan Peninsula was also left, however, in terms of character, with the effects of the *Tourkokratía*, as well as the effects of the Ottoman domination of Asia Minor upon the roughly 1.3 million Greeks who had lived all their lives there prior to 1923. Even if the *Megáli Idéa* had succeeded the Eastern influences of the Ottoman Empire would still have left Greece with a significantly hybrid mentality. And as it is, these distinctly Eastern and un-European influences are still discernible in Greek life and culture today. As Ottoman political and economic mentality naturally dominated in all those parts of the Middle East that were under Ottoman control, including Greece (and here it should be remembered that by the end of the 17th century a quarter of Athens's population consisted of Turkish Muslims), it should come as no surprise that Greek bureaucracy today is partly Ottoman in character.

🝆 🝆 🝆 🝆

There remains the question of 'the Greek language', for as Hellenism was a construct, and the link between Modern Greeks and Ancient Greeks is tenuous, as has been outlined above, how then did the beautiful Greek language that we know today manage to survive throughout the centuries, to be 'handed down' from the ancients to the modern? Surely the language couldn't have survived if there wasn't a direct line between the ancient Greeks and the people of Modern Greece?

The fact is that 'the Greek language' did not, strictly, survive. The sweet and alluring tongue that we hear today, that is referred to as 'Modern Greek', evolved, and in four distinct phases. This is not to say that the language of the fourth phase bears no similarity to the first: in fact, the grammars of the first and fourth phases have much in common. But all four phases are distinct.

Ancient Greek, of the first phase, was not itself a single entity. It was of two strands: Mycenaean Greek, of the 14th to the 12th century BCE, and Archaic and Classical Greek, of the 14th to the 8th century BCE. The second phase, Hellenistic Greek (of the 4th century BCE to the 4th century CE), is also referred to as *Koiní* Greek (pronounced kee-NEE, and creating 'Common Greek'). Next came the Byzantine phase (from the 5th to the 15th century) and it sought to preserve the purity of the written forms of Ancient Greek. In both the *Koiní* and Byzantine phases, the great works of Classical literature managed to survive by way of manuscript copies made on sheets of *pápyros*. However, while Byzantine Greek sought to preserve aspects of Ancient Greek, *Koiní* continued to evolve and eventually there existed a gulf between the written and spoken forms of the language.

The fourth and final phase of 'the Greek language' is Modern Greek, dating from the 15th century, but it too hasn't been a single entity. From the 15th century 'Modern Greek' has referred to three forms: widely varying local dialects that seem almost like different languages; *Dimotikí*, or urban, Greek, understood by all; and *Katharévousa*, a literary and academic form of the language linked by way of Byzantine Greek to Ancient Greek and which arose in the 19th century as part of the effort to cleanse local dialects of foreign elements and to standardise their word-forms according to the Classical Greek model. 'The Greek language' of today, Modern Greek, is the Demotic form, and in 1976 it replaced *Katharévousa* as the official language of government, education, journalism, and literature within Greece.

With regard to the question of how, generally and largely, the Greek language survived although the tribes of Ancient Greece most probably did not, the answer is to be found with the second phase of the evolution, *Koiní*. Alexander the Great (356 to 323 BCE), as the Macedonian who inherited rule of Greece after his father Phílip had taken control of it, was instrumental in forming the common dialect (*Koiní*) from all the related Greek dialects that existed on the Balkan Peninsula, though chiefly from the dialect of Athens, the Attic dialect. *Koiní* Greek, Common Greek, was designed to be practical, rather than academic. It was to be the language of life, not of books; its foremost purpose was clarity of communication, as opposed to elegance of style; its syntax, grammar, and inflections were simplified; and its exceptions were reduced.

Alexander's imposition of this common Greek dialect enabled his combined armies to communicate more effectively with each other, and as *Koiní* was taught to the inhabitants of all those many regions which Aléxandros conquered, it also enabled efficient communication with them as well. Thus, as a result of an imperialistic need for efficiency, Aléxandros turned Greek into a very important regional language of that time. In the wake of his exploits a remarkably uniform *Koiní* achieved a wide geographic distribution, rooting itself in urban centres all over the eastern Mediterranean, throughout Asia Minor, the Levant, Syria, Mesopotamia, Persia, as far east as India and as far south in Egypt as Abu Simbel. Hence Greek became a dominant commercial and political language, a language of government, a standard second language, a colloquial everyday tongue or *lingua franca* which people of other nationalities were very happy to take up and use alongside existing local languages. *Koiní* Greek was thus widely established before the many invasions of and migrations into Greece by all those ethnicities listed earlier, and all incomers naturally converted to the dominant language, the language of power and influence.

Another reason for the survival of Greek, despite the repeated invasions of the Balkan Peninsula by non-Greeks, is that *Koiní* also became the language of choice of that extraordinarily powerful force, the young and developing Christian Church. One of the most ancient set of documents in *Koiní* Greek is composed of the New Testament books of the Bible, for the original texts of the New Testament were written in *Koiní* from around 50 CE, when *Koiní* was the *lingua franca* of the eastern part of the Roman Empire. Consequently, *Koiní* Greek is still commonly referred to as 'New Testament Greek', after its most famous literary work. Largely because of this connection Greek thenceforward became the language of scholarship and the arts, and as such it was the medium of a vast array of philosophical, literary, historical, scientific, and needless to say religious documents throughout the Hellenistic period. Of course its widespread role in these spheres combined neatly with it having become the *lingua franca* of trade and commerce between the nations of the Mediterranean and their fringes. Thus there were now very strong religious, practical, and educational reasons for all manner of incomers to Greece to capitulate to *Koiní*.

Later, despite Greece having been conquered by Rome in 146 BCE, and Latin having been imposed as the *lingua franca* of the Eastern Roman Empire, Greek remained of great interest to the Roman élite, some of whom, like Marcus Aurelius, chose to write in Greek. Eventually, Roman Emperor Irákleios, 610 CE to 641 CE, abandoned the Eastern Empire's use of Latin in favour of Greek, thereby Hellenizing the Roman empire and adding to the chances of the language's survival. The reason for this reversion was largely that the imposition of Latin upon the common people had failed: they had continued to use *Koiní*. Irákleios was also a driving force in converting peoples who migrated to the Balkan Peninsula to Christianity. However, despite *Koiní's* survival and predominance, Slavic, Vlach, and Arabic languages remained in use amongst various communities although no such languages could rival the practicality and dominance of Greek in the eastern Mediterranean.

As the Byzantine Empire began to decline so the use of *Koiní* began to wane on the empire's outer fringes. However, after Constantinople fell to the Ottomans, the Phanariótes used the language, in combination with the Orthodox faith and notions of the classical past, to produce their potent mix that was nationalistic Neo-Hellenism. This Hellenism didn't reach as far as those outer pockets of the former Byzantine Empire of course, but in some of those places the language continued nevertheless. The huge geographical region over which *Koiní* once extended is indicated today by the fact that forms of Greek are still spoken by a small number of isolated Bulgarians in the vicinity of Suvorovo, in north eastern Bulgaria, by Muslims at ceremonial and festival times in Pontic parts of eastern Turkey, and by approximately 25,000 Italians in the Greek-speaking villages and towns of Calabria and Apulia, in Italy, where *Grekánika* or *Kato-Italiótika* (or *Grico* as the Italians call it) is currently offered as a subject in some local Italian primary and secondary schools.

▨ ▨ ▨ ▨

There are of course some Greeks in Greece today who don't accept that they aren't purely and directly descended from Ancient Greeks. They won't accept that Modern Greeks spring from a mixture of peoples, including Albanians, Slavs, Vlachs, Turks, Arabs, and all those others who have either invaded or migrated to the Balkan Peninsula and Anatolía over the course of two thousand hectic years. To assert racial purity instead, is, of course, ridiculous, for it would be remarkable, in fact it would be a phenomenon, if pure, uninterrupted, and direct lineage between ancient and modern Greeks were a fact, if somehow Greece, despite its pivotal position between east and west and all the comings and goings it has seen over the centuries, were to be the only homogenous country in the very heterogeneous and multi-ethnic eastern Mediterranean.

However, it's how people choose to self-identify that matters, and not whether they're correct in identifying themselves in any particular way, or whether they're simply participating in a comforting collective delusion. Although thousands of people can subscribe to belief, for example, that the world will end on a particular day in exactly ten years' time, and such a belief remains of course a complete invention, it is still their belief, it identifies, typifies, and unifies them, and so such believers have to be dealt with and interacted with on that basis, regardless.

If, however, young Greeks today, like those I've observed sauntering with seeming total disinterest around Greece's National Historical Museum, are inclined to reject traditional Hellenism, then they have a difficult battle ahead. For Hellenism is tightly bound up with Greece's ancient history, with a language derived from that of the ancients, and with Greek Orthodoxy, and all around, from every angle, impinging continually upon the nation's consciousness, every hour and every minute, there exist powerful reminders of each of these elements. The ancient Acrópolis and Parthenon can't be avoided, they're seen from almost every street and every roof-top throughout Athens, their images beamed daily to every television set in the land. The state educational system revels in the teaching of the nation's 'glorious' history. The black cassocked priests of the national religion also cannot be avoided, for they're everywhere. Sauntering along in beard and black, carrying home the daily milk and bread, they're an ever-present reminder that to be a true Hellene you're supposed to be a faithful follower of the national church.

This then is Greece's fundamental dilemma: is Hellenism a responsibility, or is it a burden; a positive force or simply ancient baggage acting as a national handicap? This morning's students are dressed just like kids in US films and television programmes. As they're shunted round the exhibits of the National Historical Museum half of them chew vulgarly, in the American way, on gum. Are they stuck in some sterile, bland, and homogenous middle-ground, while the dilemma goes unresolved and unanswered? Or have they made their minds up? Perhaps they're just being swept along by forces beyond their control? However they feel, I suspect that young Greeks today can at least see the lie in the Hellenic belief that somehow Greeks have richer or better DNA than any other people or nation upon Earth, or that Greece has had one long and glorious history. I suspect they realise instead that they're intrisically no better or worse than the people of any other nation, and that except for the classical era, over 2,000 years ago, this region has had a long and horrendous history.

🔲 🔲 🔲 🔲

In the early afternoon I wait on the edge of Sýntagma Square for a tram to the coast just east of Piraeus and then southwards along the shoreline to the seaside district of Voúla. Amongst those of us waiting, a number of large collared-dogs saunter passively and phlegmatically - no dog-owners fore or aft of them. Two of the creatures break off and wander along to the nearby pedestrian crossing. The light shows red and about twenty people come to a halt while the many lanes of traffic on Amalías Avenue roar past. The dogs amble up to the pedestrians, drop their behinds, and sit. When the lights turn green, off they trot with all the humans across the wide and busy avenue. The dogs however then turn toward the National Gardens. For an afternoon stroll in the park? Or for a splash in the duck pond perhaps?

There are many such *adéspota* (ownerless dogs, or 'collared-dogs') in Athens. Their collars, red for females and blue for males, are tagged so that each animal can be tracked. The city authorities have also vaccinated and spayed or neutered them. Although the *adéspota* are fed by locals, they have no close relationship with anyone, and so for company they tend to gravitate to each other. They appear to be harmless and seldom show any sign of aggression. In fact, I've yet to hear any of these dogs even bark. When they're not strolling from one place to another, they sleep, and often in unexpected spots. They seem to be treated with almost the same reverence as the sacred cows of India. In the hot months of summer they sometimes enter shops where there's air-conditioning and are kindly permitted to sleep in the cool. One morning as I passed the three grand and very expensive hotels which stand side by side overlooking Sýntagma Square, there lay, just a few steps away from the liveried doorman of each hotel, a large collared dog, fast asleep in the pleasant winter sun. They do well to choose such prestigious positions, for if they're injured or they become visibly ill there's a greater likelihood that someone may call the telephone number on their collars and summon medical assistance. Otherwise they risk being left to suffer, for *adéspota* are entirely at the mercy of passers-by and well-wishers.

Like a giant silver centipede with a massive single eye at its head, one of Athens's smart new trams creeps slowly towards the Sýntagma terminus. By 1960 the capital's traditional tram system, running on rails in the tarmac, had been abandoned, leaving the city's transportation entirely to trolleys, buses, cars, taxis, and thousands of motorbikes and scooters. The result was horrendous congestion and the *néfos*, Athens's infamous combination of photochemical and particulate smog. Thus, in time for the 2004 Olympics, the Metró, which up until 2,000 had amounted to only a single and mainly overground line from Kifissiá to Piraeus via Omónoia Square, was substantially expanded and trams were re-introduced. With the EU supplying 50% of the funding required for the system, Athens now possesses a sleek fleet of thirty-five silver Sírios, styled by the luxury Italian car-maker Pininfarina, designers of the Alfa Romeo, Maserati, and Ferrari.

To an automated announcement, in Greek and English, we all step aboard into an interior which is wonderfully spacious and very impressive. Each Sírio can transport two hundred people and as this one gradually fills up to convey Athenians back out to their homes I note that there are only two other male passengers on board! I'm surrounded by Greek women. They're of all ages and almost without exception they clutch large paper box-bags sporting the names or logos of famous Western fashion brands. They've all been doing the sales. How things have changed over the centuries, and even in recent decades, for in ancient Greece the *agorá* (the market) was only for men, the males did the shopping while females stayed at home, and photographs show that as recently as the 1940s few women frequented Athens's shopping streets. However, in 1952 all Greek women were finally permitted the privilege of being able to vote, and women's movements in Greece began to germinate. They met quite a setback though, during the Júnta, fifteen years later, when its leader Yeórghios Papadópoulos required that Greek women (particularly female students) be subservient, that they follow strict dress codes, and that they absent themselves from all mixed-sex public or social gatherings. Only since the 1970s have women in Greece begun to taste real freedom.

This afternoon most of the young women amongst the huge collection of Greek females on this Sírio are remarkably and exceptionally beautiful. Young Greek women enhance their facial comeliness by framing it with long well-conditioned and finely-cut hair (they seldom wear it short), by artistically shaping their eyebrows, and by skilfully applying quite a lot of perfecting make-up. And then, having enhanced their facial charms, they adorn themselves in stylish Western clothing. It's rare to see a Greek girl diminishing herself in Western 'grunge' or carefully designed raggedness, and I've not yet spotted a single Greek goth, of either sex, out and about in central Athens.

But as Greek women grow older it seems that, sadly, not all of them age well. It appears that after about the age of thirty-five, some have a tendency to rather fill out in certain parts and crumple in others. Many continue, however, to adorn themselves much as before. So now in this sleek silver Sírio there are dozens of women in their fifties and sixties who are plastered and pancaked in creams and face powder, rouge, eye-shadow, lipstick, and blush; still wearing very long hair, often dyed; and still sporting very noticeable designer logos - on kitsch over-large watches, or embroidered in paste diamanté upon their clothes, or writ large in electro-plated gold or silver on the broad plastic arms of the kind of big black sun-glasses in which movie-stars like to pose. Yes, even now, while wearing thick winter coats and scarves, all around me in this tram are sunglasses stamped with the names Armani, Gucci, Christian Dior, Versace, and Prada - although whether they're the real thing or just cheap replicas purchased from the many illegal Asian and African street-vendors, I'm not sure. Most of the Greek women on board this tram this afternoon appear to have much the same taste in self-presentation as wealthy women of the Middle East, except, of course, that one can actually see and appreciate most of their faces and their choices of individual clothing outside of private family gatherings.

Between central Athens and the final stop along the coast, our Sírio passes through what seems like an endless recreation of the less wealthy parts of Riyadh or Dhahran, that is, through endless five-storey cuboid *polykatoikíes*, with shops and suchlike on the ground floor and apartments above. Stacks of canopied balconies are crammed with all sorts of things from pot-plants and washing-lines through to big metal air-conditioners and outdoor cupboards. Eighty years ago Piraeus and Athens were two separate cities with several miles of open fields and meadows between them, but now there's no distinguishing between the two: they've merged into one low-rise concrete jungle, an unending cuboid *cháos*, its only regular 'beauty' being in the large lavish lettering of the signage above the shops, an imaginative window-display, or the occasional bit of horticulture on the thin reservations which run down the centres of some of the roads. The similarity to modern downtown Arabia is startling.

When the tram reaches the coast and turns to follow the land southwards, the pleasure of coming to the spaciousness of the sea is quickly marred by the state of the beach and tarmacked foreshore. For there's a great deal of litter upon both, generally the thrown-away debris of packaging and implements from *fastfoudádika* (fast-food outlets); the parking areas are often pot-holed and poorly maintained; and old refreshment structures stand rusting and abandoned beside the new. Now, in winter, a few people have turned off the busy highway that runs parallel with the tram-line, to park their cars near the beach and to walk in coats or jackets along the shore. The scene reminds me of the thousands of Kuwaitis who every late afternoon walk along unattractive parts of their shoreline, just to escape the confinement of their walled villas or their apartments, or to flee the boredom of shiny sterile shopping malls and interminable traffic.

But as the Sírio heads further south the apartment blocks become at least a little spaced. Finally, between them, there's room to breathe. But at a price! For now there are almost no older blocks, and all slight touches of interesting character or the curious, vanish. We're heading into the overspill of urban Athens. But as the tram creeps ever south, along the coast, famous luxury brand-names continue to beckon from shop-fronts lining the route, and people still get on and off the Sírio clutching large branded shopping bags. I've watched this behaviour now for just over ten miles and it makes me despair. It seems every woman in Athens has been brainwashed into participating in needless and compulsive consumerism.

The entire journey, from Sýntagma to the terminal stop in Voúla, takes roughly an hour. But for the sight of the sea, at no other point has there been any considerable note of uplift, of aesthetic inspiration. So I'm strongly inclined to remain on the tram and return immediately to central Athens. However, I've come this distance so I might as well persist, and go as far south as the southern sprawl of Athens spreads. From the terminal to the nearest bus-stop, one has to walk several hundred metres back along the tram route, while lanes of traffic in the adjacent motorway, just inches away, vroom past incessantly. This is so Arabian Gulf! So Al Khobar Corniche! I suppose Athenians though, may like to think of it as their Riviera. One interesting and significant difference, however, is that here in Athens the cars speeding by are not all expensive, new, and flash: in fact quite a lot of them are old, and there are a number of estimable little Smart cars around as well - primarily purchased, I suspect, to deal with the intense competition there is here in Athens for car-parking spaces.

After half an hour's wait in a bitingly cold wind that swooshes straight off the nearby sea, a bus arrives - packed with Greeks young and old, as well as a considerable number of men from the Indian subcontinent. I expect these many Asians are servants to the Greek wealthy who live in the plush belt of housing to which we're now headed. They probably wash windows, tend gardens, clean cars, and so forth, but as I've seen few subcontinental women here in Greece, perhaps these men also assist indoors. I alight at Vouliagméni and the bus drives off into the hills, to isolated pockets of Athenian overspill. Unfortunately the Vouliagméni seashore quickly proves to be no more than a narrow band of sand and stone, badly littered this afternoon with every possible vestige of fast-food feast or picnic. Much of the debris, embedded in the sand, is of battered plastic, left over from last summer or washed up by winter tides.

On the other side of the Vouliagméni highway are a string of upmarket restaurants and hotels, but behind them are the most well-spaced and well-kept apartment blocks I've yet seen anywhere in Athens. The streets are clean, broad, and quiet. I encounter no one out walking, but when the occasional car passes it does so at a moderate and respectful speed. And what plush cars they are! A significant number are low-slung, very expensive, sports models: convertibles with soft hoods, ideal for cruising along the sea-front in summer.

Uphill, past the few blocks of apartments, stand a row of very pukka detached villas rising from within walled gardens rich with shrubbery and trees. Elaborate verdigrised urns, and contemporary statuary, add pomp to balconies enjoying clear views of the Saronic Gulf. The pavements here are unbroken, wide, easily walkable, and pristine. When the road ends, I clamber up through rocks on the hillside, and find discarded domestic litter strewn about the grass. There's more detritus from *fastfoudádika* here as well! Presumably it's all been thrown from vehicles passing along the ridge above. I have to climb a good thirty metres further up the incline, beyond the ridge, before this evidence of human disrespect for the environment can be escaped. But then, thankfully, all about me lies a picturesque assortment of all forms and shades of rock, stone, and low-lying Greek flora, watched over, here and there, by an old and characterful olive-tree. At the summit I reach pure clean air and near-silence. This is the first time since arriving in Athens that I've completely escaped every kind of human noise, for it's quieter here than even upon the brow of Philopáppou after midnight. Gazing down upon one of the city's most select residential areas, I sit upon a rock, relax, enjoy, and then begin to peel an orange I plucked from a tree near Sýntagma mid-morning - when I was certain no one was looking.

Suddenly my mouth is flooded with vile and bitter acid! My taste-buds haven't been so assaulted since I stupidly plunged my teeth into an unripe grapefruit in the Fijian bush as a child! What foul Grecian fruit is this! It's certainly no normal orange! It's inedible and I laugh out loud over Vouliagméni. No wonder all those gorgeous 'oranges' on the trees of Athens never seem to budge! No wonder people don't bother taking them. The orange trees of Athens are clearly purely decorative and thank goodness I've a bottle of water with me and can rinse away the bitterness.

Almost the entire bay below consists of luxury housing with restaurants along the shore, and here and there a small shop, such as a pharmacy or a mini-mart. There's no hustle and bustle, no visible evidence of community, no pulsing life, and from here it's an hour and a half's very ugly journey, by public transport, to or from central Athens. Though the spacing of the *polykatoikíes*, the townhouses, and the detached homes here is reasonably generous, and the buildings themselves have some degree of individuality in terms of design and style, and there's a reasonable amount of greenery between each structure, this is a place to stay and not a place to live, in the sense of 'living' being in the thick of things. Vouliagméni offers Athenians pure air, an atmosphere of calm, and, high above the litter-line, the possibility to gaze out upon four Greek islands. For those who can afford to buy or rent a home in this extremely expensive suburb, and to commute by car each day to the buzzing heart of the city, its isolation is no doubt an enormous relief and pleasure.

On my return journey I alight the Sírio several stops before Sýntagma Square, in an area where visitors have little reason to tread. At the end of a street lined on both sides by garage-workshops and stores selling automotive accessories and spare parts, I find a simple neighbourhood restaurant in which to have an evening meal. Although I stress *lígo* and *mikró* (a little and small) when ordering a simple salad and some cooked meat, both plates come to the table piled high. The chef is clearly eager to please. And with two small carafes of most acceptable *híma*, the bill comes to just under a very acceptable ten euros. I haven't eaten and drunk so well for so little in Athens yet.

The delight of this evening is a concert performance by the singer Eléni Péta, with accompaniment provided solely by a bearded and pony-tailed young man at a grand piano. Eléni Péta proves to be a moving and powerful singer, and her accompanist a virtuoso. Ms. Péta is also a beauty. Her long brown hair falls to just below her bare shoulders, and the cuffs of her elegant long-sleeved strapless silver top drop several feet to literally fly after her hands as she gestures dramatically in song. She's a *chanteuse* of the highest calibre, quite devastating, drawing from the audience very early on in her two-hour non-stop performance a stream of enthusiastic cheers and cries of 'Bravo!' And yet I've never heard of her before. She deserves to be known far beyond the Mediterranean.

Tonight she performs mainly in Greek but with a sprinkling of songs in Italian and English. Every piece is touching. Some are slow and reflective, others are joyous. The programme climaxes with some famous *rebétika*, as well as *éntechno* by none other than Mános Hadjidákis. *Éntechno* (έντεχνο) literally means 'artistic', as in 'art song', and *éntechno* is that particular form of music which has had me ensnared for so long. It arose in the late 1950s, as the song-writers Vasílis Tsitsánis and Manólis Chiótis westernised *rebétika*. *Éntechno*'s two greatest creators, Hadjidákis and Theodorákis, went further than Tsitsánis and Chiótis and began to magnificently synthesise elements of Western classical music with Greek folk rhythms and elements of Greek melody and harmony. By thus elevating traditional Greek music Hadjidákis and Theodorákis succeeded in making it more easily accessible to the Western ear, particularly to Western ears familiar with Western classical music. Where their work involved lyrics, and it usually did, the lines had generally been written by such fine Greek poets as Constantínos Caváfy, Odysséus Elýtis, and Níkos Gátsos.

Beside Hadjidákis and Theodorákis, other significant composers of *éntechno* included Stávros Kouyoumtzís, Dímos Moútsis, and Mános Loïzos. Other renowned lyricists of the genre were Mános Eleftheríou and Tásos Livadítis. By the 1960s this sublime and sophisticated form of Greek song had become almost popular, which was irregular and surprising. The Greek film industry even appropriated *éntechno* for soundtracks. And during the late 70s and 80s the composer Thános Mikroútsikos introduced a form of *éntechno* which bears even more of a resemblance to Western classical music. This was probably because although much of Mikroútsikos's work has been in *éntechno*, he has also written opera, symphonies, chamber music, theatre and cinema music, and experimental works. Such astounding musicality in Greeks isn't rare. Although we in the West know little of Greece's composers, musicians, and singers, largely because of that massive and seemingly impenetrable barrier which is the Greek language, Greece has produced an extraordinary number of them. In fact, it's no exaggeration to say that in terms of the production of a distinctly ethnic music the Greeks are the most accomplished nation on earth.

As the concert climaxes, Eléni Péta's accompanist, Thodorís Oikonómou, rises to even greater virtuosity. Not only a fine pianist but a composer too, Ecónomou swathes Ms. Péta in an orchestra-like palette of subtle and delicate colours, a diversity of tones and timbres entirely drawn from the keys of the piano. As Eléni flies and soars at points of reverie and elation, Ecónomou's arms beat so rapidly up and down to produce a multitude of sympathetic and supportive notes that it's astonishing he doesn't hit an unintended key. In quieter moments he's so at one with the feeling of the music that his face draws within inches of the keyboard and he seems almost to writhe in passion. Aristotle said there are kinds of music that produce *cátharsis* whether or not they possess ethical value, but tonight's music clearly edifies at the same time as it uplifts and purifies the emotions.

Outside it's pouring with rain and the streets are awash with vast quantities of rushing water. I heard that Athens was hit by severe rains at the start of this winter, but found it difficult to accept that they were truly torrential. I thought the report was surely overblown. But now, while Athens is being thoroughly saturated in front of my eyes, I believe! Streams of water rush for grilles beside the roads or outlets set within paved forecourts. Buses send up splashing great waves as they career at ridiculous speeds through wide and treacherous masses of water. Athenian drivers tonight, just like drivers in Arabia during desert storms, appear not to sense or care about the dangers of driving rapidly through blinding rain and pools of water, but instead, like Arab drivers, they're revelling in the downpour. In hot dry countries like Greece water comes as a welcome marvel! But here and there on the largely abandoned streets, an Asian or an African stands completely still, forlorn, wet, and waiting, even at this late hour, in the hope of making a sale. On this most inhospitable night umbrellas hang from their forearms, often without the seller using one of them himself, to keep his own body dry from the rain. To stand sodden in such torrents and choose not to shield yourself although you've got half a dozen umbrellas for sale on each of your arms, is surely to be in a very desperate state indeed.

When I reach the hotel Roúla is on desk-duty, and upon hearing of my horrific encounter with an Athenian orange atop the highest hill in Vouliagméni she shrieks with laughter and advises that all those balls of golden delight that decorate so many of Athens's streets are known as *neránjia* and that if you cook them up with kilos of sugar they're delicious! She says Greek cooks take half a dozen *neránjia*, peel them, put the flesh away for other purposes, cut the peels into strips, roll the strips into coils, thread them onto a cotton string, and then boil the resultant 'necklaces' with a great deal of sugar. This creates a very tasty syrup in which the colourful orange coils are transformed into extremely piquant, soft, and translucent sweets. The resulting confection is a traditional Greek dessert, *neránji karouláki*, often served with thick Greek yoghourt.

Then, rather given to the pleasures of subterfuge, Roúla suddenly draws near and lowers her voice, as if about to share a conspiratorial secret. She confides that if you keep your eyes skinned, you can sometimes see people nipping *neránjia* from the trees when they're tiny and green (at which time the little fruit are endearingly called *neranjiákia*). These *neranjiákia* may then be preserved whole in syrup, to be served as a dessert, or their young aromatic peels may be used to create an essence with which to flavour alcohol. Grand Marnier and Curaçao are made like this. But there exists a far less refined role for Athens's large and fully-grown *neránjia*, Roúla discloses. When there's a riot, and we know there have often been riots in Athens, this prolific fruit, so easily plucked from countless city streets, comes in rather handy and a number of policemen and politicians have found themselves smacked hard in the head by a flying *neránji*!

◙ ◙ ◙ ◙

13

Eternal Diónysos

Monument of Lysicrátes;
Acrópolis Museum;
Greek National Theatre;
Technópolis exhibition;
Benáki Museum of Modern Art
& Yiánnis Tsaroúchis.

The magnificent 335 BCE 'Monument of Lysicrátes' stands proudly now in its own little garden beside Tripódon Street - and, in fact, in the first garden in all of Greece where tomatoes were grown. In 1658 a Capuchin monastery was established in a building adjacent to the Monument and two centuries later, in 1818, its enterprising friars introduced the first tomato plant to Greek soil. In ancient times Tripódon Street was the road along which many elegant tripods (or three-legged bronze torches) were proudly displayed so that everyone in Athens might admire them as they walked to and fro between the *agorá* and the Theatre of Diónysos. The torches were won as prizes for theatrical productions, and were then mounted for posterity upon elaborate bases. Here today at the site of this one remaining such monument on Tripódon Street, just wait for the passers-by to clear, and then one's field of vision becomes filled with pure beauty: in the foreground stands the ancient honeyed stone of Lysicrátes's monument; behind it lies a splendid neo-classical mansion of matching golden hue, with pale blue shutters, windows, and doors; and high above the towering and intimidating north face of the Acrópolis, there flutters in the breeze a very large blue and white flag, the national flag of Greece. This is one of the most stunning views in Athens.

The last surviving choragic monument of Tripódon Street was erected by the *choregós*, or sponsor, Lysicrátes after he had been in charge of employing and training a dramatic dance-chorus at the nearby Theatre of Diónysos. For his efforts and the successful performance that they produced, Lysicrátes had won a coveted bronze torch. And so with justified pride, and in the customary manner, he set out to display it: he commissioned this monument, a generous nine feet in diameter, and then had his prize, the bronze torch, fixed upon the stone acanthus flower which is still to be seen upon the monument's top. Upon the frieze he ordered depictions featuring the myth of Diónysos's battle with the Tyrrhenian pirates that he'd turned into dolphins, as a grateful tribute to the god of the grape who through the ecstasy associated with rituals and wine was considered by the Greeks to be the progenitor of all theatre. When I was studying at the Conservatorium of Music in Sydney in the mid 1970s, and in my head the voice of Mihális Theodórou continually sang the songs of Theodorákis and Hadjidákis, each day on my way through the Royal Botanic Gardens to the Conservatorium, I passed Sydney's own 'Choragic Monument'. I didn't have the slightest idea then that it was an 1870 replica, made of Sydney-side Pyrmont yellow-block sandstone, of this very Monument of Lysicrátes here in Athens. Such aspects of Ancient Greece have for long been established in even the most far-flung corners of our planet, and wherever there stands a theatre on the earth today, there stands a link to Diónysos, the temperamental Greek god of wine, *écstasis*, and *dráma*.

The last time I was in this city, twenty years ago, it wasn't so easy to locate the main attractions, or even to find a simple route to the Acrópolis itself, although of course the great rock is generally visible from almost every part of the city. But since then, the 2004 Olympics have come and gone, and there have been a great many improvements. Just beyond the Monument of Lysicrátes there now lies a fine and very broad pedestrian way to the new Acrópolis Museum in Makriyiánni, and there are several similar routes to the Acrópolis, each landscaped and with attractive seating at various points. Once you pass the Monument of Lysicrátes, the broad way to the new museum is unmissable, and despite this wet and windy winter's morning there are literally scores of visitors upon it.

The forecourt of Athens's Acrópolis Museum is grand and extensive. In large part it consists of a glass floor beneath which, and sometimes very far below it, can be seen the remains of Neolithic to early Christian buildings that once hugged the base of the great and sacred rock that is the Acrópolis. The forecourt thus roofs and protects many of the archaeological ruins below, but some parts are open to view and you can gaze upon them over a chest-high sheet of glass. Almost as dramatic as the 2,000 square metres of ancient cream-coloured ruins which lie exposed below are the 100 round grey reinforced concrete pylons which rise, well-spaced, as few as possible, to support the massive weight of the new museum. These pillars are quite narrow, and they're elegant in the way that they appear to have stepped respectfully between prominent parts of the ruins. As you proceed over the glassed forecourt and into the museum's reception area, the remains beneath your feet fall deeper and drop still further away as you move towards the heart of the museum proper, so that it becomes somewhat unnerving to look down through the glass and see mosaics, drains, and remnants of villas and bathhouses that constitute the ancient neighbourhood below.

The Acrópolis Museum is a triumph. Beautifully laid out on the first floor, to illustrate the history of the Acrópolis's development, is a very large selection of statuary from the Sacred Rock. The naked grey columns that support the roof of the forecourt also feature throughout the interior of the museum and their completely unadorned concrete yields humbly to the staggering beauty of the sculpted marbles that are all about them. The second floor presents the elegant Caryátides, as well as a shop, and a large café-restaurant. The third and final floor is truly overwhelming. Ascending to it, I suddenly realise why this topmost level appears to have been screwed some degrees anti-clockwise, so that it sits out of alignment with the floors beneath. The reason is that the rectangular uppermost storey is instead aligned absolutely parallel with the Parthenon, which, through a wall of continuous glass, you can view above you, atop the famous rock. Why such an effort to set this great glass atrium parallel with the Parthenon? Well, it enables you to compare the recreation within this top floor of all three upper decorative bands of the Parthenon with their original site, and at a glance! Here on the top floor of this museum you can examine from a distance of just feet or inches the Parthenon's *metópes*, its frieze, and its two pediments, while turning, whenever you choose, to easily see through the glass their original locations high up on *Ierós Vráchos*.

The re-creation of the fine upper portion of the Parthenon sits in the centre of the floor and you can view all four sides of it by walking around the outside of the central walled cube inside which are housed the museum's stairs and lifts. Thus you stroll between the exterior of the re-created upper Parthenon and the four glass windows of the top floor of the museum, as if you were elevated and able to walk around the top of the Parthenon itself! It's a simple but brilliant and ingenious concept, generated by the French-Swiss architect Bernard Tschumi in collaboration with Greek architect Mihális Photiádis. Parthenon panels and *metópes* which are in the possession of Greece are obvious: their creamy stone gleams with antiquity. Panels which are on display in other museums are perfectly reproduced in white plaster, the originals and the copies slotted in beside each other to create a splendid semblance of exactly how the beautifully carved frieze and *metópes* originally appeared. In places where no marbles exist at all it's because they, over the course of centuries of Greek history, have either been destroyed or lost, either atop the Acrópolis or in the vicinity.

So here you are, walking around as if high up on scaffolding, and able to view the exceptional work that once adorned the top perimeter of the Parthenon. And all the while you know which side of the re-created temple you're viewing for you've only to glance up at the Acrópolis to immediately get your bearings. In the centre of this chaotic city surely nothing else, bar the shiny new Metró system and the ancient Parthenon itself, has been so cleverly thought out and designed. It's little wonder then that on this wet, windy, and very cold winter's day, this new museum is heaving with visitors, mainly Greek adults and large parties of Greek students and school-children, although there are clearly visitors here today from all over the world. The new Acrópolis Museum is now Athens's most popular attraction after the Sacred Rock itself.

Late in the afternoon I re-enter the large Nákas music-shop on Navarínou Street to decide whether to buy a very expensive collection of Hadjidákis's songs. As on my previous visit, I'm kindly allowed to try before I buy, upstairs again in the quiet clavinova department. I find the notes to melodies that I've loved for decades, some of which, sung magnificently by Yiórgos Daláras, I never knew were composed by Hadjidákis. After all these years, these are thrilling discoveries and as I thank the assistant, who has sat quietly behind his desk tolerating my sight-reading for nigh on a whole hour, I tell him that despite its expense I've no choice but to buy this irresistible collection of songs. He smiles, shrugs his shoulders, nods his head, lifts his palms upwards, and softly says, 'Ah, but for Hadjidákis . . . the price is nothing!' Mános is a Greek icon, and the salesman is right: for such intoxicating music the high price is indeed nothing.

On Aghíou Konstantínou Street, not far from Omónoia Square, stands the Greek National Theatre, an impressive 19th century stone building which I find to be offering a production of 'Don Juan' by Molière, and in Greek. Construction of this fine and imposing building in classicist style began in the late 19th century and was completed in 1901. Its purpose was to give theatre in Athens a major and modern new home. The building was designed by the architect Ernst Ziller, of Saxony, who had originally been brought to Greece in the early 1860s by Theophilus Hansen to supervise the construction of the Academy of Athens. Both Hansen and Ziller made a great contribution to the new Greek state, particularly by way of their designs for the new capital. All of Hansen's neo-classical plans were born of his observations of the monuments and remains of the ancient city, most of which he respectfully hunted out upon his arrival. Ziller eventually became a Greek national, and by the time he died he is thought to have designed no less than an astounding 600 Greek buildings, comprising summer villas and private mansions, a variety of churches, and many public and municipal buildings, such as this on Aghíou Konstantínou Street. Several years after this theatre opened, a production of Aeschýlos's Orésteia was staged in a daring new prose translation that caused a dramatic linguistic conflict that escalated into violence. Students from the university's School of Philosophy marched into Aghíou Konstantínou Street and sought to bring a performance of the Orésteia to a halt. The clashes that followed are referred to as the *Oresteiaká*. They resulted in ten people being injured, one person being killed, and the theatre remaining closed until 1932.

Sadly this very fine structure survives in an area of central Athens which has recently become awfully depressed. Opposite the theatre stands another building of similar age and grandeur but which is clad today entirely in scaffolding, along with sheets of netting to stop materials flying out and falling upon pedestrians and vehicles below. These protective sheets are torn and tattered, with some of them flailing in the wind, as on many similar preservation projects in Athens at this time. It appears that much refurbishment in the city has recently been abandoned. Apart from the few empty shop and café spaces that I found in Kypséli, these abandoned preservation or refurbishment projects are the only significant suggestions of recession visible in Athens at the start of 2010. But it's odd that while such buildings as these stand high above the pavements, unattended and neglected, on the streets below a great consumerist fiesta is in full swing. Women passing up and down this afternoon are loaded with fashion-bags, and the many cafés and restaurants hereabout are all full and heaving.

From the National Theatre I venture south-west in the direction of a new Benáki museum, a sibling of the main Benáki Museum on the southern fringe of Kolonáki. The new one is devoted entirely to modern art. However, to avoid the extremely busy and noisy Athens-Piraeus highway, I take a long, roundabout, and jagged route through the back streets of Metaxourgheío, walking roughly parallel with the highway but well away from it. Dereliction, decay, vandalism, and piles of refuse and filth are marked and substantial. Where shop spaces are usable they're generally occupied by Chinese. There are scores of such stores, all of them being basically bare cuboid interiors sparsely furnished with stainless steel racks of cheap new clothes. Arranged beneath the racks, on lower levels, neatly and systematically, are rows of cheap new shoes. But there isn't a customer in sight. I ask one young Chinese if there's a public convenience anywhere near. He clearly understands me, but scowls, turns his head, and looks the other way. These customerless Chinese do not seem contented people. And it's fascinating that this district is in such a state of decrepitude and dilapidation when it's within easy walking distance of the heart of this great city. If there really has been a reasonable amount of wealth in the government's coffers, one would have expected a broad regeneration project to have been set in motion here. I'm beginning to suspect that for some years Greece has been turning a blind eye upon certain clear indicators of economic infirmity.

As darkness descends I penetrate once again into Gázi and am delighted to find that this time all the galleries of Technópolis are blazing with light and open to visitors. The exhibition is entitled The Human Form in Art, and most of the works on display depict faces and nudes. The collection marks the 65-year existence of the national art society known as The Chamber of Fine Arts of Greece, and the 2,000 works on display are comprised of paintings, sculptures, engravings and other forms of decorative art that have been produced by no less than 1,200 artists, including academics and past and current professors of The Athens School of Fine Arts.

Some of the pieces are absorbing for their disturbing boldness. One large canvas portrays a healthy, muscular, and clean-skinned young man sitting naked on the edge of his bed, a small portable paraffin stove at his feet, along with other drug-taking paraphernalia, and he's intently injecting by syringe a drug directly into his penis. The sheet on which he perches is bluishly clean, while all else within the frame, bar his tan skin, is some shade of seemingly deliberately meaningless grey. Within another frame, and also in shades of grey, is an old and typically Greek face lined heavily by age, by the elements, and hard work, the mouth biting deeply, hungrily, and hopefully into a large and perfect apple. In another gallery, beyond vast preserved rows of old rusted city of Athens gas-pipes that shoot up from the stone-slabbed floor with all the command and beauty of the pipes of a majestic cathedral organ, there hangs a massive canvas filled with twirling rolls of flesh, patterned like detailed Brighton Rock, and depicted as perceived through the prism of hallucination. Altogether the heaving rolls upon the canvas describe a disturbed and terrified visage, clutched and partly hidden behind anxious fingers. A bald-headed middle-aged woman, completely naked, massively-breasted, and wide-hipped, perhaps a mental patient or a person suffering the side-effects of chemotherapy, glides forward in a stainless-steel wheelchair and comes to a halt as if to confront us. Her eyebrows are carefully plucked, she was once beautiful, her features are clearly Greek, and she seems to say, 'This is simply who I now am. Will you not accept me?' A *rebétiko* player serenades her from a nearby wall, he and all around him painted deep in the dark grey gloom of perhaps an old Piraeus *hashish* den, with only the brilliant red and yellow of the accordion he plays bringing some joy into the picture, and into his life.

Elsewhere there's work by the distinguished modernist Constantínos Parthénis and the renowned Alékos Fasianós whose iconic Greek portraits sell for vast sums in the auction houses of New York, Paris, and London. The gathered work of all the 1,200 Greek artists featured in this exhibition at Technópolis proclaims that a desire to be real, and to depict reality 'warts and all', has been, and continues to be, truly alive and well in the first decade of third millennium Greece. And this particular collection provides a healthy balance to the omnipresent beauty and classical perfection which are hallmarks of most of Athens's museums and galleries.

Further down the Athens-Piraeus highway tonight, the new Benáki Museum of modern art is bathed in a soft floodlight that causes its modern rust-coloured stonework to gleam as if golden. It's a mammoth cube of a building, quite plain, but with a large open interior courtyard into which its ground-floor café can spill during the summer. Exterior stone walls that are absolutely without windows communicate the sense of a fortress or a bastion intended to protect the artistic treasure within. All daylight inside the galleries is received from the courtyard, but even so the bright light of the Grecian sky is further filtered and controlled by horizontal stained-wood slatting guarding all of the courtyard's windows.

Although this evening the museum is open until 10pm and there are two separate exhibitions to be seen, I suspect I'll only have time to view the retrospective of the work of the artist and designer Yiánnis Tsaroúchis. As I purchase a ticket the name 'Yiánnis Tsaroúchis' means nothing to me, but no sooner have I entered the first gallery than I discover that I've been regularly viewing and savouring some of Tsaroúchis's work for thirty years, without ever knowing it was his. Furthermore, I've been entirely unaware that Mános Hadjidákis had a close working relationship with this artist despite my possessing a number of the old LPs of Hadjidákis's and Theodorákis's music upon the covers of which Tsaroúchis's work is featured. For years I've enjoyed, again without knowing they were his, reproductions of some of Tsaroúchis's pen-and-ink sketches in a few of my Greek books: simple and typically Greek sketches of perhaps just a table and a chair, such as you find in a *kafeneío,* or a sailor dancing the *zeïbékiko* alone on a tiled floor or perhaps just idly smoking a cigarette while looking wistfully out of an open window. I've been completely unknowing that these wonderfully atmospheric and innocent illustrations are just minor creations of an artist who produced extraordinary work and prolifically, throughout his life, including right through his last five years enduring Parkinson's Disease.

The galleries display just under 700 of Tsaroúchis's creations. Mainly paintings, as well as a number of set-design models, they've all been brought together from museums and private collections abroad and throughout Greece. Most of the paintings and drawings have been hung, but many smaller works, on paper or in books, have been arranged in glassed tables in the exhibition's final hall. Although a good number of Tsaroúchis's paintings are of fine old neo-classical streets and buildings in Piraeus, and in his early years he painted *eikónes* in the traditional Byzantine style (he was a student of Phótis Kóntoglou, who painted the Byzantine-like frescoes of the Church of Panaghía Kapnikaréa), Tsaroúchis was clearly obsessed with the male nude. His paintings of young Greek men were numerous and marvellous. Many are of sailors, sometimes posed singly, sometimes in groups, sitting around playing cards, lying in bed or upon a couch, or dancing the *zeïbékiko*. Even though most of the subjects are fully dressed, the paintings are generally erotic. And unless all the works of Duncan Grant were collected together, I can think of no comparable collection of homo-erotic art by one artist. Why is this man largely unknown today outside Greece? His material is very Greek in nature, every picture radiates *Elláda* (Greece), but it surely appeals to the whole world.

This retrospective reveals why Yiánnis Tsaroúchis is one of Greece's most important modern artists: for he helped define modern Greek identity. He was born in Piraeus in 1910 and eighteen years later he was studying at the Higher School of Fine Arts in Athens. But it was his subsequent immersion in the bohemian Paris of the 1930s that was to focus his life and all his future output. While revelling in the styles of Picasso, Manet, Renoir, and Matisse, it seems that Tsaroúchis found in himself, while in Paris, a bravery, an honesty, and an integrity that enabled him to step outside the confines and restraints of his traditional Greek upbringing. Thus, back in his own land, as young Greek soldiers prepared themselves to fight once again for their country's freedom, firstly against the Italians and later against the Germans, Tsaroúchis began to paint them. And then once the suffering that Greece endured under the Nazi occupation came to an end, Tsaroúchis perceived a vacuum, a need for imagery, a need for a new form of *eikóna*, for paintings that examined and expressed what it was and what it meant to be Greek. Honesty and pride in his own sexuality also suffused the resultant work. This did not mean however that he then solely portrayed the Greek male: he also, though to a far lesser extent, focused upon the considerable power and the strength of the Greek woman. And beside knocking off the odd illustration for the recordings of

Hadjidákis and others, Tsaroúchis also worked as a set and costume designer. In exile during the years of the Júnta he designed productions for Covent Garden and La Scala. He died in Athens in 1989. His home, in the distict of Maroússi, has been preserved in his honour as a gallery and museum.

Of the many Athenians visiting this exhibition this evening most are mature women, in their thirties and upwards. This is somewhat surprising, for the posters around town, which advertise this retrospective, feature prominently a close-up of strong muscular hands upon a waist-belt positioned just above the crotch of a sailor in a white tunic. It's singularly homo-erotic, a deliberately alluring detail from one of Tsaroúchis's full length portraits. Beside the many mature women here tonight there are one or two young Greeks, a few pairs of heterosexuals, and several pairs of men who I think are gay though in Greece, as mentioned earlier, it's so difficult to tell. But what is effectively a celebration of the young Greek male, handsome and fine, erotic whether naked or dressed, is being treated tonight by all these visitors, led by the older educated women, rather like an exhibition of religious *eikónes*. Everyone moves around the galleries in a practically hushed reverence, as if we're all in a church.

This is a daring and innovative retrospective and it was opened only a month ago by no less an important figure than Greece's Minister of Culture and Tourism, but I sense that most Greeks don't yet feel relaxed in the presence of such a display, at least when viewing such works in a public place. Indeed this exhibition is the first complete retrospective of Tsaroúchis's work ever to be held in Athens and possibly nothing like it has been seen in the city before. In London, at an exhibition like this, at the Haywood or the Royal Academy, there'd be a palpable sense and showing of excitement and exultation. You'd hear people talking and discussing, gasping in admiration, and certainly, at times, tittering or chuckling. I find this collection so wonderful that despite hungry rumblings in the pit of my stomach, and my having already been in these rooms for almost two and a half hours, I go round each of the galleries again, in some kind of hope that a second perusal will burn these extraordinarily bold, very

Greek, and deliciously sensuous works right into my retinas, so that they'll have an indelible and long-lasting effect upon all my future thinking.

Upon leaving the new Benáki Museum, rather than heading for home I turn away from the direction of the city-centre and penetrate instead into the area that lies behind the museum, well south of Gázi's dilapidation and late-night clubs. After some time I then stumble, quite amazingly, upon a small *kafeneío* with an old interior such as Tsaroúchis himself often depicted! Its lights are bright and welcoming, and inside there are mainly older men in dark jackets, smoking, drinking, eating, laughing, and engaging in free and colourful conversation. At a couple of tables there are several women, drinking and smoking with their male friends. On one wall a brass pendulum swings behind the glass of an old wooden clock; pinned simply in position on another surface is a large unfolded map of the Greek mainland; the rest of the wall-space consists simply of a dado of quiet rural green rising from the floor to about a metre, whereat a clean cream then sweeps upwards to the ceiling interrupted only by dark green window-frames and dark green sills upon which sit luscious green pot-plants. The tables are small, the chairs are various and quirky, and all the furniture in this *kafeneío* is old, wooden, and coated in shades of dark varnish. The floor is a Greek delight. It's tiled in chequered black and white, but for one characterful red replacement, while all around its perimeter, in more intricate and smaller tiling, like the fringe of a giant rug, wanders the famous *méandros* pattern, the 'Greek fret', as found on funerary amphora dating back to 800 BCE. Upon the *méandros* design this wintry night an old-fashioned two-bar electric heater glows orange-red. The owner knows no English, and so he's delighted that I can order in Greek, and very soon he brings me a basket of bread, a splendid Cretan salad supporting a most generous slab of *féta*, a plate of grilled pork, and a large glass of *kókkino krasí*. Rippling *bouzoúkia* and the exotic melody line of an impassioned Greek singer swirl in from a radio somewhere in the sizzling stainless steel kitchen behind me, and I am once again in paradise.

After all the experiences of this day, the walk home is more like a dance, or at least a recital of every Hadjidákis melody that my level of inebriation allows me to recall. Occasionally I meet someone along the way and whereas in the UK one would instantly go quiet for fear of becoming the butt of jeers and insulting imitations, like the howling of baying dogs or wolves in the dead of night, each oncomer looks me directly in the eye, grins delightedly, and recognises that I'm embraced at that moment within something akin to sweet *tsakír kéfi*.

🔲 🔲 🔲 🔲

14

Extreme Appearances

Kolonáki;
Megális Tou Ghénous Scholís Square;
Droméas II;
National Gallery and Aléxandros Soútsos Museum;
Frissíras Museum;
Aghía Eiríni & Panaghía Chrysospiliótissa.

M y next Athenian delight is to be this city's 'National Gallery and Aléxandros Soútsos Museum', on Vasiléos Konstantínou Avenue. After shooting through the thrilling animation of the central *agorá*, between Athinás and Stadíou streets, I avoid all the hectic traffic of Vasilíssis Sofías Avenue by heading for the gallery via the lanes of quiet and swanky Kolonáki instead.

Projecting pride, confidence, and optimism from Kolonáki's multitudinous boutique windows are hundreds of chic mannequins dressed to the nines in every latest European and North American fashion, straining laboriously in their efforts to dictate style to Athens's *oi polloí*, the many. One of the male models is just far too 'casually' awash with style to inspire! A white shirt with navy stripes hangs intentionally out over his smart expensive dark trousers; within the high collar of his shirt there snuggles a rich red-and-gold satin cravat, lapping adoringly at his ridiculously chiselled jaw; a fine grey worsted jacket is held together by one button over a violet-blue Cashmere slip-over; and then to contend with the Athenian winter, he's been finished off with a voluminous coat of expensive black suede. His style is completely intimidating, but it hasn't stopped a number of young Greek gentlemen this morning from entering the shop and perusing such garments. A few doors along is a patisserie equal to the finest found in Paris or Milan, its glass and gold chrome refrigerated display cases filled with all kinds of ostentatiously configured little cakes of the one-cake-per-person variety, each priced at just over three euros.

Despite this pleasantly cool winter's morning, several broad pedestrianized back-streets are almost dark beneath wide overhanging canopies which you'd expect are meant to protect people from the scorching heat of the sun. In summer they no doubt have this effect, but in winter these canopies have another function: they turn such back-streets, which are glutted with tables and chairs, into intimate and rather alluring gathering places. This morning scores of mature men sit beneath them drinking coffee, smoking, and chattering volubly. There are only a handful of women. Now in the UK, the States, Canada, Australia, New Zealand, France, Holland, and a good number of other countries, you'd be absolutely 100% correct in immediately assuming you'd stumbled upon a gay area! But not so here. It's almost 30 years since Greece joined the European Union, but in the most sophisticated central area of Athens it's clear that Greece is still a country of the cultural Levant, of the southern Balkans, of the cross-roads to the East, a land of the Orient. For cafés full of men, and only men, are to be found all over the Middle East.

Greek men have traditionally lolled away hours each day over long coffees and cigarettes with their friends and many still do so. As I've observed in a number of places in Athens, it is Greek women, and generally Greek women over the age of 35 or thereabouts, who tend to involve themselves in cultural life, who read, who visit galleries, and who patronise the theatres. The rest of the time they're usually busy in the home. Younger Greek women, however, are generally inclined to the same popular and fashionable culture, celebrity culture, that has attracted most young women in the West, the big priority of which is to conform to a particular kind of glamorous look and be seen as 'cool'. On late Friday and Saturday nights many young Greeks of both sexes throng to bars that pump out, often at ear-damaging volumes, exactly the same Western pop-rock that is standard in young people's venues in the West. So even here on the south-eastern edge of Europe young people are being wooed into consuming and following every conceivable transnational fashion, while their dads, as can be seen here in Kolonáki this morning, are still clinging to old and traditional habits, still delighting in hours of simply chatting exclusively with their male friends.

Just opposite Athens's intrusive Hilton Hotel, designed, sadly, by a trio of Greek architects, lies the little square of *Megáli Tou Ghénous Scholí* (The Great School of the Nation). Since the early sixties, the Hilton has sat as a concrete blot, a hideous sore thumb, upon Athens's eastern skyline - despite the well-intended intervention of the artist Yiánnis Móralis, who sought to transform the entire windowless northern wall of the hotel into a semblance of a vast stone tablet incised with seemingly ancient signs and symbols. However, the adjacent square of *Megáli Tou Ghénous Scholí* calls to mind a massively more impressive and significant building than the gross Hilton. In 1454, just one year after the Turks invaded and occupied Constantinople, the Greek scholar Matthaíos Kamariótis founded what was to become, through and despite the next 450 years of Ottoman Occupation, a major Greek educational institution, The Great School of the Nation, the *Megáli Tou Ghénous Scholí*. It was in such Phanariot schools as this that the notions of Neo-Hellenism were first taught. In the early 1880s, thirty years before the Turks began to 'cleanse' Asia Minor of all Christians, whether Greek or Armenian, the Patriarchate of Constantinople rebuilt The Great School of the Nation and at considerable expense. It was replaced with a highly ornate red-brick edifice somewhat akin to London's St. Pancras Station, thus becoming known locally as The Red Castle. This very fine building still stands today, majestically overlooking the Bosphorus. Now known as the Phanári Greek Orthodox College (*Özel Fener Rum Lisesi*, in Turkish), this important school, strangely and proudly held by Turks to be 'the fifth largest castle in Europe' due to its crenellated towers, is now required by the Turkish state to provide a full Turkish curriculum (in addition to Greek subjects). Consequently, roughly a quarter of its teachers are now Turkish.

Although the impressive Hellenic institution in Istanbul is commemorated in the name of this square here in Athens, the square itself is completely dominated by a rather dirty pile of thick bluish-grey sheets of glass which rise up in the centre of the space in the form of the giant sculpture *Droméas II* (Runner 2). The many jagged pieces of glass are so placed as to create the impression of an athlete running at such speed that he or she is followed by an ephemeral trail of his or her own entity. (The gender is intentionally ambiguous.) This is the 'replacement' sculpture that was created in 1994 by the artist Cóstas Varótsos after his earlier work had had to be removed from Omónoia Square. *Droméas II*, about the height of six very tall adults, appears to have sprinted down the wide and open Vasilíssis Sofías Avenue, vehicles and traffic lights all about the runner's feet, the nation's foremost art gallery lying just off to the left, with the great Acrópolis as goal. But in fact, every November hundreds of runners from many different nations competing in the 42-kilometre 'Athens Classic Marathon' rush past *Droméas II* as they arrive from the town of Marathónas to make their way to the race's finish line inside that ancient sea of white marble, the Panathenean Stadium.

Beneath the sculpture on this bright sunny morning, jugglers and acrobats patiently wait for the lights to turn red, so that they can then take to performing on the zebra crossings, before an audience captive in halted vehicles. Pairs of jugglers keep aloft in the air six clubs or more, while solo performers on monocycles expertly manage three or four clubs each. It seems the traffic-lights around *Droméas II*, unlike most other lights in downtown Athens, stay red sufficiently long for these performers to put on a decent show and still have time left over to visit a dozen or so vehicles in order to collect donations. Two police officers sit enjoying the spectacle but when a hat is presented at their window their expressions frost over and they refrain from handing over any coins. Perhaps they get trapped at these lights several times a day.

At the entrance to 'The National Gallery and Aléxandros Soútsos Museum' - the unwieldy title resulting from the ubiquitous Greek penchant to enhance and distinguish public or private spaces by appending to them the names of notable persons - there hovers a gaggle of fifteen or so middle-aged women who are unmistakably Greek. Their identity is made clear not only because of the language they're speaking but because each one carries some hallmark of modern Greek femininity. They sport heavily coloured, bleached, or styled hair; the designer label on the handbag, clothes, or sunglasses; and in most cases a little too much cosmetic make-up. This is obviously a big day out for these ordinary salt-of-the-earth Greek housewives and they're all terribly excited! They giggle, cluck, and call, in efforts to outrage and outdo each other. I suspect that by the end of the day their enjoyment of each other's company will far outweigh their delight in the contents of the museum.

In terms of design and appearance, Greece's National Gallery is most unfortunately dull - which isn't surprising given that this space was designed by the same team of architects who were responsible for the hideous Hilton, directly opposite. The exterior of the gallery is long, low, and cuboid, and despite the building's abundance of white marble, the visitor's eye upon arrival is only rewarded by the two large bronze figures which recline in a relaxed pose beside the entrance. Unfortunately, the interior is no different: you could be inside any ordinary municipal secondary school erected in the 60s or 70s. On this particular day the first gallery is empty, it's between temporary exhibitions, and so we're ushered through to the rear, to the galleries proper, where to left and right of the point from which we emerge there stretches a very long floor of yet more white marble. But here, despite further cubic sterility in the design of the gallery's interior, there commences upon its walls an extensive panoramic presentation of Greek life from the 1600s onwards, as revealed through the development of Greek painting. At any one time there are roughly 500 paintings on display here, unfortunately less than 5% of the approximately 15,000 that are in the gallery's custody, but the works are set out interestingly and methodically, illustrating and explaining with great clarity why the styles and subject matter of Greek painting have changed so dramatically over the course of the last four centuries.

The panorama begins with Post-Byzantine Greek art - the nation's valuable heritage of the art of the Byzantine period itself being housed separately in Athens's Byzantine Museum. After the fall of Constantinople to the Ottoman Turks in 1453,

Byzantine art continued in centres which remained outside Turkish control, particularly Venetian-occupied Crete. And then when Crete too fell to the Turks, in 1669, Greek artists found refuge in Greece's Iónian Islands, still controlled by the Venetians. Thus, because of the islands' relationship with and reliance upon Venice, Byzantine style slowly became influenced by the west. Worldliness, realism, and the three-dimensional gradually began to transform images that had been limited to two-dimensions and which had focused solely upon the ideal and the transcendent, as exemplified in typical Byzantine *eikonografía*. Illustrative of the change in style, a magnificent painting attributed to Panaghiótis Doxarás, 1662 to 1729, and on permanent loan to the National Gallery, presents a scene inspired by the battles of Alexander the Great. In this work Aléxandros is gloriously depicted as a towering and rugged mountain of a man, upon his head a gilt helmet bearing a flourish of white feathery plumes, and his daunting musculature described by close-fitting garments of rich blue, gold, and white, partly draped with robes of crimson. He is shown as the greatest icon of Greece's glorious past.

Particularly illustrative of the transition of Greek artists of this period are the works of the great Doménikos Theotokópoulos, widely known as *El Greco* (The Greek). Born in Crete in 1541, Theotokópoulos began by painting *eikónes* in the style of the post-Byzantine Cretan School with influences from the Italian Renaissance, but in 1567 he left for Venice. There he studied under Titian, observed Tintoretto, and thenceforward developed into one of the most significant figures in the history of world art. Elements of the Post-Byzantine can be admired in all three of the El Grecos on permanent exhibition here at the National Gallery: 'The Burial of Christ' (painted between 1568 and 1570), 'Saint Peter' (1600 to 1607), and the somewhat ghostly, though pleasingly sensuous, 'Concert of the Angels' (1608 to 1614).

In the second half of the 18th century a new strand developed amongst those painters who were working in the Iónian Islands. The rising Iónian *bourgeoisie* triggered a flowering of portraiture. And although such works initially tended to ennoble the individuals they depicted, the Iónians gradually began to portray their subjects in relaxed poses which became distinguished by a significant psychological element which established a dialogue with the viewer.

Following the overthrow of the Ottoman Empire in the 19th century, the new and 'free' Greek State, much influenced by its imposed Bavarian monarchy, very quickly established, in 1836, a School of Arts to bring foreign teachers to Greece, and to send young Greek painters abroad, though mainly of course to Munich. This led to an explosion of European influences in Greek art, and these influences immediately expressed themselves in the production of heroic portraits and monumental historical scenes that memorialised episodes of the War of Independence. There came a wave of paintings depicting the heroism of Greece's fighters, with the old white flag and its simple blue cross nearly always a significant element of the scenes portrayed.

Theódoros Vryzákis excelled in this genre and in his famous painting 'The Bishop of Old Pátras, Ghermanós, Blesses the Flag of the Revolution' (1865) the flag is central, though not dominant. Dominance is held by Ghermanós, the bishop, who, arrayed in gold vestments and mitre, stands high on a dais to look down upon the flag and grant both it and the plan to achieve Greek independence the blessing of the Orthodox Church. All around stand Greek chieftains in rich embroidered jackets and white or red *foustanélas*, half a dozen of them raising their arms high in the air with optimism and determination. Although several women have halted near the bishop in what was probably considered for women of the time an appropriately modest and sombre mood, the rest of the canvas brims with life, animation, and drama and one can sense the feelings that were present on the cusp of the uprising against Greece's Muslim occupiers. Although this work is completely filled with the action of the church's blessing, other such depictions often required exterior backdrops and thus arose the first Greek landscape painting. Swept up in the European romance of the age, Greek artists set about portraying their land as idyllic and transcendent, a land which they maintained, in keeping with the tenets of the rising Hellenism, was inseparable from the region's classical past.

Although 1862 saw Otto and his queen fleeing home to Bavaria, following the *coup* in Athens, paradoxically, in art, the very same year marked the beginning of Greek 'Bavarianism', as fresh from the School of Munich there arrived on the Greek art scene four major Greek painters: Nikiphóros Lýtras, Nikólaos Ghýzis, Constantínos Volanákis, and Yeórghios Iakovídis. Such artists returned to Greece with high Romantic nostalgia for the East, for all of the old colour, the aesthetic extravagance, and the oriental exoticism of life before the War of Independence.

Lýtras and Ghýzis even crossed to Asia Minor, in 1872, specifically to locate the distinguishing essence of this 'Greekness'. In 'The Betrothal of the Children' (1877) Ghýzis depicted many of the visible aspects of Greek family life that he witnessed at that time in Anatolía: the tightly-knit bonds of the family; the humble dwelling of bare whitewashed walls, ornamented wooden ceiling, and arched doorways; and the colour and luxuriance in everyone's clothing despite the obvious simplicity of their lives. The artist Symeón Savvídis actually came from Asia Minor and concentrated in his work upon capturing its hues and exoticism. His 'Lighting the Pipe' (1899) reproduces a scene which is barely different in any respect from some of the paintings executed by the great British and French Arabian Orientalists. The canvas is rich with decoration; the rear wall and floor are patterned with a design still seen often in the Middle East; in the foreground is an exotic vessel like an Arabian coffee jug; and the two figures intent upon the lighting of the pipe wear head-dresses that are still worn to this very day by mountain peoples of the Middle East. The pipe itself, very long and slender, is typically Eastern. And the little fire that burns in the central hollow of a small low bronze table can still be seen today amongst the Bedouin of Arabia who use a similar arrangement for making coffee and sweet tea and for lighting their tobacco pipe, the *shisha,* also known as the *narghilé,* the *hookah,* or the *hubbly-bubbly.*

At the same time as this return to the distinguishing roots of Greekness, two other forms of painting developed. Under the government and leadership of Charílaos Trikoúpis, non-Eastern or non-Orientalist portraiture became popular as the artists of the School of Munich (Ghýzis, Lýtras, Iakovídis, Nikólaos Xydiás, Aristeídis Varoúchas, and Ioánnis Doúkas) painted those rising industrialists, bankers, ship-owners and the like who had become very much inclined towards European forms of sophistication. Landscape painting progressed too, from depictions that were heavily romantic towards a realism that was dictated by Greece's magical but highly exposing light. The revealing Grecian light required sharp honesty rather than the employment of any form of haziness or ambiguity, and so Impressionism in Greece could not, and did not, prosper. Greece's countryside is beautiful but harsh, and, dominated by the sun, its colours are strong and wonderfully vivid. Such qualities thus dominated early 20th century Greek modernism.

The harsh years of the Asia Minor Disaster, culminating in the Convention of Lausanne, followed by the Treaty of Lausanne and the horrendous population exchange of 1923, impacted heavily upon Greek art by rupturing Greek self-confidence and identity and by thus creating a further need for analysis of what precisely it was that constituted the Hellenic. Self-examination consequently led to another return to the nation's past. However, combined with this study there were continued efforts to integrate the ideas of European modernism. Thus there arose a body of work which synthesised Greekness with the styles of the European avant-garde. Constantínos Parthénis combined elements of Greek antiquity and Byzantium with modern manners of depiction. Spýros Papaloukás painted traditional Greece through the lenses of the modern. And Yiánnis Tsaroúchis sought exclusively to represent Greekness and the Hellenistic by way of brush-strokes popular amongst modern Parisians. In most of Tsaroúchis's work, and although it is so very clearly Greek in content, there can be seen the unmistakable influence, in terms of style, of Henri Matisse.

Although Expressionism was unable to really take root in Greece, due to the brilliance of Mediterranean light not entertaining the depiction of those phantoms which lurk in gloom and darkness, there were several Greek expressionists. The greatest of these was Yeórghios Bouziánis. After being immersed in the arts in Germany, Bouziánis returned to Greece in the mid 1930s when Nazism began to threaten Expressionism. And despite the Greek light he continued to work as if in Northern Europe! His very dark paintings, like 'Female Dancers' (1936) and 'The Uncle' (1950), reverberate with human passions and vulnerabilities.

Abstract art appeared very late in Greece and when it did manifest itself Greek painters were reluctant to sever their connection with visible reality. Focus on the human figure remained, though it was enriched through the prism of abstraction. After the end of the Júnta, artists felt once again free to express their own personal desires, but to this day their fascination with the human figure continues. Recently, however, there has been a significant turn towards the disturbing and the psychological, although this trend is not yet represented very strongly here at the National Gallery.

Nevertheless, this collection offers several stunning modern portraits, one of which is Panaghiótis Tétsis's 'Portrait of A.K., 1998 - 1999'. Sitting on the end of a couch, the ankle of one leg resting in a virile manner upon the knee of the other, A.K. fills almost the entire canvas as if he's just managed to fit himself comfortably within its frame. A finger of one hand rests upon his brow, suggesting deep thought, while his other arm lazes along the back of the sofa. AK wears a generous rich-maroon crew-necked jersey and close-fitting blue jeans, garments somewhat redolent, in modern terms, of the colourful gear in which Alexander the Great was depicted by Panaghiótis Doxarás four hundred years ago. To the right of AK, beneath the arm resting along the back of the couch, there's some undefined source of brilliance, a seeming furnace, a power-house, a tunnel of bright light. Like a generalised and contemporary representation of the ancient hero depicted at the beginning of this exhibition, AK seems to carry with him hope for the future of 21st century Greece.

Ever since the middle of the 19th century, all Greek artists working in Greece, and not only in the fine arts but in literature and music as well, have been wed to a hankering after Greek authenticity, dictated by a form of regional loyalty, always thinking of themselves as Greeks before viewing themselves as artists, writers, or composers. While this Hellenism has limited the contributions of Greek artists on the international level, there's no doubting that it has created for Greece a corpus of work, a cultural legacy, which is, of course, distinctively Greek. The paintings of the National Gallery and Aléxandros Soútsos Museum thus constitute a truly national collection and the people of Greece ought to be able to access it easily and for free. The works displayed here are key to Greek identity, and as such they're surely vital to the self-esteem of the nation. So they deserve to be housed in a building which is worthy of them. Why not transfer clerical staff out of some splendid neo-classical building in the centre of Athens and re-house those staff here, inside this very utilitarian space grovelling at the feet of the ugly Hilton? Or take a string of fine old mansions in Pláka and sympathetically connect them so as to provide a series of interesting and historical spaces that will allow Greece's artistic heritage to sparkle in an environment which is uplifting, inspiring, and enhancing.

What the National Gallery lacks in contemporary Greek painting, as well as in accommodation which is fitting for art, may be found at the Frissíras Museum in the Pláka. Despite its name the Frissíras is not actually a museum but a gallery. In Greece the term 'museum' is often used to indicate that works on show are not for sale, thus many Greek art galleries are referred to as museums. Anyway, in the Frissíras's comparatively small number of rooms there's a great deal of the new Greek art that's disturbing and deeply psychological. In this beautifully restored and adapted old Pláka home many of the images that I find hanging upon its walls are desperate and frightening. The contrast and incongruence between this art and its accommodation is strange, but at the same time strangely agreeable.

The Frissíras Museum occupies one of the first and finest neo-classical houses of Athens, built in 1860. Originally it had a courtyard at its centre but that courtyard has been magnificently transformed into a glass-roofed and light-filled atrium, on both sides of which are balconies and gracious curving staircases that lead up and down to the four floors. All of the rooms, most of which are connected to the atrium, are bright, airy, clean and uncluttered and painted in light colours, and this afternoon a fine and inconspicuous music system very subtly fills the entire building with a Mozart piano concerto. The atmosphere is superb. But there are only four or five other visitors here, though the streets nearby are thronging with shoppers. One can't help but consider that, surely, given Greece's current financial crisis, the citizens of Athens would be better off abandoning the shops and taking rapidly to the inexpensive and far more gratifying appreciation of art. Not that art-appreciation is always inexpensive, for in the Greek sales of Bonhams, Christies, and Sothebys modern Greek paintings often sell for prices ranging from around £5,000 to £50,000 while older works by well-known Greek artists frequently sell in the same houses for hundreds of thousands. But one can visit and enjoy art in such places without having to buy it.

The Frissíras is a most uplifting experience. On display at this particular time are works by Edouárd Sacaillán, a Greek artist born in Thessaloníki in 1957 of Armenian roots and now a resident of Athens. His work is dark in theme, tormented and tormenting, though at the same time strangely satisfying, oddly optimistic, and often colourful. Many of his paintings seem to speak of claustrophobia or detachment. He seems to suggest that the outlaw or castaway results from norms which society imposes upon the individual, but within the same images Sacaillán resolves the claustrophobia or detachment of the dispossessed or the outlawed by suggesting peace and refuge. The isolated inner self is saved, at least for the moment.

Of the 150 or so Sacaillán oils that are on display at the Frissíras at this time several feature gay subject-matter. One noteworthy canvas is entitled 'The Lovers'. It's perhaps ten feet tall, but roughly only one and a half feet wide. At the bottom, in darkness, in a grim room, are two men's faces. They are sleeping, side by side, a grey blanket up to their chins, their faces upturned towards the ceiling. I'm reminded of some grim old hotel room in the back-streets of Cairo, or some awful 'digs' in a cheap B&B in a depressed part of Britain. The top of this very long canvas shows the ceiling far above the two sleeping lovers: its elaborate old plasterwork is now cracked, dilapidated, faintly visible at the edges but more so in the centre because of the solitary light-bulb hanging by a cord directly over the bed. Because of the length and narrowness of the painting, the distance between the ceiling and the bed seems, and is, vast, but the two spaces are intimately connected in terms of relationship and experience. For this moment, at least, the two lovers in the gloom far below the dangling light-bulb are safe.

A related picture features five very masculine middle-aged male faces side by side upon the pillows of a double bed. A dull serge blanket with a toy plane and a toy car resting upon it is pulled up and onto their chins. These men too stare up towards a naked tungsten light-bulb suspended from a cord. Somehow they seem imprisoned, judged, in the dock. The picture is titled 'Aged children together in bed' (1995). Another Sacaillán canvas, 'Boat With Reader' (1991), features a small wooden sailing vessel heavy with a dozen or so very different people, some in suits, one reading, another nursing a child, another seemingly exhausted, while in the dark watery foreground a face appears to be sinking and drowning. In the distance, approaching the boat from behind, is a long trail of figures in the water. Are they following an overcrowded ark? Is this work a comment on Athens's serious overcrowding? Or might it be addressing the country's considerable refugee problem? Boats crowded with economic migrants from the coasts of Turkey and North Africa regularly enter the ports of Greek islands, and recently in the rough seas of the Aegean a number of such boatloads have been drowned. Groups of islanders have demanded that rough refugee camps set up on the edges of their towns be bulldozed and moved elsewhere. They want their islands to remain safe and isolated. They don't want the uninvited or the unwanted coming ashore.

The Frissíras claims that it is currently the only permanent museum in Greece solely for the exhibition of contemporary European painting. It has more than 3,500 works in its possession, among them pieces by Hockney, Auerbach, and Peter Blake, and the last painting I view here this afternoon is a disturbing work by the French artist Jean Rustin. It features a small freakish man, young or old you can't tell, in underpants and seaman's jersey, with long bandy legs, a tiny barrel-shaped body, a disproportionately large head, a vacuous look upon the face, and one hand clutching the crotch of his underpants. He could be 'an idiot' but for the unmistakable tenderness with which he's been painted. This work is one of Sacaillán's favourites, selected specially by him to accompany the exhibition. It's a painting of powerful intensity and one which, like many of Sacaillán's works, tells of loneliness and solitude.

Upon leaving the Frissíras I wander for a while through the Pláka. This historical area is nearly all pedestrianized now and many of its fine old buildings have been beautifully restored. The walls of one, now the home of the 'Piraeus Group Cultural Foundation', are painted in an arresting coat of rich and warm butterscotch, while a very bold dark green picks out its window-frames, shutters, and doors, and large shiny-leafed evergreen bushes lap all about the building's base. But quite a number of the Pláka's neo-classical homes still await such loving transformation. They sit, meanwhile, locked and bolted in a state of either pitiful or simply aged decay, their lower accessible exteriors often completely obliterated with graffiti. In this important heritage and tourist area the wretched wielders of spray-cans have defaced even beautifully refurbished and inhabited dwellings. Few surfaces escape their attack. It's a tragedy that this one truly beautiful and quite small area of old Athens is so deliberately and intentionally blemished and disfigured. The blots and eyesores are particularly noticeable where the houses and restaurants of the Pláka meet the ancient sites. The sites, however, are thankfully well-protected with high metal railings, but while one section of your view is comprised of the splendid columns and pillars of classical Athens, surging contemptuously towards that vision is graffitied Athens, desecrated, unkempt, and quite often filthy.

The full length of the exterior wall of the Melína Mercoúri Foundation in Odós Polygnótou has been vandalised with graffiti to a height of about seven feet. This is unfathomable, for it seems like an act of direct contempt towards the actress, singer, politician, and activist who did so much to preserve and promote Greece's cultural heritage throughout the world, who was fully aware of the privilege of living in a country where almost every inch of ground bears witness to some amazing history. For Mercoúri, Greece's cultural heritage formed a source of inner strength and pride, but it seems that Athens's custodians cannot now even be bothered to honour her memory. Why are the jewels of this city held in contempt? And why don't Athenians, and certainly local residents, if not the authorities, take action and stop the desecration? In recent years graffiti has got out of hand in some parts of New Zealand, as it has in so many other countries, and some New Zealanders have become so incensed by it that they've formed voluntary community groups equipped with paints and brushes to obliterate every graffito almost the moment after they've appeared. Action like this is needed in Athens.

Late this afternoon, directly in front of the seven splendid unfluted columns that remain of Hadrian's Library, there are fifty to sixty Africans and Asians peddling and hawking wares which they've laid out on white sheets on the pavement. In ancient times this area was the city's main commercial *agorá*, while the area further west which today is referred to as the Ancient Agorá was just as much a centre of civic business as commercial affairs. So the scene before me here this afternoon, hawkers and peddlers all over this patch directly in front of the ruins of the ancient library, is actually host to much the same activity as it saw 2,000 years ago.

All over central Athens I've come across young African men like these here in front of Hadrian's Library. They wander the streets trying to sell cheap copies of designer-handbags, sunglasses, pirated DVDs, umbrellas, and suchlike. But this afternoon there are as many Indian sub-continentals out hawking in this area as there are Africans. All have their goods laid out upon their white sheets in such a fashion that each lot may be swept up within seconds, to be thrown over the shoulder and hurried away the moment the appointed lookout signals that a band of swaggering young *astynomikoí* have hoved into view. The young Greek police stand idly around on street-corners, in groups of as many as six or seven. They chat and joke and smoke before every once in a while sauntering on a block, sending the hawkers scurrying away with their bundles of merchandise like frantic ants bearing on their backs enormous white eggs.

In Aiólou Street in Monastiráki, standing quietly back from crowds of strolling bag-laden shoppers, are several churches which aren't listed among the ecclesiastical 'must-sees' of central Athens, but which are, nevertheless, very fine buildings indeed. They're not true Byzantine churches, of which there are only a few in the old centre of the city, but are instead recent churches designed in determined Byzantine style. The excellent condition of their exterior brickwork and tiled domes betrays their comparatively recent construction. The interiors, however, appear on first glance authentically historical. In parts a great deal of candle smoke has blackened the walls and there is much ornately carved dark wood, particularly within elaborate *eikonostásia*, or rood-screens. The deliberate minimising of windows and the use of stained glass in the few apertures that there are in churches like these, fosters a mysterious internal darkness within which the glimmering gold backgrounds of *eikónes*, the cut-glass and gilt of sizeable low-hanging chandeliers, the vivid colour of many small hanging lights, and the gilt delicacy of moulded plasterwork, all dazzle, gleam, and enchant. And by the use of dark hues, and particularly dim blues, on walls and on the insides of domes, the sizes of the interiors of these churches are as if increased - a blue dome seems as high as the sky, and shallow dark ochre alcoves appear deep. These churches are truly the sanctuaries of Athens: they offer mysterious, magical, and highly theatrical interiors in which people can escape the *cháos* of the external grind for a special 'otherness'.

As you pass these places of worship during working hours it's easy to think them deserted: you seldom see anyone ascending or descending their steps. But this afternoon in both churches on Aiólou Street, both Aghía Eiríni and Panaghía Chrysospiliótissa, there are, just as I have seen in Athens's genuine Byzantine churches, solitary worshippers gliding silently and prayerfully from icon to icon, stooping to kiss the lower edge of each icon's frame before moving on to the next. There are rarely more than four or five people in each church at this time of day, and they're mainly women, but surprisingly they're not always older women. Instead they can be quite young, and often dressed in a modern fashionable manner that seems quite incongruous, and incompatible even, with the dark, godly, and antique interiors. This afternoon there are also some youngish men moving solemnly among the pillars, men in their late twenties, thirties, and early forties. They glide from shrine to shrine like the gentlest and most innocent of children, although some of them wear clothes straight out of the windows of the trendiest shops of Odós Ermoú or the most expensive boutiques of Kolonáki. One young worshipper sports a completely shaven and oiled scalp, on which are perched, in the manner of the fashionable hip poseur, a pair of expensive-looking designer sunglasses. The stylish crowds that throng the centre of Athens with their shopping bags are thus a source of puzzlement. While on the streets they appear to have been drawn into life-styles of superficiality and excessive and unnecessary consumption, caught up in the false elevation of shopping as 'therapy', their behaviour within these houses of prayer suggests otherwise. Some Greeks are clearly, though strangely, managing to balance the two extremes.

A Greek CD shop in the heart of Monastiráki astounds yet again by a display of the prodigious number of singers that Greece has produced over the decades, and which it continues still to produce. Over the years literally thousands of Greek singers have been recorded and enjoyed their moments of glory in the limelight. Music is burnt into the Greek soul, and Greeks so very often have exceptionally fine voices. While just buying a bus-ticket at a *períptero* or ordering a coffee in a café, I'm often stunned by the resonance and the sonority of the voice of the person assisting. Good vocal production seems somehow natural to Greeks. I suspect it's largely the Greek language: its strong use of vowels and their particular placement, far more in the head than in the throat, naturally encourages impressive resonance.

Anyway, this afternoon I buy several recordings of the most beautiful and most popular Greek voices that have ever been, and then learn from the very helpful assistant that sales of this kind of music are slowly dying, that young Greeks are generally losing interest in Greek music, that they want instead to be part of the 'cool' new West, part of modern 'happening' Europe and USA. And so, she tells me, young Greeks are clamouring for the thumpety-thump-thump, or even the gentler hiss-hiss-hiss, of rap and artless beatbox Eurotrash. And this kind of music they tend to download onto their computers from Internet sites, and often for free from pirate sites, some of which are based in Greece. Like their contemporaries in the West, many young Greeks don't understand why they should pay for music. They think musicians and music companies should work and produce music for free. It's as if because music is transmitted through the air they've come to equate it with air itself! Since air is free, so ought the music that somehow 'hangs' within it to be free as well, or so they foolishly think.

I end the day with an *oúzo* and a simple meal in a quiet little *estiatório* on the edge of Psyrrí, and fall into conversation with a man called Tákis at the next table. He's in his mid sixties and works as a tour guide, not only around Greece but throughout Europe as well. His English is thus very good, and, as is helpful in his line of work, he's knowledgeable and very culturally aware. We talk of many things to do with Greece and Athens and the perilous state that Greece is said to be in at this time, and Tákis agrees that *cháos* reigns supreme here. He says that in Athens disorder is now of such proportions, with the city having become so huge and sprawling, that successive governments simply fail time and again to get a firm grip upon everything needing attention. And so the *cháos* continues: many of those who earn money try every method they can to keep hold of it and avoid paying taxes, the young grow up with little trust in the system and thus express their dissatisfaction by defacing every surface they can, and more and more illegal immigrants stream into the country unchecked.

The government's coffers are empty, Greece has the greatest national deficit of any member of the European Union, there is now no money to deal with the nation's most significant problems, and millions must still be borrowed at high interest rates just to keep Greece ticking over! Billions were spent to stage the 2004 Olympics but the only legacy that has truly benefited Athens, Tákis says, is the Metró. For some reason he doesn't refer to the impressive new airport or to the fine new ring-road system that has made driving around Athens immeasurably quicker and safer. But by all accounts he is correct in dismissing the Olympic facilities. They're located far from the heart of the city and they're now largely white elephants, rubbish and debris collecting all about them while Chinese investors consider their possible development. Tákis spells out his country's situation without restraint and he's been the only person in my almost two weeks in Athens so far to do so. As he pays his bill and prepares to leave I tell him this and ask him why it is so. His answer is that it's because Greeks have an extraordinarily strong sense of national pride and it hurts them inordinately to criticise their own country, while he, Tákis, leading tours all over Europe, has come to experience a degree of detachment, a distance, an objectivity, which enables him to view his country in perspective.

Athens is a city of extremes, such as I've encountered nowhere else. One moment I'm in heaven, energised and inspired as never before, alive as I've not been for years, and the next instant I'm in despair, horrified, dejected, saddened by the realities of a place I've dreamt of for so long. And I'm beginning to perceive that this is also the Athenian state of mind: that Athenians also swing from one mood to the other, propelling themselves forward by this strange mechanism of optimism to despair and then despair to optimism, making do as cheerily as they can with whatever they have. Again tonight a good many Athenians will pass the hours right through until six in the morning in bars and clubs of all kinds, from those pulsating with Eurotrash and other sounds from beyond Greece, to those heady with *laïká* and *rebétika*. And every one of these Athenians will be seeking to enjoy some hours of *écstasis*, some escape from the hectic drudge of daylight hours in this maniacal yet totally lovable city.

◙ ◙ ◙ ◙

15

Refuge & Delirium

The young Greek on duty at reception this morning sparkles with life, and Sotíris has such a spring in his step that he seems almost manic. 'Ah, well, Mr. David', he explains, 'You see, last night I had much *tsípouro!* So then I had a very long sleep!' Well, *tsípouro* is 45% alcohol by volume but last night with my dinner I had half a small bottle of *oúzo,* and *oúzo* is just as strong, it's simply a version of *tsípouro* flavoured with anise. So how come I slept badly while Sotíris appears to have slept like a baby? One answer could be that he drank much more than I did, but I suspect the truth is that he was far better prepared, with heating and bedding, for the sudden and dramatic drop in temperature that has occurred overnight.

I head south for the Acrópolis, fully aware that my route will take me through the Sunday flea-market but determined not to waste time over endless old junk. I fail. I can't resist. Spread on the ground, or on collapsible tables, in street after street around Avissynías Square, are piles and piles of old things, alongside many carefully laid-out assortments: there are plates, clocks, Greek LPs, cutlery and utensils, lamps, bric-à-brac, in fact, almost anything! And it's generally not the same sort of stuff you see at car-boot sales or village 'antique' fairs in the UK. There's an exotic element to it: most of the bits and pieces here have emanated from Greece, the Balkans, or Turkey. Little is of Western manufacture. Some of the stalls and shops offer expensive pieces of considerable quality, while most of the sheets spread on the ground offer paltry collections of rather useless or gaudy items. All the unwanted things on sheets are sold by hopeful Greeks who must surely have travelled in to Monastiráki early this morning from who-knows-what distant areas of this enormous city. Their desperation is visible and striking.

Few people are buying from any of these sellers, though many Greeks are browsing, yet nearly every stall-holder is sipping from a large cardboard-cup or clear plastic container of coffee, purchased from one of the many nearby coffee outlets. At the same time, nearly every one of them is anxiously smoking. And although I've noted that all the *períptera* (kiosks) about town supply Greece's own brands of cigarettes, it's surprising to note the number of famous transnational tobacco brand names poking out of the jacket pockets of these clearly impoverished 'merchants'. Are these poor folk aware, I wonder, how much their poverty is a result of Greece's many decades of bargaining with American and Western corporations? Despite all the objections that there now are to the use of nicotine, Greece once had a massive and thriving tobacco-growing industry. But in exchange for Western aid and support, it was required to reduce its international exports. Thus all these ordinary Greek men and women on Monastiráki's streets this morning, desperately eking out their livings, have to some degree had their fates determined by economic blackmail, by the requirements of corporate Western interests. And although I don't smoke, I understand that most brands of cigarettes are much alike and that it's the saturated Western advertising which pervades every form of Greek media that has these merchants this morning sucking away on Western brands, in preference to cigarettes that are produced from tobacco grown within Greece.

En route to the Acrópolis, others like me, who are also out walking on this beautifully crisp but sunny morning, have paused on the quiet and pedestrianized Odós Apostólou

Pávlou (St. Paul Street) to observe a young Greek who has strung up a rope between two trees in order to perform antics upon a 'high-wire'. All the while he plays on a little harmonica which is kept to his lips by a wire frame about his neck. The melody he plays is lazy, carefree, insouciant, and balmy, and he accompanies it with correspondingly charming and dreamy movements, all performed with great skill and entirely upon the rope. He lies stretched out, gently swaying from side to side, as if having an afternoon snooze, and at points he even turns over and changes position on his rope, with as much ease and lack of concern as if he were turning over on some wide mattress or in a hammock. He adroitly erases from his viewers' minds the fact that he's entirely supported by a single taut cord. Thus people willingly drop coins in his hat, captivated and bewitched by a young Greek who is creatively using his energy and talents to earn a little income - a marked contrast to the many in this city who simply sit on the pavements and just ask for money. One can't of course deride those others in Athens who can do little more than sit begging, largely immobile because of amputated limbs or serious illnesses, but I'm not sure about the people who at this time and fully-limbed kneel on the pavements with their foreheads permanently touching the ground for hours on end, little cups held out in front or positioned just beyond their heads. You can't tell if they're disabled or not. Sometimes they keep their faces completely hidden. Compared with this young Greek working hard on his rope, or the acrobats and jugglers who perform at traffic lights, the kneeling ones often appear benumbed by their own sedentary supplication.

On this lovely, cool, clear, and sunny morning, Greeks and foreign tourists young and old, converge upon the Beulé Gate, the main entrance to the Acrópolis, unearthed by French archaeologist Charles Beulé in 1852. Most visitors approach the Beulé Gate from several wide walkways which travel up through the luscious grassy woodland that lies to the rock's north-west. But regardless of which path people take, all eyes this morning are focused upon the iconic columns and walls above, the exquisite grace and the honeyed tints of the monuments there becoming clearer with each step. Once inside the Beulé Gate everyone must now tread the same path, but twenty years ago, when I last visited, you could walk almost wherever you liked, and sit or stand on any ancient piece of stone that took your fancy. Today, and probably because of the international explosion there's been in tourism, visitors to the Acrópolis are directed by signs and barriers along a very clearly-demarcated circular route. Much of the ancient marble is thus saved from the wear of countless feet, although the entire rock and its structures still remain vulnerable to all sorts of other problems, such as the effects of air pollutants and weathering, fractures and cracks, incrustations and biodeterioration, and the failure of many earlier attempts at conservation.

However, great things are happening these days upon the Acrópolis. Very slowly and carefully its ancient remains are being repaired and restored. Following the Greek War of Independence, Greece's attention turned to the Sacred Rock as a national symbol. This was partly due to the fact that although the war had ended in September 1829 and the London Protocol of the 30th of August 1832 had fully ratified and reiterated earlier agreements regarding the borders of the newly created kingdom, Athens's Turkish governor and his garrison of Turkish soldiers had continued to occupy and live in the Acrópolis for a further seven months! They finally quit on the 12th of April 1833. Furthermore, throughout the years of Ottoman occupation the Acrópolis had been out-of-bounds to Greeks - only Turks, and foreigners who were prepared to pay for the privilege of a visit, could ascend it with ease. Consequently, once the Turks had finally left, there arose a strong desire to return the Acrópolis to its 5th century BCE state of classical purity. A mass of Turkish fortifications, several hundred red-roofed little houses, and all sorts of post-classical and medieval additions were thus to be removed.

Some of what was taken away had contributed significantly to this site being referred to as *Ierós Vráchos,* the Sacred Rock. For due to the Parthenon temple's very special nature, the early Christians had forced it into the role of a cathedral, known as the basilica of 'Mary the Mother of God in Athens', dedicated to Holy Wisdom. In seeking to coerce the worship of the goddess Athená into the adoration of the Virgin Mary while displacing Father Zeus, Apóllon, and Lógos (or Divine Reason) with God the Father, Son, and Holy Spirit, they raised a short squat bell-tower above the south-western corner of a new roof, and in constructing a semi-circular apse on the inside of the temple the Christians demolished the central section of the Parthenon's eastern pediment, so that its fine central sculptures, most probably of Zeus, Athená, Íphaistos, and Héra, were lost forever. Then with the arrival of the Turks the basilica was converted into a mosque, and sometime in the 1460s above the Christians' short squat bell-tower a very tall, pencil-like, circular minaret was erected, similar in style and height to the four minarets that the Turks placed over the course of several centuries around the patriarchal basilica of Aghía Sofía in Constantinople. After the devastating explosion caused by the Venetian attack of 1687, which destroyed the Parthenon's roof as well as much of the structure and columns of the temple's two longer sides, the Turks then built, inside the ruins and therefore open to the sky, a small stone mosque with a domed roof. Thus, long after the goddess Athená stood proudly within the Parthenon, the Acrópolis had continued for centuries to be an important site of religious worship.

In the effort to return the Sacred Rock to a state reflecting its ancient splendour, to a semblance of how it was at the time when people ascended here to pay respectful homage to Athená, there have been many completed 'interventions', many are ongoing, and more are planned. Since 1975, when the current restoration project began, the thousands of odd stones from around the Acrópolis, known as 'The Scattered Members' and which can now be seen stacked in careful piles at points all over the rock's surface, have each been meticulously examined, photographed, and catalogued. These Scattered Members include fragments of reliefs, fragments of statues, of marble vessels, and of small altars; fragments of Doric and Ionic columns, capitals, and bases; pieces of sarcophagi, and hundreds and hundreds of other unidentified chips and chunks of ancient fashioned marble. Slowly, some of these pieces are being re-incorporated and returned to their original positions within the standing monuments, and where old stonework has degenerated badly it's being substituted with new white marble from the same mountain, Mount Pentéli, from which the original marble was quarried in ancient times. Thus, there are now portions of the Acrópolis monuments which consist of perfectly cut white marble, contrasting clearly with the ancient creamy-gold weathered stone beside which it has been placed.

Altogether there are more upright standing structures to be seen on the Acrópolis today than there were a hundred years ago, but this doesn't mean that in another hundred years' time future visitors to Athens will visit a largely reconstructed Acrópolis and be able to view a Parthenon which has been entirely re-assembled. For while such a restoration might be splendid to visit, and sensational to view from points all around the encircling city, internationally-agreed modern restorative practice requires that every aspect of the Acrópolis intervention programme be reversible, that the ruins are only to be preserved, that the original structures are not to be fully reconstructed. So, we must content ourselves with simply recalling how things *were*, in the time of Periclés. When we visit the Acrópolis we can try to imagine all the beautifully and brightly painted statues that were here, the great roof of richly polished cedar over the Parthenon, and the great wealth there was of gilt decoration, glittering in the bright Athenian sunlight.

As I begin to ascend towards the Propýlaia, the monumental gateway to the Acrópolis, with the site of the Temple of Athená Níke to the right, I find I need to gently calm myself, for there's clearly a restless contagion afoot. The disturbance is slight but palpable. Amongst some of this morning's visitors there's beginning to stir a kind of competitiveness, born I suppose of excitement and anticipation. It doesn't spring from amidst the Greeks, nor from the Japanese, or Chinese, all of whom, I notice, are behaving comparatively quietly and studiously. It surges, instead, from amongst some of the many Americans, and some of the British and Germans and other northern Europeans, who are beginning now to rush greedily forwards and to the sides, with cameras and tripods.

We're passing through the Propýlaia, erected between 437 and 432 BCE, the most majestic entrance constructed anywhere in the ancient Greek world, but instead of causing people to marvel in appreciation of this wonder, it's as if the powerful presence of this magnificent gate has triggered in many of this morning's visitors a kind of mild delirium, probably born of cultural conditioning. They're suddenly seized and gripped by a fever that likely arises from their awareness of simply having made it here, at last, upon the famous Athenian Acrópolis. But unfortunately, at the very same moment, they're also seized by a determination to capture the best views that there are before anybody else does! It's completely silly and irrational, of course, because the views aren't going anywhere, they've been here for over 2,000 years, and, furthermore, about three million other people visit the Acrópolis every year and photograph exactly the same things! The fever is, I suppose, evidence of the truly iconic status that this staggering site has in the consciousness of every nation on Earth. Nevertheless, I do need to still myself and not let this behaviour detract from the specialness and sacredness of this morning's visit. I move right to the very edge of the south-west side, so that everyone else is removed from my field of vision and the delirious ones are all somewhere well behind me.

Below sits the Iródis Attikós theatre, almost 2,000 years old, with its perfectly restored marble amphitheatre, and its stone wall of arched windows granting a dramatic and antique backdrop to the stage or *orchéstra* area, despite today's façade falling considerably short of its original and more impressive height of roughly 27 metres. Gifted to the city by the wealthy Athenian Iródis Attikós, this grand and august theatre was destroyed only a century later when in 267 CE Athens was sacked by its first wave of invaders, the Heruli, a nomadic tribe which is thought to have originated in Scandinavia. It was not until 1950 that the seating of this amphitheatre was restored to its original state, following excavations in the mid 19th century. Today this stunning ancient venue, which can accommodate five thousand spectators, is much sought after for outdoor concerts in the warm months of June to September, and the theatre's custodians find it difficult to resist artists' requests to appear here, particularly given that some artists are so desirous of performing in this beautiful, ancient, and prestigious venue that they're prepared to donate all their proceeds to charity. Debates over which artists are good enough for this historic amphitheatre are fierce: who will dignify it, and who would just turn it into a night-club? Chewing-gum and high-heels have been banned, but archae-ologists remain concerned that this antique theatre simply cannot take the wear and tear of modern concerts.

When you raise your eyes from the splendour of *To Iródio*, the theatre, you see directly above it, on Philopáppou Hill, the intriguing monument to Gáios Ioúlios Antíochos Philópappos, 65 to c. 116 CE. A prince of Commaghiní, a small kingdom of Asia Minor, located roughly in what has become south-central Turkey, Philópappos was one of the most prominent Greeks of the Roman Empire. After settling in Athens and assuming civic, political and religious duties, he became a respected benefactor of this city. As a member of the Roman élite he became friends with the Emperor Trajan. And when Philópappos died, his death caused such great sadness to his sister Ioulía Balbílla, as well as to the citizens of Athens, that to honour his memory, Balbílla, along with the local population, planned an exceptional tomb and monument. It was erected at some point between 114 and 116 CE on what was then called Mouseíou Hill, the hill named, so reported the Greek traveller and geographer Pafsanías (Pausanias), after Mousaíos the companion of Orphéas who sang, died, and was buried upon it, and in whose memory, perhaps it was, I encountered several nights ago someone plucking a lýre-like instrument upon this very same slope. Made of Pentelic marble the tomb erected on Mouseíou Hill became known as the Philopáppou Monument, and from this the entire acclivity eventually became known as Philopáppou Hill. Over the centuries the tomb fell into disrepair and at points it was raided for its stone. With only the lower two thirds of the monument's original thirteen metres of height now remaining, it's a curious, strange, and incomplete structure that stands today upon the crest of Philopáppou Hill.

As I proceed along the south side of the Acrópolis, the Parthenon, the great temple of Athená Parthénos, the Virgin Goddess, looms magnificently to the left. With barely a single straight line or perfectly flat plane within its construction, with corner columns that are slightly larger in diameter than all of its others so as not to appear smaller, with all of its columns tilting slightly inwards, with a floor that is not a perfect rectangle but slightly bowed on all four sides as well as slightly raised at its centre, and with many other similarly deliberate distortions integrated throughout the building, this entire edifice, though wholly, of course, of rock-hard marble, possesses an astoundingly 'living' quality: a fluid, vibrant and dynamic naturalness. And herein, upon a pedestal in its nave, once stood sculptor Pheidías's great 'statue' of the Parthénos (the Virgin). About 10 metres in height, and so beloved of the citizens of the ancient city, Athená was actually no more than an intricate web of thin but beautiful plating, carefully affixed upon a large hollow wooden frame. In 2 CE Pafsanías beheld and described the Virgin's robes, spear, and helmet as being of glistening gold, while her hands and face were of ivory, a combination and composition described as *chryselephántine*.

When I come eventually to look down upon the neighbourhood of Makriyiánni to my right, and the quirky twisted top floor of the modern Acrópolis Museum that is sited there, the behaviour of certain other visitors suddenly tempts me to fury. The morning tranquillity and the sacredness of this rock is shattered and disturbed by the loud voices, all at once surrounding me, of several parties of young Americans, aged roughly between fifteen and twenty-five. They're of that particular kind who don't for a moment think of the sensitivities or feelings of other people. Their speech and cries are straight from the sitcoms and trashy teenage Hollywood movies that now blot practically every television channel under the sun, including the dozens of stations broadcasting here in Greece. They are quite the antithesis of the studious young people to be seen passing in and out of 'The American School of Classical Studies at Athens', beside the foot of Mount Lykavittós.

Here, this morning, on this marvellous, historical, and ancient Acrópolis, teenaged girls from the States are mainly concerned with clinching themselves together against any column or pile of scrolls they can find, so as to grin inanely and exhibit perfect rows of teeth while holding their heads at an angle, long hair draping downwards, in automatic imitations and projections of sweetness and innocence. They're so appallingly good at posing and fakery. They flutter from one magnificent view to another, take a quick gasp at whatever they see, and then immediately, giving their backs to the source of their excitement, they assemble into a pose and proceed to giggle at their friends' cameras as if ecstatic. I suppose they are. But not for the best reasons. They seem to be 'stealing' this site, using it, exploiting it, as a backdrop for their own egoistic excitement. They're behaving just as they would in some plastic fantasyland back in the States, in Disneyland, or on some Californian beach.

Their boyfriends, meanwhile, or at least the young American males accompanying them, are given to striking solitary heroic poses in imitation of classical statues. Doing an impersonation of the stunning seven-foot muscled athlete with arms raised as if about to thrust a thunderbolt, a javelin, or a trident, the bronze discovered in the waters off Cape Artemísion in 1926 and preserved now in the National Archaeological Museum, is clearly a very popular pose. Several of the young men instruct the girls to photograph them leaping through the air, camera shutters clicking so as to capture them while their feet are well above the ancient marble. Thus they use these rocks of ages as mere props and background, to create records of themselves, flying through the air not only high above Athens but above the iconic Acrópolis. Back home it'll be 'Look, this is *me*, flying through the air on top of that big rock in Greece!', instead of 'Look, here's a photo of some ancient Athenian scrolls!' If they were permitted to turn tricks on skateboards and mountain-bikes atop this rock, I have no doubt they would. How 'cool' that would be.

The young Greeks here this morning are so markedly different. They stroll around their *Ierós Vráchos* quietly and respectfully, with dignity, discussing this aspect or that of the various structures or the views below, or simply conversing quietly about other things. I'm surprised they don't show any sign of being offended by the superficiality of the raucous invaders. Perhaps because of their history of repeated occupation and the endless streams of millions of tourists, Greeks have become long-suffering and tolerant, perhaps too generous. I exchange a few words with a young Greek couple, male and female, who are leaning with arms around each other upon the parapet of the Belvedere, the small and rather dramatic look-out or terrace at the north-eastern end of the Acrópolis, created in the 19th century on the site of a Turkish tower for the pleasure of the Bavarian royal family. Above us flutters the same Greek flag that can be seen blowing high above you when you're way down below in the streets of the Pláka, looking up, like a tiny ant. The young couple tell me that this particular part of the Acrópolis occupies a very special place in Greek hearts, because here on this very spot there once occurred acts of gallantry comparable to the heroic feats of the Greek gods.

Hours after the Germans entered this city in 1941, one of the Nazis ordered a Greek *évzon,* or sentry, named Constantínos Koukídis, to haul down the blue standard so that the Nazi swastika would be seen flying over Athens instead. Koukídis had little choice but to comply, but as soon as the flag was free of the ropes, he suddenly wrapped it about his body, and threw himself over the parapet and down the side of the cliff, to certain death on the rocks below. The tale leaves me speechless. The two young Greeks nod their heads and smile. But there is more, they say, and they translate for me the inscription upon the plaque near the base of the flag-pole. It commemorates Manólis Glézos and Apóstolos ('Lákis') Sántas, two young students from the nearby university, who, on the night of the 30th of May, soon after the earlier event, safely bypassed Nazi guards stationed on the Acrópolis by ascending through a narrow cave and secret passage they'd read about in a book of ancient history. Armed only with a torch and a pocket-knife, it took the young men three hours to scale the 50-foot flagpole and cut down the huge swastika. They then tore five pieces from the detested Nazi flag for themselves and friends, dumped the rest in a well inside the cave, and fled, though not before they had been stopped at the foot of the Acrópolis by a Greek police officer who demanded to know all they had done, but who then let them hare off into the night.

Next day, after the Gestapo launched a manhunt with the stated intention of executing the perpetrators, there was extensive front-page coverage in Athens with editorials 'condemning' whoever was responsible - so causing the young men's mothers to hurriedly burn their sons' diary of their exploits and the five pieces of swastika. The news thus marked the beginning of the Greek Resistance; within hours the BBC broadcast to the world that the first national resistance against the Nazis had begun; and throughout the rest of the war the two students' courageous and spirited behaviour gave inspiration to all of those Greeks who resisted the Nazi occupation. The facts of how the flag of the Third Reich had been removed emerged only after the war when the Greek police officer who had accosted Glézos and Sántas stepped forward and revealed all. In 2008, at a session in the Greek Parliament specifically held to honour the two men, a resolution was passed stating that their act had been 'the first gasp of resistance', that the two young heroes 'saw a symbol and decided to become symbols themselves'. Both men continued to lead political lives right into the 21st century and have received numerous other awards. Manólis Glézos remains politically active despite having been injured by tear gas at an Athens protest in March 2010, at the age of 87, and in April 2011 thousands of Athenians turned out on the streets to honour Apóstolos Sántas as he was carried to his grave.

Many Greeks have not forgotten the horrors of the Nazi period. They've not forgotten the 300,000 who died as a result of Nazi Germany's occupation of their land over the course of four long years. Nor have they forgotten that Germany has yet to fully and directly compensate them for looting all of the gold that was stored in the Bank of Greece, or for the terrible trail of damage that the Nazis inflicted upon the country's infrastructure. For following the liberation, war damage to Greece's infrastructure, proportionate to the nation's population, was found to exceed that of every other war-damaged country in Europe. Although in 1960 Germany paid Greece about 115 million Deutschmarks to compensate victims of the Nazi occupation, it has refused all subsequent demands for further compensation. It has, however, given Greece around 33 billion Deutschmarks since 1960 in the form of financial assistance to a fellow member of the EU, as well as having contributed to the approximately 60 billion euros that the EU has granted Greece for the development of infrastructure and archaeological sites, and for the improvement of skills and productivity, not to mention additional funds for farming.

Still, for the horrors they suffered during the Nazi occupation, Greeks have every right to remember, for the effects of occupation and domination are profound and long-lasting. As I drift away from the young couple lolling on the spot where three young Greeks displayed bold defiance of the Nazis, I recall how, along with 2,000 other Britons, my grandparents on my father's side were transported to German prisoner-of-war camps in Southern Germany when they were both sixty years old, accompanied by my uncle who was then aged thirty. The Nazis had already ejected them from their farm on the island of Jersey in the Channel Islands, leaving them to take refuge for two years in a spare room in the home of a St. Helier well-wisher. Their additional three years behind barbed wire in Germany, in appalling prison-like conditions, particularly in winter, and with war-planes regularly roaring overhead, were enough to disturb the three of them so severely that soon after liberation my grandmother and my uncle were admitted to a hospital in Lincolnshire. They remained there for the rest of their lives. My uncle 'lived' in that hospital for 33 years, until he died in 1978. Such are the untold but lasting psychological effects of war. Furthermore, my grandparents and uncle never received a single Deutschmark of compensation - nor to this day has any other resident of the Channel Islands who suffered under the Nazi occupation.

Sometimes people mistakenly think that the pain of war dies out when those who were directly involved pass away. But this isn't so. The effects linger on. I know very well that until the day my parents died they were psychologically scarred and haunted by the traumas that were inflicted upon them by the Nazi's looting of their own home in St. Helier, and by my father's horrendous five years as a rear-gunner on RAF bomber flights over Germany, as well as by their knowledge of the physical and psychological suffering endured by my uncle and ageing grandparents in prisoner-of-war camps. And of course because the war so badly affected my parents, it also affected the day-to-day life of our isolated little family in far-flung Fiji and New Zealand, and so to an extent the Second World War also affected me. But at least my imprisoned grandparents and uncle were revived occasionally by the odd Red Cross food parcel from home. Unlike thousands of Greeks in Nazi-occupied Greece, my relatives didn't suffer the agonies of starvation that result in death.

The stones of the Acrópolis are impressive but so too are the views of what lies below and around it, hugging the rock's circumference. Beneath us, the red-tiled roofs of Anafiótika, sandwiched between Pláka and the vertical rock-face of the Acrópolis, reveal the tinyness of its dwellings and how small it is as a community. And away to the north-west, like a smaller but complete version of the Parthenon, the intact Temple of Íphaistos, known now as 'The Theseíon', sits solidly and proudly amidst the luscious winter green of Athens's Ancient Agorá.

As I approach the Eréctheio and its famous portico supported upon the heads of six draped maidens, the famous Caryátides, so named because they were modelled upon women from the village of Karyaí in Lakonía, the final stage of my visit to the Acrópolis is marred by an American who I noted earlier, holding court. He's in his late forties or early fifties and he's not only representative of those people who must loudly 'own' anything of value that they find anywhere upon the face of this earth, but he is a true caricature of the type. He has clearly read a great deal about the Acrópolis, and now, here, today, he must, simply must, declare his knowledge to all who can hear him. Loudly, and with that aggression that is part and parcel of the vigour of the All-American Male, he insists on disseminating much of what he has read, as if the Acrópolis were his own property, as if his family has owned this site for generations. He delights in informing his listeners that the Caryátides which they see before them 'are all fakes!' (Certainly they are indeed all copies, or casts, the four existing originals being now safely and splendidly displayed in the new Acrópolis Museum.) And no sooner have his listeners taken on board that the beautiful stone maidens before them are all modern cement 'fakes', than he follows up with 'And, hey, I bet you'll never guess what the Eréctheio used to be used for, by the Turks!' Of course, his listeners can do nothing other than await the answer. 'It was their hareeeeeeeem!' he blurts, signalling and savouring the salaciousness of the fact. Probably because this learning is so strongly and unavoidably declared, if not somewhat hurtfully, one young American woman walking in his group seems to attempt to side-track him.

'So, hey, tell me, you really know your stuff, don't you! Like, when was it, like how did you start, like getting interested in all this kind of, like, archaeology thing?'

Oh, big mistake, young lady, for off he'll go again so that dozens of us will have to endure yet more of the same.

'Well, OK, you see I was, like, a History Major, yeah? At college, yeah?'

And then off he launches into the depths of his CV, fully engaged in self-adulation right up here on the Acrópolis. I fear few visitors of his kind actually experience anything profound on this great rock. To them the Acrópolis is just another stop on a tour of all the world's 'historical theme-parks'.

A dozen or so paintings at the Benáki retrospective of Yiánnis Tsaroúchis were of fine streets of neo-classical buildings in old Piraeus, so to try to find them, I leave the Acrópolis and its crowds and make my way down to Monastiráki to take the Metró to the port. The ride to Piraeus is not a long one, and once the train has pulled into the fine old station, it's thrilling to walk out into the salty air and immediately see, just upon the other side of the road, the vast white ships that wait to cast off for sparkling Greek islands. Piraeus is one of the largest ports in Europe and with just under twenty million passengers passing through it every year, it is the third largest passenger port on Earth.

A fine modern suspended footbridge, complete with escalators, enables pedestrians to pass easily over Piraeus's busy harbour-front highway, to the many quays and ships on the other side. But I head south instead, and over the hill to the small exclusive waterside streets that are spread between Mikrolímano and Pasalimáni, the latter being also known as Marína Zéas. Between these two charming, quiet, and clean little harbours and around the tip of the stony hill of the Prophet Elías, one hundred metres above sea level and the highest point in Piraeus, lies the prosperous and somewhat picturesque area of Kastélla. Beside all the usual *polykatoikíes*, Kastélla comprises a considerable number of neo-classical mansions that feature elegant balconies with elaborate wrought-iron railings and windows that are protected by characterful narrow wooden shutters. The wealthy who inhabit these fine homes also own some of the pristine crafts that are moored in the two little bays below.

But many of the old neo-classical buildings of Kastélla are in ruins, receiving until such time as they're restored only the attentions of graffitists. At least they're now protected by preservation orders. Above them, on top of the hill, stand the picturesque church of the Prophet Elías and, for secular entertainment, the outdoor Veákeio Amphithéatro, from where views of the waters of the Saronic Gulf provide a backdrop to summer entertainments upon its stage. From many points in Kastélla one can look out to the islands while also looking down upon the two plush little harbours packed with luxury yachts and the wonderfully complicated criss-cross of masts and riggings. To the south east the coast trails off to the far distant seaside areas of Voúla and Vouliagméni.

But what of the larger part of Piraeus, to the north of the railway station? Emerging from a belt of ugly warehouses and storage depots as are to be found near every large and busy seaport, I find myself again in streets very similar to those of most areas of Athens. There are blocks and blocks of five-storey apartments, streets cluttered with parked cars, and unfortunately a far greater litter problem than I've seen anywhere else in Athens except for that generally dilapidated area formed of Psyrrí, Kerameikós, Metaxourgheío, and

Gázi. Here on northern Piraeus street corners, even immediately adjacent to well-maintained dwellings and expensive new cars, there are occasional heaps of garbage and refuse, the agglomerations of many weeks, if not months. Household rubbish stuffed into scores of multi-coloured plastic shopping-bags spills out of unemptied skips and down upon broken household appliances or bits of broken furniture or even whole couches and mattresses. And almost as if to emphasise that these occasional corners have become unofficial tips, the first six feet or so of adjacent apartment-block walls are covered with layer upon layer of graffiti. It's all hideous, and it's obviously been like this for months, if not years.

But hopeful that some of the fine buildings that Tsaroúchis recorded still stand on this side of Piraeus too, I zigzag north-west, towards the locality of Keratsíni. A large antique shop appears, an oasis of interest, closed at this hour but full of all sorts of curious things from old Greece, including a complete old dentist's chair with, standing separately, a beautifully elaborate matching rinsing-fountain. There are characterful old oil-lamps, antique glass lampshades, a considerable amount of authentic nautical brass bric-à-brac, salvaged from old Greek ships, and a flourish of wind-up gramophones with trumpets of verdigrised brass or of thin opaque leather bound tightly over metal webbing.

This mid-afternoon people are indoors, at home, resting, and the roads are fairly quiet. Windows at street-level are nearly all shuttered, but through the shutters there penetrate the sounds of radios and televisions and people talking. It must be very dark within, for the shutters are nearly all of the roll-down metal variety, solid and unperforated, and so admitting absolutely no light. Presumably they're needed for security, most particularly in the summer, during July and August, when many in Athens and Piraeus flee to the cool of the islands or the mountains, but no doubt such shutters also simulate night during the *ypnákos*, or siesta, by very effectively blocking out every ray of brilliance. And such metal shutters, unlike the old slatted wooden ones, need little maintenance.

Nevertheless, with all of these closed metal shutters about, it seems to me, just as it has often struck me in similar parts of Athens, that streets of *polykatoikíes* like these are somewhat like the halls and corridors of an expansive and very free open-prison. Of course there are pleasant, leafy, and spacious suburbs in Athens, like Vouliagméni and Néo Psychikó, but in areas like Kypséli and Keratsíni choices are limited. You can spend as little time inside your 'cell' as you please, you're entirely at liberty to venture out to the shops and cafés below, and you can join with the mad traffic and travel to some other point in the unending sea of concrete *cháos*. But if you wish to taste true freedom, you need to strike out for the coast, or for the far distant hill-tops, or the ferries and the open sea. I haven't met a Greek yet who hasn't sighed with longing when hearing of the idyllic rural seclusion and tranquil beauty of the valley in which we live in the Welsh Marches. But Athenians seem to need the extreme communality of life in Athens and I suspect the average Athenian would go quite potty after more than just a couple of days in the very isolated hills of South Shropshire. Nevertheless, I've come to learn that a great many Athenians dream of change and yearn for escape.

I've noticed that of all the community meetings advertised in the weekly Athens newspapers, about 30% of them tell of support groups that deal with drugs, alcohol, or over-eating problems. It could be, of course, that help agencies in Greece more regularly and more visibly advertise their services than do similar agencies in the UK, but I wonder to what extent life in this vast sea of almost uniform blocks of concrete, this relaxed and exotic form of 'open-prison', is indirectly responsible for what may be a high prevalence of addiction to state-altering behaviours. For example, the EMCDDA (The European Monitoring Centre for Drugs and Drug Addiction) has reported that in 2006 in a study carried out among members of the population aged between 15 and 64 in Athens, Thessaloníki and Irákleion, 19.3% of respondents reported prevalent 'lifetime' usage of cannabis. While this statistic seems worryingly high and figures for other addictions in Greece may perhaps not be as pronounced, it's a fact that people generally form such habits when they feel there's no better way to improve their situation, when they feel that there isn't much else that they can do. And, indeed, I've heard the passive expression *'Ti na kánoume!'* (What can we do!) so many times over the past two weeks here in Athens that I've been reminded of Arabs shrugging their shoulders and sighing *'Allahu Almusta´aan!'* to indicate exactly the same thing.

After four hours of searching, and finding only the very occasional simple old house, single- or two-storey, surrounded by five-floor apartment blocks, and always abandoned and dilapidated, I finally chance upon one solitary and splendid specimen. It's all characterful 'gold' stone, recently cleaned and very smart, with fine new wooden shutters in a traditional style. Aside from its spectacular incongruity with every structure that surrounds it, the building is, in its own appearance, impressive. A young woman passes and in answer to my enquiry as to whether this building is lived in she chuckles and tells me it's been converted into a special venue for community events, for concerts and suchlike. I say how delightful it looks, and how I'd hoped to find more of the same, but she frowns and shakes her head. 'There is no historical centre now to Piraeus. All has been replaced with modern. Only here and there you will find old buildings. It's so sad.' It seems that but for the sprinkling of mansions remaining in Kastélla, and but for old photographs and the brush-strokes of artists like Yiánnis Tsaroúchis, bulldozers have erased most of the reminders of Piraeus's better past.

However, as I near the main port again, towards the end of this afternoon, I do find a section of old Piraeus, except that unfortunately it's not a remnant of the city's neo-classical past but simply a couple of intact short lanes from perhaps the 1930s or 40s. Its buildings have a few touches of Art Deco about them, and if they were smartened up they'd look good. Some of the upstairs balconies are gracefully curved and some bear intricate wrought-iron railings. But the lanes are strewn now with garbage, they're derelict and utterly foul but for a couple of straggly lantana bushes, gallantly sprouting from between broken slabs of concrete, their brightly-coloured florets bringing a touch of sweetness to the general squalor. Downstairs windows just above the pavement are mostly stopped up with old sheets of rusty corrugated iron, to prevent unwanted entrance. A couple of old sofas have been dumped outside front doors. And the graffitists have had a field day, although somebody at least is holding out hope: one building amongst this shambles stands substantially painted in recent virgin white, though the effort appears to have been abandoned a metre or so short of the roof. And then I hear the sound of Eurotrash pulsing from speakers behind the peeling wooden concertina shutters of an upstairs window. People are actually living in this slum.

Just minutes away is an extremely flash men's clothes shop, breathtakingly at odds with the nearby squalor. Its windows display suggestions for men's evening-wear. One mannequin advocates donning first a long-sleeved jet-black shirt, buttoning it at the neck and then adding a tie of brilliant red diagonal stripes upon a background of silver-blue silk; following this, don a second long-sleeved shirt in brilliant vermilion, leaving it entirely unbuttoned and swept open so that the tie and black shirt beneath are fully visible; and then, finally, turn up together the two sleeves on each arm to just short of the elbows, so that the forearms are exposed but finished off with a wide band of bold black. The effect is stunning, luxurious, and theatrical. And it whisks me back to Cairo. For in that city, where there is intense and widespread poverty, and where most of the buildings are old and decayed and the streets are dusty and often filthy, young Egyptian males seek escape in the purchase of inexpensive but elegant shirts and trousers. The number of shirt shops in central Cairo is staggering, and they play a very important role: they offer young Egyptians a way of freeing and cleansing themselves of *cháos* and poverty by literally enveloping their bodies in affordable presentability, freshness, and newness. I suspect that this Piraeus shop and many other such stores here and in Athens are offering a similar commodity, though not so much for gentle walks along the Glyfáda sea-front, in the manner of young Egyptians strolling up and down along the banks of the Nile on weekend evenings.

The 'escape-industry' in Athens is considerable, despite the heavy grip maintained upon Greek life by the Greek Orthodox Church. Though Athens is certainly not a European 'sex-destination', until 2010 it offered its residents between

three and four hundred sex shops. And there's a considerable number of brothels as well, clustered mainly in particular
areas like Metaxourgheío and around Fylís Street. Several fine
old cinemas have been turned into porno flea-pits. The Greek
airwaves, cluttered with TV channels, broadcast programmes
of very low escapist quality including pornography. But I
suppose a positive way of viewing these options for escaping
into the worlds of dreams and fantasy is to see them as simply
yet another aspect of the Greek love of *eleuthería*, freedom.

The night-clubs and *bouzoúkia* of Athens function as a very
important central safety valve. They provide an escape from
the drudgery, the monotony, and the ugliness of most of the
city streets. They offer places where young Greeks may revel
in sheer delight. They provide late nights and early mornings
of music, laughter, dancing, and, most important of all, *paréa*
- the pleasure of one's circle of friends. Such places in Athens
are, in function, expensive and modern elaborations of the
simple dingy night-time *rebétika* dens of old Piraeus. They
present modern young Athenians with wondrously and richly
theatrical places of nocturnal flight and liberation, spaces of
delirium where dreams may take wing. Some Athenian clubs
feature chandeliers, swathes of plush curtaining gathered up
theatrically as if upon a stage, lavish couches with punched
and silken cushions as of an immense Eastern harem, and
enchanting lighting produced by the most sophisticated
lighting systems currently available in Europe. Such clubs
are palaces of glamorous escape from the mundane. Their
bars stock almost every form of liquor imaginable. One of the
most famous night-clubs in Greece, situated on the seashore
in Voúla, includes a luxurious restaurant offering gourmet
dishes with champagne at 100 euros a bottle. In summer its
bars and dance-floor can accommodate up to as many as 3,000
young revellers at a time. So if when you go to a club such as
this, or to any of the sixty or so *bouzoúkia* in Athens, you really
want to impress and make your mark, then you need to arrive
dressed as smartly as the mannequins in the windows of the
most stylish of the city's clothes shops.

At about 5pm I'm welcomed into one of the many restaurants that look out upon the Piraeus quays, and the gigantic

ferries that are moored there, by a very attractive young Greek woman who then with great kindliness and patience lifts the lid of each of the dozen or so delicious-looking dishes she has gently simmering in her kitchen, so that I can make my choice. This wintry night the dozen or so tables of this quay-side *estiatório* are empty but for that of a very interesting-looking woman who appears to have arrived only a short time before me. The four big paper box-bags to her side suggest she's probably just returned on the train from a shopping expedition up the line, in central Athens. While she's being brought the usual array of little dishes that many Greeks appear unable to resist ordering, I settle just a table away so that I too may enjoy the fine view of the ships opposite. As she tucks in, I sense from her manner a strong independent career woman of reasonable means and who probably lives alone. I suspect she's also much the same age as myself. When my plate of novel Greek 'fusion food' arrives, a wicked slice of *Μπενγκάλι Μουσακάς* (Bengali Mousaká), steaming with aromatic cumin, coriander, turmeric, chilli and masala, ginger and garlic, aubergine and lamb, lemon, curry, and cheese, I catch her stealing a helpless and curious glance at it. We exchange smiles and speak, and of course, like me, she's keen to learn what it tastes like! So after a few pleasantries regarding its absolute deliciousness and as she begins to pour herself a glass of wine, I'm encouraged to lean over and ask if she'd mind helping me out on a couple of rather puzzling questions concerning the many Bengalis, Pakistanis, and other Asians who now live in Greece. She beams in response and says she'd be delighted. Now could I, or would I, ever be so daring in a British restaurant? I don't think so. But in Greece, you can.

I tell how I've been staying for the last two weeks in a hotel in the historic centre of Athens and how I've observed that for most Greeks streets like Socrátous, Sophocléous, and Evripídou are no-go areas, teeming with immigrants involved in unfortunate activities. I relate how passing through this area I've often seen half a dozen policemen lining up immigrants along a wall or shop-front and forcing them to take off their shoes and jackets and to answer questions. Then before I can move on to ask if she knows what the policy of the Greek government is towards these immigrants, my fellow-diner is shaking her head and saying that such behaviour from the police isn't acceptable, that this isn't the way to deal with the problem, and that Greece needs to make some very important decisions.

'On New Years Eve, were you here?' she asks. I wasn't. 'Well, five police officers beat up a thirty-year-old Chilean man inside the Acrópolis Police Station and all because he asked to be allowed to make a call to his lawyer! In the end he had to be taken to a hospital!' She relates that this incident was yet another case, one of many, where underlying frustration got out of hand because Greek authorities are desperately trying to cope with a continual stream of migrants, the police are under enormous pressure, and nobody has decided what's to be done. She qualifies this by telling me she's a psychologist, that she understands the police's frustration, and that the problems of immigrants often crop up in her work. I appear to have struck gold. After sharing a little of my own background in psychology and education, I discover in response that I'm talking to a psychologist of considerable experience. Her name is Chryssoúla.

Chryssoúla goes on to relate that generally migrants tend to arrive in Greece by way of the country's islands, where detention centres are overflowing. I know this is true, for I've read that Greece, being as it always has been on the cross-roads between east and west, is literally the front-line for migration into Europe. This nation's thousands of miles of mainland and island shorelines are simply unpatrollable. Every day smugglers are dumping up to 500 people on Greek islands close to the coast of Turkey. These migrants are from all over, from places in the east such as Afghanistan, Kurdistan, and Iraq and from many parts of Africa. But most of them dream of getting all the way across Europe to the UK. In the meantime, they're here in Greece, and most simply get used to it, and then for one reason or another they decide to stay. When I relate that I remember seeing nothing of such a problem twenty years ago, Chryssoúla confirms that it's only existed since 1991.

'It all began with the Albanians', she advises. Now, I've been aware for years that Greek feelings towards Albanian immigrants are overwhelmingly negative, and Roúla at the hotel has told me that at one stage Greeks were repositioning their clotheslines because penniless Albanians were reaching across fences and balcony railings and stealing underwear. Chryssoúla says many Greeks fear that a significant part of the Albanian *diasporá* in Greece remains loyal to Albanian nationalism and that many of them are Muslim, thus some Greeks believe that a hostile minority is being allowed to take root within Greek borders. Well, one has to remember that Greece has been over-run and occupied many times in the past, and thus a fear of 'the Balkan predator' is not without justification. Furthermore, following the tragic 'population exchange' between Turkey and Greece in 1923, both countries spent many more years seeking to homogenize their lands, rooting out and seeking to obliterate nearly every trace of each other. During the Ottoman era both lands had been multi-ethnic but after the population exchange the over-riding thrust was towards consolidating two mono-ethnic states, and in both countries numerous agreements and much time, effort, and money were directed towards this end. Hence, the West's expectation today, that Greece should treat uninvited foreigners, illegal immigrants, with respect, goes against all those efforts of the early 20th century that were actually encouraged and endorsed by the West.

When I then ask Chryssoúla why Greece has been 'flooded' in recent years with Albanians she says that in a nutshell it's all due to the underlying problem of there being no coherent immigration policy, that the lack of policy simply allowed Albanians to walk in. Added to that, she says, there have been historical precedents. For when the north of Greece was liberated from the Turks in 1912 it had not at that time been inhabited solely by Greeks, but chiefly by Jews and Muslims who had lived in the region of Thessaloníki for centuries. These people were left in a state of fear when their Ottoman protectors were sent fleeing by the Hellenic Army in 1912, and so the government of Elefthérios Venizélos had assured them with a promise of complete racial equality; they were to be treated as new citizens of the extended Greek nation. And in 1925 Albanians (who were at that time predominantly Muslim) were allowed residency in Greece provided they could show Albanian papers and had no Turkish sympathies.

'But why should Albanians today wish to come here?' I ask. Chryssoúla explains that when communism began to crumble in Albania in 1991, about 90% of the centrally controlled factories of the régime began to close, and so hundreds of thousands of Albanians were left unemployed. Eventually the prisons were opened and the thousands more who were thus released also found themselves without work, and money, and often without even a roof over their heads. So about a quarter of a million Albanians trekked, illegally, across the rugged and unpatrollable mountainous terrain that lies on the border between Albania and Greece. Others made by sea for Italy, until such time as Italy developed methods of fending them off. When I ask Chryssoúla why Greece too simply didn't return illegal Albanians to their homeland she reminds me that Greece just had no immigration policy at that time, that the problem had never presented itself before. But, she adds, there were other reasons for Greece 'being soft' on Albanian immigrants. Firstly, the Albanians were desperate, not only for themselves but for their families back in Albania, and so they were prepared to undertake the least desirable forms of work and for very little. Next, Greece had to be mindful of what could befall the considerable population of ethnic Greeks who reside in Albania. Also, with the collapse of Communism, Albania offered Greece significant trade and investment opportunities. And lastly, Greece has always been fearful of Muslim influence from Turkey reaching over to Greece's north-west, to Albania, a substantial portion of whose population is Muslim and which country has at times shown itself quite willing to develop its relationship with Greece's former occupier, Muslim Turkey, instead of developing a relationship with Greece.

At the same time as the Albanian influx, economic migrants began trickling into Greece from Asia and Africa and this additional trickling was permitted to occur simply because of the government's difficulties with regard to the immigrants from Albania. The Greek government didn't feel it could treat one set of immigrants one way and the other set by a different method. And so as the economic migrants kept arriving, concern and tensions developed, until in 1999 a young Greek took a gun to the streets near Omónoia Square and shot at people. He killed a Georgian and an Iraqi Kurd and injured seven Asians and Africans, most of whom he rendered wheelchair-bound for the rest of their lives. This young Greek was a member of *Chrysí Avghí* (Golden Dawn), an organization founded by Greek extremists and whose members often used to wear large crucifixes around their necks and claim that they were *Éllines*, the so-called 'purest form' of all Greeks. In court the killer said he acted as he did as 'a service to the nation'. Chryssoúla advises that since this incident Greece has seen a dramatic rise in attacks on immigrants. She tells me the Pakistani community not far from us here in Piraeus has been brutally attacked several times by groups of men protesting against illegal immigration, and that in December 2009 roughly 25 members of one such group descended on a local house, forced their way in, and then attacked and injured 6 Pakistanis. Chryssoúla says that following such attacks as these government ministers have failed to immediately condemn the behaviour and neither has there been any public outcry. The issue goes unresolved.

Although Greece became an EU member in 1981, it continued to treat foreign workers right up until 1997 in exactly the same way that many Arab countries treat them: immigrants had to be sponsored by an employer, they couldn't change jobs, they had to renew their permits each year, and they had no rights. It took sixteen years of pressure from the EU before Greece even started to think, in 1997, about giving legal status to immigrants. Greece, historically and geographically on the edge of Europe, has still to swing fully to the European side in this regard despite its membership of the EU. Its indecision stems largely from the understandable attitude that formed after the Greek War of Independence, that Greece was once again for Greeks. If Greece were to leave the EU, the Council of Europe, and

NATO, it would feel vulnerable to its Muslim neighbours. So while it welcomes the protection of Europe, it still can't bring itself to obey EU rules regarding immigration. The thought of Muslim Turkey being admitted to the EU and Greece being therefore required to allow the free passage of Turks back into its land is understandably distressing.

Although immigrants currently make up roughly 10% of the Greek population they continue to have very few rights. Even asylum-seekers and political refugees in Greece are denied justice as listed under the Geneva Convention. Greece is regularly shown to have ignored agreed EU standards with regard to the right to legal representation, the right to trial, and the right to due processes. Immigrants can't vote or stand at elections, but they must pay taxes. They can only acquire Greek naturalization and citizenship after more than ten years' residence, and pending payment of a 1,500 euro fee, as well as satisfying other requirements. But before this stage can even be reached, they must acquire long-term resident status. However, this can only be applied for after five years of legal residence and will only be granted if the immigrant can demonstrate a high level of fluency in the Greek language and considerable knowledge of Greek history and culture.

I'm unsure whether at the end of the day Greece will actually grant full rights to those who are prepared to work for it long enough and hard enough, so I ask Chryssoúla if she thinks a coherent policy ought to be in favour of immigrants. She says she's reluctant to answer my question. I ask why, and she tops up her glass, clearly thinking carefully as she does so. She then fixes me in the eye and asks, 'Do you think we are racists?' I say I've no idea, that I'd just like to know what she thinks. She replies that there are two definitions of racism: one that belongs to countries like the United States, the UK, and France, and one that is more general and appropriate for countries like Greece and Italy. Greece, she reminds me, is not like Britain, France, Spain, and other countries which have gone out all over the globe in recent centuries and conquered and colonised other lands. In her opinion Greece's problem is that as a member of the

EU it's being forced to wrestle with a definition that is only appropriate to countries where racism describes the treating of members of an invited resident race as inferior. But this definition can't be applied in a country where immigrants arrive uninvited and unwanted. Greeks, Chryssoúla says, can't be described as racist because they really don't think of immigrants as being inferior. She reminds me that Greece is famed for its traditional *philoxenía*, its hospitality or, literally, its love of strangers, and she tells me many Greeks have given much help to immigrants, particularly by providing food and clothing when they turn up on the islands. And, indeed, I've witnessed several Greek restaurant owners giving food free to immigrants who simply stop and ask for it. So Greeks are well-disposed to visitors but draw the line at those people who seeking to populate their country without permission or invitation. 'To your country,' she says, meaning the UK, 'your government invited many people from India, from Uganda, and the Caribbean. To invite them and then to treat them badly, now that is racism! But to not invite immigrants and to not wish that they force themselves upon your country, that cannot be called racism! Just because we belong to the EU we don't have to behave exactly like the UK and France.'

When I ask how close the Greek government is to determining a policy on immigration Chryssoúla rolls her eyes and says that both parties, PASOK and Néa Dimokratía, occasionally discuss the matter, but right now, of course, they have important economic matters to consider. And so it goes on. 'It's crazy!' she says. 'You know, in summer we used to sleep in our yards or on the balcony but now we are frightened. Now we have bars and shutters on the windows and alarms on the walls! Where there used to be openness and warmth now there is fear! But,' she smiles, 'on the other hand, as things are at the moment, if you're well-off then all your housework is done for you by your Filipino maid, your garden is looked after and your car gets washed by a Pakistani, and when your pipes leak you just call the Albanian plumber!' She laughs. 'So, you see, the longer we leave this problem the worse it's getting!' I thank Chryssoúla immensely for her time, her openness, and her honesty, and once again I'm off on my way overwhelmed by the warmth and friendliness of practically all the Greeks I have met.

What have I experienced this evening, following a rather fruitless walk of north Piraeus, but *philoxenía*? The charming *philoxenía* that I've encountered time and again during these extraordinary days in Athens. How could anyone not fall in love with these people? Perhaps that's the problem. Perhaps all those immigrants who intend simply to pass through Greece become charmed, and see that they'd be very foolish to move on! Maybe they simply react to Greeks as many of we Westerners have over the decades: they too fall madly in love with the land and its people and then want to stay forever. But it seems that many who seek to stay on then discover, rather like guests who come to one's home for a few days, that although they're welcomed and embraced for a reasonable period, naturally enough they're eventually expected to leave and move on.

Nearing Piraeus Station at about 7pm for the journey back to Athens, all is dark but for the glow of the street-lamps and the headlights of the endless noisy traffic rushing along the ceaselessly busy Athens-Piraeus highway and the road that edges the harbour. As I pause at lights to cross to the station, I notice just a couple of feet away, huddled against the front wheel of a parked motor-cycle, four large dogs: two Labradors and two Alsatians. Like the *adéspota* up in the centre of Athens they're all wearing collars. Yet here they are, at rest in this most exposed part of Piraeus, traffic whizzing past at a distance of just several feet, and a bitingly cold wind rushing in off the sea. Pathetically, they've settled skin-to-skin for warmth, on a thin layer of discarded sheets of newspapers. They appear to be hoping for some protection from the wheel of the motor-cycle. Weeds grow up through the slabs of the pavement around them. It's a wholly piteous scene. I speak to them slowly and quietly and they raise their heads and look at me, timidly, sadly. Although they are four large 'wild' dogs there's no reason for me to feel any danger from them. They don't seem to have the will or energy for either aggression or enthusiasm. Have they been whooping it up, all along the quays all afternoon, and now want simply to be left in peace, for a bit of kip? I don't think so. But at least they look well-fed. Travel a little outside Athens, to poorer areas, and the picture is apparently quite different. Animal welfare groups report that there one can see strays that are horribly skinny, sick, all too often injured and completely uncared for, and that at the time of writing no Greek court has ever found anyone guilty of inflicting cruelty upon an animal. So life as a highly visible stray under a municipality scheme in Athens has at least some benefits. But of course there are owned dogs in Athens today who are greatly loved, and a little dog's grave that was unearthed during the digging of the Metró proves that some citizens of the ancient city also cherished their pets.

There are maintenance works on part of the line, so the train-ride back to Athens is interrupted by a short spell on a linking bus, on which I find myself sitting opposite a man in his late thirties or early forties who looks part Asian and part Arabic. I catch him watching me, a curious and intent look on his face and a slight smile on his lips, so I nod my head and say hi and he eagerly responds with the same. I ask where he's from and he tells me he's Iraqi. He asks where I'm from and when I say I live in the UK he tells me he used to live there too. His English is quite good. So I ask why he's living in Greece. 'Well, I did not have the papers to stay in Britain, I tried but they make me go, and so I must come back here,' he explains, with a shrug. He probably means he originally entered Greece from Iraq as an illegal immigrant, at which point he may or may not have made himself known to the Greek authorities by claiming asylum. In all likelihood he then proceeded to the UK where he either declared himself or was picked up by the police. He probably asked for UK asylum but was rejected (usually due to insufficient evidence of good reason for doing so). Following this, the odds are that under the terms of the Dublin Convention he was then returned to his European 'country of arrival', in his case Greece, for consideration and appraisal here. Thus now, in 2010, Greece is struggling to cope with large numbers of immigrants and asylum seekers who have been returned from

EU states which have rejected them - in addition to Greece coping with hundreds of fresh new arrivals from Asia and Africa, via Turkey, every day of the week.

His eyes twinkle and he keeps smiling at me. Several scenarios appear likely. He could just be a nice guy. But time and again in Kuwait and Sa'udi I've had Pakistanis and Indians approach me, pursue me, and even cling to me, in the hope that they might make a friend, a connection that would somehow help them get a footing on UK soil. And it's also possible this guy is gay and simply fancies me. So I continue with the rather bold 'Your country is not a good place for gays', to which he responds, not with annoyance but in full confidence, 'We have no gays in Iraq. Gays is a Western problem'. Of course I then look him directly in the eyes and make it clear to him, in no uncertain terms, that proportionally there are as many gay men and lesbians in Iraq as there are in the UK, in the United States, and in any other country, but that to dare to be open about one's homosexuality in any Muslim country is usually to volunteer to live in a state of continual fear. He looks amazed, stunned, his face completely blank. 'Don't you know that in Iraq, as in Iran, they often kill gays?' I ask. Evidently he has no idea of the systematic hunting-down, torture, and murder of gay men in his country.

As the bus rejoins the train-line at Pháleron Metró station, and we all rise and make for the doors, there are enough passengers for me to turn and give my Iraqi companion a cheery 'Goodbye! And good luck!' and to then weave my way off into the crowd, some of whom are heading, like me, towards the Metró station, while others stride towards the massive new Karaïskáki football stadium, right beside the station. This is a ground that can accommodate just over 33,000 spectators and at this very moment, from all the surrounding streets, as well as from the station and buses, hundreds of men and boys are swarming towards it.

Karaïskáki is the home of the most successful club in Greek football history, *Olympiakós*, and it's named after Yeórghios Karaïskákis, a general in the Greek War of Independence who was killed quite close by. The stadium is constructed mainly of concrete but all around it are fourteen blood-red towers of criss-crossing metal tubing that can, if required, support a translucent membrane over the entire structure. Tonight it's undrawn and thus from inside the arena, from the contagion of passion and frenzy, from yet another form of escape and delirium, there now freely erupts into the clear night-sky a mighty roar of male singing. Floodlight too escapes into the atmosphere, and caught within that light is a great billowing cloud of greyish-white smoke, a massive swirling dusty fog, created by the fireworks and flames that are part of the tribal, testosterone-fuelled, preliminary rituals performed in the build-up to 'the big game'.

Despite the chanting and all the clamour, I can just about hear Hadjidákis turning uncomfortably in his grave. During the early years of the 1967 to 1974 Greek dictatorship, Hadjidákis had lived in exile, in New York, but after returning to Athens in 1972 he'd opened an exciting new café-theatre. It was called *Polýtropon*, meaning 'Of Many Ways', as in 'clever' or 'crafty'. It flourished, with its patrons savouring their famous composer's musical experiments and delighting in some of the finest work that he ever produced. But then in 1974 the Júnta ended, democracy returned, and Greek society began to change. By and large people began to slowly shed their earlier concerns. The thought-world of Hadjidákis's edgy café-theatre was gradually displaced by the more enticing but superficial preoccupations engendered by the nation's desire to see Greece accepted as a full member of a prosperous European Union. And so, with regret and sadness, Hadjidákis began to remark upon his country's gradual turning away from the concerns of art, politics, the theatre, and the concert hall for the manic consuming delirium, the phenomenally exhilarating hysteria, and the easy tribal belonging that are typical of the modern football stadium.

🔲 🔲 🔲 🔲

Undercurrents & Shadows

*Monastiráki Square; Tzistarákis Mosque;
Ancient Agorá, Stoá of Áttalos, Theseíon,
Church of the Holy Apostles, Altar of Twelve Gods;
Valliános National Library;
City of Athens Central Library;
Kifissiá, Goulandrís Museum of Natural History;
& Pallás Theatre.*

The city of Athens consists of buildings designed and painted to reject heat rather than retain it, and as a harsh and penetrating wind from the north has chilled the city overnight, the temperature in my room has plummeted. Breakfast television reveals parts of northern Greece are now deep in snow and that snow lies even on the ridges surrounding Athens. I had an awful night's sleep but I'm not sure my slumbers were disturbed only by the cold. My mind spent much of the night replaying sections of my conversation with Chryssoúla, but at about three, my torso juddering with the chill, I was finally driven to rise and spread all my clothes upon the bed in an effort to warm up, and also to take a chair to the air-conditioning unit, high on the wall, to climb up and try to coax some heat out of it. It refused, unfortunately, and the night didn't improve. Sotíris promises that later today he'll leave two extra blankets on my bed and have an engineer attend to the AC.

Despite the bitter cold this morning, there are half a dozen Chilean musicians, all wrapped up in colourful alpacan capes and scarves, performing to a camera crew in Monastiráki Square. I suppose they're quite used to this temperature in the Andes. But given my bad night's sleep, it's uncanny that I should find them filling the square with the beautiful sweeping melody of Hadjidákis's *Kourasméno Palikári*, which roughly translates as 'Oh, Weary Laddie'! It's also astonishing to hear Hadjidákis soaring out of this Greek square from Peruvian flutes, but such is his international fame and popularity.

Monastiráki Square takes its name from Panaghía Pantánassa Church, which is commonly referred to as simply Monastiráki, meaning Little Monastery. The small church that can be seen here today, though rebuilt in 1911, once flourished as a convent, and perhaps as long ago as the 10th century, though all that is certain is that it was initially established by monks from the monastery of Kaisarianí, high up in a valley to the east, on the side of Mount Ymittós, and that later it came to be associated with nuns who cared for the local poor and who supported themselves by weaving. It's now partly sunken, due to the floor of the surrounding square having been raised to accommodate the important Metró station that lies beneath.

The square's other historical focal point is the restored Tzistarákis Mosque, which now houses the Kyriazópoulos Collection of the Museum of Traditional Greek Ceramics. This mosque, also referred to as The Mosque of the Lower Fountain, because of the little font that once stood below it in the square, is one of many mosques erected in Athens during the Turkish occupation. It was built in 1759 by local official Mustafá Agá Tzistarákis and embedded in the wall above the elaborately decorated arch of the main entrance, a rectangular marble plaque presents the visitor with eight small panels of Arabic script. Such script was used throughout Greece during the long period of the Ottoman occupation, and a sharp eye can spot occasional remainders of beautiful Arab calligraphy over old doorways and upon discarded stones throughout the country. Only when Mustafá Kemál, also known as *Attatúrk* (Father of the Turks), established the Turkish Republic in 1923 did the Turks abandon Arabic script and officially replace it with our Latin alphabet, as a way of indicating modern Turkey's admiration of, and determined alignment and involvement with, the technologically superior West.

A relatively small building, the Tzistarákis Mosque has recently been restored. It has not however been handed over for the use of Muslims now resident in Athens. Instead, it has been imaginatively and pleasantly adapted to house ceramics many of which have a considerable and observable connection to Greece's long-time occupier. This 'ex-mosque' consists now of a spacious ground-floor and a specially-created u-shaped mezzanine that hugs all of the walls except for that which accommodates the fine *mihrab*, the niche that points in the direction of the *ka'aba*, that huge block of grey granite in Mecca which has become the focal point of Islam. Natural light reflects off arched expanses of whitewashed plasterwork to fill the interior of this old mosque with a luminescence that greatly benefits both its exhibition of ceramics and, here and there in the walls, small patches of original plaster and original stone, and even fragments of old fresco.

It's possible that some of the small patches of original plasterwork that can be seen in this mosque today have quite an impressive history: for Tzistarákis, having once been commander of the Turkish garrison stationed upon the Acrópolis, had connections and power in Ottoman Athens sufficient for him to be permitted to blow up one of the columns of the Temple of Olympian Zeus in order to provide plaster for the interior of this mosque. And this was after he had demolished several other ancient edifices in order to acquire basic building blocks for the structure itself! Perhaps some of these pieces are displayed in the pattern of large mounting brown stone arches that climb, amidst the whitewashed plasterwork, one on top of the other to the dome. Regardless, the grace and elegance of these mounting rounded arches now resonate harmoniously with the voluptuous bellies of all the many pots and vases which are displayed below.

Greek ceramics of recent centuries haven't reached the sophistication or refinement of the work that was produced in the classical age, nor even the sophistication of work produced contemporaneously in Persia or North Africa, but nevertheless they do possess an appealing vigour, sensuality, and earthy rawness. The Tzistarákis collection features work mostly from the first half of the 20th century, and since many of the early 20th century Greek potters came from Asia Minor there are distinct Arabic and Turkish qualities to a considerable number of the pieces which are displayed here. So it's fitting then that they are exhibited in an Ottoman mosque. Many of these ceramics bear brilliant and vivid glazes of intense blues and dark greens, colours that predominate in Islamic ceramics throughout the Middle East. However, some pieces have a wonderfully casual and modernist feel to them, despite an essentially rustic quality. One large and very simple pot, statuesque and with a traditional handle on either side, has been decorated firstly with an all-over coat of pure white, upon which there have then been added seemingly random and casual brush-strokes of bright blue and vivid red. It's a vase which speaks of the sunny, breezy, and carefree days of a Greek-island summer.

Not far from the Tzistarákis Mosque is the Ancient Agorá, also known as the Athenian Agorá, a large and gently undulating stretch of greenery and ancient stonework that lies just below the north-west corner of the Acrópolis and north-east of Philopáppou Hill. After all these years, I'm finally about to enter the marketplace and civic centre of classical Athens, the site of the ancient city's nitty-gritty, of bargaining, buying and selling, workshops, administration, judiciary, religious worship, bathing, gymnasia, entertainment, and gossip! Xenophón and Pláton tell us that roughly 2,450 years ago this is where Socrátes delighted in being, particularly early in the mornings, when no doubt the market was at its liveliest and in summer not so hot as later in the day. The entire site, heavily populated with ancient carved stones, is immediately spectacular, but three of its attractions sing out above all the rest.

The first of these is the most intriguing. Its long red pantiled roof is clearly visible from Mount Lykavittós, from the Acrópolis, and from many points on Philopáppou Hill. Occupying almost the full length of the eastern side of the *agorá*, it is the fully reconstructed and massive Stoá of Áttalos, a shopping arcade built in the reign of King Áttalos II of Pérgamon, 159 to 138 BCE. In 197 BCE the city of Pérgamon (now Turkish Bergama) had aided Athens, Rome, and Rhodes in the defeat of Phílip V of Macedonía, and Áttalos subsequently demonstrated his veneration of Athens by gifting the blossoming city with this magnificent *stoá*, 11 metres high, 20 metres in width, and a stunning 115 metres in length.

After two decades of investigative archaeology followed by meticulous planning, the Stoá of Áttalos was completely rebuilt in the early 1950s by the American School of Classical Studies, which now uses the entire upper floor. In ancient times this building was full of little stalls and shops: 42 in total, in dedicated rooms as well as in the open area at ground level. Today the enclosed section along the eastern side of the ground-floor is home to The Museum of the Ancient Agorá. Collected there, from excavations throughout the grounds and adjacent land, is yet another fantastic Athenian display of fine ancient artefacts and statuary. The greater part of the ground-floor consists of a long open and airy arcade, its beamed ceiling supported upon two extensive rows of stately columns. Very wisely, this open side of the *stoá* faces west, away from the burning summer sun, and towards the Theseíon, the second great attraction of the Ancient Agorá.

The Theseíon was originally called the Iphaisteíon, due to its being dedicated to Íphaistos, the god of the forge, known in Latin as Vulcan, who in ancient times aided the blacksmiths, potters, and bronze-workers who plied their trades in this particular section of the *agorá*. However, as Íphaistos was lame, and was therefore thought grotesque, and as reliefs in the temple also featured Theséas, founder-hero of Athens and brave decapitator of the Minótavros (the 'Minotaur'), Athens preferred to call this handsome Doric temple 'The Theseíon'. Dating from 420 BCE, and consisting almost entirely of fine Pentelic marble, it's smaller than the Parthenon but still greatly inspiring - because after nearly two and a half thousand years it stands almost completely intact. However, it's not as pleasing to the eye as the Parthenon, as the Theseíon wasn't constructed according to a perspective-design like the Parthenon's. Although the Theseíon is inarguably very fine, there's a rigidity and a stiffness about it when compared with its younger brother atop the Acrópolis. Some archaeologists have speculated that perhaps it was actually because of the Theseíon's slightly unpleasing rigidity that optical illusions were incorporated into the building of the Parthenon.

However, with all of its 34 columns safe and sound, only half of its front pediment damaged, its *metópes* depicting 9 of the Twelve Labours of Iraklés and 8 of the Deeds of Theséas, with a further exploit of the latter being shown in its frieze, Athens's Theseíon, together with the temples of Héra at Paestum, and Omónoias at Agrigento, both in Italy, is one of the three best preserved temples of Ancient Greece. Sadly though, of all the figures in the *metópes* and frieze, only the figure of the gruesome Minótavros, part man and part bull, is intact: all of the other 'pagan' figures in the marbles were defaced by raging Christian fervour early in the Byzantine period. But sitting on top of the little hill of Agoraíos Kolonós, the Theseíon still rises magnificently, amidst pomegranate, myrtle, laurel, and the lush green grasses which have sprung up all about since the end of summer. Excavations have led archaeologists to conclude that in ancient times there was a garden on this spot also. And, indeed, according to Pláton there grew near the temple and the adjacent foundries the fine Garden of Íphaistos.

The third substantial attraction of the Ancient Agorá stands on the site's southern slope: the 'Church of the Holy Apostles', *Aghíon Apostólon*. In the mid 1950s this exquisite place of Christian worship, the first to be constructed in the *agorá*, and specifically to commemorate the apostle Paul's teaching here, was stripped of all structural additions that were subsequent to its erection at the beginning of the 11th century. Thus, today we may appreciate its original appearance, and on its internal walls and in its dome can now be seen many sections of the church's Byzantine frescoes, as well as several 16th and 17th century paintings transferred here from other churches. Contrasting dramatically with the plain cream plasterwork of all the surfaces which required restoration, are the deep wine-dark reds and blues of the original intricate designs. As in most Byzantine churches, the dome and roofs feature terracotta tiles and the exterior walls are composed of attractive alternating strata of thin reddish bricks and cream stone. The brickwork is particularly decorative over the west *nárthex*, or portico, where in stylised profusion it imitates 'Squared Kufic', an angular elaboration of the earliest script of the Arabic language, developed on the banks of the Euphrates in 7 CE.

This exceptional trio of structures stands within the fourth and final attraction of the *agorá*: its grounds, in which, amidst flourishing emerald-green grasses, shrubbery, trees, and the occasional vivid yellow, orange, white, crimson and purple of lantana, lies an almost endless assortment of ancient scattered stones. These stones indicate where once there stood the city's civic buildings, like the new and old Vouleftíria, or parliaments, wherein met the Council of Five Hundred; the Thólos, the circular building wherein met a committee of 50 senators; the Heliaía, the city's most important court of law; a library; the city mint; and, of course, a jail. Other stones indicate places of worship, like the Metróon, a sanctuary dedicated to Rhéa, the mother of all the gods; a small temple dedicated to Apóllon, father of all Athenians; and a temple dedicated to Áris, the god of war. Elsewhere are the sites of a temple thought to be dedicated either to Démetra or her daughter Persephóne, or possibly even to both, and a circular temple of unknown dedication and made of Thessalian marble. Then there's the site of The Triangular Shrine, possibly dedicated to the departed, and the Leokórion, a shrine to the three daughters of Leós, a son of Orphéas.

Also in the Ancient Agorá are stones marking places of cleansing and relaxation, such as a gymnasium and several bath-houses and fountain-houses. There are remains which indicate that in addition to the Stoá of Áttalos, the *agorá* offered no less than 10 further arcades - most of them providing accommodation for further shops and stalls. There lies amongst the luscious growth of this time of the year evidence also of productive buildings like a flour-mill, an olive-oil factory, and the house and shop of 'Simon the Cobbler', a contemporary of Socrátes who is referred to in the writings of Ploútarchos, Xenophón, and Dioghénis Laértios. There's a pedestal which once bore a statue of King Áttalos, to honour his donation of the *stoá*. There are the remains too of the Great Drain that saved the *agorá* from the massive amount of water that ran off the limestone hillside above during heavy rains, and which channelled it into the nearby Iridanós brook.

Perhaps the most visually impressive of all these assorted smaller ruins here in the *agorá* are those remaining in the vicinity of the Odeíon of Agríppas, a massive roofed theatre, taller and slightly larger than the Parthenon and which, 2,000 years ago, could accommodate a thousand Athenians. Today the remains of a stone giant and two *trítones*, monsters that were, respectively, either half-man and half-serpent or half-man and half-fish, stand sentinel on the north side of the theatre, while three of Athens's plump *adéspota* (ownerless dogs), sprawled out where once an audience sat, snooze in the winter sun, seemingly completely unfeeling of the cold biting wind that's blowing in from the north.

This *agorá*, set just below the Acrópolis, is nothing less than magnificent, and it's wonderful to experience it on an exceptionally cold day for such weather keeps it largely free of other visitors. From the front of the Theseíon there is this morning a totally unpeopled view: a view that glides over the scattered ruins and the rich green grass, over the trees of the wood beneath the Acrópolis, across the jumble of the red-tiled roofs of the Pláka, and up to the Parthenon glowing atop the Sacred Rock. Here is an Athenian vista that is largely classical, romantic, entirely without flaw, and overwhelming. From this point no litter or graffiti is visible anywhere. Tranquil and dappled with sunlight, this prospect is so perfect it puts one in mind of the imaginative compositions of the French painter Claude Lorrain. The ancient buildings here were, of course, created and positioned by the Greeks of antiquity, but credit has also to be given to the American landscape designer Ralph Griswold who in the 1950s and 60s so magnificently oversaw the careful placing and planting of nearly all of the trees and shrubs that today so grace this Ancient Agorá.

As I depart, one small and unimpressive ruin cannot go unobserved. Just west of the northern exit, to Odós Adrianoú, and peeking out at ground level from beneath the stone wall that forms the northern perimeter of the grounds, there are to be seen the simple remains of the south-western corner of a courtyard. Beside this seemingly unremarkable and bare arrangement, humbly indicated in the grass by a thin right-angle of old stone slabs, lies a marble base which once supported a bronze statue and which bears the inscription 'Léagros, the son of Gláfkos, dedicated [this statue] to the Twelve Gods'. The sad little corner which is adjacent is thus all that is visible today of the remains of 'The Altar of the Twelve Gods', a walled and stately courtyard that was open to the heavens and at the centre of which once stood a majestic marble altar. Here in this enclosure, between the Temple of Áris and the Stoa of Zeus and directly beside the Panathenaic Way leading up to the Acrópolis, the people of ancient Athens prayed and called upon the *Dodecátheon*, the twelve great gods of Mount Ólympus: Zeus, Héra, Poseidónas, Démetra, Hestía, Apóllon, Ártemis, Íphaistos, Athená, Áris, Aphrodíte, and Hermés. And within the walls of this sacred sanctuary anyone in ancient Athens could acquire asylum from those who pursued them. According to Thucydídes, the Altar was dedicated by Peisístratos the Younger, son of Hippías, in 522 and 521 BCE. The Persians destroyed it in 480 BCE, but in 5 BCE it was rebuilt. Then by 600 CE this central Athenian focal point of 'paganism' had been vandalized by the Christians.

The Altar of the Twelve Gods was thus one of the 'holiest' and most important shrines in Greece. Consequently it was used as the milestone from which all distances in and from Attica were calculated. It was therefore literally at the geographical heart of the region and at the emotional and religious heart of the people. Yet for decades now nine-tenths of this courtyard have been allowed to remain beneath the unsightly Piraeus-Kifissia railway line, just the other side of the wall that runs along the northern boundary of the *agorá*. Archeologists have advised that trains rattle not only over the courtyard but right over the position of the ancient altar itself. So you'd think the authorities would revel in this site, that they'd excavate it, re-route the railway over or around it, and make something special of this shrine to those great mythological figures who inspire such wonder in every corner of the globe. You'd think they'd at least jump at the revenue to be made. But the site goes ignored, and an unmistakable incongruency is apparent: while in the heart of Athens an extremely important archaeological site remains deliberately buried beneath a railway track, year after year a massive amount of emotion, energy, time, and expense is spent by some who seek to replace Greece's perfect facsimiles of other sites with originals which are in the care of foreign museums! It's also possible that the powers that be fear that if The Altar of the Twelve Gods were resurrected, as the important centre-piece that it undoubtedly was, if it were to be showcased in grand style and savoured every year by millions of visitors, it would also prove a magnet for devout Hellenic Polytheists.

Back in the bustling *cháos* of the city's modern *agorá*, in an electrical shop run by a charming middle-aged Asian gentleman, I try to replace a malfunctioning electrical adapter. The man is pleased to talk English and tells me he has relations in Leeds, in the UK. We fall into discussion about the many non-Greeks like himself who now populate central Athens and before long he's volunteering an off-the-cuff list of all the different ethnicities there are, and it's interesting to note his perceptions. They don't correlate with government statistics, but they show what this gentlemen genuinely perceives to be the reality around him, here in the heart of Athens. The largest group of immigrants, he believes, are the Chinese. And certainly south-west of Omónoia Square there are a great many shops run by Chinese. He says this group is followed in number by Pakistanis, and then Bangladeshis, with only a comparatively small number of Indians. But Asians, he says, are to be found mainly in the outer areas - and presumably in those outer areas where, as Chryssoúla related, there have been attacks by Greek extremists. The third most numerous group, he believes, are the Africans. I ask exactly which parts of Africa they come from and he lists Ghana, Nigeria, Tanzania, and Somalia as being their main places of origin. Lastly in number, he says, come the Arabs and Afghanis, mostly from Kurdish Iraq, North Africa, and of course Afghanistan. These are the guys, he says, who loiter outside his shop every night of the week, urging passers-by to purchase their cannabis, their *ganjha*, their *hashish*. I thank him for his break-down and then tell him, as pleasantly as possible, that I know for a fact, from government figures, that the greatest number of foreigners in Greece at this time are Albanians, Bulgarians, and Romanians. Then I ask him why it is that this isn't how it appears to him. 'Ah, well, *they* are all invisible!' he says. 'You see, those peoples, from Albania, Bulgaria, and Romania, they all look much the same as the Greeks!' 'That may be true, but I dare you to say that to a Greek!' I answer. His eyes pop at the thought, and he chuckles.

In nearby Odós Menándrou, off Odós Evripídou, there's a swarming going on. The street is full of Asians, Afghanis, Arabs and Africans, all of them hawking just a few things each in the middle of the road. There are no Greeks here at all, and no traffic passes through. The immigrants appear to have taken the street over! There are hundreds of them. They're all just standing, or leaning, talking or waiting. As I pass through the dense crowd, avoiding contact but stealing glances at the things for sale, I note one guy standing there with just five or six different bottles of shampoo and nothing else. Another pitiful young man is holding up a shirt, one solitary shirt, his only merchandise, hoping to sell it to someone in the crowd. There are no women in the street, no tourists, and there's an element of danger in the air. Several cheeky and slightly aggressive men call to me 'Hello-how-are-you!' but I pass on quickly into the crowd as if I've not heard or understood. Against the boarded-up face of an abandoned building, two Arabs or Afghanis are shooting up with a syringe, entirely unconcerned that everyone can see them do it. A little further along another two Arabs or Afghanis are leaning over the bonnet of a car. From off the paintwork one of them is clearly snorting a line of something, while the other waits and watches. And then I notice that from the forearm skin of the one who's snorting there's a syringe dangling, in mid-air, by its needle! The sight is chilling. I hurry out of the street glad not to have been harmed or mugged.

Near Panepistimíou Street, in yet another attractive and well-organised bookshop, with all of its volumes in Greek, I enquire after a title I'd like to take back to the UK. The young pony-tailed assistant is attractively pierced with a diamond to one side of his nose, and another just below the left of his bottom lip. He has also two diagonal and parallel thin shaves passing attractively through his right eyebrow. He speaks fine English and is absolutely charming and businesslike. As a number of books in the current window-display are clearly about things holistic, green, and ecological, I dare to ask if there might be a gay and lesbian section also. Without batting an eyelid he instantly replies 'Unfortunately, no. And I'm very sorry.' I tell him I've been surprised to find no gay or lesbian sections in any of the many fine general bookshops I've visited so far in Athens, and he then passes me on to a more senior employee who eventually proves delighted to assist although her initial reaction seems scornful and mocking.

'So should we not also have a section for all authors who are black?' she retorts. 'Should all French writers be separated from English writers? That would be separatist!' she snaps. Then seeing me left speechless by this assertive response, she melts, smiles, and explains that any gay or lesbian titles they have are incorporated into the shop's various collections. She then kindly adds that she understands that separate sections are a great help to minority readers.

Before I then dare to suggest that the shop should give it a go, she draws me over to one of the shelves and points to four volumes by Cóstas Tachtsís. She says that none of them features any 'gay content' and that this author, even in his late years, often spoke out against gay liberation. It seems like a pretty good argument to bolster a position against 'separatism'. But then her eyes twinkle and she says, 'And you know what? He was known to regularly dress up in drag and hang round Omónoia Square looking for guys!' I'm amazed, thrown off-balance, and I laugh. Cóstas Tachtsís was a transvestite and a fine author, and I know that the story is not actually this simple. But for the moment I go along with it and ask this very communicative bookshop manager if she's suggesting that Tachtsís was a hypocrite. Without missing a beat she replies 'Of course! Of course! Total hypocrisy!' But then she grins again, shrugs her shoulders and adds, 'But this is Greece! What do you expect!'

I relate that I've heard that in fact what Tachtsís really railed about was the fact that in Greece so many gay and lesbian people are fearful of coming out, and thus they leave what little fighting is done for gay rights to those who can rarely *not* be 'out', the committed transvestites. She's not surprised and asks me if I know that in 1988 Tachtsís was found murdered. I had no idea. 'No one was arrested, the crime remains unsolved, the police have just forgotten all about it!' This articulate and educated middle-aged Greek woman, yet another, astounds me, and I realise I've been presented with a further opportunity too good to pass by. I tell her many things have been puzzling me during my time here in Athens and ask if she'd be so kind as to give me a few of her views. 'Of course!' she replies. 'But why don't we go outside. I can have a cigarette, and you can fire ahead with your questions!'

I ask why, despite the perilous economic situation, boutiques proliferate in the city and outer districts, and why Greeks are relentlessly shopping and purchasing luxury goods. Her answer is that people are simply refusing to accept that the country is teetering on the edge of bankruptcy. Their heads are in the sand, the spending goes on, and the debt is simply getting worse, she says. When I ask her opinion on the source of the money, she tells me it's either the credit card, the wealth of established families, 'or it's simply black money'.

Her name is Elpída and she suggests we sit at a café table a couple of doors along and have a quick coffee. Once we've ordered I ask her to explain this Greek 'Black Money'. She says I'll understand best if she gives me an example, and so refers to the many night-clubs and discos down on the sea-front, south of Piraeus, where thousands gather at night to party and dance. She says that in Greece you're now supposed to be given a receipt for every drink you buy, and indeed I've noticed the way some Greeks are issuing receipts, almost ceremonially sometimes, and even for slight things, such as postcards. However Elpída informs me that what actually happens at these clubs is that you may only get a receipt for your first drink, and then perhaps for every third or fourth drink after that. This means that at the end of the night the club has records of taking, she suggests, perhaps 10,000 euros, when in fact they have also taken, and pocketed, an additional, unreceipted, 30,000 euros.

Such 'black money', undeclared, and therefore untaxed, allows the rampant and extravagant spending that I've been seeing everywhere in Athens despite all the publicity about

Greece's near-bankruptcy. The other day I bought another twenty-euro CD from an elderly man in a pleasant little shop and noticed that he didn't give me another big and detailed receipt, printed off laboriously on an old printer he keeps in the corner, as on a previous visit. A restaurant I ate at for a second night did the same thing: lots of smiles, flirtation, camaraderie, and warmth, but no receipt on the second occasion. A meal in another restaurant came to 18 euros, but when I looked at the receipt the following morning, just before tossing it in the bin and not having bothered to examine it the night before, I noticed it stated that it was for food totalling just 4 euros! So, indeed, almost everyone appears to be at it.

The philosophy seems to be that one should follow the rules a little, but not always; declare something, but not everything; and avoid the keeping of accurate records. And this city, Athens, is so massive and chaotic, so difficult to organise, that there's little accountability, little control. If you can get away with hiding a good part of your income, you simply do. Elpída's words remind me of what Andréas tried to convey some days ago, but which at the time I didn't really grasp. I suggest to Elpída that it must be awfully frightening to be always walking this knife-edge, to be ridden with guilt, to know you're tax-dodging. 'Oh, yes!' she exclaims. 'But this city is riddled with guilt! We live on guilt! Everybody in Greece lives on guilt!' All of a sudden I'm wondering if this is why people are so friendly. Are they just covering themselves, seeking to give a good impression? Surely not. I don't like it, I don't want to believe that at heart Greeks are not genuinely warm and friendly. I can't accept that the extraordinary kindliness I've encountered these past days has sprung from something dishonest. It has to be more complex than that, surely.

During this astounding venting of frank and helpful truths, my informant has apologised and confessed that she's a nicotine addict. She's almost got through two cigarettes already. And now, after twenty minutes or so, another employee has come down from the shop to ask, apologetically and in Greek, if Elpída would kindly return because it's his turn for a cigarette break! So we quickly pay the bill and oblige. At least in this shop, and actually in most Athenian bookshops, the no-smoking ban of July 2009 is being respected. There's scant deference towards it in many other places, however. And a lot of people believe that the government is now willing to turn a blind eye upon the ban, as a palliative, to soften the period of austerity ahead.

I tell Elpída how impressive I think her bookshop and all the bookshops of Athens are, particularly given the warm Greek climate and the natural prevalence for outdoor interests, and she informs me that Greek bookshops are actually now finding it very difficult to survive, and that some have recently closed. Reasons for this are that in the past few months rents have begun to increase substantially, and due to the fiscal situation not so many Greeks are buying books as previously. There has also been a great cultural change in recent years: many Greeks have succumbed to the allure of celebrity interests, glossy magazines, luxury goods, and football mania - in short, the lifestyle and 'concerns' of the compulsive and passive consumer. Bearing in mind the books in the window, I'm clearly talking to an opponent of excessive consumption, so I tell Elpída of my own fears of the 'affluenza' that has gripped vast swathes of the globe. Elpída says her problem, and the problem of all bookshops at this time, is that there's little they can do to fight it, for it's not the efforts of booksellers that encourage a population to read good literature.

Although Greece is a small country with no particularly great reputation as being a land of readers, recently nearly 850 Greek publishers have produced just under 10,000 new titles per year, of which just under 2,000 were Greek works, although only about 10 of these publishing companies are major players, each producing between 150 and 350 titles annually. The rest are often small family businesses. Regardless, it seems that all the publishers of Greece wield considerable power, for Elpída relates that to preserve their income they recently united and succeeded in having a piece of legislation pass through parliament. As a result, the discount that Greek shops may give on any book that is within two years of its date of publication is limited to no more than 10%.

Moreover, Greek publishers obviously have a monopoly on books printed in Greek and so the Greek-reading public has little control over the titles from which they can select. Worse still, the 60% of all books which are translated into Greek from other languages are often poorly translated. Elpída refers to one Nobel prize-winning writer of fiction whose novels have been translated by a Greek whose best qualification appears to have been his personal relationship with a member of the local embassy representing the homeland of the writer! Elpída says that people of that particular foreign country who are fluent in Greek have been appalled by the poor quality of the resulting works, reporting that they offer embarrassing representations of the original. Such practice therefore doesn't encourage Greeks to read beyond Greek writers, unless they're able to read works in their original languages. And of course though most Greeks are able to deal with you in English over shop-counters and suchlike, not a great number have the confidence or ability to persevere through an entire book of English. The average Greek reader is therefore unfortunately rather trapped.

With regard to civil rights, Elpída confirms that the domination of the Orthodox Church is considerable, despite, she says, there having been a number of scandals exposing its clergy's involvement in 'clandestine homosexuality'. So, because of the religious domination of the state, the attitude from top levels of government downwards is that you may do in Greece as you are inclined in all the realms of gender and sexuality provided you do not do it in a manner which is publicly declared or which demands public acknowledgement. Thus the small number of brave and bold individuals who organise women's groups, feminist groups, gay and lesbian groups, and so forth, are not widely approved-of, and not only by the powers that be, religious and secular, but by the population in general. There often exists in Greece an exasperating 'double-think'. In the late 1990s many Greek gays and lesbians were not surprised to learn that a prominent Greek figure, also much liked by many gays and lesbians worldwide, had voted in Brussels on four separate occasions, during a five-year stint as a Member of the European Parliament, against moves granting human rights to homosexual people in a number of different European contexts. There are numerous such examples of well-known or important Greek figures towing the conservative church line in public, while at the same time appearing to be genuinely tolerant and accepting in private.

The double-think extends also to the way that the machinery of government and bureaucracy operates on a daily basis. Elpída informs me that in getting anything done via any authority in Athens or elsewhere, such as the processing of documents, it is generally publicly accepted now that bribery ought not to be practised. However, at the same time, if you still produce a brown envelope, it'll be quietly and gratefully taken and things will move a great deal faster for you! The workings of Greek society are lubricated by *méson* and *rousféti*, connections and mutual favours, and unless one capitulates to these 'mechanisms' it's very difficult to make any headway in Greece. I suggest at this point that corruption, with a little c, is widespread in this country and Elpída looks aghast. 'Oh, yes, for sure, widespread, one hundred per cent!' she replies, her eyes almost popping, 'But, please, make that with a capital C! And add to it cronyism, nepotism, impunity, and the most ridiculous bureaucracy you can imagine!' She assures me that all of Greece's government ministers and members of parliament are automatically immune from arrest, detention, or criminal prosecution for so long as they are in office, and that any crimes which they are thought to have committed may only be adjudicated once they leave office and their immunity therefore lapses, or if parliament decides to meet specially (extraordinarily) to impeach the member! Greek MPs are only answerable to civil suits - cases which may result in no more than an MP having to compensate a plaintiff or make good for some form of loss incurred by the MP's behaviour. I understand now the words of a noted and native Greek writer who I was in touch with shortly before leaving the UK. Amongst other things, he said, 'Greece is absolutely wonderful, but, be warned, it can drive you totally crazy!'

Some ten minutes after leaving Elpída's shop, I open the door of a small pharmacy amongst all the government buildings and banks of Panepistimíou Street, in order to buy a remedy for a slightly sore throat. And in this of all places I move instantly into a fog of cigarette smoke! It's yet another example of Athens's *cháos* and *anarchía*, the philosophy of 'Do as you please!' But the pharmacist, like every Greek I have met during these two weeks, is utterly charming and helpful. He dispenses me a pack of strong antibiotic analgesics for which I suspect in the UK I'd need a doctor's prescription. This city is a paradox. It's full of contradictions. Its people are beguiling, but their 'system' is mad, crazy, chaotic, corrupt, and frightening, particularly for those who expect, or who are used to, a high level of transparency.

As I cross a side street just beyond the pharmacy, a very old Greek lady, perhaps in her nineties, leans back against the bonnet of a car. She appears to have walked down the centre of the street, so as to avoid the vehicles parked upon the pavements. She has no bag or purse with her, and she's simply leaning there in a plain dress, shoes, and cardigan, with the fingers of both her hands splayed out for support upon the bonnet of the car behind her. She looks at me with wide, intense, pale-green eyes. There's a look of terror, crossed with wonder, upon her face. She soaks me in, and then, just as I pass, for an extraordinary few seconds that I'll never forget, it seems that she and I peer into each other's inner selves! She's so thin, stick-like, and frail that she looks as if she might break. I can feel her fear. Where is she going? How on earth will she cope with the roaring traffic of the wide and busy road beside us if she attempts to cross? I imagine she's come from some apartment high above us. She can't have walked far. In Athens aged people like her must fear descending to the streets, and I suspect that this lady has seen enough frenetic reality in just the last fifteen minutes or so to last her a good many days to come. I pause to look back at her from a little way beyond, when suddenly the door of the pharmacy opens and a young assistant calls to her in Greek. Thankfully somebody is looking out for her.

So many Greeks, on hearing that I come originally from *Néa Zealandía*, have immediately swooned and asked for my confirmation that *Néa Zealandía* is indeed beautiful. And then, after I've told them that it most certainly is, they ask for my advice on the best time to visit. They dream of New Zealand as being clean, green, calm and peaceful, and full of open airy spaces - everything that almost every part of New Zealand is, in fact. Some Athenians have even told me that they'd love to live there. But what they fail to consider is that New Zealand cities, rather like the main towns of Shropshire and Herefordshire, offer very very little of the electrifying buzz, the intense almost maniacal twenty-four-hour excitement of the city that they inhabit here. They do not imagine that on any night of the week they would completely fail to find street after street crowded with long strings of convivial cafés, bars, and restaurants, and that certainly from Sunday to Thursday, even in the four major cities of New Zealand, they'd be very lucky indeed to find more than just sporadic sparks of night-life. I warn them that were they, as Athenians, to move to New Zealand, they might eventually feel rather bereft and inclined to flee over the Tasman Sea, for just the same reasons as caused almost half of the 1970s Greeks of Wellington to eventually disperse to the larger Greek communities of Melbourne, Sydney, and Adelaide. Wrapped up and absorbed in their massive beehive of a city, I don't believe Athenians appreciate just how much they actually depend and thrive upon the excitement and closeness of the Greek *metrópolis*.

Earlier in the week I enquired in several bookshops as to the whereabouts of public libraries. Although this question was met by puzzled looks, I was eventually directed to one of the three stately Bavarian buildings of neo-classical style in Panepistimíou Street. But after climbing one of the two very fine curved marble stairways which sweep up to the portico of the building indicated, and after then passing between its majestic Doric-style columns, I found this library to hold only a large reference collection. It is, however, an important and a historical collection. It includes roughly 2,500 books from the 15th and 16th centuries and all are housed in an enormous, galleried, and very impressive central Reading Room in which antique desks are illuminated by a massive glass ceiling high above. This is the picturesque Valliános National Library, part of the so-called Neo-Classical Trilogy of the City of Athens, the trilogy's two other components being the nearby Academy of Athens and the equally fine University of Athens building. An imposing marble statue of Panaghís Valliános, who financed the construction of the magnificent library, stands protected between the two sweeping arms of the steps.

A librarian at the Valliános did however give me an address in north Athens, and today I emerge from the Metró into the somewhat decrepit area that is immediately beside Lárissa Station. And here I locate 'The City of Athens Municipal Library'. It's late afternoon and the library's big heavy wooden doors seem locked. Fortunately they give under pressure, and then, but for one slight young lad in a far corner, I find myself in a seemingly deserted interior. The lad insists on taking my bag. He stows it with charming but excessive care and ceremony in a locker, and then very politely issues me with a small numbered token. Newspapers, he advises, are down the hall on the left, with books down on the right. I venture through a brightly lit white marble corridor, past display cases of children's written work and crayon drawings, and in one long room discover many bare tables and empty chairs, some encyclopaedic-looking volumes on shelves at the far end, and one elderly suited gentleman engrossed over a tome. Other rooms seem either largely empty or clearly not meant for members of the public, and in one of them sit three members of staff, quietly chatting. I nod, smile, and pass on, but a man calls after me. He explains that the reason why the library is now empty is that members of the public tend to use it in the mornings. Now isn't that when most people are at work?

Anyway, how does a public library in Athens operate? Well, it seems you need to know exactly which book you want before you arrive. Here in the city's Central Library the public cannot browse the actual collection. Recent Greek publications are available but unless you already know the title that you wish to borrow, you must sit at one of two bulky old TV-type computer monitors and examine the catalogue. You then put in your order and if the book is available it will be fetched for you. I suppose you're then able to examine it and possibly reject it, but no doubt the assistants won't welcome visitors who constantly send them scurrying back and forth from the stacks with books that are not, in the end, actually checked out and taken away! A number of bookshop assistants have suggested to me that this is the only public library in Athens, but I'm assured by the librarian who helps me here today that there are others, and that they all run on similar lines to this, the main one. My exploration of the public library system in Athens need go no further.

I've been told that Kifissiá is an outer suburb well worth seeing, a very pleasant place quite close to Athens, and a highly desirable area in which to live, particularly during the summer when its air is clear, clean, and cool, due to the area's considerable distance from congested central Athens and its greater height above sea-level. The journey there, by Metró, takes about 45 minutes, and for the greater part of that period, almost as far as Eiríni Station and the Olympic Stadium, the walled sides of the overground track are continuously covered with wild and loud graffiti. The Olympic Stadium, with all its high white sweeping arches, then sweeps into view as a welcome relief, a pleasant surprise, a stunning modern architectural jewel - which is unfortunately set far from the centre of Athens. And sadly, Spanish architect Santiago Calatrava's showpiece is now something of a white elephant, a white elephant that, like the entire 2004 Olympic Games, must surely have contributed to Greece's current economic disaster. Get too close to the Olympic Centre in Eiríni these days and I'm told that despite efforts being made to use the complex for football matches, concerts, and theatrical shows like *Cirque du Soleil*, you're confronted with graffiti, decay, and corners filled with windswept litter.

Eventually the train terminates at Kifissiá, and while making my way to the town centre I pass a number of very stately detached villas and mansions, evidence that this area has been a retreat for the wealthy of Athens for centuries. But the centre of Kifissiá is pure downtown Riyadh! There are wide white marble footpaths, much elaborate street-lighting, and a great maze of boutiques ablaze with light and filled with mannequins bedecked in expensive Western gear. One model, in particular, halts me in my tracks, for she's wearing practically the same outfit as a woman who sat opposite me on the train, except that the woman on the train wore her hair, and the same clothes, in a heavily moderated manner compared to that being demonstrated here by the mannequin. The woman on the train wore her long luxuriant bleached-blonde locks plainly, letting them fall quite simply, but the model's are puffed up, blown all over the place, like a great cloud of candy-floss torn this way and that, and quite obviously fixed with a great deal of lacquer, to massively increase the size of her head. The stylish grey woollen top with a foot or so of concertinaed roll-neck, was all gathered up neatly and uniformly on the train, but in the window it's sluttishly unravelled, pulled about to create a deliberately sloppy and dishevelled appearance. This cold night the woman on the train had her thick woollen coat zipped up for warmth to just short of her roll-neck collar: the mannequin has hers unzipped and deliberately pulled apart, clearly to reveal the full curve of her ample breasts. So, while Athenian women are clearly buying the fashions exhibited in boutique windows, they're mostly not wearing them in the very daring manner being so blatantly demonstrated. Thankfully, a strong sense of modesty seems to prevail, and no doubt many a Western fashionista has despaired at the way Greek women tone down such heavily sexualized creations.

Between the clothes shops are jewellers, shoe stores, and boutiques specialising in luxury wrist-watches. Up and down the streets every glossy brand name of Paris, Geneva, Milan, and Rome is writ large in brazen neon signage. This Kifissiá *agorá* is sterile and soulless. Down one arcade is the only noticeable bookshop, a very small branch of a national chain. A supermarket offers nearly every luxury food that can be purchased in such UK chains as Waitrose and Sainsburys, including all the famous brands of English tea. Kifissiá is obviously home to many of Athens's wealthy, and for those content to live amongst glamour and high-end consumerism.

While in summer Kifissiá provides a welcome refuge from the heat of the densely packed concrete of central Athens, throughout the year it has at least one other positive draw: The Goulandrís Museum of Natural History. I locate its impressive buildings in a leafy side street just beyond

Kifissiá's centre; they stand in a stunningly modern design as well as in neo-classical marble. The complex was begun in 1964 by Níki and Ághelos Goulandrís, of the wealthy ship-owning Goulandrís family, specifically to promote within Greece interest in the natural sciences, and to bring to people's attention the need to protect the country's natural wildlife habitats, as well as those species living within them which are in danger of extinction. To date, an enormous amount of collecting from all over Greece has enabled this museum to exhibit birds, mammals, insects, reptiles, rocks, minerals, shells, and fossils. The botanical collection consists of over 200,000 different species, including Greece's own 6,000 native wildflowers, and the museum's library currently contains almost 16,000 scientific volumes, along with 45,000 journals. It's also pleasing to observe that these things are not just being collected and stored, as is often the case in the wealth-endowed libraries of the Arabian Gulf. I'm told that the Goulandrís is very much a working museum, and important research is conducted here in such specialised departments as Entomology, Herpetology, and Biotechnology.

On the train back to central Athens, the seat directly opposite me remains free until we pull into Eiríni. There, it's taken by a woman in her late fifties, or early sixties, who, I note, as she settles herself before me, possesses unusually lively eyes. I'm the only non-Greek in the carriage, and of course she's spotted it and she's intrigued. It's winter, and she's probably wondering why I'm here, what I'm about. She wears a faint smile upon her lips, and like a boy and girl at their first school dance, it becomes a case of which of us will dare to make the first move! I'm just about to venture a comment, when an automatic safety announcement is repeated through the carriage's speaker-system, words along the lines of 'Passengers are reminded to keep their personal possessions with them at all times, in the interests of security'. We've both heard this message on at least five or six occasions already, and my 'companion' now looks at me directly and declares in perfect English, though with a slight trace of an American accent, 'Honestly! The tone of her voice! It's almost like a threat!' I laugh in acknowledgement, and the ice is broken.

She and her husband lived for twenty years in Chicago, but returned to Athens 'for the buzz', which, she assures me, even Chicago cannot match! I share with her my impressions of the centre of Kifissiá, and she says that nearly all of the many boutiques I've seen are simply 'fronts', that the reason many of them exist is to provide an excuse for the acquisition of 'black money', to avoid tax or to collect subsidies. 'But is that really possible?' I ask. 'Why not?' she responds, factually. 'If they can do it, if no one stops them, then they will!' She tells me that tax evasion in Greece goes right back to the time of the Turks, that it was seen as a rightful form of resistance against the occupying power. She's not the first one to have told me this. Life under the Turks had been bearable for roughly the first 300 years, but in 1760 the status of Ottoman Athens dramatically altered: the Sultan took the city as his personal property, and citizens had not only to purchase their land back (on a lease-for-life-only basis) but with the addition of exorbitant taxes. Then in 1772, when the Anatolian Turk Hadji Ali Haseki took control of administration, the taxation became extortionate. Greeks unable or unwilling to pay were thrown into jail, or left on the streets to starve. Evasion of taxes thus became habituated when Otto's Bavarian régime imposed taxes no less burdensome than the Turks'. Estimates of the underground Greek economy today range at the very least from 30% of the officially reported economy, to as much as 60%! And indeed, the Bank of Greece has estimated that in recent years the country's tax evasion has amounted to about five billion euros a year. Thus, finally am I beginning to understand how the spending sprees of a considerable number of Athenians are being funded.

After consuming a hearty platter of tasty *mezédes* at a little *ouzerí* downtown, I make my way to the much lauded Pallás Theatre, in Voukourestíou Street, to see one of Greece's great divas. This evening the plush extensive foyers are flowing with expensively-clad men and women, nearly all over forty though a small number are in their twenties and thirties. They're nearly all wearing the latest gear, out of boutique windows from Kifissiá to Vouliagméni. For evenings such as this, black is clearly the fashionable colour of the moment.

And for the women it's often black sparkling with sporadic threads of silver or gold. There's also, this evening, much ostentatious display of women's jewellery, as well as oversized excessively-butch watches on the wrists of many of the men. Perhaps this spectacle of fashion is engendered by the luxury and grandness of the setting, so that audiences always feel the need to dress up for performances at the Pallás Theatre? For the lower walls of the foyer are tiled with impressive green marble from the island of Tínos, the striking columns are of streaked marble from Éuvoia, the monumental stairs are formed of fine white marble from Chíos, and all about there are sparkling fixtures in Art Deco brass.

A very sniffy and disdainful young male usher, in black bow-tie and suit, examines my ticket and then condescendingly dismisses me with a wave of the hand to the circle, upstairs. Evidently, only peasants can't afford to sit in the stalls. He's little different from those arrogant peacocking individuals who often usher at theatres in London, who feed off the adulation and excitement of the audience and who somehow mistakenly think that they're every bit as important as the stars upon the stage. When I then arrive at my row in the circle, I find six middle-aged ladies all settled between me and my seat, large expensive designer handbags lodged upon each lap. I smile, say 'Kalispéra!' and 'Sygnómi!' (Good evening! Excuse me!) and could I possibly get past to my seat, 'Parakaló, kai efcharistó?' (Please, and thank you?). But they all look back at me blankly! They stare as if I must be out of my mind! It's ten minutes before nine, ten minutes before the concert is scheduled to begin, there's plenty of time, the curtain isn't about to rise, so I can't understand why they should be so reluctant to assist and allow me to pass! They then confabulate a little, but tightly, out of the corners of their mouths with their eyes kept firmly frontwards. And then they continue to ignore my request! What am I to do? I stand and look at them, aware too that everyone seated above is now focused downwards upon this gripping confrontation. Eventually one of the ladies cracks and volunteers to respond on behalf of the rest. She raises an arm, and then, gesticulating in a rather muscular and unladylike manner, she indicates that I should ascend past the remaining fifteen or so rows behind her, to then pass along the back of the theatre before returning down the side to my seat! Clearly these dames have every intention of not budging. So I smile, give them a nod of agreement, and then ascend the rake, only to find that there's no unblocked passage along the back and that people in some other row will have to be inconvenienced instead.

As a number of Athenians have excitedly told me during the past two weeks, the Pallás Theatre has recently been expensively refurbished. Unfortunately, however, once in my seat I observe that within the auditorium the designers have consummated their efforts with a hideous, massive, and unavoidable crown of vulgar *nouveau-riche* glitz. In the centre of the ceiling, high above the stalls, it seems a giant jelly-mould has been pushed up through the ceiling and that the three undulating metre-high inner sides of this mould have then been lined with sparkling gold tinsel. This unfortunate affair is partly a left-over of what was once a significant decorative element of a very smart 1930s cinema. When the rectangular cupola of three wavy walls was layered into the cinema's ceiling at the time of its construction it was justly considered something of an Art Deco marvel. But sadly the designers of 2006 decided to highlight it, and in the most garish and excessive manner imaginable. Rather than subtly respect the feature with sober tones, they've lined its inner walls with optical fibres, and though these fences of fibres cast, in total, a very pleasant and gentle light upon the auditorium below, the cheap three-layered crown of glitz above totally dominates the space. Together with four ghastly large mirrored disco-balls, which hang suspended from within the highest part of the mould, the illuminated walls impose a very strong and specific character. What reaction then, I wonder, did this décor elicit recently in members of the Berliner Ensemble, visiting Athens to present Brecht's Threepenny Opera! Did the big sparkly crown upon the ceiling assist their projection of social and political commentary, conflict and disturbance? Perhaps they were grateful: maybe the glitter of the ceiling actually aided them in their Brechtian battle against suspension of disbelief.

I have read that it is thought by some in Greece at this time that the Greek establishment has plunged this nation into the worst pseudo-glamorous decadence to be seen on the entire planet. I'd love to say that I, however, have seen kitsch glamour in the Arabian Gulf which diminishes the interior of Athens's Pallás Theatre to a mere peccadillo. But unfortunately I can't. I've never before beheld in any theatre anywhere anything as hideous.

Downstairs, the great stretch of stalls is slowly filling, and between the front row and the stage, in several bunches, are fifteen to twenty professional photographers with large cameras and flash-guns. When I arrived, they were all at the top of the foyer staircase. They had momentarily glanced at me before looking hungrily away for a face which they recognised. Now they wobble like clusters of agitated bumble-bees, from left to right of the stage, and back again, as more and more of the worthy take their seats in the front rows. The celebrities are clearly delighted, and from up in the circle, at the back of the theatre, we watch them striking poses, throwing their arms around each other and grinning at the lenses, some even getting up to go and join other celebrities in other rows purely to strike further poses for tomorrow's papers. This goes on for well over half an hour, until, shortly after half-past nine, about thirty-five minutes after the scheduled starting time, a bell sounds and the clusters of photographers suddenly and frantically wobble off left and right as if to avoid a catastrophe, or as if the most astounding theatrical happening ever is about to commence!

The lights begin to dim, and exotic music that has roots in Asia Minor, softly filters into the auditorium. It's neither *rebétiko* nor traditional *laïkó*. It's been given a modern, updated, contemporary feel. It plays for some considerable time, creating a feeling of suspense, until, in darkness, half a dozen musicians make their way upon the stage and seat themselves behind their instruments. Slowly and indiscernibly they pick up the curling interweaving melody lines of the pre-recorded soundtrack, and then slowly bring this 'cool' interpretation of traditional music to a crescendo. The lights come up slowly on each musician, and then into a sudden splash of illumination steps the Greek diva. The theatre erupts into long, polite, applause.

The diva walks slowly to the microphone, fixes her gaze upon the back of the stalls, and then, after a minute or so, joins with the music. Her voice is sombre. It moves sedately from note to note, remaining most of the time amongst tones of quite a low range. Song follows song until the singer begins to move a little with the rhythm of the music. Her exquisite robes flow with beguiling pliancy, though I think it'd be better if she remained still. However, as the performer perseveres with her programme it becomes clear that there are many in this theatre who appear to very greatly delight in her delivery. Unfortunately for me, I find little of it entrancing.

Nevertheless, this is a fascinating experience, and worth a discreet photograph - without flash, of course. But just as I'm about to press the shutter, all at once, in the darkness, my hands and camera are criss-crossed, in wild and vexatious manner, by bright blood-red laser-light! Someone, somewhere up at the back, is monitoring! It's frightening. I'm instantly put in mind of the barricades and watch-towers of a jail or prisoner-of-war camp. And it's particularly riling because from the moment the singer stepped upon the stage, two young women directly in front of me have been recording every one of her songs on glowing high-tech mobile telephones! But unlike myself, who dared to raise his camera a little for a good sight-line, I now note that they're holding their equipment very close to their chests. Although they were alarmed by the spill-over flashes of red that were inflicted on me, and they turned their eyes upon me like everyone else in the vicinity, the incident hasn't perturbed them in the least, and they continue heedlessly to record.

I know that the diva has been considered brilliant, that her voice has been said to soar and sparkle with voluptuous sensuality, but here tonight I've heard enough. Apart from one ballad of achingly touching melancholy, for which her style seems superbly suited, no other song has captured my interest. So at half-time I collect my things from the cloakroom and make to leave. But as I descend the grand staircase connecting the upper foyer to the entrance, I find that several hundred members of the audience, all in their plush blacks and dark greys, have already exited from the stalls and are now standing massed under and around the portico, blocking my way. They are largely silent, and all well and truly stuck into cigarettes. They're desperate for them. These two hundred or so people have fled the stalls more quickly than I have fled the circle, in order to light up and get the fix. The hour-long first half must have been an agony for them. I think of halting and pointing my camera at this mass of smartly-dressed silent smokers, but do not dare. Instead, I weave my way through the smoke, quit the Pallás Theatre, and head for home.

Hurrying through dark Psyrrí, I notice that the restaurant I visited two whole weeks ago, on my very first night in this extraordinary city, appears to be full of people. I ask the young guy on the door if the *rebétika* players are in. *'Nai!'* (Yes!) he replies. *'Nikólaos kai Aristotéles?'* I ask. (This night may yet be saved!) But he doesn't know the musicians' names. So I make it clear I won't be eating, only drinking, and he says that'll be fine: *'Típota!'* (You're welcome! No problem!). And in I go.

I pass a pillar, my eyes following the long neck of a *bouzoúki* emerging from the other side of the column until its player is revealed. 'Áris!' I cry, delighted. Instantly they all cease playing. The diners all turn and the restaurant falls momentarily silent. 'David!' returns Áris, delighted. They each shake my hand enthusiastically. With the big dip in the winter temperature the band is now warmly clad in thick jerseys, and Aristotéles has a woollen scarf draped elegantly about his neck. Very briefly I relate the evening's unrealized expectations. 'Ah, but she is now not so young!' exclaims Nikólaos, clicking his tongue in a kindly philosophical manner. They tell me her singing has been adored for decades, so that I wonder for a moment if perhaps I've misguidedly walked away from a more interesting second-half.

The waiter urges me to take a little table quite close to the musicians, and as further Greeks arrive, to eat and enjoy the *rebétika*, this night is indeed redeemed! How very lucky I am! A rare and curious old chap, large, strong and fierce-looking, sits drinking, eating, and smoking a cigar, all alone.

He wears a white roll-neck top and a seafarer's navy-blue cap. From a delicate silver chain around his neck, a silver medal of the Blessed Virgin hangs proudly out over the white top. And with his little well-trimmed moustache, he looks as if he's just nipped up from the boats in Piraeus. He probably has. He claps along to the rhythms of the rippling *bouzoúkia*, and each time a chorus comes around he raises his rich strong voice like some great creature looming from the depths of the ocean. We recognise each other's delight in the music, and soon we're seated at the same table and chatting. He's been to New Zealand! Many times! He knows Wellington Harbour well! He's sailed every ocean on Earth with the Greek merchant navy! I tell him of the wondrous Greek liners I used to boldly board and prowl around in Wellington Harbour during my lunch hours in the early 70s. 'Maybe, you came on board one of *my* boats!' he says. And maybe I did!

The room swells with the divine music of Greece, and cries of *'Ópa! Ópa!'*, and *'Yeiá sou, David!'* and *'Yeiá sou, Andrea!'* and *'Yeiá sou!'* to everyone else! And every so often everyone at every table turns to the band and sings along to a rousing chorus. There's laughter and gaiety and merriment. And song after splendid song I rejoice in these dedicated and exceptionally talented musicians, who perform this fabulous music night after night in all the many such *estiatória* and *tavérnes* of Athens, and for very little return beside the intoxicating and revivifying exhilaration of it all.

🔁 🔁 🔁 🔁

17

To Démetra & Cátharsis

'Public';
Monastery of Kaisarianí;
& Manólis Lidákis.

Whathat on earth is happening to me? I've had another awful
night. They've given me two extra blankets, making four
in all, but I still felt cold, right through until rising, and I got
very little sleep. With the temperature having plummeted
to that of a bitter British winter, I asked them to see to the
heating, and they did, but then, oddly, they requested
me not to move the setting above the indicated 24 degrees
centigrade. And I haven't. But surely the machine is pumping
out air no 'warmer' than about 10! Or has my sleeplessness
been the result of that particular half litre of *híma*, drunk
last night in the *mezedepoleío*? Or is it just this extraordinary
city again? Maybe it was the drama at the Pallás Theatre!
Followed, perhaps, by the high excitement of hearing once
more the music of Áris and Nikólaos. My brain is bursting
with over-stimulation. All night long it seems I've been
replaying my experiences; thinking about the contradictions,
the joys, and every one of the madnesses. So this last day in
Athens must be a free one. I really need to wind down. And
I need to get away, to try to view this city from afar, to get
things in perspective. Today must be simply for wandering,
and relaxing, and preparing to say goodbye to a city which
has lifted me off the ground, thrilled me, shocked me, and
inspired me.

This morning's local news is that the government may try to reduce its horrific accumulated public debt of at least 300 billion euros by slashing the public sector and pension rights and by radically reforming the country's chaotic tax system. A Herculean problem requires such a Herculean solution, but there seems to be great uncertainty in the air. It's as if ordinary Greeks can't conceive of the seriousness of this crisis, nor how to deal with it.

To try to push my sleepless night behind me, I indulge in a cup of good strong coffee from one of the hundreds of outlets which are part of Athens's prolific café culture, those little places where thousands of Athenians sit daily, and into which thousands more call briefly to take away a coffee in a cardboard cup, or a *café frappé* (iced coffee) in a sturdy transparent plastic capsule with a clear dome-like lid. As the assistant mixes this and that in preparation, and the right proportions are driven through the large and impressive stainless steel valves of a great coffee-making machine, the production of my *caffé látte mikró,* the smallest available, seems to take forever. And once it's all done and I sit down to enjoy it, well, to be frank, I don't see what all the fuss is about. The Nescafé I've been making myself each morning with a good dash of the local condensed milk tastes just as good, if not better, and is certainly stronger.

A wander into *Public* on Sýntagma Square is a revelation. This very popular store consists of six levels, including a café on the roof, and is set in a wide refurbished space behind a handsome old beaux-arts façade. It's the flagship of a dozen Greek 'microelectronics-supermarkets' initiated by business-man Pános Ghermanós in 2005. The floors are crammed with CDs, DVDs, players and recorders, digital cameras, mobile phones, satellite navigation systems, portable computers, a vast array of flat-screen televisions, computer and TV games, and elaborate big black padded racing-seats for simulations of events like Grand Prix races to be experienced in front of gigantic 'home entertainment screens'. Moreover, the Sýntagma branch of *Public* has a massive book department that offers everything from the latest rubbishy American comics through to modern Greek treatises on classical philosophy.

There's a Greek music CD and a Greek film that I've not been able to hunt down anywhere in Athens so far although I saw just before leaving the UK that legitimate copies of both can be purchased easily from Greek shops in Australia and the USA. So, in this vast modern emporium of every form of medium available in Europe it's worth having a final try. The assistants are all very easy to spot: they wear a casual uniform of dazzling orange. But as I approach two of these orange people in different departments, I note the slow turning of the head, in a kind of aloof and weary disdain, despite the time being only mid-morning and there not yet having been much 'annoying' customer foot-fall. On both occasions my '*Sygnómi, miláte anglicá?*' (Excuse me, do you speak English?) brings only a weary '*Nai*' (Yes), as if yet another member of the public is about to burden them with an imbecilic question. The answers I receive are laced with superiority and dismissiveness, though they are still, just, acceptably polite. Few smiles. Little graciousness. The thinking in this place appears to be: 'We're where it's at! We're the high-altar of all things high-tech! And we've had thousands of beggars like you in here already!' It's what you can expect these days in most shops along Oxford Street, in London, and it's such a pity the same attitude is clearly rooting itself here in the very centre of Greece's capital. I'm authoritatively informed that both the famous Greek CD and the famous Greek film are simply 'No longer available!' I politely advise both assistants that in fact each item *is* still available, in Australia and the United States, and am then pleased to note at least slight diminutions in their projections of self-importance.

In capacious atria between *Public's* floors the air-space has been filled with giant theatrical displays which hang suspended by almost invisible wires. In one of these areas, Elvis Presley, larger than life-size and in full white lavish cabaret apparel, complete with blue-lined cape, a stuffed crotch of ludicrous proportions, and a chain of Hawaiian flowers swinging from his neck, sails through the air while standing upon a giant flying guitar. Far below him orange assistants hawk thirty or so of the latest netbooks, notepads, and laptops to prospective customers. In a similar atrium, a pile of enormous ancient-looking tomes, probably hollow and made of fibre-glass, appear to hover, centre-space, to provide a crouching spot for a devilish-looking, blood-red, life-sized model of Spider Man. On shelves below him are hundreds of 'Graphic Novels', or 'Adult Comics', from the USA.

Turning a corner of a large square concrete pillar, I'm surprised to find, against one of its four surfaces, a high and wide bookstand above which, in bold large letters, are emblazoned the words 'GAY and LESBIAN'! In all Athens, except for sex-shops I suppose, such a sign appears only here, in this cavernous temple of everything Western and American, this place for the worship of every up-to-the-minute electronic gizmo currently purchasable upon the planet. On closer inspection, however, I find this section to be in reality no such thing. Its shelves are loaded with mainly picture books: coffee-table volumes of photographs of nude, or largely nude, women in exotic poses; guides to heterosexual Kama Sutra-style sex; and other lavish books of mainstream erotica. The most there is in terms of gay material are several books featuring only tasteful photographs of the male physique. There's no gay literature here whatsoever.

So what's happened? Has someone had hopes too high? Has a bold start been abandoned? Or is there a plan to alter the shelves' contents by a steady mixing of caution and stealth? Have they decided to kick off by just getting the most with-it members of the Greek public used to the signage alone? Elsewhere in this store they haven't held back in pushing every latest foreign concept, so why so squeamish about the gay and lesbian? Or are they having trouble, as in Islamic Middle Eastern countries, getting imported consignments past the censoriousness of customs officials? It's perfectly feasible. For 'The Greek Council of Radio and Television' is known to have fined certain local stations for broadcasting during afternoon hours television programmes which have included only very slight and subtle references to human beings who are not heterosexual! And in 2003 the same council fined the private Greek television network *Mega Channel* roughly £70,000 for showing two men simply kissing. So unfortunately every media outlet in Greece has reason to be cautious.

But how come sex-shops and big sleazy porn cinemas can be so easily spotted right in the centre of Athens yet no mainstream bookshop in this city can handle even a modest and conservative Gay and Lesbian section, offering at the very least the works of Thomas Mann, Proust, Gide, Virginia Woolf, Radclyffe Hall, James Baldwin, Genet, Yourcenar, Wilde, Waugh, Isherwood, Mary Renault and Gertrude Stein? I'm so vexed I feel a sudden urge to hot-foot it up to Omónoia Square just to see inside one of those grand and massive old-world cinemas up there which have been converted into dual porn-palaces, showing both square and gay erotica. For there's clearly a gay underworld in this city and one can't help wonder how it expresses itself. But every city on Earth has its seamy side, even where openness of mind and lack of repression enables bookshops to stock a wonderfully liberal breadth of material.

So no, for my final afternoon in Athens I shall keep to my plan and catch a bus to Kaisarianí, just over two miles from Sýntagma Square, to re-visit that magical hillside which so enchanted me twenty years ago, but also to try to get above it all, to see Athens from a distance, and to get all my thoughts about this city into some kind of perspective. As for whatever delights remain to be seen at the Athens Municipal Gallery, the Benáki Museum of Islamic Art, the Gennadius Library, the Cycladic Museum, the Hadjikyriákos-Ghíkas Gallery, the Epigraphical Museum, Daphní Monastery, the Athens War Museum, the Numismatic Museum, the Theocharákis Gallery, the Vorrés Museum, the Pierídes Museum of Contemporary Art, the Exile Museum, the Katakouzenós House Museum, the Piraeus Archaeological Museum, the Hellenistic Maritime Museum, and the Piraeus Municipal Art Gallery, and so many other interesting places in this rich and overwhelming city, they'll all have to be seen on future visits!

The Kaisarianí bus terminates just short of a vast and crammed cemetery where hundreds of little votive candles twinkle on well-tended tombs even in the full light of day. From here, there follows a walk of a further mile up into the mountains, to the Monastery of Kaisarianí and the splendid slopes that surround it. But I'm very quickly lost! Where twenty years ago there was just one, quiet, and simple lane, there's now a very busy system of several roads, whizzing continually with single-occupant vehicles. Athens's urban sprawl has been relentless, and the entire range of Mount Ymittós is now surrounded by housing. New passages have been carved through the foothills so that roads now pass over and under each other, criss-crossing or meeting at large interchanges all along the western side of the great mountain, to eventually connect to the wide new Attikí Odós freeway which arcs north from Spáta to Elefsína. The banks of the gorges which have thus been carved through the foothills are lined in part with large concrete slabs to keep the earth from the road. All of these slabs are graffitied with the scrawls of vandals and juveniles, each panel daubed with symbols, names, words and slogans in car-spray-paints of every glaring colour. It's all an inarguably ugly mess and so dissonant with the shrubbery and trees of the beautiful Forest of Kaisarianí lying immediately above.

Only two decades ago you stepped off the bus and were immediately in quiet pastoral paradise. As you slowly made your way up to the ancient monastery, amidst bird song and near-heavenly peace, bee-keepers quietly tended hives in the beautiful tree-covered strand to your left. The Kaisarianí and Mount Ymittós beehives have been famed for centuries for their fine thyme honey, and hives are still here today, beside the rushing roads, although most are in poor condition and appear to have been abandoned. And no wonder, for the passing traffic is relentless, the air is tainted with exhaust fumes and the floor of this early section of the forest is now littered with rubbish, tossed from the perpetual torrent of passing vehicles. The globally ubiquitous, super-thin, blue plastic bag is torn and snagged all about on branches and rocks, while the many on the ground spew household garbage. Amongst the luscious green grass of the Greek winter there's every kind of non-compostable and non-biodegradable detritus imaginable: all the polystyrene trays and cups and plastic knives and forks that are handed out willy-nilly by *fastfoudádika* for that one single meal on-the-fly; along with tins, glass bottles, even small old unwanted domestic appliances. It's all so depressing, and it continues for roughly half a mile of the route to the monastery - as far as that point at which visitors take a turn to their right and finally escape the traffic rushing to and fro the busy Perifereiakí Ymittoú. This wintry afternoon I appear to be the only visitor approaching the monastery on foot, and all the detritus and debris that I've had the misfortune to encounter is probably hardly visible from speeding vehicles. What they do not see, it would appear most Greeks simply don't care about. But unless this behaviour stops, then in years to come even the people inside the vehicles will be faced with the accumulation of rubbish.

Thankfully, as I walk further uphill litter and the roar of engines lessen dramatically. Bird song is heard and the air becomes sweet, scented by the aromatic herbs, bushes, and tall thin cypress trees and other conifers that are growing all about in great profusion. Despite it being cold winter, here are all shades of green from the silvery greyish verdure of olive trees, to the deep dark emerald of the cypress. I leave the road and follow up through the valley a simple winding clay and stone path which takes me higher and higher towards the monastery. This, at last, is what I remember. It's magic. It's a tonic. It's sublime.

This is where, at the end of a thrilling day or fun-filled night in the buzz of Athens, one needs to retire to. The monks who once lived in this secluded spot surely savoured their privilege. Not that 'holy' men would have availed themselves much of the exciting and pleasurable places of central Athens, but you never know, there must have been a few who were adventurous. And, of course, it was the monks of Kaisariant who established the little Panaghía Pantánassa Church in Monastiráki, in the heart of the city. That little dependency no doubt provided a good lodging place for any monk who found he'd left his return to the side of Mount Ymittós till too late at night! However, one suspects that regardless of the invigorating delights of the city below, the monks of Kaisariant must have much preferred their hillside monastery, its peaceful solitude, its glorious location, its mellow stones, its beautiful roofs and domes of terracotta, and their little Byzantine church all aglow with candles, the gleam of *eikónes*, and the resplendent oranges, golds, and ochres of its magnificent 14th and 17th century frescoes.

The Monastery of Kaisarianí was originally a temple dedicated to the goddess Démetra, whom the ancients believed was responsible for the fertility of the land, and consequently for good harvests. Roman columns on the site indicate that a temple existed here at least two thousand years ago, and a nearby spring, known as the Kallía Fountain, was probably the spur to the temple's construction, as it fed the River Ilisós, which conveyed water to crops upon the plain below. This spring, still running, and now called the *Aghiasmós* (Sanctified Water), feeds the Roman ram's-head fountain which trickles into a sarcophagus-cistern in the monastery's eastern wall, just to the left of the entrance - though actually this fountain is a copy, and the 6th century original is now on display in the National Archaeological Museum. In the 5th century, a Christian church was built where once the shrine to Démetra had stood, and then in the 11th century today's monastery was erected over the ruins of the former church.

In its hey-day the Monastery of Kaisarianí was home to over three hundred monks. It was a flourishing institution. In 1456, when the Turks had Athens surrounded and there was no chance of resisting them, it was the Abbot of Kaisarianí who was chosen to step forward and surrender the keys of the city to the invaders. As a result, the Ottomans looked favourably upon this monastery for most of the Occupation, allowing it both tax exemption and independence. The community here thus continued to prosper and Kaisarianí became the most important monastery in Greece. It kept a fine library, and the monks were renowned not only for the quality of their honey but for the medicines that they prepared from the many splendid herbs that to this day grow wild and profusely upon the hillsides. However, in 1792 Neóphytos VII, Ecumenical Patriarch of Constantinople, placed the Moní Kaisarianís within the jurisdiction of the Metropolitan of Athens and this caused the monastery to lose both its status and its privileges.

Within ten years the monastery was abandoned, and it remained so until after the War of Independence, when, until

1855, it was used as a nunnery. When the nunnery closed the hillside was once again forsaken and the monastery fell to ruins. During the horror of the German occupation, nearly a hundred years later, all of the trees on the sides of Mount Ymittós were cut down to provide wood for heating and cooking. Then between 1949 and 1963, 'The Athenian Friends of the Trees Society' replanted the 750 acres surrounding the deserted monastery with all of the varieties of trees, shrubs, herbs and flowers which had originally populated this hillside. The society also restored the monastery buildings.

If it weren't for the hundreds of tall and elegant cypress trees that now stand like great majestic candles all about, I could be back at home, walking in the South Shropshire hills, or in some beautiful mountainous area of Powys or Gwynedd, in Wales. The cypresses here at Kaisarianí are in some areas so numerous that they cut visibility to about 25 metres, so one is dwarfed in a magical maze of slender emerald trees with thousands of herb bushes sprawling at their bases. In spring this hillside is ablaze with all kinds of wildflowers. Red and orange poppies abound. This is the kind of environment that regenerates the human condition. Surroundings like this are oxygen, food, and drink to the mind - to the poetic 'soul', and to the romantic 'heart'. And to think that only a few years ago, in 2007, this luscious valley was at risk of destruction, when the world watched nightly TV reports of nearby areas of Mount Ymittós being ravaged by summer fires and razed to the ground. Firemen and dedicated volunteers worked tirelessly to ensure that this magnificent hillside was spared.

Despite the cold and the dusting of snow on the summit above, I'm one of only a handful of people who have journeyed up here this afternoon to savour this splendid and singular antithesis of the frantic concrete warren of the city below. A couple of women pull up and open the doors of a people-carrier to let three large dogs rush ecstatically along the hillside tracks. A pair of young men, possibly students, speaking some language of Eastern Europe, emerge from a forest path to clamber onto motorbikes and roar off back down to town. Several hundred metres above the monastery, two young Greeks sit on a rock looking out over Athens, quietly talking. As I pass up the trail, through trees and bushes, they offer me the usual friendly Greek greetings, we share pleasantries regarding the view, and then we drop into comments about the other side of the city below.

Chrístos is a student at the university in Zográfou, just beyond a ridge in the Kaisarianí foothills, while Phótis, about ten years older, is a technical writer who works freelance. I ask what they think will happen, and instead of either of them answering they both just shake their heads. Then Phótis eyes me carefully, pauses a moment, and says, 'The system is corrupt. The officials are corrupt. They're all political cowards.' He says he's studied and worked in the United States and coming back to Greece has filled him with embarrassment. He says Greeks know they're in trouble but they're still being profligate. He says each government comes to power promising to put the situation right, but time and again they shrink from enforcing real and permanent change. He says almost everyone in Greece right now is just sticking their heads in the sand and hoping for the best. And he can't understand why we, the other members of the EU, simply don't expel Greece from 'the club'!

I'm humbled by the honesty, and I can feel their pain, so I ask Phótis what in his view ought to be done, to save the economy. They exchange a grin, and chuckle.

'Ha! So you think, we have only one economy, yes?'

'Well, maybe two, if you include the black economy?' I reply, hoping to impress.

'Ah, but we have three!' Phótis responds mischievously. 'And you think the black economy is just something on the side?' When I nod, he pounces.

'No! The first economy of Greece, our main economy, is our black economy, a massive percentage of everything!'

To keep things even, I assure Phótis and Chrístos that even in the UK we have something of a black, or, to use the politically correct term, a 'shadow' economy. But Phótis says I should understand that Greece's shadow economy, unlike the UK's, is not confined to drug-dealers, pimps, a few tradesmen, and companies using sophisticated accounting tricks to lessen their tax. 'In Greece', he says, 'the black economy includes doctors, dentists, lawyers, and it continues right down through the work-force to the taxi drivers and all the people who work in the hotels, the restaurants, and the cafés!' He confirms what Elpída told me yesterday.

Phótis then moves on to the Public Sector, the second of what he holds to be the three true sectors of the Greek economy. 40%, he says, of the national budget goes towards allowing Greek Public Sector workers to live a life of comfort. He says this sector has become so bloated with exaggerated bureaucracy and excessive positions of employment that one out of every four people working in Greece is an employee of the state. He says that in addition to very good salaries, Greek public sector workers enjoy large untaxed fringe benefits; their pensions are excellent; their working day is just six hours long; they have good holidays; they have access to free child-care; and they get fixed home loans at very low rates of interest. Furthermore, he says public sector workers are well known to claim many hours of overtime that they've never actually worked. So it's little wonder then that the brightest and most ambitious of Greeks seek positions in the nation's state sector, that the 'dream job' in Greece is perceived to be a cushy occupation in a state institution.

The attractiveness of the Public Sector therefore deprives the third Greek economy of the nation's talent, that third economy being the equivalent of other countries' normal and predominant economy of goods and services, the usual power-houses of productivity and wealth. Phótis says that not only is this third economy small in Greece, but it's shackled by red-tape: by restrictions on rates of pay, on who may do what, on how many hours people can work, and so forth. The most successful parts of this third economy, he says, are tourism, shipping and construction, and that Greece is very weak at generating other ventures. I tell them that in my sixteen days of walking the streets of Athens I've indeed seen little visible evidence of bold enterprise, and Phótis explains that because of people's realisation over the past few months that the books were cooked by the previous government, Néa Dimokratía, they're less willing now than ever to gamble with ventures. And anyway, there's no way the third economy could ever get Greece out of its troubles while the other two continue to operate as they have.

Phótis suggests that what has really puzzled me since my arrival in Athens are only the outward appearances of the main problems: tax evasion, nepotism, and corruption. When I ask what he thinks of the idea that everyone in Athens is living with guilt, an idea that I still find incredible, he says it's true. He says everyone knows that billions of euros never reach the government because everybody knows that they themselves are party to the belief that Greeks have a right to take and keep as much money as they can. When Phótis then confirms that this thinking stems all the way back to the 400 years of *Tourkokratía* it occurs to me that whenever I've heard tax evasion being acknowledged in Greece, it's been blamed on that long rough ride beneath the Turkish yoke. But Michael Llewellyn Smith, in his revealing account of Athens's evolution, cites an example of detestation of tax-collection occurring shortly after 1180 CE, almost 300 years before the Turkish occupation, when the last Metropolitan Bishop of Byzantine Athens, Michaél Choniátes, complained that the city's tax-collectors made their calculations by measures capable of setting a value on the very footprint of a flea!

When I suggest that surely Greeks can escape this mind-set, Chrístos says he thinks it's become so ingrained that change will only happen with great difficulty. He gives a couple of examples. He says that the most recent census revealed that thousands of pension cheques were still being cashed for individuals who'd been dead for years. People try to withhold from the relevant authorities any notification that their relatives have died. And secondly, despite nearly 30,000 motorists having simply refused to pay this year's vehicle registrations, so far there's been no indication from the government that people won't get away with it. Phótis adds that a similar mentality underpins the public sector problem, in that when Greece overthrew the Turks in the 19th century, Greek politicians wrongly but quite understandably regarded the freed and regained state apparatus as Greek property, their personal property, and not as a state service - a service of government belonging to, and provided for, the people.

The major problem for Greece, Chrístos says, is the belief that 'If you're honest you're a fool, because no one else is being honest!' I'm dumbfounded. I haven't heard such condemnation and ridicule of one's own country since I sat, many years ago, with some of my 18-year-old Arab students in Dhahran one evening after a Ramadan feast, and they told me honestly that they had almost no respect whatsoever for their Sa'udi royal family or the government that it maintains. 'You've heard of *fakelákia*?' asks Phótis. I shake my head and they both chuckle. They're enjoying themselves. I sense this encounter with a foreigner high above the city is like a kind of blood-letting, a purging, that they're enjoying seeing my shock, and that my shock provides them with a kind of sounding-board, a source of assurance that their perceptions of the situation are right.

Phótis says that if you want a doctor to help treat somebody who is ill in hospital, the doctor may well indicate that a *fakeláki* of something in the region of 1,000 to 2,000 euros will help. He says a similar figure is often needed to acquire a building license or to 'legitimise' an already constructed house. *Fakelákia* means 'money in small envelopes', the brown envelopes Elpída referred to yesterday. And apparently you simply don't question it. You quickly get the money from wherever you can, and you discreetly hand it over!

In this regard the organization 'Transparency International' reported in its 2009 Corruption Perceptions Index, which ranks and scores countries according to their perceived level of public sector corruption, that the Greek public sector was perceived to be one of the most corrupt in the European Union, along with those of Romania and Bulgaria. Then in 2011 the Greek chapter of Transparency International released findings estimating that between 2007 and 2011 corruption in Greece was highest in 2009, when an estimated total of 787 million euros' worth of bribes or *fakelákia* were paid in the private and public sectors combined. Encouragingly though, the total of bribes paid in 2011 was estimated at 'only' 554 million euros, a decrease, or improvement, of 233 million euros on the estimate of 2009. The Greek chapter also observed that individual payments over the entire period, 2007 to 2011, were to the value of 1,476 euros each, on average, with most *fakelákia* being paid to medical personnel, followed by tax officers, planning personnel, legal practitioners, and so on down to engineers and plumbers.

Raised in New Zealand, I find all this frightening, for I was fortunate to grow up in the land that year after year Transparency International has listed as being perceived to be the least corrupt country on the face of the globe, usually followed by Denmark and Sweden. This isn't to say, however, that there is never inappropriate behaviour in New Zealand, and when Phótis starts telling me that the Greek government is thought to be looking at cancelling its debts by selling off Greek assets, such as property and institutions, I'm able to warn him that this is unfortunately what the New Zealand government did in the 1980s, forgetting that when a nation sells its property it sells itself, because a nation *is* its land and its property, and outside buyers remodel their purchases according to the values of their own cultures. New Zealand society took a tragic turn when it invited the transnationals in, and there's been a determined effort ever since to buy back Kiwi ownership of Kiwi property.

This has been quite the most extraordinary exchange I've had in Athens yet, and my mind is reeling with it. It's now absolutely clear to me that since Greece joined the EU it's been living far beyond its means, wallowing in the superficial glamour of being a European country while paying scant attention to the little that Greece actually produces and creates. And as deficits have grown, successive governments have just kept on borrowing - to try to pay off the debts, and to continue importing far more than Greece exports. It's all been one wild excessive fiesta of consumption, and which to this very day is still going on, despite everyone's awareness that the nation's finances are in serious disarray.

I draw the conversation to a close by airily suggesting that hopefully the coming tourist season will assist Greece considerably.

'Ah, but you've already forgotten our black economy!' Phótis laughs. 'Tell me what incentive there is for tourists to demand receipts while they're in Greece! And when you do get a receipt, how do you know it's genuine?'

Apparently, some Greek businesses run two systems. They give a receipt for the correct amount, but then fabricate in a parallel system a separate receipt for the eyes of the tax office, a receipt that suggests that a lesser amount was received. The 'cleverness' of Greece's tax evaders appears to be without bounds. Confirming the brief facts that Andréas advised me of during my first week here, Phótis says that in December 2009 the Greek government announced all workers would be required to substantiate claims for the standard tax-free allowance of 12,000 euros, which previously had been granted automatically to everyone, and, at the same time, all citizens are now being used to try to flush out the country's black or shadow economy by forcing them, when buying, into coercing sellers to issue receipts. Greeks must now provide the tax office with a high number of receipts each year, at the risk of being penalised if they don't. But tourists often don't bother about receipts, and if they do they usually just throw them away, so that while tourism and shipping together are thought to provide just over 20% of Greece's Gross Domestic Product, their real wealth isn't known, and is probably much higher. Furthermore, given the crisis and the uncertain future, all of those tightly knit Greek families, large and small, which dominate both tourism and shipping will now be more eager than ever to pocket as much undocumented money as they can. So much for my suggestion that next summer's tourists will help save Greece's bacon.

How determined is the Greek government to devise and apply methods of detection which will absolutely stamp out tax evasion, bribery, and corruption? Are Greece's politicians even capable of launching such methods? Many say that the officials are so used to corruption that it's beyond them, that corruption is now 'in their blood'. Such thoughts are depressing, so I put it to Phótis and Chrístos that generally Greeks are extremely industrious, that the electric activity of Athens is evidence of this, and that Greek creativity is just ill-spent. They agree that Greeks ought not to squander their energies in the work of restaurants and cafés, but herein is another root of the country's crisis. Greeks are not naturally inclined to imitate Western competitiveness, the discipline and the cut and thrust of capitalism, although they are, naturally enough, happy to absorb into their traditional lifestyle the luxurious aspects of advanced consumerism. Altering their pleasant communal culture, born of centuries of life under a scorching sun, does not, and will not, come easily. Thus, membership of the EU has resulted in the pseudo-glamour of Athens. Instead of being really productive and creative, many young people are sitting around, posing, looking chic, and, from mid-morning onwards, lazing away their hours in idle chatter in cafés. Genuine Europeanization doesn't appear to be appropriate to the Greek climate. And the hearts of the people aren't really in it. And why should they be? Greece is as partial to Europe as it is to the East, and since the dawn of civilization Greeks have sought to maintain their own identity.

Before I go, Phótis insists on returning to the question I initially asked: what might actually happen to 'the economy'? He wants me to know that there are many in Greece who dream of Brussels walking in, taking over, and sorting out the whole country. He says many believe that Greeks just can't be trusted to keep their own system under proper surveillance, that every aspect of Greek financial life needs to be disciplined from the outside. So I ask him what the EU would gain from such a take-over (for there has to be a return), other than the satisfaction of transforming the country into a state that's no longer a liability. He thinks the question isn't worth asking: he doesn't believe the people of Greece would ever let it happen, that they're too proud, overly proud. He says Greece's 'problem' is its cultural difference with all the dominant countries of the EU. And he points specifically to Germany. Germany, he says, is a land of forward-thinking Lutherans who are happy to suffer, while Greece, on the other hand, is a sun-drenched, pleasure-loving nation where the family and quality of life is more important than anything else. 'Isn't that why so many Germans and English come to us for their holidays?' he asks. He's right. Greeks are happy to be European in so far as it enables them to stroll glamorously around town in all the designer-wear of Paris and Milan, but

Greekness is fundamentally at odds with the systematization that typifies the senior members of the EU. The Greeks are essentially a Levantine people and to become truly 'European' would necessitate a massive alteration of mind-set and nature, not to mention climate. And if such a transformation of mind-set be forced upon them, as to an extent it already has been, there can only be serious consequences for many of the finest features of Greek culture.

I thank Phótis and Chrístos profusely for their honesty and their openness, and as I leave and make my way further up the mountain, I know I've just met yet more utterly exceptional Greek people. I can't imagine ever having a conversation of such quality with a couple of young Brits I might happen to pass on some public footpath back in the UK. Whatever happens to Greece in the future, I feel it won't be all bad as long as there are people like Phótis and Chrístos around. And for sure, there are many people like Phótis and Chrístos in Greece. Greece's greatest hope is its people.

And then another significant thought hits me. During these sixteen wonderful days in Athens, during all the incredible interaction I've had with Athenians all over this city, not a single person, male or female, has ever asked me if I'm married! Nor has any Greek ever given the slightest indication of trying to work out my marital status or sexuality. There's never been a hint of such a question even being considered. In this Greeks are most certainly unlike Middle Easterners, for 'Are you married?' is one of the first questions that every Arab asks another male. It's automatic. It's also a dominant question in the Western *psyché*. Westerners are always trying to work you out, to discover your status, 'which way you swing'. I cannot say that the occasional Greek hasn't turned just slightly faint if I've needed to indicate I shouldn't be presumed to be heterosexual, but every Greek I've met has been entirely respectful. Perhaps the reason why I've enjoyed so many conversations with people here in Athens is that they don't seem to let any obsession with a person's sexuality or marital status get in the way. They don't erect that barrier. They don't allow it to prevent them from making and enjoying satisfying and delicious human contact.

From higher up the Kaisarianí mountainside, a fine panoramic view of Athens unfolds below from north to south. Behind, up on the ridge of Mount Ymittós, 1,027 metres above sea level, stands a rank of well over 50 tall television, radio, and mobile masts: all the communication towers of Athens's 'transmitter park', a tier of metal towers, some of them fifteen to twenty metres in height, some with dishes, some with antennae, some with both, all of them conducting telecommunications to and fro the ceaselessly distending city below. The tranquil song-filled air of this ancient monastic mountainside is clearly now shot-through with microwaves.

Far in the distance, a little Acrópolis squats in the middle of a vast carpet of creamy-white concrete that radiates, undulating, towards every point of the compass, lapping at the bases of Lykavittós and Philopáppou and surging on to the surrounding hills like a vast barrel of magnolia emulsion that's been poured upon the floor. It's astounding to look down on the city from this vantage point and consider that in the early 1830s, immediately after the War of Independence, this city that now has a population of just under 4 million consisted then of just under 3,000. In a little less than 200 years, the population of Athens and the population of New Zealand have increased almost identically in terms of total numbers, though the former is one city and the latter an entire country which is larger than the UK.

As one descends the Kaisarianí hillside, views of the slopes surrounding the little monastery below are sublime. The variety of shallow growth is abundant: there's sage, lavender, thyme, and juniper, to name just a few of the hill's wild herbs. Above this, and up to a height of roughly 15 feet, are many different species of larger shrubs and bushes. Then shooting from amongst that taller shrubbery, at regular intervals and all over the undulating hillside, are the majestic slim candles of Mediterranean cypress, beautiful exclamation marks that punctuate the folds of the hill and reign supreme at heights close to 30 metres. According to the Roman poet Ovid, the cypress was named after Kypárissos, a favourite of the god Apóllon. The young Kypárissos accidentally slew a stag that was much loved by Apóllon, and he was then so overcome with sorrow for what he'd done that he beseeched the gods to punish him. In compliance they transformed Kypárissos into the first cypress tree.

It's time to say goodbye. I pass the monastery and its adjacent wood of pines, maples, almonds, and poplars, and follow the long winding driveway down to the junction at which it joins an artery of the real world. There's a road sign there that faces vehicles that are about to drive up to the monastery and approaching this sign from its rear I see that someone, probably a person leaving this paradisical place on foot as I'm doing, perhaps it was even Phótis or Christos, has used a thick black marker-pen to write very deliberately and boldly all over the plain grey of the sign's reverse side 'Like a bird in the tree, we must be free'. Clearly, at least one person, possibly an Athenian, has left this magical oasis, this antithesis of the *metrópolis* below, determined to preserve and savour *eleftheria* (freedom), so that I wonder if the crazy unpredictability of Athens, the unceasing activity of its nights and days, is actually the result of such a determination.

My days in Athens are to end with a concert by the singer Manólis Lidákis. Again, the foyer of the theatre is packed with Greeks more than forty minutes before the performance begins. Everyone's standing around hoping to socialise, to talk, to greet, to call out and wave to others whom they recognise, or just simply to be there, to savour all the excitement and anticipation. And tonight, in this particular crowd, there's a wide variety of people, from late teens through to pensioners, as well as, I suspect, a real mix of backgrounds. There are men who look like artists or poets, with long hair, berets, or the kind of seaman's cap that the artist Yiánnis Tsaroúchis used to wear. There are sophisticated older women, who are beautifully and theatrically made-up. The foyer is so densely packed it's almost impossible not to catch someone's eye and strike up conversation.

On a lower landing, just below the foyer, standing all by themselves and not participating in any of the interaction, but just observing it, are three people who form a very interesting unit. I first see the two who are older: a very ordinary Greek couple, middle-aged, and probably husband and wife. I then notice that the person who is with them is clearly transgender, and whether transvestite or transsexual, I can't tell. She's much taller than the couple, she's no older than thirty, and her clothing is very feminine and somewhat lavish in variety so that only her hands and face are visible. Her hair is long and luxurious, and her make-up is a very carefully-applied all-over work of art. Every visible inch of her, the clothed and the unclothed, is the product of meticulous intention and design. The ghost of masculinity, however, unfortunately remains. Her eyes and mine suddenly lock. We gaze into each other. I smile. She smiles back. Her expression toward me is timid, but brave, and her eyes widen with a knife-edged mixture of curiosity and anxiety. Stupidly perhaps, I feel I've unmasked her, conveyed to her that I know her secret. I feel embarrassed. In hindsight, I wish I'd immediately gone to her and spoken.

But our eyes just as quickly unlock, and within seconds I've become engaged in conversation with a very smart woman pressed close against me by the huddle of the crowd. She says she has no ticket and is hoping for a spare. She looks for all the world like one of the most fashionable women of central Paris. Her hair is immaculately coiffured, she wears a stylish thick navy blue winter coat, its collar raised high around her neck, and her face is beautifully made-up and finished off with a flare of brilliant red lipstick. As upon my first night at a Greek concert here in Athens, this lady too is overwhelmed when I relate that I, a New Zealander from Britain, am here because I love this kind of music. I briefly tell her of my exhilaration in Athens these past days, and then dare to suggest that it's surprising to see that people are still flocking to evenings such as this despite the country's state, news of which has day by day been growing worse. She draws her head back a little, smiles beautifully, and says,

'So what do you think we *should* be doing?'

I say I only meant that perhaps people might be getting a little nervous, feeling that maybe they ought to be tightening their belts?

'No!' she replies, with sophisticated charm and assurance, 'We cannot just accept austerity measures!'

'But wouldn't they help to pay off the debts?' I suggest, slightly nervously.

'Any austerity measures that the government impose upon the people would be punishment, and completely undeserved! Most of the debt is illegal. It has been incurred by corrupt politicians.'

These denials are delivered so calmly that, somehow, they're redeeming, they have a stamp of authority about them. Placidly, though not unstirred, she then explains that the state of Greece's economy is not the fault of its people, that, instead, Greece has been driven into the state it's in against its own wishes.

'I am a Communist!' she announces, with complete confidence and pride and no drop in volume.

And I'm inclined to laugh. For by her fashionable clothing and luxurious manner of self-presentation this woman gives every sign of thoroughly enjoying Athens's excessive consumption as much as thousands of others. But maybe I don't know enough Communists, or at least enough Greek Communists. Perhaps I'm wrong to expect them all to dress in the working-class, casual, and often scruffy mode of the Socialists and Communists I used to know in Manchester.

Anyway, this charming educated middle-aged woman then proceeds to tell me that which I've suspected myself these last two weeks: that multinational companies have swarmed into Greece in the last twenty years and imposed on its people a consumerist value system which is fundamentally at odds with their traditional culture. I ask if she thinks there are others here tonight at this concert who are similarly concerned for Greece's identity. She thinks it's likely, and then asks how well I know Lidákis's music. I confess that unfortunately I can only appreciate its sound, grasping the meaning of just the occasional word amongst the rush of lyrics. She tells me to look forward to music that it is very Greek. Her final words are then delivered almost as a kind of confidence. She draws her head a little towards mine as if intending to share a secret.

'You know, there are many of us who do not agree at all with the EU!'

I take it she means to say that there are many Greeks who regret that Greece is an EU member, and I can understand why. But as I watch this lady go off to hunt down a ticket, I also can't help reflect on her gorgeous attire, as fine as that of any wealthy female habitué of Kolonáki or Kifissiá. It seems as if every Greek, despite whatever reservations, and even if Communist or Socialist, has become addicted to the illusion of 'the good life'. And if and where the good life ends, it seems they segue immediately into the delirium and oblivion of dreams. But the addiction to compulsive consumerism has to end, just as it has to end elsewhere if human life is to remain worth living. Will Greeks volunteer to give it up? Despite her better judgement, this particular Communist here tonight doesn't really seem inclined.

When the inner doors of the theatre are finally opened and the audience surges forwards to take their seats, the excitement is almost tangible. Again, I'm up in the circle, and again at the end of a row. Happily, however, this time I have an aisle seat, so I'll not have to disturb anyone. Five young men in 'cool' or 'hip' Western gear, with designer stubble-beards, the odd small diamond sitting beside a nose or just offside a lip, and hair jelled upwards as if shocked into place, file into the row directly in front of me and proceed to talk animatedly in Greek about the instruments set out on the stage below. Then suddenly, just minutes from the concert's beginning, a middle-aged couple who appear to have just been issued with some spare tickets come noisily down the steps of the aisle to find seats. The usher clearly explains to them that there are no more free seats side by side anywhere, but it seems they can't cope with the notion of being split up and sitting separately. An altercation then erupts. This causes the usher to abandon the pair and flee. And then, in front of us all, these two late-comers launch into a full scale row! The woman then abruptly turns away from her companion and plonks herself down in a spare seat, just two rows in front of me. Her partner heads back up the rake, as if leaving. She then turns around to catch him trying to persuade people right at the back to get up and move so as to create two free seats side by side. But as I unfortunately experienced myself last night, once Greeks are settled in their allotted seats, it seems they're not greatly amenable to moving! No one's willing to co-operate with him. So he starts to beg, and loudly, but for all his pleading nobody will budge!

Then all at once, the woman, down at the front, lets out a frightening screech of loud and furious Greek, accompanied by much finger-pointing and angry waving of the arms, presumably ordering her husband to desist and to just sit down and stop making such a fuss. Her outburst is immediately met by hissing disapproval from nearly everyone in the circle! Objections can even be heard spiralling upwards from people down in the stalls! The whole theatre is in momentary uproar. It's thrilling! She must have used some very choice language. Then six young women, all with gorgeously long flowing hair, and rattling with fashion accessories, suddenly rush down the rake and seat themselves in pairs upon the steps of the aisle immediately beside me. The lights dim, and in a swiftly receding babble of whispered excitement, everyone's attention turns to the spectacle about to unfold upon the stage. After the unexpected 'warm-up act', the anticipation is now overwhelming.

Manólis Lidákis's eight musicians enter from the wings to strong applause, and then simply settle themselves at their instruments in silence, in the manner typical of a classical concert. After a little tuning and adjustments to music-stands and microphones, they then proceed to fill this theatre with all the intricate and exotic sounds that sing of the musics of the East, the Balkans, and of North Africa. During this entrancing piece of introductory scene-setting, the one 'blower' switches from one wind instrument to another several times, performing equally stunningly on each. At various points the 'strummers and pluckers' change from guitar to *bouzoúki*, or to oud or *baglamá*, and then back again. As the drummer and pianist focus intently upon their instruments, the violinist, amplified in his solo passages, drives an enrapturing vein of Eastern sensuality right through the collective heart of the audience. At the height of this rich and glorious tapestry of magical sound, Lidákis enters, and of course he's met with rapturous applause. He then adds his voice to the music as just another thread, as just another rich and satisfying strand, and the bewitching fresco of sound is driven onwards and outwards, enveloping us all in a kind of communal passion. It's so reassuring. And we all know this amazing pleasure is going to continue for at least two hours.

After a dozen poignant and thrilling songs, Lidákis introduces a new young singer, a well-known and popular television presenter who just a couple of months ago sang on a television show and struck people with the quality of her voice. So tonight she appears in a totally new guise, as a serious *chanteuse*. Dressed in only a simple grey dress, she's beautiful and delicate, with long blonde hair and a deliciously charming smile. She sings ballads in keeping with those of Lidákis, and with a voice that is as powerful and a heart that is as feeling as his. All around me everyone's whispering into ears, remarking on this splendid surprise. The aged man beside me rings out a string of bravos at the end of each of her songs, while at the same time cheers erupt from every part of the theatre. Every night at concerts like this, Athens is transformed, renewed, and reborn. At gatherings like this, the deep inner heart of this city pulses and pounds. It's ecstatic, rejuvenating, completely fulfilling, and utterly Dionysian. You forgive and forget anything and everything that made you grumble or even curse this city during the course of your day.

The performance began at nine and it goes right through to just after eleven, increasing in excitement along the way with more and more dramatically emotional songs. Most of the music is all so extraordinarily 'Arabic'. It puts me in mind of the mesmerising songs of Enrico Macias, the Algerian singer who shot to stardom in Paris in the sixties and who also became very popular in Greece and Turkey. While Macias sang mainly Judeo-Arab and Arab-Andalusian songs, and generally in French, Lidákis's music is similar, though of course always in Greek. The intricacies of Lidákis's melodic lines are utterly entrancing. Up and down the necks of *bouzoúki* and *baglamá*, the fingers of his accompanists fly with astounding skill and accuracy, and when the melody lines of the singer and instrumentalists are as complex and rapid as they often are in these songs absolute concentration is paramount. The degree of hard work that this music requires in order to create its spell, and to seem effortless, is massive.

The man beside me says that Manólis Lidákis is Cretan and this partly explains the music, for Crete is close to the north of Africa, and therefore close to the musics of Egypt, Libya, Tunisia, and Algeria. Furthermore, Lidákis is a musician with a deep appreciation of serious music. Born in 1961, he was studying at the Irákleion Conservatory of Music (in Crete) by the age of nine, and was later a member of two symphony orchestras. To date he's recorded twenty-two CDs, although most of them consist not of his own compositions but traditional Cretan songs and works by other writers. An educated and a thinking artist, he's become one of Greece's finest and most respected singers. Perhaps it's his intellectual side that's attracted here tonight a good number of arty poetical-looking sorts, including at least one transgender person, and a very stylish Communist.

The concert is stupendous. It's a tonic. It revitalises and charges both the emotions and the mind. It's an epitome of all the elements that constitute a night of fabulous Greek song. In this auditorium, dazzling with lights of changing hues and swirling with mesmeric music, I see all the Greeks around me happily losing themselves in the words and melodies of songs they love, submerging themselves in such exquisite sophistication, where profound human feeling is expressed in sounds of the most pleasing delicacy and embedded in artful compositions of the most refined qualities. Such music isn't to be found anywhere in the West, though similar pleasures arise from a great deal of Western classical music, and occasionally from French chanson. In this particular form of creativity, the unique modern art-song of Greece, the Greeks of today are absolutely unmatched and peerless.

Greece has been in the midst of crises for centuries. In fact, *kríseis* and *cháos* are where the Greeks of today have come from. Greece has defaulted, either officially or in one instance by way of severe devaluation, six times (in 1827, 1843, 1860, 1893, 1932, and 1953) since acquiring independence, and during the same period has endured a horrendous trail of wars and political upheavals. Greeks therefore accept, as we all should, that into unpredictability they, and we, cannot but unavoidably head. They're used to it, and they've come to know that life will go on. They've seen far worse before. And thus for two continuous hours, without break or interval, in this sea of glorious sound and dreams and imaginings, there's no thought of the frantic concrete jungle outside, or of all the disheartening *cháos*, or of any of the immense difficulties with which Greece appears to be deeply afflicted at this time. Everything that is painful or paltry in life is now spiced out of mind. The music is like a medicine, a drug. It provides a complete intoxication. It is part of this city's intrinsic Dionysian inebriation. Most of all, it offers *cátharsis* and enables Athenians to look another day fully in the face. For everyone here tonight it is precisely as one ancient Greek, Aristotéles, stated 2,000 years ago, in his 'Politics' (Book Eight, Part Seven).

καὶ γὰρ ὑπὸ ταύτης τῆς κινήσεως κατοκώχιμοί τινές εἰσιν, ἐκ τῶν δ' ἱερῶν μελῶν ὁρῶμεν τούτους, ὅταν χρήσωνται τοῖς ἐξοργιάζουσι τὴν ψυχὴν μέλεσι, καθισταμένους ὥσπερ ἰατρείας τυχόντας καὶ καθάρσεως: ταὐτὸ δὴ τοῦτο ἀναγκαῖον πάσχειν καὶ τοὺς ἐλεήμονας καὶ τοὺς φοβητικοὺς καὶ τοὺς ὅλως παθητικούς, τοὺς ἄλλους καθ' ὅσον ἐπιβάλλει τῶν τοιούτων ἑκάστῳ, καὶ πᾶσι γίγνεσθαί τινα κάθαρσιν καὶ κουφίζεσθαι μεθ' ἡδονῆς.

we see those persons, by the application of sacred music to soothe their mind, rendered as sedate and composed as if they had employed the art of the physician: and this must necessarily happen to the compassionate, the fearful, and all those who are subdued by their passions: nay, all persons, as far as they are affected with those passions, admit of the same cure, and are restored to tranquillity with pleasure.

🁢 🁢 🁢 🁢

18

Afterword

In the spring of 2010, as the magnitude of Greece's debt crisis came to be understood, and very reluctantly accepted, there developed in Greece a steady escalation of anger. The Prime Minister, Yiórgos Papandréou, told the Greek people that as the country's public debt was believed to stand at about 300 billion euros, a wide range of major austerity cuts would have to be implemented, and that these 'great sacrifices', as he termed them, were necessary in spite of the multi-billion rescue loan to be granted to Greece by the Eurozone and the International Monetary Fund (the IMF). The Prime Minister advised that immediate measures would include a freeze on all government salaries; rises in many and various taxes; significant reductions in bonuses, overtime, and expenses; and cuts to the numbers of public workers and to the salaries of private employees. The measures would also include the lifting of the age of retirement for both men and women, to 65 years, and an immediate reduction in pension payments.

However, even before the first 'tranche', or portion, of the initial bailout of 110 billion euros was approved by the Eurozone, in May 2010, it became very clear that Greece's finances were in such disarray that the country would need much more assistance. Also, if Greece failed to repay its vast debt to lenders, almost half of which institutions were Greek but located in a total of eight different countries in Europe and around the world, it was feared that those institutions would probably collapse, and that governments too would be seriously stretched, with possibly calamitous effects for people in Europe and beyond. And so three regularly-visiting non-Greek representatives from the European Commission, the IMF, and the European Central Bank (the ECB), began to visit Athens to oversee consideration of all further loans, to recommend additional measures, and to generally monitor and supervise Greece's public finances.

Many Greeks saw the arrival of this 'Tróika' (a term meaning *triumvirate* but with overtones of Soviet-style power) and the austerity procedures listed in the Memorandum of Understanding of the 3rd of May 2010, as agreed between the Hellenic Republic and the Commission acting on behalf of member states of the Euro Area, as foreign interference, as an affront to their nation's sovereignty. Consequently from the 5th of May 2010 central Athens became the scene of days of protests and riots, with over a hundred people arrested, dozens injured, and three people killed. During the next seventeen months Sýntagma Square, as well as the park around The White Tower in Thessaloníki, saw further and regular mass demonstrations until in late October 2011, as the Greek parliament barely managed to pass further austerity measures in return for a second vast EU bailout loan, popular feeling exploded again into violence. Amid ferocious battles between police and protesters, the area around Sýntagma Square became a battleground of hurled rocks, broken glass, tear gas, and petrol-bombs. Two policemen and several demonstrators were set ablaze.

Later that month, on the 27th of October 2011, European leaders and Greek debt-holders reached an agreement with lenders to write off roughly 50% of Greece's enormous debt. At the same time, the second bailout was upgraded from an intended 109 billion euros to 130 billion, to be loaned by the EU, the ECB, and the IMF. In return the European Union required, amongst other things, commitments to further cuts and taxes, and a 50 billion euro privatisation plan. Lenders even went so far as to set out a detailed list of Greek assets which they thought suitable for purchase, as well as a timetable for their sale by 2015. But many Greek citizens believe that selling any of their national assets is an inferior method by which the country may generate revenue, and that islands and cultural monuments must not be included in such sell-offs or 'fire sales'. People are concerned about what their government could negotiate behind closed doors. A further condition of the second bailout was that EU officials be permitted a continuing presence throughout Greek government departments whereby they may oversee discipline and ensure changes and improvements are actually enforced. Since September 2011 a special EU Task Force, headed by Horst Reichenbach, German Vice President of the European Bank for Reconstruction and Development, has been set up in Athens specifically to battle with the nation's endemic tax evasion and to implement widespread structural reforms.

Probably because such conditions as the above are perceived as posing a threat and an affront to Greece's pride and sovereignty, on the 31st of October 2011 Yiórgos Papandréou unexpectedly resurrected his earlier desire for a referendum, whereby the Greek people could decide for themselves whether to reject or accept the considerable terms of the second bailout. EU leaders, mainly France and Germany, were immediately aghast at Papandréou's move, fearing that an overwhelming Greek '*Óchi!*' (No!) and a consequent Greek default would cause a catastrophic domino-effect throughout Europe. And so three days after Papandréou announced there was to be a referendum he withdrew it, thereby losing the confidence of his country and being forced to resign as Prime Minister. Meanwhile the EU suspended the sixth tranche, of 8 billion euros, from the first bailout loan, without which the Greek government said it wouldn't be able to pay salaries and pensions beyond December 2011. The EU also gave Greece an ultimatum: its major parties had either to pledge support for all of the terms of the second bailout, and in writing, or forgo the second loan of 130 billion, as well as the immediately-needed 8 billion, not to forget the remaining 37 billion still to be granted from the first bailout loan.

On the 11th of November 2011, following days of tense private negotiations, Lucás Papadémos, a former Vice-President of the ECB, was sworn in as Interim Prime Minister of a Government of National Unity, in a ceremony conducted before eight

Greek Orthodox priests arrayed in black stovepipe hats and various vestments of silver and gold. Mr. Papadémos then declared his intention to pursue Mr. Papandréou's plan to avoid default by ensuring Greece received the much-needed 6th tranche of 8 billion euros, to be followed later by the remaining tranches of the first bailout, as well as the eventual release of the second. However, Mr. Papadémos's problem lay in maintaining the support of the different political factions that existed within the interim administration and in having them co-operate. In November 2011 Antónis Samarás, leader of Néa Dimokratía, declared that he would not express his agreement to the terms of the EU's Memorandum for the second bailout in writing, saying that the 175 billion euros' worth of loans which remained on offer to Greece should proceed upon his verbal agreement alone, out of respect for the dignity of Greece and the value of his word. For a whole week Mr. Samarás had Greece, Europe, and the world on a knife-edge, waiting to see if he would eventually comply. Meanwhile, his supporters objected that in exchange for economic assistance Brussels was effectively demanding the full commitment of all future Greek governments, thereby castrating Greek politics and making charades of future elections. When on the evening of Sunday 12th February, 2012, the Greek parliament met to vote on Brussels's terms for delivering the second bailout, 100,000 citizens took to the streets of central Athens in protest against further austerity measures and roughly 150 shops were looted while 48 buildings, including several very fine neo-classical edifices were set ablaze. Inside the *Voulí* 22 PASOK MPs and 21 ND MPs were expelled from their parties for not having voted in favour of the bailout measures as their party chiefs had ordered them to do. Greece seemed about to explode. Nine days later, on the 21st of February, the Eurozone assented to lending Greece the further 130 billion and Greece agreed to the establishment in Athens of a more elaborate 'European Union Task Force for Greece' to monitor, control, and to guide progress and reforms.

The nation's plight at this time, mid 2012, is horrendous. Although by the end of March 2012 the reductions agreed in October 2011 had slashed central government debt from 367.9 billion euros (in December 2011) to 280.3 billion euros, Greece is still running at a loss. It has negative economic growth, it's paying out more than it can make, it's surviving on monetary 'life-support' provided by the EU and the IMF, which it obviously can't rely on forever, and because it is shamed and desperate, exploitative and profiteering international financial institutions are charging it exorbitant rates of interest. Consequently, it's extremely difficult to see how Greece might ever escape its downward spiral. Additionally, over the course of the last two years Greece has been the subject of such intense scrutiny and analysis that the entire world has come to learn that its culture and practices, not to mention its history, actually have more in common with the country's former Eastern Mediterranean and Middle Eastern neighbours than with its Eurozone counterparts in northern Europe. But heavily Orthodox-dominated Greece is not of the same prevailing religion as any of its neighbours, and sporadic Turkish belligerence towards Greek territory continues even at this time. Hence for this as well as other reasons many in Greece are fearful of ending any one of the nation's arrangements with the European Union.

And so the nation currently hovers between three main options. Firstly, it may try to survive the crisis by further austerity and bailouts, although it's difficult to imagine such a path won't eventually end grimly and require some extraordinary solution. Alternatively, it could choose to default in an 'orderly' manner, repaying much of its debt but doing so at a slower pace, over many decades to come. However, this option would still mean continued reform and further austerity. Or there is the solution most feared of all: that Greece just does a 'disorderly' default, repays none of its debts and is therefore forced to leave the Eurozone and return to its former currency, the *drachmí*, and then, left entirely to its own devices, face an unknown future, possibly reforming itself and possibly not. In the end, whichever path Greece takes, analysts the world over tend to agree that there'll be inescapable and painful repercussions for people and institutions in a wide number of other countries.

Significant in determining how this crisis will actually play out is the fact that a great many people in Greece are now seriously suffering, so much so that there exist well-grounded fears that unrest could develop into an uprising, a revolt. After two years of intense concern that at any moment Greece might default, instantly lose access to all sources of external credit, find its cash-machines empty, and erupt into unforeseeable *cháos*, the Greek index of misery has become truly shocking, and deeply numbing. There has been a doubling of the total number of unemployed to just over 24% of the entire labour force. Joblessness in the 15 to 24 age-group stands at a staggering 54.9%. Since the beginning of 2010 industrial production has fallen by roughly 10%, and from the start of 2011 about 42,000 workers have had to accept their full-time contracts being converted into part-time contracts. In 2010 bankruptcies throughout Greece rose by almost 50%, compared to the years immediately prior, and then in 2011 bankruptcies exceeded the 2010 figure by a further 27%. Since the beginning of the crisis a total of 68,000 small and medium-sized enterprises have been driven out of business, with a similar number expected to fold shortly. Recently the foreign chains FNAC, Carrefour, and Aldi have pulled out of Greece entirely.

One third of all Greek families now count as suffering from material deprivation, and since January 2010 there has been a 25% rise in the number of people who are homeless. As a result of the deprivation, there's been a nationwide surge in theft and violent crime, along with a considerable increase in illegal prostitution and drug trading. These practices, in turn, have contributed to a massive rise in HIV infections. New HIV cases reported in Greece in 2011 surged 57% beyond those of 2010, while among drug users, the rate rocketed by a horrifying 1,450%. According to *Médecins sans Frontières Greece* this was possibly due to government cuts to needle-exchange programmes, as well as ingrained social stigma. Amongst the entire population, the economic crisis has led to a doubling of Greece's normally low suicide rate, with police figures indicating that from 2009 to 2011 no less than 1,727 Greeks took their lives.

In the twelve months leading up to April 2012, ordinary Greeks withdrew approximately 44 billion euros from the country's banks, for fear of it being lost or wiped out, and roughly 10% of the population have quit Greece to live elsewhere. The vulnerable left behind, such as the disabled, the elderly, and those whose health is dependent upon medical treatments, are struggling with many more difficulties than they usually have to deal with. In addition, they live in fear of what will come with further austerity measures. There have been reports of some who suffer from terminal diseases having to rely on the kindness of other patients sharing out their own medications. And in a chilling short film released in June 2012 by the Greek documentary-maker Áris Chatzistefánou, an unemployed young man explained how some Greeks suffering from HIV have actually stopped taking their vital medications in order to allow their CD4 cell counts to drop to life-threatening levels, below the 200 mark, just so that they may then qualify for minimal benefit payments and thus be able to buy something to eat.

Meanwhile, it's believed that since the middle of 2010 many wealthy Greeks, including politicians, have withdrawn roughly 250 billion euros from Greek bank accounts to deposit their money mostly in either real estate in England or bank accounts in Switzerland. Several reliable British newspapers have reported that estate agents covering expensive inner-London areas like Kensington, Mayfair, Knightsbridge, and Baker Street have sold houses and apartments costing upwards of a million pounds to scores of well-heeled Greek visitors who have been so eager to invest their cash in British bricks and mortar that many of them have dispensed with having their purchases checked and inspected by a building surveyor.

In the Greek general election of Sunday the 6th of May 2012 Néa Dimokratía received only 18.86% of the vote, while a comparative new-comer, formed only in 2004, the Coalition of the Radical Left (*Synaspismós Rizospastikís Aristerás*, or SYRIZA), took an unexpected 16.77%; PASOK received just 13.18%; the right-wing Independent Greeks 10.6%; the Communists (KKE) 8.48%; and after having campaigned almost entirely on the issue of illegal immigrants, *Chrysí*

Avghí took an alarming 6.97%, thereby gaining these brutes a shocking total of 21 seats in the 300-seat Greek parliament. The 'winner', Antónis Samarás of Néa Dimokratía, immediately declared he'd try to form 'a government of national salvation', but failed, largely due to the response of Aléxis Tsípras, the youthful, tieless, and dynamic leader of SYRIZA, who maintained that his party's agenda was incompatible with that of both ND and PASOK. For SYRIZA held that since 2010 Greece's leaders had negotiated bailout loans in return for austerity measures and privatisation of the nation's assets without the mandate of the electorate; that cuts alone can't cure recession; that international auditors should decide how much of Greece's debt may be 'onerous' and ought therefore to be written off; and that the terms set out in the Memoranda of Understanding (the bailout agreements) would either have to be re-negotiated, while the country continued to receive rescue funds, or Brussels should be told the agreements were null and void. Although SYRIZA said it would prefer Greece to remain in the Eurozone, it was widely believed that if the party came to power it could quite easily declare a unilateral default and propel Greece into what at this time commentators began calling 'The Grexit'. Against this background it thus fell to Tsípras, as runner-up in the election results, to try to form a workable coalition with other groups who were similarly 'anti-bailout' and preferably of the left.

With all parties and the Greek President rightly excluding from coalition talks the coarse *Chrysí Avghí*, and with SYRIZA and KKE being vehemently opposed to each other, Tsípras's endeavour to create a coalition had little chance of success. Nevertheless, the young leader set out a stall requiring a handful of bold changes including the immediate abolition of MPs' immunity from prosecution. Meanwhile Míkis Theodorákis, the legendary cultural icon of the left, announced his full support of SYRIZA's efforts to substantially modify or even terminate the requirements of the bailout agreements and to recover Greece's sense of national sovereignty. Several days later the eighty-six-year-old composer even declared he was willing to take action himself, 'on the front-line'. Another famous member of SYRIZA, and a new MP as a result of the

May election, was the eighty-nine-year-old Second World War hero Manólis Glézos, who with Apóstolos Sántas tore down the swastika from atop the Acropolis in 1941 and so signalled the beginning of the Greeks' Resistance against the Nazis.

At the end of Wednesday the 9th of May, Aléxis Tsípras announced that he too had not been able to locate sufficient allies to form a government, and two days later Evághelos Venizélos, of PASOK, was forced to concede the same. So the task of trying to cobble together a coalition fell finally to the President, Károlos Papoúlias, but largely because both Tsípras, of SYRIZA, and Phótis Kouvélis, of the Democratic Left party, couldn't accept themselves as functioning effectively alongside parties that were pro-bailout and pro-austerity, even the President's attempts to form a coalition ended in failure. Thus, as prescribed by the Greek Constitution, on Wednesday the 16th of May Mr. Papoúlias appointed Panaghiótis Pikraménos, president of Greece's 'Council of State', the nation's highest administrative court, as the country's new Prime Minister and the Republic's 184th leader in the 190 years that have passed since 1822. Mr. Pikraménos had agreed to maintain a caretaker-government until the second election on the 17th of June 2012.

In the weeks that followed, polls published by major Greek newspapers revealed that roughly 80% of those surveyed wanted Greece to remain in the Eurozone, while in the next election as much as 30 to 40% of the vote could be won by SYRIZA. It therefore seemed that the majority of Greeks wanted both to stay in the Eurozone but not to abide by the austerity agreements to which earlier Greek leaders had committed them. Divergent opinions also began emerging elsewhere. On the 15th of May, after having campaigned on a platform for growth rather than austerity, François Hollande was inaugurated as Prime Minister of France and then immediately flew to Berlin to address with Germany's Chancellor, Angela Merkel, the desire of French Socialists to move the Eurozone's emphases from programmes of austerity to programmes of growth. And while Germany's Finance Minister Wolfgang Schäuble and its Foreign Minister Guido Westerwelle warned that Greece wouldn't receive any further tranches unless it kept to the schedule of cuts and reforms to which it had agreed, the German economic adviser Peter Bofinger publicly opined that countries like Greece and Spain were 'saving themselves to death' and that the Eurozone ought to supplement austerity with some kind of softening or corrective action. Even the IMF seemed gradually to be inclining towards a similar view. However, with powerful figures like Angela Merkel and the President of the Euro Group, Jean-Claude Juncker, maintaining that Greece must abide by its agreements, Greece's second election, in June, promised to be, in effect, a referendum by which the Greek people would decide, and hopefully with finality, whether to remain in the Eurozone or not.

Unfortunately, however, late on the evening of Sunday the 17th of June, the results of Greece's second election in 43 days proved far from decisive. Although support for SYRIZA had increased to an astonishing 26.89% of the vote, SYRIZA fell just 2.77 percentage points (170,556 votes) behind the winner, ND. And despite 52% of the total number of votes cast having been won by the many parties that were very clearly against the bailouts and the conditions of the Memoranda, the two largest pro-bailout pro-austerity parties, the long-time rivals centre-right Néa Dimokratía and socialist PASOK, gained sufficient votes to be able to hold a parliamentary majority. So despite the Greek people's expressed dissatisfaction with the terms of the bailouts, the task of forming a coalition fell to ND with its 29.66% share of the vote. PASOK had gathered 12.28%; the right-wing anti-bailout 'Independent Greeks' (ANEL) took 7.51%; Chrysí Avghí 6.92%; Democratic Left (DIMAR) 6.25%; KKE 4.5%; and the remaining parties 5.99% combined. The world's press interpreted these figures as indicating that Greeks wished both to remain in the Eurozone and to re-negotiate the Memoranda. Berlin, however, hailed the results as showing not only that Greece had decided to remain in the Eurozone but that Greece intended also to respect the conditions of the bailouts, which Berlin maintained were signed, sealed, and non-negotiable. ND's and PASOK's written commitments to the second bailout had earlier been carefully included by Eurozone administrators in the

13-page document filed at *www.ec.europa.eu/economy_finance/ eu_borrower/mou/2012-03-01-greece-mou_en.pdf*.

On the 20ᵗʰ of June 2012, Antónis Samarás was sworn in as Modern Greece's 185ᵗʰ Prime Minister, to lead a coalition consisting of ND, PASOK (led by Evághelos Venizélos), and Democratic Left (led by Phótis Kouvélis), but with the two partner parties having decided to support ND 'only in confidence' and not to participate in its cabinet of ministers. And although the two larger parties, led by Samarás and Venizélos, broadly back the bailouts, and ND and PASOK have committed themselves to the bailout conditions, Mr. Venizélos announced several hours before the new Prime Minister's swearing-in that the top priority of Greece's new government would be the formation of 'a national team' to rewrite the terms of the 130-billion-euro second bailout!

Mr. Samarás now faces an extraordinarily arduous task. In co-operation with ND's long-time opposite and rival, PASOK, he must now steer the Greek people, the greater part of whom are not in favour of his plans, through an indefinite period of great difficulty. And this he must do when to the exasperation of the larger part of the electorate the nation's new government is seen to be dominated by that very party, Néa Dimokratía, which was in power from 2004 until 2009 and which was therefore responsible for overseeing the final five years of Greece's slide towards catastrophe. Additionally, the coalition's two most prominent figures, Mr. Samarás and Mr. Venizélos, are perceived by many as being part of the problem: the nation's corrupted establishment. So, with little authority Greece's coalition is weak, and even if its 'national team' succeeds in persuading the EU and IMF to soften just a few of the conditions of the second bailout, the new government is bound by Samarás's own written commitments, of the 23ʳᵈ of November 2011 and the 15ᵗʰ of February 2012, to implement yet more painful austerity measures, although in both letters Mr. Samarás reserved the right to 'policy modifica-tions' that 'might be required' at some point in the future.

Greece's new Prime Minister now walks a tight-rope. If he presses the nation's creditors too hard, all of those further bailout tranches which Greece so desperately needs may not be forthcoming. And if the population resists further austerity measures, if it protests, or even yet again riots, the coalition could collapse and Greece could soon require a third election. On the other hand, the remarkable rise of the comparative new-comer SYRIZA, following the recent victory of France's Socialists, has revealed such a swelling demand for social justice and a strong change of direction that, just possibly, the Eurozone and the IMF may bend sufficiently for Greece to eventually reverse its downward spiral. But in the meantime, for most of the Greek population the nightmare and the struggle continue.

◻

Shortly after dawn on the morning of Tuesday the 4th of May 2010, one hundred or so radical and politicized Greeks cut through locks on the gates to the Acrópolis and proceeded up through the Propýlaia to the southern edge of the rock. Directly below the pediment and columns of the Parthenon, and at a point visible above the arches of the Iródis Attikós Theatre, they draped over the wall of the Acrópolis two enormous white cloths bearing the simple message,

ΛΑΟΙ ΤΗΣ ΕΥΡΩΠΗΣ ΞΕΣΗΚΩΘΕΙΤΕ

PEOPLES OF EUROPE RISE UP

Dozens of press photographs and video footage of the two banners, with the iconic Parthenon as backdrop and the arches of the ancient theatre as foreground, were immediately transmitted and viewed all over the world. Tourists continued to visit the Acrópolis as usual but the banners remained fixed in place for weeks. This dramatic occupation of probably the most famous archaeological site on Earth, just several hundred metres from the very spot where ancient Greece introduced its form of democracy to civilization, proved both poignant and deeply inspiring. As global markets at that time plunged in fear of the effects of staggeringly large bailouts for Greece from the EU and the IMF, the occupation of the Sacred

Rock sent out a call not only to the peoples of Europe but to peoples everywhere.

First and foremost the protest upon the Acrópolis was against harsh measures being inflicted upon ordinary men, women, and children in Greece and elsewhere while the international financial élite, failing to accept blame and continuing to draw disgracefully excessive salaries, bonuses, and pensions, were rescued and saved. The protesters of the Acrópolis also called on people to resist those forces primarily concerned with self-interest, exploitation, and profiteering, forces which are ruthlessly establishing themselves in almost every corner of the world while offering in return very little that's truly positive. Such powers claim that they 'protect the national interest', that they 'encourage foreign investment', and that they 'promote free trade', while, in reality, the desire for perpetual 'economic growth' is causing the steady depletion of the world's resources, addiction and enslavement to excessive and needless consumption, continuing pollution of the planet, and homogenization that spells the end of the world's diverse cultures.

As a dozen municipalities throughout Greece have indicated that on behalf of their communities they'll resist some of the austerity measures (and at least one Greek court has found in their favour) 'The Greek Debt Crisis' has become just one part of 'The European Sovereign Debt Crisis' which, in turn, is now seen as a significant component of a serious global problem, involving even the United States. Meanwhile the *Indignant Movement* which began in Spain during the summer of 2011, and which then spread to Athens and Thessaloníki, and then to Italy, has given rise to the worldwide *Occupy* movement, which sprang to life in New York in September 2011 as *Occupy Wall Street*. The intentions of the global *Occupy* movement have been broadly twofold: firstly, to protest against corporate greed, whereby roughly 1% of the world's population keeps to itself nearly all of the wealth which it extracts from the rest, from the 99%; and, secondly, to campaign for a better form of capitalism, a capitalism that will be ethically and internationally regulated and which will respect our planet and everything and everybody dependent upon it.

The occupation of the Acrópolis in May 2010, followed by an identical protest there a year later, in June 2011, called upon peoples everywhere to make a stand, to say, just as the people of Greece have so powerfully said in the past, *Óchi!*, 'No!' And people everywhere have responded. By November 2011, *Occupy* had become a highly visible campaign in no less than 951 cities in 82 countries, with a tented community beside St. Paul's Cathedral, London, to encampments all around the world, even to tents upon the green of The Octagon in Dunedin, the city where I was born, in the far south of New Zealand. Although at the present moment, international media attention has drifted away from both *Occupy* and the *Indignant Movement*, the recession across Europe has worsened, and general dissatisfaction persists.

July, 2012

By the end of May 2013 the level of unemployment amongst Greeks between 15 and 24 years of age had risen to 62.5%, with general unemployment nudging 28%. In spite of this, however, Greek politicians have suddenly begun to speak with assurance of a 'Grecovery', as opposed to the much feared 'Grexit'. Their optimism appears to ride largely upon their selling-off, or 'privatizing', Greece's national assets, such as its railways, its energy companies, its airports and harbours, and some of its islands. The purchase of these assets involves a battleground of wealthy investors from outside the EU - from China, Russia, and the Arabian Gulf. And it's believed that these investors may be jostling not so much for opportunites to make profits in Greece but in order to acquire footholds in what they perceive as being an open gateway to the wider and more lucrative marketplace inside the European Union. A recent announcement by the Greek government that it intends to create a large mosque in Athens, 90 years after Greece and Turkey's devastating 'population exchange' of Christians and Muslims, is thought to have been assisted by an inclination of the Greek government to please investors from the oil-rich Gulf.

June, 2013

Acknowledgements

I offer my thanks to all those people in Greece who have been so honest and open with me. If it were not for their warmth, friendliness, and generosity, I wouldn't have come to learn anywhere near as much as I have. During the period in Athens which is described in this book, I had no idea that I would eventually come to write of the experience. So I've given pseudonyms to most of those I met, and if by chance those people read this book and recognise themselves, I can only hope that they'll perceive and accept my sincere gratitude.

For their kind assistance in helping me to try to ensure accuracy in the finished text, I am indebted to the generosity of Evaggelía Sofianoú, Níkos Dramountánis, June Strátas, Aléxandros Moustákas, Menélaos Aligizákis, Beatrice Cántzola-Sampatákou, and, with regard to an important detail regarding Greek food, the cookery writer Aglaía Kremézi. Any errors or inconsistencies that remain are my responsibility. And although the subtitle of this account is 'The Truth' I fully accept that it only records *my* truth, all of that which I happened to see, hear, and perceive in Athens during a single two-week window. All opinions expressed as being my own are entirely that, mine alone.

For the extracts, statements, and other items that have been cited in this text, I would like to thank the following: Transparency International *(transparency.org)*; Transparency International - Greece *(transparency.gr)*; Médecins sans

Frontières Greece; The European Monitoring Centre for Drugs and Drug Addiction, Lisbon; Human Rights Watch for data contained in the report 'Denying Human Rights and Ethnic Identity: The Greeks of Turkey' (at *hrw.org/sites/default/files/reports/TURKEY923.PDF*); Project Gutenberg for William Ellis's 1912 translation of Aristotle's 'Politics'; archive.org for Francis Allinson's 1921 translations of Ménandros's fragments; and Oxford University Press for allowing me to include a statement from Professor Rosen's entry on the London Greek Committee in the Oxford Dictionary of National Biography, edited by H. C. G. Matthew and Brian Harrison (2004) and published in association with the British Academy. The translation of part of Constantínos Caváfy's poem Ιθάκη is my own.

I should also record that there are a few other professional sources, Greek and based in Athens, which unfortunately I can't thank due to my having encountered the byzantine behaviour of gladly granting full verbal agreement to the inclusion of materials while simultaneously providing a succession of 'explanations' over the course of several months as to why those agreements have not been delivered in written form. (The word 'byzantine' is used here according to the definition referred to near the start of Chapter Three.) I have of course excluded from this book the few items in question.

General non-fiction that has been informative, and in some cases invaluable, in the preparation of this book includes the Encyclopaedia Britannica, numerous volumes from the Oxford University Press reference collection, the Penguin edition of 'Description of Greece' by 'Pausanias', John Freely's 'Strolling Through Athens', Diane Shugart's 'Athens By Neighbourhood', Mimíca Cranáki's 'Greece', Elizabeth Boleman-Herring's 'Athens', Michael Llewellyn Smith's 'Athens', 'Greece' by Dána Fácaros and Línda Theodórou, 'Athens and Attica' by Marianne Mehling, Evangelos Konstantínou, and Gerhard Rebhan, 'Athens' by Stephanie Ginger and Christopher Klint, 'Pagan Cult to

Christian Ritual' a paper by Gerald Lalonde, and a number of Athens newspapers, including 'Kathimeriní', 'Athens News', and 'To Víma'.

Regarding the events of the Asia Minor Disaster, Giles Milton's 'Paradise Lost', Bruce Clark's 'Twice a Stranger', and Mark Mazower's 'Salonica' were all exceptionally illuminating - and I think have to be read by anyone with a strong interest in Greece.

For their insights into the spirit and nature of Greece I am indebted to Colin Simpson's 'Greece - The Unclouded Eye', Patricia Storace's 'Dinner with Persephone', Patrick Leigh Fermor's 'Mani' and 'Roumeli', Henry Miller's 'The Colossus of Maroussi', James Davidson's 'Courtesans and Fishcakes: The Consuming Passions of Classical Athens', Kevin Andrews's 'The Flight of Ikaros', Lawrence Durrell's 'The Greek Islands', Robert Byron's 'The Station', Ralph Brewster's brief but totally rational and objective exposé 'The 6,000 Beards of Athos', and Sofka Zinovieff's 'Eurydice Street'.

Also of interest were two recent but very different books titled 'It's All Greek to Me', one by Charlotte Higgins and the other by John Mole. Yiánnis Bólis's beautifully illustrated book on the life and work of the painter Yiánnis Tsaroúchis is a pleasure to leaf through. John Purkis's 'The World of the English Romantic Poets' sheds light on Greece's considerable power to inspire. Edward Said's 'Orientalism' reveals how the West came to perceive the East. Frank Snowden's 'Blacks in Antiquity: Ethiopians in the Greco-Roman Experience' demonstrates the Ancient Greeks' respect for Africans. David Brewer's very recent 'Greece - The Hidden Centuries' provides a highly informative survey of the 400 years of the Turkish occupation. Vangélis Calótychos's 'Modern Greece - A Cultural Poetics' is a sprawling but assuring tour of Modern Greek history by way of some of its literature. And Michael Lewis's 'Boomerang - The Meltdown Tour' (2011) helps to put Greece's current crisis into global perspective.

Tákis Kalogerópoulos's 'To Lexicó tis Ellinikís Mousikís', Dimítris Papanikoláou's 'Singing Poets: Literature and Popular Music in France and Greece', the commemorative volume 'Mános Hadjidákis' published by 'Eleftherotypía' newspaper, and Níkos Papandréou's 'Míkis and Mános' have all shed light upon Greek composers, musicians, and singers.

Tales that I have enjoyed have included the excellent collections of short stories 'Good Friday Vigil' by Yiórgos Ioánnou, 'Woof, Woof, Dear Lord' by Sotíris Dimitríou, Níkos Bakólas's 'Mythology - Twelve Tales From a Life', and Christóforos Miliónis's 'Kalamás and Achéron'. Yiánnis Rítsos's three volumes of poeticized autobiography, 'Iconostasis of Anonymous Saints', superbly translated by Amy Mims-Argyrákis, paint a vivid picture of life in mid 20th century Athens as Rítsos experienced it. Didó Sotiríou's novel 'Farewell Anatolia' is an arresting recreation of the horrors that befell Asia Minor in the build-up to the 1923 population exchange. Other novels I've enjoyed include 'The Maze' by Pános Karnézis, 'Four Walls' and 'Stolen Time' by Vangélis Hatziyannídis, Ménis Koumandaréas's intimate novella 'Koula', Chrístos Tsiólkas's 'Dead Europe', and of course Níkos Kazantzákis's 'Zorbá the Greek'.

Of verse, Kímon Friar's translations in 'Modern Greek Poetry' and Robert Fagles's translations of 'The Iliad' and 'The Odyssey' are all beautiful.

For the artwork created for this book's cover I am grateful to the very talented and highly imaginative Paris-based artist Laurent de Commines. I asked Laurent to depict the magical *mýthos* of Athens, that vision that I conjured up as a child and with which, to some degree, I approached the city at the start of my visit, and which by the end of my stay I found to be still, happily, an aspect of the modern Greek capital.

My greatest thanks are reserved for Giorgio Landon, my partner of 21 years, my 'Civil Partner' since 2009, and, pending the outcome of passionate debates in the UK parliament at this time, hopefully, soon, my husband, as I shall be his. Giorgio is a long-time visitor to and lover of many of the Greek islands and throughout the roughly 5 years that it has taken me to get to grips with the obsession of most of my life-time, and to start and to complete the writing of this book, he has been a source of steadfast, loving, and massive support. I cannot thank him enough.

I have also to thank all those other people who since my arrival in the UK in 1979 have in one way or another supported, or at least supportively tolerated, my fixation with Greece. As I set off for Athens, and then returned, it was such a pleasure to share the excitements and discoveries of the adventure with Denys and Monica Sharrocks, both of whom had a close association with Greece for many years.

And for all the countless hours of exquisite pleasure that I've enjoyed over the decades by way of the music of Mános Hadjidákis, delight and enchantment which I hope to enjoy for many more years to come, I have of course to end by thanking the great Greek composer himself.

Thank you, Mános!

Index

CPSIA information can be obtained at www.ICGtesting.com
Printed in the USA
LVOW05s2023220514

386948LV00003B/119/P

9 780955 209031